LIFE IN ONTARIO

ONTARIO

A Social History

Drawings by
Adrian Dingle

University of Toronto Press

LIFE IN ONTARIO

A Social History

G. P. deT. GLAZEBROOK

© University of Toronto Press 1968

Reprinted 1971

Printed in the United States for
University of Toronto Press,
Toronto and Buffalo

ISBN 0-8020-1513-1 (cloth)

ISBN 0-8020-6116-8 (paper)

LC 72-392684

Preface

"SOCIAL HISTORY" is a phrase which can be interpreted in a number of ways. A distinguished writer in this field, G. M. Trevelyan, suggested that it be defined as "the daily life of the inhabitants of the land in past ages," and to describe that life is the purpose of the present book. Because of the infinite variety of people and circumstances it is an ideal which can never be fully attained. Nevertheless an attempt has been made always to start from the point of view of people—their needs, problems, interests, means of livelihood —and to move on to the activities in which they engaged and the institutions which from time to time they created or had thrust upon them.

Within a broadly chronological order some individual subjects are isolated. To do so is to distort people's lives, which are not in compartments labelled "occupation," "religion," "food," and so on; but any other method would lead to infinite repetition. By "Ontario" is meant the territory included within the present province. For that reason, and to avoid changing nomenclature applying to different boundaries, the word Ontario is used throughout, even though it may be technically an anachronism.

Some indication of sources for the social history of Ontario is given in the bibliography. I am indebted to members of the staffs of the Public Archives of Canada, the Archives of Ontario, the University of Toronto Library, and the Toronto Public Library for their help. Officials of several departments of the Government of Ontario have given ready assistance, as have those of the Dominion Bureau of Statistics and the Canadian Pulp and Paper Association. Mr. T. Ritchie generously allowed me to read his book, *Canada Builds*, in manuscript. To many others who answered appeals for information and advice in this wide field I can only express my thanks in general terms.

J. M. S. Careless and S. D. Clark were good enough to read the text in draft form and to give me the benefit of their sage advice. Miss Francess

Halpenny, Managing Editor of the University of Toronto Press, has encouraged and guided my faltering pen. Adrian Dingle's drawings are not only a delight in themselves but tell the story of Ontario better than words can do.

Uxbridge, Ontario
January 1968   G. P. deT. G.

Contents

Ottawa River

Mattawa River

NIPISSING

Pembroke

Hawkesbury

PRESCOTT

RENFREW

RUSSELL

Ottawa

CARLETON

GLENGARRY

STORMONT

LANARK

DUNDAS

Cornwall

HALIBURTON

Smiths Falls

GRENVILLE

Perth

Rideau River

Prescott

LEEDS

Brockville

PETERBOROUGH

LENOX AND ADDINGTON

FRONTENAC

St. Lawrence River

VICTORIA

HASTINGS

Trent River

Kingston

Lindsay

Peterborough

Napanee

Belleville

Trenton

DURHAM

NORTHUMBERLAND

Picton

Cobourg

PRINCE EDWARD

Port Hope

Bowmanville

Oshawa

Whitby

Lake Ontario

Catharines

Niagara Falls

LLAND

Hudson Bay

KENORA

Albany River

Moose River

Lake Abitibi

COCHRANE

Kapuskasing

Cochrane

Lake Nipigon

Timmins

THUNDER BAY

Kenora

Dryden

TIMISKAMING

Lake of the Woods

Fort Frances

ALGOMA

SUDBURY

Ottawa River

RAINY RIVER

Port Arthur

Fort William

Rainy Lake

Lake Superior

Lake Huron

Lake Ontario

Lake Erie

Scale of miles

0   400

Lake Michigan

Part One

TAMING A WILDERNESS

CHAPTER ONE

Indians and
Fur Traders

THE EUROPEAN EXPLORERS and fur traders who first came into Ontario from south or north quickly realized that they were in a land of great distances. It consisted, as later became known, of 412,582 square miles of which 68,490 were fresh water, the whole being about twice the size of European France of the early twentieth century. From the most southern to the most northern points, and from the eastern to the western, was, in each case, a distance of approximately a thousand miles. Those who came into the south in the early seventeenth century saw, stretching upward from the St. Lawrence and the lakes, what was to become in time the richest and most populous part of Ontario, where agriculture and industry were to find their main base. North of Lake Simcoe was the Precambrian or Canadian Shield, an area inhospitable to agriculture except in the stretches of clay soil interspersed with the ranging and knobby rocks. The rivers that ran north from this east-west watershed flowed through a third region, the lowland surrounding James Bay. There from the late seventeenth century were the English adventurers who braved the perilous passage of Hudson Bay in their little ships. This area was flat but without the lush soil or giant trees of the south. The winter was long and forbidding, with the temperature sliding to fifty degrees below zero, but one great advantage was access to salt water on a shoreline of about 680 miles.

Such are a few facts of the geography of Ontario. It might seem immutable but some provisos should be attached if its social significance is to be understood. In the first place, of course, all the facts became apparent only gradually: the existence of waterpower, for example, in major or minor quantities at innumerable locations, or the presence of minerals beneath the forbidding surface of the Canadian Shield. Such benefits, however, had no practical meaning until they were exploited by man. Farming and the construction of buildings were greatly facilitated by grist and saw mills, and in a later generation the same waterpower brought light, power, and heat to factory and farm. Mineral wealth changed the Shield from a liability to an asset, although its value could be measured only in relation to the availability of means of extracting and transporting the minerals. The effects of distance and climate on social life could be modified by technology. Man, moreover, could not only take advantage of nature but also upset its balance. The forest had to be cut down if crops were to be grown and lumber produced, but an incidental effect was to interfere with the whole water-table, causing floods and drought. Certain of the early mining operations destroyed vegetation for miles around. Thus, in any meaningful sense, a geographical setting for the story of the people of Ontario cannot, except for a few basic features, be painted in fixed colours. It is constantly modified by many factors, such as the size and distribution of population, knowledge of the resources of the area, changing demand for these resources, improvements in transportation, and a series of inventions.

The land of Ontario had for many centuries—no one knows how many—been inhabited by the peoples that Europeans, because of an early geographical error, called "Indians." They, like the aborigines of all the Americas, were descended from migrants from Asia. There being no verbal record—for at no time did these people have a written language—it has been left to anthropologists to deduce the story of this migration from other evidence, and that being very incomplete, the conclusions are inevitably tentative. It does seem certain, however, that the first human beings in the Americas were primarily Mongoloid, though with some other strains apparent; that they came by way of the Bering Straits; and that the time of the first move was some 15,000 to 20,000 years ago. It has further been deduced that, as groups fanned out into the continent, they reached Ontario in undetermined numbers some 10,000 years ago. For the sequence of their story in the period before they were first seen by white men the available evidence is sketchy and there was no constancy in the location, power, size, or even existence of a given tribe. The principal characteristics of Indian society in the last days of their sole possession of the area, however, are known in part and they help to explain their relationships with Europeans and their place in the social fabric of Ontario from the time when written records began. Even here evidence is uncertain for much of the available information is in letters or books written by Europeans who could hardly detach themselves from the standards and practices to which they were accustomed. Moreover, such men were writing for European readers, people who would be interested in what they regarded as the peculiarities of the Indians.

All Indians were in some degree hunters and fishermen, but there is a distinction between the sedentary agricultural tribes on the one hand and the nomadic tribes on the other. The Hurons and their cousins of the Tobacco nation, who had perhaps the most advanced civilization in Ontario, were examples of the first. They lived between Lake Simcoe and Georgian Bay and had a population of some 50,000 souls at the beginning of the seventeenth century. Their crops were corn, beans, and squash and it has been estimated that at that time they had 23,000 acres of corn under cultivation. Like other Indians they supplemented this produce with nuts, fruits, and berries, and with game and fish. North of the great lakes were the Chippeways or Ojibwas who were, with minor exceptions, nomadic hunters. They were relatively numerous too, perhaps rather more than half the numbers of the Huron-Tobacco group at its maximum. North of them again, and in immediate contact with the Hudson's Bay Company, were those skilled hunters and trappers, the Crees.

None of the Indian tribes, sedentary or nomadic, had advanced far in European terms. They lived still in the stone age, had not discovered the wheel for transportation or pottery, had to endure smoky dwellings as they had not thought out the chimney, had no conception of sanitation or the virtues of privacy, had no written language and consequently no recorded literature. On the other hand they had largely mastered the environment in which they lived. They knew the ways of the forest and of its birds and animals. They used the waterways in the bark canoes they had invented. Their pottery, if made under difficulties, had taste in style and decoration. They might depend in part on witch-doctors but they had learned many of the beneficial effects of herbs, as the first European visitors found to their advantage. Even if they could not write they could create music and folklore and pass them on from generation to generation through the elders of the tribe. They were a courageous and on the whole an energetic people who invented little but lived with nature on terms that left no room for physical comfort. Their houses were simple in the extreme but easily erected, and could readily be replaced when the time came to leave accumulated dirt and exhausted supplies of firewood. The life was not that of the noble savage so dear to European romanticists of the eighteenth century; neither was it that of the slums of a European city. Political, economic, religious, and scientific thought as it developed in Europe passed the Indians by. They did, however, understand the forests of Ontario. It remained to be seen what marriage could be made between the skills of the Indians and those of the incoming Europeans.

By a purist the Indians of North America could be considered immigrants since they are known to have come to an empty land from northeast Asia. The time of the move, however, is so remote that they can reasonably be classified as aborigines. The first Europeans to touch on the shores of Canada were evidently Norsemen, but if they ever were in Ontario—which seems improbable—they made no mark on it. The beginning of white occupation came when the explorers of France found their way in by the St. Lawrence entry and those of England by Hudson Bay. It was in pursuit of the trade in furs that the nationals of the two countries established residence of a kind in Ontario. They were not settlers in the usual meaning of the word, but because their business interests required continuous presence at a number of strategic points they were, willy-nilly, inhabitants and subject to many of the problems of pioneer life. In contrast with colonists proper they did not come to re-make their lives in a new location; indeed they did not expect to live there for any long span. The employment of this male society was in a trade that would be positively damaged by the advance of civilization: for them there could be no vision of smiling fields to be left to their children, of productive activities supported by a flow of immigrants; no struggle to build roads, mills, schools, churches, or shops as for the orthodox settler. Theirs was the life of the wilderness, and they would keep the land that way; but to stay alive they needs must in some respects act as if they were settlers.

There were differences between the French and English establishments in Ontario. The French were moving inland and westward from a base in Montreal. It was their ambition to pull the fur trade, the life blood of the colony, away from the Hudson River to the St. Lawrence. A necessary part of the plan was the establishment of posts at strategic points on the waterways over which the trade must move. They were expensive to build and to maintain. They had to be fortified and to house such soldiers as could from time to time be spared. Frontenac, the first of the forts set up on Lake Ontario, was also the earliest shipyard: sailing vessels were essential for the carriage of furs and trading goods, building materials, and supplies of all kinds. Boat building began there in 1673 and was carried on at irregular intervals. Four ships were sailing on Lake Ontario before the famous *Griffon* was built above the falls at Niagara. In 1725 two barques of fifty tons burthen were laid down at Fort Frontenac, and although they, like most French vessels of the day, could carry guns, they were in demand as transports. Bearing Kingston limestone to Niagara for the fort there proved to be too heavy a task, but they were replaced and by 1747 there were four sizeable sailing ships actively engaged on Lake Ontario.

Thus Simcoe was not the first to attach importance to naval and mercantile shipping on the lakes. By his time it had a hundred years of history. The ports on Lake Ontario had also been chosen. Kingston and Toronto are directly on the French sites. The old Fort Niagara was on the east side of the river and so fell into American hands, but Newark was not far away. Parts of southern Ontario which were the first to be settled were already identified and Europeans moved into, and to some extent resided in them.

There was a real French presence in Ontario, but could it be called colonization? Was this the first chapter in the pioneer settlement in the south of the province? With Detroit that could be said to be the case; or, to be more exact, it was the case for that part of the population which spilled over on to the Ontario side of the river, and which will be more fully described in the next chapter. Meanwhile it is pertinent to note that Detroit was designed not only as a staging point and depot, as all these posts were, but also as a producer of food for the more western posts. After its first few years it had a surplus of flour and other produce. The same was never true of Niagara, which was dependent on the provisions sent from France and laboriously hauled up from Montreal. Consignments might be late or the food in them might be bad; and if so it was not easy to replace them from already-scarce crops grown in the St. Lawrence Valley. There were sometimes quite large numbers of people at Niagara: men engaged in building or rebuilding, soldiers, sailors, traders, and some families of officers (the last contrary to regulations). A few things were grown, corn and fruit certainly, but never on a scale sufficient to make the post nearly self-sustaining.

In the French régime Toronto was a minor trading post, placed to interrupt the flow of furs southward to Oswego. At times it looked as if Fort Frontenac might become the centre of an agricultural settlement. When it was founded in 1673 some land was cleared, wooden buildings were erected, and domestic animals introduced. La Salle secured the area as a seigneury and in 1675 moved in with masons, carpenters, and blacksmiths. The fortifications were improved and a chapel and forty cottages built. Land was cultivated and crops reaped. During Hennepin's stay (1676–79) he claimed that a hundred acres were under cultivation. This is probably an exaggeration since La Salle's talk of a seigneury barely disguised his real interest, which was the fur trade. Frontenac became a busy place, as a shipbuilding centre, a depot, the residence of traders, and the point at which expeditions to the west, military or commercial, were mounted. Like Niagara, however, it had to be supplied from outside, and that was a process both dangerous and expensive. The route from Montreal was vulnerable to Iroquois attack, and transportation in the westward direction took from twelve to fifteen days and cost from eight to twelve francs a hundredweight.

Not one of the posts that has been mentioned directly paid its own way through the fur trade, but if there was a loss it was deemed to be justified by the danger of seeing the whole trade fall into the hands of the English colonists. Little attention seems to have been directed to building up agriculture with the one exception of Detroit, which was to feed the far western posts. Neither the Canadian authorities nor the Canadian people were looking for more land. The population of the St. Lawrence Valley was small and there the farmers could not consistently supply even local needs. None of the usual pressures leading to colonization existed.

In their wide-ranging expeditions as far as the extreme west and north of Ontario the French carried out much detailed exploration though they had no reason to initiate civil settlements. Relations with the Indians in this land were important because of the needs of the fur trade and of forest life and travel. Whether at the larger and established posts, at smaller and perhaps temporary ones, or on trading trips the French had—it is generally recognized—a gift for understanding Indians and making common cause with them whenever that was possible. One result of good relations, less conspicuous in Ontario than on the prairies, was a race of half-breeds or *métis* who added a small but interesting element to the population. Because, however, of the English–French–Indian triangle the relations of the French with tribes could not always be easy. If the fur trade could at times be a bond it could also be a source of friction. Commercial competition became linked with inter-tribal and international rivalry to allow only a few periods of peace in which the potentially good relations with Indians could become a reality.

The posts of the Hudson's Bay Company had much in common with those of the French or their English-speaking successors after 1760. Both were for commercial purposes; neither group was directed to settlement or development of the country. The "forts" of the company, however, had more of the characteristics of pioneer communities anywhere in Ontario. Yet the techniques that the company's men learned at an early stage seem to have had little, if any, influence elsewhere. The only contact between the Bay and the lower great lakes was commercial rivalry, and there seems to be no record of the company's being consulted in London by officials concerned with Loyalist settlement. Probably it was taken for granted that there was nothing in common between the frozen wastes and the St. Lawrence Valley, between the fur traders and the settlers. If that was so, the assumption was only partly justified. Nevertheless from the point of view of the company what they knew of Canada, whether under the French or the English crowns, was not to their liking, for they saw only unpleasantly successful inroads into the trading country in which they considered they had a monopoly. At times even military operations were added to the commercial contest.

Neither at that time nor since has the Hudson's Bay Company been credited in the history of Ontario with much more than exploration and the management of an export. Nevertheless, in the story of those who came to Ontario and of their life there the comparatively large groups living, for well over a century, at points on Hudson Bay and James Bay cannot be dismissed in such simple terms. It is true that the centres in the north were placed there only for trade; but, whatever the purpose, men were living in them, and to survive were obliged to devote much of their time and energy to solving the problems of existence in that environment. The physical conditions were not easy. The winter was long and cold, a good deal worse than in the south of Ontario where it was seen as harsh by European immigrants and visitors. The outstanding contrast with the south came after farms and villages began to appear there. In the north there were none until much later, although in a sense rural and urban life were combined in a company post. The difference was isolation. In the south it was possible for outlying groups to maintain communications by one means or another throughout the year. The St. Lawrence entry may have been seasonal and the further waterways partly frozen in the winter, but the summer was not short and the towns and farms in the older parts of Quebec had at least limited capacity to forward the necessities of life. It may now seem very convenient that the posts actually on the Bay had sea-going ships arrive at their very doors. They could come, however, only once a year at best; and if that one voyage was not completed —as it was not in 1716—the posts were on their own for another twelve months. The ships had to carry the bulk of trade goods together with personnel, food, tools, building materials, and many other things, including even prefabricated ships. As the company moved farther into the interior and set up a series of posts hundreds of miles from the Bay further demands were made on the space in the ships of the day.

There were a dozen arguments in favour of the doctrine that the posts must be as self-sufficient as possible. Economy was a major consideration, but the overriding one was that the men in the posts could be sure of surviving in no other way. They had, by instructions and by reason, to live as far as possible on the country as well as in it; to create quite complex little communities, blending native and imported means. Reading through the daily journal of a post one might almost forget that its business was to trade with the Indians for furs. Shelter and heat, food, clothing, care of the sick, travel, and defence, together with some lesser attention to religion, education, and recreation: these are the subjects that seem to have occupied most of the time. There was plenty of paper-work too. Journals had to be entered, accounts kept, correspondence conducted with London and with other posts. One way of judging the activities of a post is to see how its personnel establishment was made up. In 1783 Moose Fort (which was an important port) together with its dependency, Brunswick, had a chief and a second, a surgeon, two "writers" (clerks), a carpenter, a cooper, a bricklayer, two tailors, an armourer, fifteen labourers, a sloopmaster, a shallopmaster, a shipwright, a "shaloper," a sailor, a sloopmate, and six "sloopers." Almost every day's entry in the journal describes how "the people" were employed. Here is an example, the entry for May 24, 1784:

Wind variable clear weather A.M. a Canoe came down from the upland Boat to acquaint me that they had unfortunately run her aground on a shoal ripple a little below Hancock's Creek on Saturday Evening and tho they endeaviored all day yesterday, have not been able to get her off, immediately dispatchd. Mr. Turnor with 2 men and two Indian lads in the small new Batteaux, Cooper and 4 men preparing the foundation logs for the new flanker, Armourer mending and cleaning Musquets, and Pistols, Leask making Trading coats, three with 2 Boats fetch'd home the Geese and Goose hunters from the Northwd. one Chiefs servant, one cook, one Ruptured and one Lame, the others in the Garden and occasionly assisting at the new Building Recd. 60 Geese.

Here is an account of a November day:

Wind North Sleet and Rain Shipwreck and four men breaking up the old Sloop Cooper helving and grinding Hatchets. Peter McFerlin making Sleds, A. King preparing Methy hooks, Armourer cleaning trading guns Steward at work for Mr. Brand, 2 Cooking, one tending the hogs, one Chiefs servant six away hunting, the rest collecting poplar firewood which was fallen around the plantation in the Summer.

On other winter days the armourer and his mate were making nails out of old iron hoops and four men were on an island sawing planks. In the summer some of the men were making hay for the cattle while the scythes were being repaired by the indispensable armourer, who is later found making locks and hinges, and also ringbolts for the shipwright. The carpenters were kept busy on repairs and new construction, but it seems to have been the cooper who made bedsteads. Quite often there was plastering to be done, and so there was a lime kiln to supply and attend. Cutting, collecting, and transporting firewood were frequent tasks. Chimneys had to be built and kept in good repair, for adequate heating was a necessity during several months of the year, but accidental fires could bring exposure and death. In 1784 the chief at Albany was facing the identical problem to that so often encountered by settlers in the south. "My Chimnies," he wrote to his colleague at Moose,

are all so bad that we dare not light a fire in them and our Bricklayer so ignorant he cannot repair them or at least not in sufficient time for the Winter Use, therefore would be very glad if you could spare Thos. Harcro, I have been last winter under great anxiety of mind concerning them, the Men's House having once been on Fire & I dread to pass the approaching winter wth. them in the same state.

The highest priorities were shelter and food. A portion of the latter always came from England, but that portion was limited in quantity, variety, and condition. It was not pleasant to find maggots in salted meat. Nature offered a good deal. Wild fruit flourished near some of the posts. Fishing was usually good but game was considered more important. Geese, ducks, plover, and partridge were fairly plentiful. The goose hunt was a crucial annual event, and when it went well provided a considerable stock for salting. Venison was sometimes available. European domestic animals—cattle and pigs—were imported, and from time to time found their way into the diet. Some vegetables were grown in gardens adjoining posts though in what quantities is not clear. Oatmeal was ground locally and flour came in the ships, but sometimes it became scarce. Bread was baked in the main posts. The margin of safety was not wide and there was always the danger of a serious shortage. "I had," wrote the chief at Moose Fort at the end of January 1785, "a tolerable Goose hunt having salted 20 casks and I have received a few rabbits from Indians during the winter, with which, and the Beef and Pork killed we have been pretty well off for fresh food till Christmass since which we have lived almost wholy on salt." In winter, though apparently not at other times, food was put in the cold water to "freshen" it. Liquor was an important item at posts.

From England came brandy, essential to the fur trade and sometimes an escape for bored or unwell servants of the company. Wine and beer were also imported. "Small" (weak) beer was regularly brewed at the posts. The records suggest that the appetite for food and drink of these men engaged in hard labour was healthy enough, and it seems that, in one way or another, it was generally satisfied. Yet the danger of shortages, even of starvation, brooded over the area. Nature, it seemed, was fickle, and the comings and goings of animals and birds were unpredictable.

The Moose Fort establishment included, under various titles, a number of sailors employed on inter-post transportation on the Bay. Unless the needed sloops were brought in parts from England they had to be built locally, as was the *Phoenix* in 1744. Sails were supposed to be imported but if they were forgotten substitutes had to be improvised out of whatever canvas could be found. Buoys and beacons were set as aids to navigation. Small boats and batteaux (the distinction seems to have been one of size) were also built on the Bay. They were used to carry trading goods and building materials to the inland posts and were alternatives to canoes. It was realized that canoes had great advantages but the English employees did not take readily to their use and had no skill in building them. For this the aid of Indians was sought.

In these various ways, but within a limited range, the centuries-long presence of the Hudson's Bay Company in the most northern regions can be seen as part of the social history of Ontario, and in particular as an approach to pioneer life. That the English there were not a mere handful is illustrated by the proposed establishment for Albany and its dependencies for 1792, totalling 212. (A few of these, in the categories of transport crews, may have been Indians, but most, probably all, were white.) The character of the posts varied according to their location, age, and functions. No one is typical of them all. The smaller inland posts have the least relevance to this theme, but the larger ones—which meant some of those on the Bay—have points of distinct similarity to contemporary and later settlements in the south.

Moose Fort, at "the bottom of the Bay," which was one of the largest, has already been in part described. As the headquarters of an area it has been seen to have a varied and quite large staff, and it combined elementary industry with even more elementary agriculture. Nearly always some men were on the sick list, often with scurvy from the unbalanced diet or ruptures or broken limbs; the walking wounded, however, were put to light tasks such as picking oakum for the boats or weeding the garden. There are no direct references in the journals to ague, that bane of the southern settlements, but some of the ills described might refer to it. As a large post Moose had a resident surgeon, who also visited those neighbouring ones which had not. The company did its best to maintain a standard of behaviour and morals, and evidently social distinctions were rigidly maintained. Drunkenness was —largely unsuccessfully—frowned on. Religion was not to be forgotten. "You will," wrote the chief at Moose to a subsidiary post, "daily perform divine service on Sundays and all the proper occasions and in order further to promote religion and virtue among their Servants the Honourable Company have sent out a parcel of Religious Books, part of which I have sent you to distribute gratis amongst your men. . . ." There is no indication that the company also supplied secular books for the long winter evenings but many of the officers had books sent from England and welcomed newspapers and periodicals no matter how late they came. The New York *Albion* was a favourite there as it was in the Kingston or York of the early nineteenth century. Organized recreation is not often mentioned. On one Guy Fawkes day the men were given a holiday with the entertainment being "shooting at a Mark," followed by a bonfire "round which at night they with grog made merry." Guy was duly burned. Boxing Day brought "foot Ball and other exercises," and on St. George's Day it was traditional to have target shooting for prizes, with imported beer for all. Such were the lighter moments, but on the whole it was a hard life in a hard environment, and until later years unenlivened by female society other than that of squaws who were not supposed to be within the gates.

The meeting of Indians and Europeans, representatives of strikingly different civilizations, brought a series of contrasting results, some good, some evil. Warfare, of course, was one; but much of that was associated with intertribal disputes and not therefore simple racial friction. Apart from this it is possible to distinguish between the situation when the white man was living in an Indian environment and that when the red man was exposed to, or threatened by, the European way of life. The second situation did not occur in the north until well into the nineteenth century and hardly at all in the south of Ontario during the French régime. Huronia was to some degree an exception, for in that organized and well-populated community the French missionaries had some expectation of introducing Christianity and a modicum of education. However, Huronia was cut to pieces by the Iroquois in the mid-seventeenth century. The conflict between cultures came in serious degree only in the late eighteenth century when agricultural settlement began in southern Ontario and when land was bought from the tribes for that purpose. The problem of the co-existence of Indian and white man in settled areas dominated by European concepts of society belongs to that later period. In the late seventeenth and for most of the eighteenth centuries it is the first situation which applies throughout Ontario, life in the Indian mode.

The fur trade imposed a quasi-nomadic life on both sellers and buyers of skins. It assumed Indians engaged in hunting and trapping, ranging from one district to another according to the presence or absence of fur-bearing animals; and for Europeans the role of what the French called *coureurs de bois*, modified by the existence of permanent or semi-permanent posts such as have been described. In a life on the rivers and in the forests survival itself depended on the ability to counter the dangers of a harsh environment: accident, starvation, or freezing to death. Trade was on a basis of barter, a system not very different from the usage in southern Ontario later except that money did not appear in the fur trade at all. The Hudson's Bay Company calculated value in so many "made beaver" (winter skins in good condition). The practice of giving presents to Indians was an adjunct to barter, rather like the bowl of free whisky on the counter of the general store.

Exchange of skills between trader and trapper was beneficial to both. Travel by water is a good example. The manufacture, operation, and repair of the birch bark canoe, together with the technique of portaging, were native skills and basic; but the Europeans added rowboats, sailboats, the astrolabe, and some elementary cartography. For land travel the European could have offered wheeled vehicles drawn by imported horses or oxen; but as there were no roads the Indian knowledge of how to travel through the forest, on foot in summer and on snowshoes in winter, could alone be employed. Both sides contributed to medicine, in Indian herbs and imported drugs; and to clothing in furs and woollen articles. Much of the food was Indian—fish, fresh meat, pemmican, corn, and maple syrup; and to these the Europeans added wheat, flour, beef, pork, and additional vegetables. Nothing affected the Indians so much as being translated from the stone to the iron age. It gave them cooking-pots, awls, hoes, knives, hatchets, steel traps, fishhooks, and muskets. Thus their cooking, agriculture, trapping, fishing, and hunting were revolutionized; but the change facilitated their semi-nomadic life rather than replaced it with something different. Broadly the Indian benefited up to the point that he could apply European technology to the kind of life he understood, while the European gained so long as he too was living under the conditions that the fur trade imposed everywhere except in the larger posts. When the emphasis shifted from that trade to fixed farming operations and urban centres a divergence, and sometimes a conflict, of interest arose.

There were other interrelationships besides those of techniques. European diseases and liquor had devastating effects on a people that had no opportunity of building up resistance to them. Whole villages were wiped out by smallpox; alcohol could drive an Indian into temporary madness. Some Indians were converted to Christianity. It was not to be expected that youngish European males would be disinterested in the only women in the vicinity. Individuals from all ranks consorted with the Indian girls, sometimes in casual relationships, sometimes in the equivalent of common-law marriages. A number of both French and English traders became deeply attached to their Indian women and half-breed children, and one Hudson's Bay officer renounced his return to England because he was not permitted to take his children with him. Others, of course, had less devotion or sense of responsibility. Some of the half-breed children were employed by the traders, others found their way back into the tribes with which they were connected and where they were accepted without difficulty.

It has been common to contrast the attitudes of the French and English toward the Indians, the French being regarded as free from racial prejudice and the English as intolerant or lacking in sympathy. This contrast is largely true if applied to New France and New England but it is not true of the English in the north. The Hudson's Bay men might themselves exaggerate the difference between Canadian and their own success in getting on well with Indians, and at times it even looked to them as if the Canadians— French or English—were rather too friendly. "The Canadians," read a letter from Albany in 1776, "have great Influence over the Natives by adopting all their customs and making them Companions, they drink, sing, conjure, scold, etc. with them like one of themselves, and the Indians are never kept out of their houses whether drunk or sober, night or Day." In the competition for Indian co-operation the Hudson's Bay Company may have come off second best, but it was still in the race, and on the whole its relations with Indians were helpful to both sides. The company had always insisted that they should be well treated and its men on the spot apparently carried out that policy consistently. Starving Indians were fed even if a post itself were short of food, and in the terrible smallpox epidemic of 1781–82 the Hudson's Bay staff fearlessly fed, tended, and buried the Indian victims who came for help. No doubt it was an interest, a necessity, to have good relations with the Indians if the fur trade were to be carried on, but a self-regarding motive need not cancel out a benign result. Over the long range of the history of Ontario the unfortunate aspects of the meeting of two races have tended to hide the limited phase during which the two were partners, often, admittedly, uneasy partners, in the first combined exploitation of the great forest land that was Ontario.

CHAPTER TWO

Pioneers

AT THE MIDDLE OF THE EIGHTEENTH CENTURY Ontario was still a wholly un-developed expanse, silently awaiting—as it had for centuries—the men and women who would come to make their homes on its broad acres and fertile soil. It was not an unknown land, for explorers and fur traders had made their way over its lakes and rivers from one extremity to another. Nor was it in an absolute sense uninhabited. But the tribes of Indians and the fur traders had done little to alter this forested region; and the groups of Frenchmen living at points on the lower and upper lakes or of Englishmen on Hudson Bay were there for purposes other than homemaking. Near the eastern end of the province a few French families were residing on the west bank of the Ottawa River but most of them were to be separated from Ontario by the boundary of 1791.

Virtually an empty land, Ontario could be peopled only through immigra-tion and that assumed the existence of political pressures. The first coloniza-tion was caused by the desire of the government of New France to encourage agriculture in the Detroit area. In 1749 and 1750 proclamations were read in the parishes of the St. Lawrence inviting farmers to accept grants of land, with rations and equipment added, provided that they did in fact devote themselves to agriculture. The terms were generous enough: the land itself, food for a year and a half, agricultural implements, domestic animals, roofing nails, powder, and lead. Those who accepted the offer were a mixed lot. Some came from around Montreal and these included *voyageurs* who already knew the area. There were also applicants from Detroit itself, disbanded soldiers and merchants with an eye on the main chance. Evidently there were pros-perous individuals in the group since some held slaves, Africans or *panis* (Indians). The tenure was, of course, seigneurial but apparently in a diluted form. Each occupant paid a yearly rental and an alienation fee. Since this was all French territory no distinction was made between the two shores of the

Pioneers 17

Detroit River, and therefore the exact number of settlers in what before long came to be part of Ontario is not known. But it is estimated that at the time of the American Revolution a hundred families lived on the Ontario shore. Some of those who first went there drifted away but left a substantial nucleus who made permanent residence.

Were they bad farmers as has been charged? The land was good so that crops of wheat, barley, oats, peas, buckwheat, corn, and potatoes could be raised with little effort. A feature of the area was the number of orchards growing pears, peaches, plums, and apples. But the impression is of lack of diligence, and there are stories of heavy drinking (not unique in North America), and of diversion into more adventurous paths such as the fur trade. The first British commandant at Detroit found these people "in great destitution of all things" but the years of war may well have impeded their progress. Writing in 1776 the lieutenant-governor of Detroit, Henry Hamilton, said that the farmers were lazy and backward and yet gives a pleasant picture of the life there. J. F. Hubert, appointed to Assumption church in 1781, found the farms neglected but expressed the opinion that the better market for wheat would lead to improvement. It was an uncomplicated society and the British conquest did little to change it: the farmers kept their land and their religion. No provision for education seems to have been made until 1786 when a small school for girls was established with the aid of teachers from Quebec. All too little is known about this first white agricultural community in Ontario. It was not large, and indeed was begun only a few years before the war with England upset the plans. Nevertheless it was clearly deep-rooted, for the descendants of those who came to live near the Detroit River in the seventeen-fifties remained to form a lasting and distinctive group in Ontario.

The Seven Years' War changed the sovereignty of the Detroit area but for some time the settlement that had grown up was left isolated in otherwise unoccupied territory. A royal proclamation of 1763 invited British subjects, whether at home or in America, to take up land in the new dominions but Ontario was held back as reserved for Indians. In any case few people took advantage of the offer and those who did were mostly merchants of some kind. The older colonies in America were more attractive to emigrants from Britain, and those who already lived in those colonies saw no advantage in moving north. It took another war to change that situation. Meanwhile the Quebec Act of 1774 put Ontario back into the colony of Quebec.

Opposition to British policy in many of the colonies soon after took the form of armed resistance, with opinion so divided that the resulting revolution has been described as a civil war. All those who did not favour rebellion were likely to be grouped together under the general name of "Tory," though in fact they varied from extreme conservative to doubtful and pacifist, as they did from the wealthy and highly placed to the simplest farmer and the Indian. Some Tories did not make themselves conspicuous and others recanted in time to save their futures without dislocation, but for the known opponents of the revolutionary cause there was neither forgiveness nor tolerance. They were regarded as enemies of the new state that was emerging, and were subject to the penalties of the loss of property and even of life. Thus they perforce became political exiles, driven to find refuge where they could. Over a number of years thousands of them came to Ontario, some in organized evacuations, some overland, some after temporary residence in Nova Scotia.

From their own point of view, and understandably, the Loyalists merited the highest consideration by government, and their claim was accepted without question. At the time and since the British response has sometimes been ascribed to a sense of guilt arising out of the failure to protect the Tories in the terms of the treaty of peace. Perhaps this was an element, but it is difficult to imagine what more effective protection could have been provided. True, more explicit promises might have been wrung from the American negotiators but in the climate of opinion that obtained the chance that promises would have been implemented and enforced by the individual states was notably thin. Having failed by the route of international agreement (for even the clauses that were included were ignored) the British adopted three ways of aiding those exiles who were to be known as United Empire Loyalists. One was temporary financial help; another was compensation for loss of property, office, or professional income; and the third was assisted settlement in those colonies which had not joined the revolutionary cause.

A sampling of the evidence placed before the commissioners by those who left the United States and claimed compensation indicates that the largest number had been full-time or part-time farmers and the same description would probably apply to the loyal regiments. Quite a number were in trade —as shopkeepers, tavern keepers, blacksmiths—and some of these also owned land, though it is not clear whether they cultivated it themselves. There were a few millers, scattered surveyors, shipowners and operators, and a handful who had held judicial appointments. All in all the Loyalists came close to being a cross-section of North American society. Some—the minority —had financial means, professional skills, and social status, but the majority had none of these. Most of the migrants had lived in communities in which distinctions were real and generally accepted, and some of the privileged were loud in their demands that the advantages they had enjoyed should be carried over into the land of adoption; that, for example, their lands be better placed as well as more extensive. All the Loyalists were satisfied that they were entitled to be well treated and did not hesitate to voice complaints. The circumstances of the migration were unique for Ontario: later there were to be groups of political exiles from other countries, but the Loyalists had come from the king's own dominions which they had striven to preserve for him. They came with bitterness for the past and expectations for the future. For the most part they were not "democrats" in the sense in which this term came to be used, either politically or socially. They were believers in British institutions as they had known them to be practised in the older colonies and expected to enjoy them again in their new home. But it was important, too, that all of them were accustomed to North American conditions, and therefore could adapt themselves more readily than could the later immigrants from the British Isles. This does not mean that all of them had been pioneer farmers, but a large proportion had had experience of that kind of life.

The United Empire Loyalists were those who could satisfy the special commissioners that they had in some way or another upheld the royal cause, and it was such people who received the benefits mentioned. Others came to Ontario from the Thirteen Colonies as a result of the revolution but from a mixture of motives. Mennonites, whose principles would not allow them to support rebellion, moved to Ontario, some of them because their attachment to the revolution was suspect, some because their political principles led them, some who were apolitical because they were looking for land. As pacifists the Quakers were technically neutral in the revolution although some of them had sympathized with one side or the other, but they were people who were migrating in large numbers toward the receding frontier. The opening of new land also attracted other categories of people who were not influenced by political considerations.

The political entity to which all these immigrants came was the Province of Quebec, which for practical purposes then consisted of two parts: that from below the town of Quebec to above Montreal, with established farms and towns; and the western section, Ontario, in which there was as yet only one genuine white settlement, the small one along the Detroit River. Some of the Loyalists were placed in eastern Quebec but most of those who came to the province were located on the upper St. Lawrence and the great lakes, from below Kingston to Niagara. This meant breaking into a wilderness. The land had to be surveyed, sometimes too quickly for accuracy, and was allocated to individuals in lots ranging from fifty to five thousand acres. The families had to be moved from barracks to their lots and provided with rations, tools, seed, and stock. All this was done as a quasi-military operation, and with a speed and precision which reflect great credit on the governor, Haldimand, and the army officers and officials working under him. The influx of Loyalists and the other contemporary groups went on for several years and in that time they were the only immigrants. On their heels came an increasing number of others, the first waves being mainly from the United States up to the War of 1812, and after the war principally from the United Kingdom.

Now that Quebec had a western section with the nucleus of a population, and one that was English in speech and customs, there was an argument for dividing it into two, one which took effect in 1791. Ontario thus found its first political being as the Province of Upper Canada. Its first lieutenant-governor, John Graves Simcoe, anxious to see the province develop and believing that there were in the United States more loyal British people, opened the door of immigration more widely than some of his contemporaries thought safe— they, with some justice as it proved, being apprehensive that not all those who might respond to offers of cheap land would necessarily have sound political views. Whatever defects it might prove to have, the policy did at least produce numerical results, for the population figure of eighty thousand in 1812 is explained largely by emigration from the United States.

In the interval between the two American wars, however, came the beginning of immigration from the United Kingdom and Europe. One of the earliest groups to be brought, in 1786, consisted of some five hundred people from Glengarry in Scotland, who gave the same name to Glengarry County where they settled, as well as in the counties of Ontario and Stormont. At the western extremity of settlement, in Kent County, the Earl of Selkirk received a substantial grant of land on which he planned to have a home farm worked by indentured servants from Scotland and also farms for other families in its vicinity. The operation began in 1804 at Baldoon in the County of Kent but proved to be a sad failure. Selkirk was unfortunate in his local representatives, his colonists, the area, and the weather; and in less than ten years he wound up an expensive and unsatisfactory experiment. Not far away Thomas Talbot, an ex-army officer who had come to know Ontario as a member of Simcoe's staff, had a year earlier begun a single-handed project for colonization. His methods were arbitrary from the points of view of both the local government and the settlers. Toward the former he could be high-handed if he chose because of his direct line to London; to most of the settlers his benevolence more than offset some despotism. A settler in Talbot's domain had to build a house and to have, within ten years, ten acres under crops. Furthermore he was required to build a usable road along half his frontage. All these conditions had to be met before Talbot would enable him to get a patent. Within a generation the results, both in quantity and in quality, were to be remarkable. Writing to the lieutenant-governor in 1831 Talbot commented on his own methods:

> I was the first person who exacted the performance of settlement duties, and actual residence on the land located, which at that time was considered most arbitrary on my part, but the consequence now is that the settlers I forced to comply with my system are most gratified and sensible of the advantage they could not otherwise for a length of time have derived by the accomplishment of good roads, and I have not any hesitation in stating that there is not another settlement in North America which can, for its age and extent, exhibit so compact and profitably settled a portion of the new world as the Talbot settlement. . . . My population amounts to 40,000 souls.

That population, at about the time of the letter, was spread over twenty-eight townships, comprising more than half a million acres which extended for about a hundred and thirty miles along Lake Erie and northward to the boundary of the Canada Company's Huron Tract. Although Talbot was inclined to ride roughshod over local officials and at times may have been unreasonable with individual colonists, he largely eliminated, in a big area, the evils of absentee ownership and speculation in land. He emphasized the necessity of having decent roads, saw mills, and grist mills. That such a result was difficult to attain is illustrated by the failure of Selkirk, a man who was as sincere as was Talbot in his desire to effect a genuine and prosperous settlement.

It was after Waterloo that emigration to Ontario got into its stride and it was mainly from the British Isles. Although occasional people emigrate from a love of adventure, and more to escape objectionable political or religious régimes, the most common motive is the hope of economic betterment. The dislocation following the long war, the industrial revolution, and the pressure of the enclosure movement on the small farmer combined to produce unemployment and widespread misery in the British Isles. Many of those who suffered from such conditions saw emigration as their only hope, but to set out on a long voyage into the unknown and to find a means of livelihood at the end were not easy for destitute people with no influence and scanty knowledge. There were, it is true, others who, while seeking to improve their lot, did not have to start from zero; but it was on the helpless ones that a debate began to centre. To some of those who interested themselves in such problems or who were involved because of their official positions the British Isles were over-populated and therefore the answer was to move the excess to the colonies, which were under-populated. To another school of thought such a course was an expensive and ineffective solution.

Individuals and groups in Britain made emigration possible and at times government helped to finance the passage. Substantial sums were sent back by persons already in Upper Canada to assist their friends and relatives to follow. In broad terms the categories of immigrants were those who came in organized groups, with or without provision for settlement; those who had help for travel only; those who individually made their way; and those who responded to the advertisements by land companies. There were a great many emigration schemes and they were of all sorts and descriptions. An example of one which was well executed was that for people from southern Ireland conducted by Peter Robinson, who was appointed by the Colonial Office for that purpose. This was not a project for dumping indigents on Canadian soil but for helping and directing their settlement and looking after them in the early and critical days. The emigrants were accompanied to their destination by a doctor and were issued beds, blankets, carpenter's tools, agricultural implements, and even cows. To judge by their various memorials the settlers were appreciative both of the British government's interest and of Robinson's "indefatigable exertions and unwearied diligence." They were, they wrote, pleased by their judicious locations (near Peterborough) and by the arrangements for a school and mill. They would welcome further immigrants to the empty land.

The value of this plan was that it was properly organized and designed to do the complete job, or in other words it was colonization and not just transportation. The land companies could also design and look after settlement, and they were a continuous operation. The largest was the Canada Company, a commercial corporation founded in 1824 for the purposes of buying crown land and selling it at a profit. This it did on a big scale; but although its "court" kept an eagle eye on dividends it was concerned to sell to settlers rather than to speculators and to encourage and aid public improvements. Early sales were encouraging if not dramatic, and in an advertisement of 1832 the company offered 2,233,000 acres under three categories. The first was made up of former crown reserves. "They are scattered in almost every township throughout the Province, which gives Emigrants who have friends or relations already settled in the Colony the means of choosing a situation in their vicinity." The "farms" were of two hundred acres or could be subdivided. Secondly were blocks of land in an area of which Guelph was the centre. There were, it was said, already conveniences—mills, stores, taverns, a school, mechanics and tradesmen, and resident or visiting clergy—and a good class of emigrants already established. The Guelph region was recommended for persons of moderate capital. The third category was the Huron Tract, with the town and harbour at Goderich and with roads "cut," but it was not as far advanced as the Guelph section. The company had its ups and downs but did make real progress. By 1837 it had sold some 100,000 acres of land to real settlers, opened more than a hundred miles of roads, and spent about £87,000 on improvements. The fact that dividends were also comfortably accruing to the shareholders did not prevent a real advance in orderly settlement.

Through the twenties and thirties a considerable number of immigrants arrived and settled in the southern fringe of the province. Ireland was heavily represented and many came from England and Scotland as well. The *York Almanac and Provincial Calendar for the year 1821* gave the total population of Ontario as 104,982. A glance at the breakdown by counties shows that Essex, the scene of the eighteenth-century French settlement, had not grown quickly. In the neighbourhood of Kingston, York, and Niagara the numbers had risen briskly, but some of the more northerly counties had yet to advance far. Looking at the population question from the point of view of immigration, the official figures for 1834 (a high year) show a total of 22,210 as going to Upper Canada. In the detail much the largest figure (8,000) is that for Toronto and the Home District. The table then lists the losses, including some who had returned to the United Kingdom and a substantial number who had gone to the United States. This last drain, which the emigration officials struggled to stop, was an early chapter in a long and sad story.

The majority of immigrants were of British origin, either coming direct or at one remove (an important distinction politically) from the United States. To this generalization there were some interesting, if minor, exceptions. By no means all the early immigrants at the time of the American Revolution were of British stock. William Berczy had a plan for a large settlement of Germans at Markham, which collapsed after only a few families had been placed, and the Comte de Puisaye placed a group of French émigrés near

Whitby which dwindled to a mere handful. A more successful movement was that of German Mennonites to Waterloo County where they took up a considerable tract of land. A number of other immigrants were brought from Germany to the County of Perth. There was thus some diversity in national origin but the province was mainly inhabited by people whose mother tongue was English.

Emigration being a subject of some interest in Britain dozens of travellers and residents in Ontario set out to describe the mysterious, forested colony, and to turn an honest penny thereby. To a reader of today most of their accounts have finally a wearisome sameness: batteaux on the St. Lawrence; bad roads, crude inns, and grim tasks in the bush; alternatively the land of hope where anyone could rapidly become an independent farmer. Some were more analytical. Others set out to paint an attractive picture or to refute it. Perhaps the most famous in the last group was Susanna Moodie, of the Strickland family, whose *Roughing it in the Bush* reflected as much her own distaste for pioneer life as a caution to middle-class people thinking of following in her footsteps. In a jungle of publications some balanced advice can be found. John Langton, who was to emerge from farming into the office of auditor-general, answered an inquiry from England in 1835. It was best, he wrote, to buy a partially cleared farm, say with twenty acres cropped and laid down in grass. This you could get for £150 within five to eight miles of a market. To that amount add £50 for a house and barn. All the provisions for the first year should be brought, and in most years the first crop would not cover the cost of clearing new land. Unless a man was prepared to work hard himself and had grown sons to help him he would need not less than £1,000. T. W. Magrath answered a similar inquiry by taking two cases. The first was of a two-hundred acre farm in the bush, thirty miles from York, with an open road for twenty miles. He estimated its cost at £178, including £100 for the land, £32-10-0 for clearing and fencing ten acres, and £20-10-0 for a log house and a road. The alternative, which he obviously favoured, was a farm of the same size and distance from York, in a settled township, ten acres cleared, and apparently an existing house. The land would cost twice as much, other expenses would be negligible, and the total would come to £207. Running through several of the more sensible letters and published books of the time was the warning that immigrants, poor or not, should have the will to work and to accept conditions as they found them.

With the exception of the small enclave along the Detroit River it was not until the last quarter of the eighteenth century that land, as providing for farming, development, and even for future wealth, came into its own in Ontario. Yet what the province clearly had was land—millions of acres of it. Any emphasis on the value of the timber came slowly and for long there was only talk of minerals. For the genuine farmer land was the necessity; for the privileged immigrants it promised prestige; for the state it was a pool from which could be drawn aid in support of churches and schools when there were few other sources. Governmental land policy was consequently of paramount importance for it affected almost everyone, rich and poor, town or country dweller.

A starting-point was that not all these wide acres were to be considered as unoccupied for much of the land was in the possession of Indian tribes and their rights to it were firmly recognized by the British government. The principles followed here (with a modification in one case to be noted later) were that private individuals or corporations were not permitted to buy Indian lands direct; and that only the crown could make purchases, for which proper negotiation and agreement with the tribes were required. The object, of course, was to avoid unjust transactions. Connected with transfer was the setting aside of "reserves" which were not subject to white occupation. Elimination of Indian rights by what were known as purchases or treaties began in the areas close to the St. Lawrence and Lake Ontario where the first settlements were made. A different type of transfer was of the tract on the Grand River purchased by the government from the Mississaugas for the placement of the Loyalist Iroquois. This case illustrates some of the possible complications. The description of the land transferred was in general terms, six miles on each side of the river and from the source to the mouth. In fact, however, no one knew exactly where the source was or that it was so far from Lake Erie. This was one cause of argument and another arose when the Iroquois found that they could not alienate land except to the crown. Joseph Brant, the able Mohawk spokesman, protested bitterly that they had no more than the rights of "sitting down or walking on the lands."

The Six Nations had not been of one accord in their attitude toward the revolution, but those of them who had fought on the British side could find no future in the United States and, like the white Loyalists, had no option but to migrate to British territory. Joseph Brant set his heart on a territory he knew, the land around the Grand River. Not all the Iroquois leaders were of the same opinion and a smaller group went to the Bay of Quinte. However, the majority did accept Brant's choice so that portions of the Mohawks, Onondagas, Tuscaroras, Senecas, Oneidas, and Cayugas found their way to the Grand River. Brant, who continued to call the tune, gave a kind of land grant within the tract to a number of white men on the theory that their skill in agriculture and development was necessary. By steady pressure, and at a time when the continued loyalty of the tribes seemed questionable, he succeeded in persuading the authorities, against their better judgment, to allow him liberty of action with the result that thousands of acres were sold. It was a confused and unsatisfactory operation with the minimum benefit to the Indians and the huge tract intended for their sole use was rapidly disappearing. Finally, in 1841, the government intervened with the proposal that the Six Nations surrender their lands to the crown, retaining the farms they occupied, and with an additional twenty thousand acres reserved. Profits on the rest were to accrue to the Indians. This accepted, a long controversy came to an end.

The process of extinguishing Indian claims to lands proceeded and seemed inescapable on the twin assumptions of Indian rights and the needs of white farmers. It was made no easier by the inevitable absence of Indian titles or even their own detailed descriptions of what they occupied and therefore were considered to own. Nor was it possible to assess the value of such land with any hope of even comparative accuracy. At first payment was made in goods and cash and later in cash or in an annuity or a combination of the two. A list of lands surrendered by Indian tribes in the period 1790–1836 shows a total of 13,331,580 acres, covering a long list of counties. Other areas were added later of which perhaps the largest was that purchased from the Ojibwas, between the northern shores of Lakes Huron and Superior and the watershed of Hudson Bay. At the same time as the purchases were made reserves continued to be set aside, and other measures were taken toward the protection of the Indians. An Act of 1835 continued the policy of preventing the sale of intoxicants to them; and in 1839 the chief justice ended a long argument by ruling that the Indians had no claim to a separate nationality, but that on the other hand the ordinary courts were open to them. Later on an important step was taken when a procedure was established for the enfranchisement of individual Indians. The result would be to make such persons ordinary citizens, losing the protection of measures intended for the benefit of Indians living on reserves.

Into the lands vacated by the Indians and into others came the immigrants. In the first few years when Ontario was included in the old Province of Quebec grants were made in seigneurial tenure. Just why this was done is not clear since the Quebec Act of 1774 provided that free and common soccage could be used. The seigneurial system was unfamiliar to the Loyalists and they complained of it, though without stopping to show that it was inconvenient or burdensome. In practice it was a strange form of that tenure since there were no seigneurs, the king taking their place direct. The Constitutional Act of 1791 provided that all new grants in Upper Canada were to be in free and common soccage and it appears that previous grants were converted subsequent to the adoption of English law by the first legislature of the new province.

The problem then shifted from the character of tenure to the policy, or series of policies, under which land was granted. The story as a whole is a complicated and changing one, but a few points in it will be sufficient to indicate the bearing of the policies on those who came to live in the province. For a limited period land could be acquired free either by privileged persons such as the Loyalists (who were also immune from the normal fees) or by men considered deserving, such as those holding public office or officers of the armed services. The amount of land granted free varied in extent. The original Loyalist grants, for example, were scaled from fifty acres for a private soldier to five thousand for a field officer. By extension it was deemed appropriate that the upper classes should have larger estates than the lower in accordance with the norms of eighteenth-century society. Little as the Ontario landscape might resemble that of contemporary England it would have been surprising if those in authority had suddenly denied their whole upbringing in favour of an unknown and unattractive egalitarianism at the very time when they were meditating on how the forces of conservatism and order had disastrously broken down in the Thirteen Colonies, with the first extensive colonization of Ontario as the direct result. Land was also allocated for the support of the Church of England and of schools, not in itself an unreasonable provision in the light of the vast acreage that was unused and of the absence of adequate revenue from other sources. The transfer of land from original grantees to purchasers finally began to upset the free-grant system which was in any case much criticized, not least because a rising level of fees payable contradicted its name. In 1826 the government of Upper Canada, accepting a British suggestion, switched over to sales, saving the claims of Loyalists and allowing for small grants to indigent immigrants on a basis of quit rents.

Such were the main features of a system of land-granting in which the weaknesses, however glaring, were further magnified by the more violent critics. Even if it were accepted that those holding the keys should release enormous amounts of land to their friends and to each other it could not be denied that withholding such lands from settlement and keeping them waste and undeveloped was an impediment t) the progress of the province. Such withholding practices created big blank spaces in the region of good soil, hindered the making of roads, and made it difficult for colonists to be close to each other. Similarly, while it can be argued that a church established in England should have preference in Ontario, that it was in the public interest that it be supported financially, and that this could be done only through land, the Clergy Reserves produced much the same results as did the holdings of the absentee owners. When Robert Gourlay sought answers on the factors that retarded the improvement of Upper Canada the one most frequently mentioned (in twenty-four reports) was the holding of land by non-occupants, and the second (in nineteen replies) was the existence of crown, clergy, and other reserves. Some twenty years later Charles Buller, Durham's Commissioner for Crown Lands and Emigration, was highly critical of the method of granting land. He explained that

the most striking proof of the early improvidence of the Government in its disposal of the waste lands of the Province is to be found in the fact, that from 1763 to 1825, during which the population had slowly grown up to 150,000 souls, the quantity granted or engaged to be granted by the Crown was upwards of 13,000,000 acres, while during the thirteen subsequent years in which the population increased from 150,000 to 400,000 the quantity disposed of, including the sale of the clergy reserves, is under 600,000 acres.

His main point was "the enormous disproportion between the granted and cultivated land." Too much land was held as waste for future appreciation in value, and thus there was discouragement of immigration and encouragement of emigration. Squatters, it is true, tended to solve the problem pragmatically but that was not good enough. Items from Buller's breakdown of the grants illustrate the discrepancy between ownership and development: clergy reserves, 2,395,687 acres; United Empire Loyalists, 2,911,787; magistrates and barristers, 255,500; executive councillors, 136,960; legislative councillors, 48,475; surveyors, 264,950. Complaints about land-granting became about as numerous as the acres involved; but except in rare cases they were predicated not on a theory that all men should be equal, but against absenteeism and the related abuse of authority for the benefit of officials and their friends.

With few exceptions, the immigrants who were building up the population of the province took up land not as a future asset but for the immediate purpose of making a farm. Their first problem was to get themselves and whatever goods they had brought to the particular acres of forest that were to be their homes. Water transport was used as far as possible. All those who came up the St. Lawrence, and most of them did, were carried in batteaux, large open rowboats. Part of the carefully organized plan for the Loyalists included this mode of transport, although the officials were handicapped by the persistent disappearance of some of the batteaux at the western end of the trip where they were diverted to local use. When sailing vessels became available on Lake Ontario toward the close of the eighteenth century they greatly added to the comfort of travel, but even if the newcomers found the batteau trip rugged it was luxurious compared to any land travel they had to face. Rare indeed are kindly remarks about the early roads of Ontario; but if nothing can be said in their favour there are explanations of their deplorable state. The predominance of wooded terrain made heavy cutting necessary and at the same time cutting created damp or swampy areas. Some of the early roads were merely tracks through the forest with stumps in place and bridges not. Attempts to exploit the presence of trees produced the corduroy road, that is one with logs laid across it; but if this saved a vehicle from disappearing into a bottomless pit it automatically created an unhappy series of bumps. A more sophisticated version was the plank road, first introduced in 1835, but it proved not to be durable.

The effect of a small population on the road system was exaggerated by the waste blocks between settlements, as was illustrated conversely in the Talbot settlement where road-building was more effective than in most areas. Scarcity of public funds encouraged the system of statute labour under which most landowners were let loose on work they barely understood, directed by men who were not much further advanced. The traveller used water transport as far as he could, and by a kind dispensation of fate travel by land was much easier in the winter through the good offices of frost and snow. The fact that the roads were never better than passable and frequently so bad as to challenge his supply of adjectives shocked the immigrant on his first arrival and created a barrier between his isolated farm and the mill, market, post office, doctor, clergyman, and every other institution or person not near at hand. In 1818 a petition to the Assembly from the Justice of the Peace and more than a hundred other men near Perth complained that, in addition to ignorance of farm conditions in Ontario, severe climate, and crop failures, three thousand people suffered from being cut off by the absence of roads, and prayed that a sum of money be granted "to render their access to Brockville practical, it being now utterly impossible."

As time went on partly cleared farms were offered for sale and by the twenties newspapers carried advertisements of them, couched in language markedly similar to that of the present day. Thus some immigrants could escape the tough stage of cutting the trees, which meant that someone before them had started in the bush on what was seen as a farm only by those with the maximum optimism and imagination. By luck or design it might be on a river or a lake; and equally it might contain unwanted water in the form of a swamp, in which case the pestilential black flies and mosquitoes would be at their hideous worst, pursuing the unhappy humans day and night, indoors and out. To provide the "indoors" was the immediate task before the first settler on the land. Temporary arrangements might take the form of a tent brought with the luggage, a primitive wigwam type of shelter made of bark or branches, or a simplified cabin made of round logs with no windows, an opening without a door, a hole in the roof in place of a chimney, and plenty of daylight between the logs. Such a building could be put up by two good axemen in about two days.

The log house proper, as distinguished from this kind of shanty, was constructed not in the manner used in the French-Canadian settlements in Ontario but in that common in the Thirteen Colonies before the revolution and brought to Ontario by the Loyalists. Log buildings became larger and more refined but their essentials are found from the seventeen-eighties. The average one was quite small, about sixteen by twenty feet over-all, and one storey high though sometimes with a simple loft. It was usually made of logs squared by hand and keyed at the corners in one of several ways. The gaps between logs were filled with wooden wedges and clay. A common weakness was the absence of any adequate foundation, the logs being laid on the ground. As a result they rotted and at the same time the house settled unevenly. The roof could be of hand-made shingles, but earlier ones were more often of halves of cedar logs hollowed and overlapping, laid alternatively top and bottom up. Doorways and openings for windows were cut after the walls were up, and if the owner was lucky he had one or two glass windows and a door instead of a curtain.

No stoves were used in the early days, so that heating and cooking were both dependent on a fireplace set in a chimney which at best was wholly of stone and often was a mixture of stone, logs, and clay. Even given the bountiful supply of wood (and it was there for the cutting) the log house was nearly always draughty and hard to heat. Sometimes the floor was of packed earth and sometimes of rough planks or machine-made boards if there were a mill nearby and if the owner could afford to take advantage of it. The log house was dark in the daytime and at night was lit by the fire or by homemade candles. Since the windows were seldom of a kind that opened ventilation was left to the doorway or the many crevices in the walls. The cost of construction of the basic house was not great even if workers were hired, while building with the voluntary aid of neighbours involved little outlay of money. Glass was expensive and not always obtainable, and the same could be true of boards. The logs were at hand, and free except for the time in squaring them. Usually some kind of log shelter, perhaps the original and temporary house, was supplied for the draft oxen; but this was often beyond the means of the early farmer, making it difficult to keep a cow or a pig through the winter.

Not all the farmers lived at any time in log houses and many of those who started that way moved, or their children moved, into other types of houses. As early as the last years of the eighteenth century there were a few brick or stone houses but frame ones were much more common. The choice often depended on the availability of materials, of skilled workmen, and of financial resources. There is a suspicion, too, of social pride in having a house not made of logs. If Robert Gourlay was an accurate reporter the difference in cost was considerable, for he gives the price of a good frame house as £125 to £250 (Halifax currency), of a good frame barn as £125, and of a log house as £25. All that the average immigrant could hope for was a roof over his head, provided, with luck, before cold weather set in. He had no thought of luxury or of the charm of fine architecture. For most people there was no time for frills, but a minority brought with them memories and traditions of solid construction and good style which, without the aid of professional architects, were translated into houses, churches, and public buildings of solidity and beauty. Until the forties and fifties, however, the flowering of such ideas belonged to the towns or the oldest settlements. In early days the average building in the rural areas was just plain shelter, and if it had some attractive features they came from accident or the good taste of the odd individual.

Furniture was of almost every conceivable kind. A few houses in the country had fine pieces brought from England or the United States or others, of varying quality, made in an Ontario town. At the other end of the scale was the crudest sort of furniture knocked together by immigrants possessing, often, the minimum knowledge of carpentry. Many cottagers of recent years will remember this as a familiar experience—and also that chairs, tables, and beds intended to be temporary somehow survive for years. Between the extremes of expensive hardwood furniture and improvisation came the softwood pieces made in many small shops throughout the province. This is the pine furniture which disappeared later into barns and attics to be retrieved a generation ago by moderns impressed by its beauty. It was made by local craftsmen with a few tools and apparently faultless taste. Some, probably most, of it was painted when made (with red as the prevailing colour), offering many hours of exercise to those later buyers who scrape down to the lovely wood.

We have given to the average immigrant buildings of a sort; but at the outset he was a farmer without a farm. His land was the prisoner of trees which had to be cut down before any crops could be grown. A few of the trees were used in building and for firewood, and where circumstances were favourable others could be used for lumber. When burned in the field or the fireplace they would also produce potash which was a marketable product. For the most part, however, trees were enemies. From this attitude, understandable as it may be, came the appalling destruction and waste to which attention has often been drawn and from which the province has never recovered. To the would-be farmer the forest seemed boundless and inexhaustible and the effort involved in clearing even a few acres was not calculated to make him a lover of trees. Ontario was not actually a solid forest for there were comparatively open areas known as "oak plains," but these were not considered best for cultivation so that to the pioneer farmer there was an appearance of unbroken bush. It was only when the settlers were multiplied many times in numbers that any serious reduction of the forest took place, with that process being hastened by lumbermen.

The first stage in early farming, then, was to clear some land, or clear it sufficiently to scratch the soil around stumps. This a man could do by himself, or by hiring "choppers," or by the co-operative endeavour of neighbours known as a "bee." Once cut, the trunks and brush were placed in piles and burned. At times these great fires set the whole forest ablaze and the wonder is that the destruction was not greater than it was. The agriculture that followed was extensive rather than intensive, since land was plentiful and labour was not. Rotation of crops, fertilization, and elaborate cultivation were for some time almost unknown. Implements remained crude until the second quarter of the nineteenth century except for improved ploughs and the introduction of the grain cradle. For most field work oxen rather than horses were used. The first crop was sown by hand between the stumps where decades of falling leaves had left a good bed of humus. Harvesting, done by hand, was a problem because of the shortage of labour. Threshing was done with a flail until the first threshing machine turned up in 1832, a monster that enslaved eight horses and a dozen men.

The major crop was wheat, but rye, oats and buckwheat were also planted together with Indian corn and supplementary vegetable gardens. Strenuous efforts were made by the government to encourage the production of hemp, which was needed in great quantities for British sailing vessels, but the offer of seed and instructions, bounties, and prizes failed to bring substantial results. It was not that hemp was difficult to grow but that its preparation for market called for too much time and skill. Orchards were planted on an increasing number of farms. When cattle and pigs were acquired they were left to run loose in the summer and in the winter got the minimum protection and fodder. There were few sheep. Most of the livestock was of American ancestry or from French Canada. On the whole the animals were not impressive but they were hardy. By the last decade of the eighteenth century there was a surplus of wheat in Ontario, and in the next few years the long story of exporting it to Britain began. The mechanics of this were in the hands of the merchants in the towns and will be examined in that context. For the moment it will be sufficient to note that prices varied wildly, dropping, for example, a few years after peace in 1814 to half the wartime mark. Cattle were quite extensively sold in the United States and could be moved there under their own power. In the days when wheat was king the farmers of Ontario had their good and bad years, just as they did in later times.

Although the emphasis continued to be on wheat there were signs of the mixed farming that was long to be characteristic of Ontario. Other field crops became more important than formerly and a market for fruit began to develop. Domestic animals, for draught, meat, or dairy products, became more numerous and of better quality. Vegetable gardens were given more attention and the women of the family found time to grow flowers. Clearings around the houses became more attractive. The fields looked more as if they were intended for agriculture as stumps were pulled out and stones piled. Both were often used for fences.

The early immigrants experienced some of the most difficult conditions, such as the absence of cleared land, maximum difficulties in travel, few schools or churches, and no nearby villages in which they could buy and sell. On the other hand they had opportunities of securing the best locations and the best soil. The softening effect of time was modified by the need for new arrivals to move further away from developed areas and on to less good soil. Much depended on the location of the farm. Travel by water might be available or, as in the Talbot settlement or the domain of the Canada Company, there were some relatively usable roads. There might or might not be a mill nearby. Neighbours could be agreeable and helpful or the opposite; or there could be none at all because of absenteeism.

It is impossible to draw a simple composite picture of rural life in Ontario in the period from the immigration of the Loyalists to the 1830s. Conditions varied by time, place, and the circumstances of the landowner. "Pioneer farming" is a phrase that can be taken to include a number of factors. If the agricultural implements in Ontario were crude so were they in most developed countries. There was a time-lag in their reaching the colony and fewer farmers could buy them, but in other countries manual labour was only slowly giving way to mechanization. On the other hand it was a new experience for immigrants from Britain and for some from the United States to have to convert part of a forest into a farm. That requirement, together with some other conditions of early life in rural Ontario, constituted what was peculiarly pioneer farming in the province. It applied in full only to those who first broke the land and in varying degrees to all other farmers. A few landowners—probably only a handful of town dwellers—had their farms operated by managers. A sizeable number of immigrants were able to buy farms that were partly developed and, with or without that advantage, to hire labourers. The scale then ran down all the way to the indigent immigrant who might work his way through to comparative comfort or live miserably. What could be said of almost every farmer, however, was that, with or without help, he had to apply his own muscle to agriculture. He could be a gentleman and a farmer but not a gentleman-farmer.

Contemporary and later writing dwells so consistently on one aspect of pioneer farming life that an unduly simplified picture emerges: the solitary immigrant emerging from his doorless log cabin to guide patient oxen amidst the rotting stumps of the trees he had laboriously cut down, returning exhausted in the evening to share salted pork with wife and children. The "life in the bush" and "emigrant's guide" type of writing of the eighteen-twenties and thirties almost invariably concentrated on the sides of Ontario life that were novel to British readers. A principal target was the simplest farm occupied by semi-literate peasants who could be represented as unwashed and crude characters or splendid, determined types making a new country. It was all true enough in itself but even from the earliest days it was only one thread in a mixed texture. Both the immigrants themselves and the modes in which they lived showed considerable variety. Many of the Irish immigrants of the famine years had no possessions and no money, were dependent on charity for travel and needed immediate employment in the province. Other newcomers from the British Isles and the lesser number from Europe had some capital, and even if that were small it made their early years much easier. A contemporary claimed that at least one-quarter of the Scottish immigrants of the twenties were able to bring some money with them, amounting in some cases to considerable sums. Many of the professional and business men and artisans went to the towns but a proportion took to the land.

For a few emigrants adventure was the motive but the great majority were influenced by the hope of a better life in the new world. Thus the comparison between personal circumstances in the land of origin and those encountered in Ontario is important. The half-starved, ill-housed Irish peasant living on the margin of subsistence had no money and few skills to take with him and he often had to face a hard life in the Ontario bush. On the other hand he usually got better food than formerly and could obtain temporary employment. If he was enterprising or lucky he could take advantage of opportunities that he would not have met in Ireland. The middle class families of moderate means, from any part of the British Isles, also migrated in the hope of economic betterment, although they were less ready to admit it. Those amongst them who went in for farming could sometimes obtain partly developed land with buildings of some kind. They were able to pay for labour, though they themselves had also to perform unaccustomed tasks. A minority were critical of pioneer life and claimed that they had been misled as to what to expect, but most accepted strange conditions with good grace. In the early stages they might well be less comfortable than they had been at home, but many found the road to modest prosperity a little later.

Every kind of individual was to be found from the very poor to those with substantial worldly possessions. Scattered across the province were groups who lived in various degrees of luxury and even in high estate. Such were those, mainly former officers of the army and navy, who after the French wars received thousand-acre grants in March Township on the Ottawa River. A civilian among them, Hamnet Pinhey, a merchant who had acquired merit by running the French blockade, built by stages a fine stone house in which he entertained at formal dinners and balls. It was said that Mrs. Pinhey was driven in a coach-and-four, though one wonders what roads allowed for such a vehicle. But if Pinhey and his neighbours lived in some style they were genuine residents, not speculators in land, and they set about making farms with a will. To Otonabee Township, further west, came well-educated families—the Stewarts, Stricklands, and Langtons among them—who had private means and ready pens.

Where Dundas Street crosses the Credit River was Erindale, the farm of the Magraths who had migrated in 1827, bought seven hundred acres of land, and before long built themselves a three-storey frame house. In the Huron Tract, in Goderich and into Colborne Township, was another group of immigrants who lived in considerable comfort. William—"Tiger"—Dunlop was one; Henry Hyndham, a barrister; the architect Henry Lizars and his publisher brother; a Belgian baron; some English army officers and others completed the complement. They had large houses, good furniture and glass, butlers, and generally formed a sophisticated society remote from log cabins and the simple life. Such a standard was, of course, the exception; but moderate comfort was less rare and gradually became more common. On the other hand there were few residents indeed who did not have to work hard to attain that comfort. Men and women needed to be Jacks and Jills of all trades, and even those unaccustomed to manual tasks—whether carpentry and stonemasonry or cooking and sewing—found that minimum skills must be developed quickly. Thomas Talbot, former army officer and present autocrat, was proud of his competence in the domestic arts and particularly as a baker. The average farm household had to be largely self-contained, both in the fields and in the house. Writing to Dublin in 1832 T. W. Magrath was cheerful about the life he led:

When we first came here, our hands were soft and delicate, as those of a lady, from being unused to laborious occupation, but seeing everyone around us employed at manual works—magistrates, senators, counsellors and colonels, without any feeling of degradation, we fairly set to, in the spirit of emulative industry, and we have already exhibited pretty fair specimens of our efforts in clearing land, and afterwards ploughing it.

My brother Charles can take, what is termed here, a great *gap* out of a field of corn, with a cradle scythe; he and his brother James once cut down two acres of Rye before dinner.

The latter makes all the waggons, sleighs, harrows, &c. and when I am not superintending the emigrant settlements, my time at home is occupied in shoeing horses, making gates, fences, chimney pieces, and furniture. Indeed my mechanical labours are so multifarious that I can hardly enumerate them, but you may form some idea of their versatility when I tell you that I made an ivory tooth for a very nice girl, and an *iron* one for the harrow within the same day.

By no means all the middle-class immigrants were as cheerful: Mrs. Moodie, for example, was prone to forget that she and her family had come to Ontario for their own benefit, and she had a weakness for writing of the "Canadians" as if they were of some inferior race. The fact was, of course, that many sorts and conditions of people, from several countries, had migrated to Upper Canada, and amongst them were those whose speech was no more pure than that of the London cockney. Every conceivable description has been given of the population of early Ontario. No doubt there were plenty of queer characters but lots of others too. William Proudfoot, a Presbyterian minister and a man who could be critical, gave this account to his daughter in Scotland in 1832:

> The people are very hospitable and in general very polite.—Canadians speak very well but late settlers from every country speak just as they did at home, and when you go into a Scotch settlement you see the same dress and hear the same dialect as you would do were you to visit the place where they come from. In some places nothing but Gaelic is spoken or understood—in others nothing but Dutch, in others nothing but French—and there are many who *guess* and *calculate* and *expect* from Yankeeland. In this country a person may place himself amongst a people where he will feel just himself as if he were at home. . . .
>
> The people here are not poor.—At present the majority of them who came into the country with scarce a dollar in their pockets are struggling with difficulties connected with settling in a new country.—Every year they are becoming more comfortable—even rich.

A few people lived in large houses, staffed with servants and well furnished. They and some others of very moderate means had imported clothing. Those who could afford to had regular supplies sent from Britain. In Otonabee Township Mrs. Stewart, a woman who cheerfully did much for herself, found a dearth of wearing apparel and sent to Ireland "for a chest of useful material every year. These consignments were various and wonderful; among the contents being cloth for men's clothing, material for winter and summer dresses, linen, flannel, boots, shoes, stockings. . . ." There were many cases like this but curiously few references to shopping expeditions in the towns where a variety of material was available. The poorer settlers had no money for purchases abroad and seldom saw the towns where they might have bought clothes in exchange for farm products if they had a surplus. For everybody to some degree and for many people almost entirely clothes were made at home. In some cases a family would perform every stage from processing flax and making cloth in a loom to cutting and sewing garments. For those who raised sheep and had a spinning wheel woollen clothes could be added. One set of precious buttons might be transferred from a discarded garment to its successor. Many women and men treasured "party" clothes but the average rural costume was simple and famed more for its warmth and endurance than for style. Proudfood kept warm when sleighing but must have looked a little like a mummy.

One needs to be very well clothed for riding in a sleigh,—a large pair of stockings drawn over the shoes and coming over the knee, then a pair of mocassins over all. . . . Then over a great coat must lie a buffalo skin—a bear skin over the knees—a fur cap with pieces of fur to come over the ears—and on the hands gloves lined with fur inside, and covered with fur outside—or if these are not had, then mittens or pawkies are used—Gloves of leather or wool will not do. Then a shawl tied round the neck, and a sash round the waist to keep all tight. Dressed in this manner a person may laugh at the cold. I stood the cold remarkably well. I had on two pairs of trousers, two flannel shirts, two waistcoats,—a pair of large stockings with leather soles to them to cover over my walking shoes, a pair of pawkies—a piece of flannel over my ears,—In this way I was perfectly comfortable in a sleigh. . . . In winter nobody cares for appearances, *comfort* is the thing.

In the country dinner was usually at noon and supper at six. The elaborate meals served in the towns were seldom seen in the country, and some of the records suggest that in the latter there was an endless procession of plates of salt pork varied only by potatoes and corn. Very often such a dreary diet was inescapable, especially in the winter. During much of the year, however, nature offered game, fish, many wild fruits, maple sugar, and edible wild greens. When the busy farmer got around to planting vegetables he could grow roots and store them for the winter. When Magrath built a barn, about 1830, he placed a root house, an ice house, and a summer dairy beneath it. Milk depended not only on having the price of a cow but on food and shelter for her during the winter. Buttermilk was drunk when available. Tea was expensive and substitutes were sometimes used, but it was served at inns and in houses. Coffee was less common. Apples were dried and various fruits preserved. The meat of pigs roving in the woods and living largely on nuts was excellent (and is now a rare luxury), but beef and mutton from the same simple conditions were tough. Bread was made at home by various methods and could be very good. For those who came from comfortable surroundings in other countries the food was lacking in quality and variety but for those who had been poor it was the opposite. Quantity of meat was a new phenomenon for many a British family.

The tasks before the early farmer and his family were compelling and strenuous. They filled long hours but by no means all the days. In the winter, when there was the least outdoor work, were also the fewest opportunities for recreation. Here educated people with some means had an advantage. Many of them brought books with them and could add to the stock by boxes from London or purchases in the Ontario towns. Henry Hyndham's library in Colborne Township held more than two thousand volumes and his was not unique. Pianos were imported—with no little difficulty—and sheet music could be sent from London or bought in a town. Card games, especially whist, filled many a long evening.

The poorer households had limited possibilities. Featherstone Osler, a Church of England clergyman, started a circulating library in his rural parish: "I have just established a kind of lending library. . . . Tis very popular and I expect there will be about 80 or 100 members. I have named the annual payment one dollar so that none might be excluded by poverty. . . . As a commencement I have given fifty volumes." There are not many references to similar enterprises. Mrs. Oille wrote that in childhood in the Niagara Peninsula there were no books for children and few for grown ups. What was in her house was "heavy and hard to digest": "Finney's Revival Sermons"; "Edwards Sermons"; "Baxters Saints Rest"; "Doddridges Rise and Progress of Religion"; and "Fox's Book of Martyrs." What a diet for a small girl! But she found the last to have "thrills all the way through." In a simple family the winter evenings could induce a boredom for which quantities of inferior whisky seemed the only cure. The pedlars who roamed the countryside carried not only an astonishing line of goods but also news of the outside world. Even in very early years there were enough of them to require a scale of licences and by 1816 seventy-six holders of licences were listed.

The months during which gatherings were possible provided opportunities for fun and games. The many bees were accompanied by meals as large and as sumptuous as the host could muster and were washed down with generous draughts of whisky. Very often such a day ended with dancing. Horse races were often included in agricultural fairs; and at them, as on other occasions, trials of strength, often taking the form of fights for which the rules were not conspicuously strict. Travelling circuses and menageries were common in the twenties and thirties. They stopped at many small places so were often near enough for the country people to attend. Theatres and concerts were mostly in the larger towns, but picnics and regattas in the summer drew participants from many miles away. Weddings and funerals were occasions for people to get together and were not hasty proceedings but accompanied by gaiety for the first and solid food for both. Fishing and many kinds of hunting interested people of all kinds and were readily available. The Methodist camp meetings should not, perhaps, be classified as recreation but they did form one means by which people could gather together, and they added some drama to life. Life on an isolated farm could be dreary and depressing, with many discomforts and few amenities, with illness, monotonous food, and sometimes sheer want. Much of the organized entertainment described in letters, books, and newspapers could be enjoyed only by those who could provide for the care of their children while they were away for long hours or days, who had neighbours, and who had the means of travelling. Extremes were evident in the realm of recreation as in all other aspects of Ontario rural life. For the poor, uneducated settler monotony was hard to break; for a very few families there were formal dinners and balls; in between were those who had opportunities for more modest pleasures. As time went on more and more people fell into the middle group.

In addition to farming, which was the occupation that claimed the majority of the country population, two others were important and they concerned increasing numbers. Lumbering was by its nature rural. By stretching words it could be said that almost everyone had something to do with timber, even if it was no more than cutting down trees or squaring logs for a house. In early Ontario, however, there was not the drain into commercial lumbering such as seriously prejudiced farming in New Brunswick. The exceptions to this rule were people near waterways along which rafts could be sent to Quebec for shipment to Britain. Some settlers on the St. Lawrence left their farms for employment in the lumber trade and others, in several districts, farmed in the summer and worked at lumber camps in the winter. John Langton of Sturgeon Lake operated a modestly profitable lumber business, but the most famous example was Philemon Wright, an American who led a group of people to the Ottawa River in the early years of the nineteenth century and began what was to become an extensive commercial business in an area that was better suited to lumbering than to agriculture. Lumbering was to be prominent in the forties and fifties, but before that the typical involvement of a settler was to take logs to a nearby mill, have them cut into boards, and as payment leave a portion—usually a half—for the operator of the mill. For the most part the settlers were more concerned with the destruction of the forest than its exploitation.

Mills, whether for lumber or wheat, and often for both, were links between the farming and the commercial worlds; between the country and the towns. They depended at first on water power and in several cases villages grew up where they had been placed, both to take advantage of the mill itself and to have a supply of water. In 1823 the editor of the Niagara *Gleaner* wrote of a steam mill just erected in Chippawa which was believed to be the first in the province. The engine was six horse-power and used two cords of wood in twenty-four hours. In that period it would grind enough wheat to produce twenty-five barrels of flour. It was operated by one miller and one fireman, both of whom worked sixteen hours a day. It was possible to make flour without these mechanical means, and the "plumping mills" in which corn, wild rice, and (with greater difficulty) wheat were pounded by hand-power into flour were common. Grist mills, however, were very much in demand and slowly a network of them came into existence. The first seems to have been near Kingston and the second in the Niagara district. Talbot got one erected in his empire and gradually they appeared in various areas until they amounted to about six hundred in 1836. Soon after that the great age of milling began, based on exports to the United Kingdom and with its success symbolized by gracious brick houses dotted throughout southern Ontario. The mills, whether grist or lumber, first appear as community services; but they were looking forward too to the developing commercialism which was centred in the little towns.

CHAPTER THREE

Shoes —
and Ships — and
Sealing Wax

WHEN TOWNS BEGAN TO BREAK the unending line of forest in southern Ontario any suggestion of similarity with the cities of the older civilizations from which the residents came would have seemed laughable; and yet these little communities had two characteristics which for centuries marked the towns of the old world. They were the domains of the middle class, and their life blood was commerce.

Writing toward the end of the period with which this chapter is concerned, the compiler of the *York Commercial Directory, Street Guide, and Register* for 1833–34, a man not handicapped by verbal restraint, pictured the change from the "mere wilderness" of forty years earlier. Now, he announced triumphantly, York

luxuriates in the solid evidences of a well directed industry, and from the precosity of enterprise every where pre-eminently conspicuous in efforts to inspire with life and activity our inexhaustible fund of now inert wealth, mechanically conveys to the mind, anticipations of future consummations calculated to illustrate even the brightest pages of future histories of Commerce.

A less colourful way of making the point would be to note that the towns had, not long before, started from nothing; that they had made some commercial progress, and would make more.

The sites of the first towns—Kingston, Niagara, York—echoed the judgments made by French authorities up to two centuries earlier. As the line along the St. Lawrence and Lake Ontario was filled in at such points as Brockville, Cobourg, or Hamilton, the significance of water transport was continually emphasized. When settlement spread inland other towns, such as

Perth, Peterborough, Dundas, London, and Brantford, arose, bringing further problems of contact with their neighbourhoods and the world beyond. And that contact was essential: an isolated town can neither live nor thrive.

For long distance transport of bulk goods little dependence could be put on travel overland. Even if the roads had not been so desperately bad traction by horses, far less by oxen, would have been of little avail for carriage of what was to be exported or even to be moved within the province. Until the railway age transport by water was the most practical method. On the river and the lakes sailing and steam vessels multiplied with the decades, some of them built and owned in the United States but many others of Canadian construction and register. Although none of the lists of ships can be assumed to be completely accurate they sufficiently indicate the character and dimensions of the merchant fleet. In 1800 three schooners and a sloop are shown on Lake Ontario. During the War of 1812 many naval vessels, of from three to a hundred guns, were hastily built, most of them at Kingston. Some were lost in action and the remainder were broken up not long after the end of hostilities. It was then that large numbers of ships were built for commercial purposes, principally to carry freight but also passengers.

Shipbuilding was itself an important industry scattered over a great many river and lake ports, such as Prescott, Brockville, Kingston, Cobourg, York, Oakville, Hamilton, and Niagara. Most of the shipyards built both sail and steam vessels, ranging from small to quite large. Wood, including white oak, was readily available and of the best quality. A steamship of 150 tons laid down in 1832 had bilge timbers of tamarac, half the top timbers of red cedar, and "the body of the best white oak and pine." To judge by such descriptions as there are and by the number of vessels prematurely broken up, not all were of seasoned wood or the best workmanship; but some of the master builders and their shipwrights did skilled hand work, although perhaps few attained the perfection found in Nova Scotia. Shipwrights were paid, according to their skill, from seven shillings and six pence to ten shillings a day.

Few of the sailing ships were large, 150 tons being about the maximum. Most had schooner rig. One of 50 tons needed a crew of three or four, those up to 100 tons, five or six. The pay was from £3 10s. to £5 a month. In some of the little towns once famous for making vessels retired lake captains were still found in the early twentieth century, ready to tell stories to wide-eyed children. Probably the last sail boats, other than pleasure craft, to survive were the stonehookers, clumsy-looking vessels into which were loaded flat stones taken from the bottom of the lake in shallow water (and sometimes pulled illegally at dawn out of the bank).

Steamships steadily overtook the schooners although it was long before the latter surrendered to their mechanical rivals. The *Frontenac*, built in 1816, was the first steamer constructed in Canadian waters to ply the lakes. It ran between Prescott, York, and Niagara until it was burned, the fate of many of the early steamships. By the twenties a number of steamships came off the ways, the *Queenston* of 350 tons, *Niagara* of 400, and *Alciope* of 450 being the largest until *Great Britain* of 700 tons was launched at Prescott in 1830. There is a long list for the thirties of steamers ranging from 100 to 500 tons. Several of them were tow boats. Few seem to have had a peaceful end, being listed as wrecked, burned, or broken up. They followed a number of routes on the lower lakes, some of them stopping (weather permitting) at the smaller ports, others concentrating on the main ones such as Toronto and Hamilton, others again going to American ports like Rochester, to Oswego for the Erie Canal, or down the St. Lawrence with lumber and wheat for export to Britain.

River and lake ports were often the focus of trade for an area running miles inland. An interesting case was that of William Chisholm who had been buying timber all the way along the shore of Lake Ontario from Burlington Bay to the Credit River. He was struck by the point at which the Sixteen-Mile river emptied into the lake and bought nearly a thousand acres of land around it. His plan, which he largely carried out, was for a town and a port, using the river both to carry timber down from the back country and to provide power for a grist mill and a saw mill. A curiosity of the arrangement was that he built and owned the harbour, being reimbursed by dues for a period of fifty years. The principal exports at Oakville were white pine, squared white oak, and oak staves. To provide transportation Chisholm built a number of schooners and later of steamships which carried, amongst other things, the wheat which he bought from farmers not far from the lake. Oakville was but one of many ports which fulfilled such functions. They were active little towns, with their eyes turned both inland and offshore, and drew to themselves the business and services which go with an urban community.

External trade and the shipping business thus went hand in hand, each dependent on the other. Agricultural products, especially wheat and cattle; potash, the saleable by-product of clearing land; wood in the form of squared timber, boards, and oak staves for making barrels were the principal items. Manufacturing still had a very junior status. Carriages and agricultural implements were made in many places, sometimes in very small places, often starting as a sideline for a blacksmith and in a few cases growing into substantial concerns. A Toronto newspaper of 1837 asserted that a particular firm there built carriages as good as any to be found in England. Similarly there were a number of firms, mostly small, making furniture. A statute of 1826 offered a premium of £125 to the first person to manufacture paper, won by James Crooks who lived near Dundas. Soon after other firms made paper in the Don Valley, at Belleville, and at Georgetown. Salt and glass companies were incorporated. The earliest known manufacture of glass was at Mallorytown, from about 1825. Out of local materials were made bowls, pitchers, flasks, and other containers.

Tanneries were here and there. Distilleries and breweries were as general as the public taste for alcohol. Heavy industry was in its infancy but in 1833 a foundry opened at York with provision for the manufacture of steam engines.

For the building industry there were many lumber yards, and in 1826 the press noticed that one J. Brown had begun manufacturing nails in Port Hope. Some tools were made. Stone quarries were in a number of places and brickyards at many. Up to the middle of the century, when mechanization was introduced, bricks were made by hand. Clay and water were placed in long shallow troughs and mixed by the hooves of oxen. Bricks were then formed in wooden moulds and exposed to the sun. When dry they were put in a kiln and heated for about six days by a wood fire.

Iron ore was early found in several places and efforts were made to exploit it. In 1799 one ingenious character petitioned the executive council for the privilege of erecting iron works "upon the waters of Niagara." The council, perhaps translating the request correctly, replied that he could not have exclusive possession of the river bank. Only a month later a group of associates expressed their desire to manufacture iron in the County of Leeds and petitioned to have crown land granted them to cover the cost of the equipment which would have to come from the United States; land also for the workmen, presumably in lieu of all or part of their wages. Nothing seems to have come of this particular scheme, but in 1800 a blast furnace—the first in Ontario—was erected on the Gananoque River at what is now Lyndhurst. The ore, which was of inferior quality, had to be drawn a considerable distance and the enterprise was abandoned after two years.

Two other iron works turned out better. The first was in the County of Norfolk at a site on Lake Erie from which products could be shipped and where a small river furnished power for the machinery. The furnace was begun in 1813. After a few years, and under a second management, production began of castings which were shipped by water or road to towns where they could be used in the manufacture of agricultural implements and household utensils. Some surplus was sold in the United States. The second was at Marmora in Hastings County. The first furnace was built in 1820 but for more than twenty years financial difficulties overpowered the enterprise of successive owners. When, in 1837, the provincial government considered acquiring the Marmora Iron Works for the employment of convicts the commissioners appointed to investigate found two smelting furnaces, a casting house, a forge to manufacture iron bars, saw and grist mills, blacksmiths' and carpenters' shops, a store and houses. The government decided not to buy and nothing came of the project in private hands until the middle of the century.

Retail trade was conducted in two ways, public fairs and shops. The former date from the beginning of the nineteenth century and were under the authority of proclamations which named the persons responsible and defined the conditions under which the fairs were to be held. A typical petition for a fair came from "sundry inhabitants" of the County of Glengarry in 1802. Young as the country was, they said, "it now yields some superfluities which might be turned to greater advantage by being sold or bartered within itself than being disposed of even at a higher price in the Lower Province, considering the loss of time consequent on going thither, and the perpetual drain of money which the country suffers by depending solely upon the Montreal Market." Already it would be possible to barter cattle, horses, sheep, leather, wool, yarn, butter, sugar, homespun cloth, and linen; the general development which a fair would assist would in turn enlarge its own scope. Fairs soon became common and remained as institutions in towns.

Shops appeared at an even earlier date. As time went on a few developed branches in more than one town, but most of them were small personal businesses found in only one place, though they might move from one to another. Even a brief survey of the towns of the province suggests certain characteristics in these shops. Many of them resembled something between a village general store and a later department store; that is to say, they carried goods of different types but included more sophisticated items than the simpler general store. Together with such shops were others which specialized in one line, so that there could be a tailor, a hatter, a hairdresser, a shoemaker, a watchmaker, an apothecary, and a butcher. There were shops selling material and clothes, groceries, and hardware. In Niagara, for example, one shop sold drugs, confectionery, paints, oils, dry goods, groceries, crockery, and hardware; another hardware, groceries, and crockery. A wide range of goods was offered for sale, and it is noticeable that this applies in quite small towns where the customers did not include government officials or military officers. Advertisements show not only that almost anything in common use could be bought in a town of average size, but also that customers demanded the kinds of food, drink, clothes, and other things that would be quite surprising if Ontario were thought of as no more than a simple pioneer society.

To illustrate what was for sale, or, to put it in another way, what townspeople used, some of the advertisements are revealing. A shop in York advertised in 1805 that the following articles had "just arrived from New York": ribbons, cotton goods, silk tassels, gown-trimmings, cotton binding, wire trimmings, silk belting, fans, beaded buttons, block tin, glove ties, cotton bed-lines, bed lace, ostrich feathers, silk lace, black veil lace, thread lace, fine silk mitts, handkerchiefs (including silk ones), black, blue, white, and yellow Belong, striped silk for gowns, Chambray muslins, printed dimity, split straw bonnets, cotton wire, Rutland gauze, band boxes, cambric, calicoes, Irish linens, plain muslins, laced muslins, blue, black and yellow nankeens, jeans, fustians, long silk gloves, velvet ribbons, Russia sheetings, India satins, silk and cotton umbrellas, parasols, white cottons, bombazetts, black and white silk stockings, damask table cloths, napkins, cotton, striped nankeens, bandana handkerchiefs, catgut, Tickenburg, brown holland, Italian lutestring, beaver caps for children.

On the grocery side: Hyson teas, young Hyson, green, Soulong and Bohea, loaf, East India and Muscovado sugars, mustard, essence of mustard, pills of mustard, capers, lemon-juice, soap, indigo, mace, nutmegs, cinnamon, cassia, cloves, pimento, pepper, box raisins, prunes, coffee, Spanish and American Segars, Cayenne pepper in bottles, castor oil, British oil, pickled oysters.

The hardware department: chinaware in small boxes and sets, suwarrow boots, bootees, and an assortment of men's, women's and children's shoes, japanned quart jugs, tumblers, tipped flutes, violin bows, brass wire, sickles, iron candlesticks, shoemakers' hammers, knives, pincers, pegging awls, awl blades, shoe-brushes, copper tea kettles, snaffle bits, leather shot belts, horn powder flasks, ivory, horn and crooked combs, mathematical instruments, knives and forks, fish hooks, sleeve links, sportsmens' knives, lockets, earrings, gold topas earrings, gold watch-chains, gold seals, gold brooches, cut gold rings, plain rings, pearl rings, silver thimbles and teaspoons, shell sleeve buttons, silver watches, beads.

In stationery: pasteboard, foolscap paper, secondpaper, letter paper, black and red ink powder and wafers.

Of the wide range of goods sold in the shops some, including meat, flour, and other farm products, could be obtained locally; but as the advertisements have indicated most manufactured goods were imported from England or the United States. Importing could, but did not necessarily, mean direct purchase by an individual shop. Ontario's dependence on Montreal in almost every aspect of business, trade, and finance was lifting only slowly during the early nineteenth century. There were wholesalers and middlemen in Ontario but they could not yet wholly stand on their own feet. Richard Cartwright, a Loyalist who lived in the principal town, Kingston, and who was in partnership with another leading merchant, Robert Hamilton of Niagara, was obliged in 1797 to turn down an offer by a London firm to act for him. He explained that both exports and imports were handled by correspondents in Montreal, for a commission, and that he could not have direct relations with London. "This mode of business," he added, "seems necessarily to be imposed upon us by our inland situation, but the terms upon which it has hitherto been conducted will become less burdensome when the mercantile capital of the country comes to bear a greater proportion to the trade of the country than it does at present."

The Montreal merchants had begun as fur traders and before that trade had left the St. Lawrence in 1821 had branched out into shipping, banking, and general export and import business. What was called "forwarding" was a combination of importing, wholesaling, transport, and financing the whole. Montreal was a port, a financial centre, and the principal centre for wholesale trade. It was to be long before any town in Ontario could compete seriously in any of these functions. Much of the purchasing was done in Montreal by Ontario firms—whether they were wholesale, retail, or both—and there for a time that business was financed.

Retail trade in Ontario was necessarily governed by the undeveloped financial structure in the province as a whole. Transactions with the public could be in any one of three forms: barter, cash, or credit. The first was generally acceptable to both parties although it imposed on the shopkeepers the necessity of selling, as it were, in two directions. Credit had the same risks as continued to obtain and could be as disastrous to the shopkeepers of the early nineteenth as to those of the early twentieth century. Empty coffers induced bargain sales, threats of legal action, and some bankruptcies. The shopkeepers yearned for cash payments and increasingly called for them, but cash was a rare commodity. In purchasing the retailer and the wholesaler were in turn largely dependent on credit.

Barter was widespread. The simplest form was the exchange of farm products, say wheat and pork, for groceries or hardware. The merchants then re-sold the farm products to their town customers. This kind of barter lingered longer in the country districts than in the towns. Alternatively barter could be in the form of labour or professional services exchanged for goods. A step in the direction of currency was in the merchants' notes or "bons" which could be redeemed in goods to the amount shown on their face. This last was similar to the system of tokens used by the Hudson's Bay Company or by some later industrial firms. Land was granted in part payment of judges and government officials.

There was very little currency and that little was a strange jumble of the real and the imaginary. British accounts in Canada were kept in sterling but for a time payment to their troops was in Spanish dollars, which owed their prime position on the continent to the old trade between the colonies and the West Indies. The so-called Halifax and New York, or York, currencies were no more than ratings of that dollar, the one at five and the other at eight shillings. They were not represented by coins or paper money. In early days prices in Ontario were commonly shown in pounds, which usually meant Halifax pounds, sometimes identified as "currency"; in country districts the reference could be to York although that currency lost any official recognition. Sometimes prices or accounts were in dollars, and not infrequently in a mixture of pounds and dollars. Some British silver was imported from time to time but it quickly disappeared in payment of overseas debts. Spanish, French, or Portuguese coins circulated to some extent and included some discards from the United States. There were various kinds of tokens, including even brass buttons hammered smooth. During the War of 1812 the British introduced army bills for purchasing supplies. They were legal tender and—except in the smallest denominations—carried interest. Promissory notes signed by one individual and counter-signed by another circulated and were discounted either by private firms or by banks when they existed.

Before there were banks the larger trading concerns performed several of their functions. They held money on deposit, handled credit, and collected debts. The firms in question were mostly in Montreal. Forsyth, Richardson and Company, for example, had wide interests in Ontario and for a time held the official funds of the province. In conformity with its role as financial centre it was Montreal which had the first bank in British North America. The Bank of Montreal, which began operations in 1817 and received a charter from the legislature in 1822, showed the influence of the First Bank of the United States as did later banks. One of the most important of these borrowed principles to be incorporated in charters was the absence of restrictions on the establishment of branches. Long after it ceased to enjoy a position of monopoly the Bank of Montreal dominated finance in both Upper and Lower Canada, but other banks did appear quite early in Upper Canada. The first foray was in Kingston but it was not successful and it was the Bank of Upper Canada in York, chartered in 1821, which was first active and which had the support and approval of the provincial government. Kingston then recovered its lost position in 1831 with the Commercial Bank of the Midland District, and five years later the Gore Bank got under way in Hamilton. There were no other chartered banks for a time but some that were ordinary joint stock companies. One of these, the Agricultural Bank, was noteworthy both as being the first bank to allow interest on deposits and for its failure, disastrous for depositors and holders of notes. Other unchartered banks were more stable, one being the People's Bank whose manager, Francis Hincks, was later to achieve wider financial fame. None in this category, however, had long lives. The Bank of British North America, organized in Britain, was authorized by the province to conduct all kinds of banking business. It opened a branch in Toronto as in cities of the other provinces. The banks accepted deposits but for some time this was a minor part of their business. They issued bank notes in dollars thus alleviating the shortage of currency, lent money, and discounted notes. At the same time legislative action was taken to prevent the issue by any unauthorized persons of anything "intended to pass as money."

The Home District Savings Bank, organized in York in 1830, was not similar to the commercial banks but more like the later penny banks. It was "for the Earnings of Journeymen, Tradesmen, Mechanics, Servants, Labourers, &c." and was open every Saturday to receive deposits of any sum over one shilling and three pence. Suggested by the lieutenant-governor, Colborne, its object was to provide a means of making small savings. Interest of 5 per cent was paid on deposits, the money being lodged in the Bank of Upper Canada. The managers, who had volunteered their services, were eight prominent business men.

One of the most essential institutions in Ontario was for insurance against fire. In days of wooden houses, some unreliable fireplaces, great hay barns, and sketchy fire-fighting services the hazard was serious. To a lesser extent life insurance was in demand. The earliest insurance seems to have been written by English companies through their agents and American companies were also early in the field. In 1832 fifty business men and artisans of York petitioned the lieutenant-governor for incorporation of the British America Fire and Life Assurance Institution. They argued that "there is annually taken out of this province into England and the United States a sum little short of one hundred thousand pounds currency" in premiums for fire insurance alone. If that was true there must have been a substantial number of subscribers. They also argued that delays were caused by the remoteness of the companies. Whether or not either claim was accurate the petition was allowed and the new company began its career. Evidently there was a general interest in encouraging local companies since not long after, in 1836, a statute authorized any ten freeholders in a district to call a meeting to consider whether it was expedient to establish a fire insurance company "on the principle of mutual insurance."

For the people of those days the cost of goods and services was as of much interest as to any later generation. Since so much was imported the cost of transportation and the fees of middlemen constituted important elements. In 1792 Simcoe told Henry Dundas that the price of goods at Detroit (then still in British hands) was 50 per cent over that of Montreal; Thomas Radcliff, writing from near London in 1833, said that "any thing of British manufacture is here nearly double the price it is in the mother country." Elizabeth Russell, sister of the administrator of Upper Canada, was not usually unduly critical, but in 1799 she wrote of the "high prices of every necessary of life" and the "dearness of labour of all kinds." Some price control was attempted, the Justices of the Peace being authorized in 1825 to fix the price of bread, basing it on the average for the previous fourteen days. It is difficult now, however, to attempt any assessment of the level of prices. Not only is there often uncertainty about which currency is involved but the real value of money from year to year cannot readily be seen in modern terms. Raw information is voluminous, and although a glance at some of the lists shows obviously high prices for some items, no intelligent judgment can be made of the whole.

Towns were the centres of trade, of industry, and of finance. From them were managed the export of staples, chiefly agricultural and lumber products, and they supplied the rural areas with manufactured goods. All these functions were in the hands of the middle class and it was on that class that the progress of a town depended. The social structure of a town, however, did not so obviously reflect this priority. The stigma of "trade" was less a barrier to high society than in contemporary England and men who started as small merchants might find their way into the upper social echelons. Bankers and large importers were socially closer to the top of the ladder, but the non-commercial groups made up the largest part of the "upper class" or "society." The composition would vary from one town to another. Where garrisons were stationed the officers held unquestioned status and apparently had, in years of peace, plenty of time for dining and dancing, for riding and hunting. Politicians were less certain. Tories were more likely to find favour in society than were Reformers but exceptions existed either way. In York high government officials were prominent. Everywhere the Bench, the Bar, and the Church of England supplied many of the social leaders. Other professional men—doctors, teachers, and engineers—were often in the inner ring, together with a smattering of journalists and those described in directories as "gentlemen," who presumably were retired or had private means.

The towns in which such people lived, and in which, of course, they constituted small minorities, were described by visitors in language varying from ill-concealed disgust to enthusiasm. One would dwell on the remaining shacks, muddy roads, a disproportionate number of taverns; another would report new buildings, enterprising merchants, and general signs of progress. Perhaps the European travellers, accustomed as they might be only to the dignified sections of large cities, had never explored the less attractive urban scenes at home. In Ontario a short drive revealed all.

Even for the well-to-do residents problems arose. Plank sidewalks were some protection against deep mud but they would be on only a few streets. Sanitation was not far advancd in any part of the world and certainly not in Ontario. Domestic animals had a weakness for wandering about the town, but almost worse were the harum-scarum drivers of carriages. Hooligans and robbers, then as later, disturbed the peace. Fire was an ever-present menace in towns built largely of wood, having stables of hay, and no proper arrangements for the disposal of rubbish. In 1800 the Court of Quarter Sessions studied the problem of fire in York and decreed that every householder should provide two buckets especially for the purpose of extinguishing fires and should keep handy two ladders of specified lengths. In 1802 the *Upper Canada Gazette* expressed gratitude for a fire engine provided by the lieutenant-governor, noting that the citizens would subscribe to a building in which it could be placed. Citizens meanwhile were required to serve on bucket brigades, but in the twenties and thirties volunteer fire departments were organized. In 1837 the City of Toronto Fire Engine Company had two engines and seventy members, and the City of Toronto Hook and Ladder Company had sixty members. Members of both were exempt from military duty and from serving as jurymen or constables; but until much later they were voluntary workers. The same sort of problem and development is found in other towns. In 1817 the inhabitants of Amherstburg and Sandwich petitioned the Assembly. These towns, they said, had increased in population, and "as the houses are mostly built of wooden materials they are very subject to fire; and no provisions being by law now in force affording adequate power to the Magistrates to make regulations and impose the same," this situation should be remedied.

Fireproof or not, the most conspicuous features of a town were the buildings. The proportion of log buildings declined as time went on but this form of construction was too economical to be dropped quickly. The transition from logs to boards was in the form of a combination of the two, as illustrated in the specifications for a gaol to be built in Charlotteville:

To be built with squared logs of white Oak Ten Inches thick, on a foundation of Black Walnut Logs, so deep in the ground that the lower Floor of the building may be below the surface of the Earth: The Building is to measure Thirty four by Twenty feet from out side to out side, and Ten Feet from floor to floor, and to be divided into Three Rooms of Twelve feet by Ten each, and the remainder to be an Entry, to be lined on the outsides; the Partition Walls to be made with squared Logs Six Inches thick; the whole Building is to be Weather boarded with good Inch and a quarter boards not to exceed Ten Inches in Width, and to be lapped with feather edge; And the whole building is to be lined with good Two Inch White Oak Plank to be lapped, halved or groved at each joint and spiked with such spikes as are usually made use of for such purposes: The Building is to be covered, first with Inch and quarter White Oak Plank, then with good Shingles, the Plank to be lapped with feather-edge. The Logs of the Floors are to be squared with Oak Ten inches thick, and laid close together side and side, and the Floors over those Logs to be Two Inch white oak plank, to be lapped halved or groved as aforesaid. There is to be a good Brick Chimney in each of two of the Rooms with a Three feet back to each, with the Customary Fleer; The Four Doors, one outside and Three inside, are to be made of Two Inch white oak plank doubled and spiked in the usual manner; with a Lock and Key, to each door of the usual size and strength; There are to be a Window in each of the two rooms, with Iron Grates to each window. . . .

When, three years later, in 1803, it was decided to build also a court house in Charlotteville the logs were dropped and plans drawn for a frame building. It was to be of two stories, forty by twenty-six feet, with shingles on white oak. Frame buildings became more common as saw mills were generally available, and especially as the faster and more powerful steam saws were introduced. Stone was used principally where it was found in suitable form, as in the Kingston and Guelph areas. Individual brick houses and other buildings were erected before the end of the eighteenth century and by the twenties and thirties were probably found in every town. Robert Gourlay gave the price of bricks as £1–10–11 (Halifax currency) per thousand. A few years later a St. Catharines newspaper carried an advertisement to buy 500,000 bricks to be used locally in the next spring. The walls of a brick house were at first twelve inches thick, and it was only when the form of construction changed later in the century that brick veneer was practical.

Scattered through Ontario were some beautiful buildings, whether of frame, brick, or stone: churches, public buildings, and houses. There are few references to architects, the designs usually being made by artisans or owners working from books or from memories of buildings in England and the United States. In the best examples the taste and proportion were conspicuously good and the details reflect skilled craftsmanship. Georgian style predominated.

In the *Emigrant's Guide* George Henry commented favourably on what he saw in York in 1831: Government House, Upper Canada College, the commodious hospital, the court house (then occupied by the Assembly), and "many elegant private residences." Apparently anxious to draw the pleasantest possible picture he paid no attention to the less attractive buildings which formed the majority. A surviving contract for the woodwork in a stone house to be built near Napanee describes a ground floor of five rooms with a hall and a second storey of four bedrooms. All the mantelpieces were to be made "in a most substantial manner" and the specifications for the other work suggest simplicity combined with quality. Houses of this size and larger were not found on every street but probably in nearly every town.

As in the country there was a great variety of furniture, but in the towns there was a larger proportion and greater range of the more expensive types. Although the records of the contents of the poorer houses are scarce it seems clear that in such houses simple softwood pieces were the rule. William Proudfoot, a Presbyterian minister, wrote to his daughter in 1832 that he had found a small house a mile from York (the rent of which was $5 a month).

For it he bought some wooden chairs for three shillings and eight pence each, and from his description they were probably the pine type common in the country. To them he added a black walnut table for twenty-five shillings. "Everybody here," he wrote, "who is not in the very highest class has just as little furniture as will possibly do. The better class have things just as in Edinburgh, only less of it and not so costly." The "better class" bought their furniture from England, the United States, or from the numerous local makers.

Furniture was made in virtually every county of southern Ontario by scores of firms, mostly small, in many towns. Several local woods were used. Pine, found everywhere, was easily worked as was basswood. Ash, birch, chestnut, elm, hickory, oak, maple, butternut, cherry, and walnut were all at hand. Mahogany and rosewood were imported. Advertisements in a Cobourg newspaper of 1831 are typical. Three firms offered to sell pieces from stock or to make anything to order. One of them listed as always available sideboards, escritoires, sofas, bureaus, bedsteads, and tables. They would accept produce or lumber in payment. Evidently business was good as one of the firms was separately advertising for two journeymen cabinet makers. A little earlier a St. Catharines "cabinet factory" was looking for similar employees.

There is ample evidence of good workmanship but little of any distinctive Ontario style. The makers had an advantage over builders of houses in that, although both could and did copy from books, furniture was imported and houses were not. Little of the surviving furniture can be attributed to particular makers, partly because similar designs were followed by many firms. The Sheraton style was popular in the early nineteenth century and a little later was combined with ideas of the French Empire. All the successive stages of Victorianism were faithfully reproduced.

The Ontario householder of even moderate means did not take lightly the furnishing of his home. The house of William Firth and its contents were put up for auction in York in 1811. The house, on four acres of land, was a large one. The contents, which took a page of small type to list, included both a harpsichord and a piano, and a great number of what appear to have been good-quality beds, tables, chairs, china, glass, and so on. A York newspaper of 1826 referred to a fire which had destroyed a brick house there, and gave the value of the house and contents as £2,000, a considerable sum.

The inventory of the contents of a house owned by a storekeeper in Thurlow Township in 1829 suggests modest comfort. It included a black walnut desk; six Windsor and six other chairs; a cherry bedstead, one with curtains, and two others; great numbers of blankets and quilts; linen and cotton sheets; curtains and valances; various kitchen items; dishes, decanters, and wine glasses; and a number of books, mostly religious.

In 1837 John Macaulay and his bride were busily engaged in setting up house in Toronto. Helen worked from the English end where she bought some "handsome glass," knives and forks (dear but good), a plain tea set, and a common dinner set. At that time all china and most pottery had to be imported. Brownware was quite extensively made in Ontario and some of it was in excellent taste, but it had distinct limitations from the point of view of a middle class Victorian family. There were a few silversmiths in Ontario but most of the silver used was made in England or in Montreal.

John explored in Toronto and Rochester. Wallpapers were a problem but he collected samples in both places. Carpets, he found with regret, would have to come from England. The inevitable crimson damask was ordered for the dining room although the Toronto furniture firm of Jacques and Hay (who appear also to have done some interior decorating) tried to interest him in drab damask. Apparently the furniture was all bought from two makers in Toronto, and by the end of the year the house was ready. In a list of contents drawn up for insurance purposes these are the principal items: mahogany dining table; sideboard, of mahogany with marble top; one dozen hair-bottomed mahogany chairs; two arm chairs covered in crimson damask; $32\frac{1}{2}$ yards of carpet; crimson damask window curtains; mahogany bookcase; child's mahogany table and chair; rosewood writing desk inlaid with brass; mahogany piano; cherry bedstead; walnut dressing table and washstand; child's bedstead of mahogany.

Two years later Macaulay was buying some furniture in Toronto for his mother in Kingston and he wrote to her:

I am glad to know that the side board reached you in good condition and that you are pleased with it. I thought you would like it and that it would [fit?] the corner of the dining room very snugly. I have great hopes of it bearing stove heat well, for the best New York glue, which is better than English glue has been used in the veneering. I have agreed with Wilson for table of black walnut. It is to be a Pembroke table with two narrow leaves and will cost about three pounds and be made of the best wood. It will be ready in the course of three weeks, when I will send it down with the Secretary, which Jacques and Hay are making.

In addition Macaulay bought in Buffalo a cooking stove for his mother, which, he said, was better than a "Rotary stove." He seems to have been a busy shopper as a few years earlier he had told his sister that he was sending her a piano. Replying enthusiastically, Ann said that it would be the wonder of the natives and the first to reach Hallowell (later Picton).

Sitting at their mahogany tables in comfortable houses and waited on by servants, the well-to-do townspeople ate well, even in earliest days. For breakfast porridge was evidently not common (a fact lamented by some Scots) but eggs and ham went well with homemade bread, tea or coffee. Dinner was the serious meal and was usually about the middle of the day or up to three o'clock to accommodate the office workers who finished their labours by then. On occasion, however, dinner was in the evening. What was known as supper in the country and in the simpler households of the town and was at about six o'clock was dignified as tea in the wealthier families and moved on to about eight o'clock. The menus had least variety in the winter. Some people dried or bottled fruit. Root houses existed but are seldom mentioned. Refrigeration was in use at least by 1830 but evidently not widely.

In the summer townspeople could get supplies from their nearby farms and others had fruit and vegetable gardens attached to their houses. Alexander Macdonell, for example, grew in his York garden vegetables, apples, pears, plums, cherries, peaches, and grapes. During her stay in Toronto in 1837 Mrs. Jameson was unimpressed by the Toronto market but observed that the "higher class of people" got meat, poultry, and vegetables either from their own farms or from particular suppliers. She went on to say that,

Our table, however, is pretty well supplied. Beef is tolerable but lean; mutton, bad, scarce, and dearer than beef; pork excellent and delicate, being fattened principally upon Indian corn. The fish is of many various kinds and delicious. During the whole winter we had black bass and white fish caught in holes in the ice, and brought down by the Indians. Venison, game, and wild fowl are always to be had; the quails which are caught in immense numbers near Toronto, are most delicious eating: I lived on them when I could get nothing else. What they call partridge here is a small species of pheasant, also very good; and now we are promised snipes and woodcocks in abundance. The wild goose is also excellent eating when well cooked.

Other diners called the beef plain tough. Earlier accounts included salmon, once plentiful but apparently not so by Mrs. Jameson's time in spite of efforts at protection. Perhaps the fullest record of menus was that by Joseph Willcocks whose diary in 1800–1801 daily describes what he had for dinner in York. For our generation the meals are frighteningly large, but they do show variety as well as plenty. Beef, salmon, chickens, ducks, ham, veal, mutton, perch, pheasant, calves' head, pork, beef's head, trout, hare, and venison all appeared on tables and usually three or four of them for each meal. At Christmas there was turkey. It seems that vegetables were scarce in the winter, but in the summer there were cauliflowers, cabbage, parsnips, carrots, beets, asparagus, and peas as well as potatoes. Puddings were also seasonal, with bread pudding and custard appearing for months; then came plum pudding and mince pies for Christmas; fruit and fruit pies brightened life in the summer. This great array of food applies to private houses but the officers' mess did no less well. Willcocks wrote also of wine. On one day he took into a cellar a cask of port, a cask of Madeira, and one of rum. He kept a bottle of rum in his room so that he could give a glass each morning to the servant who lit the fire. Wine was consumed in quantity as well as variety, for Willcocks several times refers casually to himself or his friends as being helplessly drunk.

Such food and wine were seen only by a minority, probably a small minority, of the people of the town; the same would hold true long afterwards, and at the time applied to England and other countries. Unfortunately there is very little record of what the poorer classes had to eat in a town.

A good deal is known about the clothes of the late eighteenth and early nineteenth centuries but in some respects the evidence is misleading. In the previous chapter an indication was given of country costume, which for most people was simple, utilitarian, and homemade. It probably can be assumed that the average resident of a town wore equally simple clothes but probably of materials bought locally. What the artisan or clerk in a shop, or their wives, wore seems to have escaped the eyes of the many travellers. From advertisements, books, and letters of the period it becomes evident that the professional and merchant classes in the towns were well dressed. For both men and women most of the clothes were made locally by tailors and dressmakers or, in the case of women, often at home. Small articles and to some extent dresses, coats, and men's suits were imported, principally from England. Some of the articles for sale in shops have already been noted. In 1826 a shop in St. Catharines offered the following materials for ladies' costumes: broadcloths (all colours and qualities); cassimeres, satinetts, flannels; pelissecloths, baizes, fearnaughts; tartan and caroline braids; bombazettes, bombazeens, velvets; beaverteens, fustians, Circassians; vestings (a great variety); steam-loom shirtings; a genteel assortment of calicoes, French and Indian silks, cambriels; imitation, merino, cassimere, silk, and cotton shawls; silk and cotton handkerchiefs; mull, jaconet, leno, and book muslins; dimities, ginghams, cravats; leather, silk, and kid gloves; woollen, cotton, and worsted hose; buckskin mittens; ribbons, laces, threads, tapes; galoons, suspenders. Quite a lot could be done with a stock like that.

Mrs. Stewart, visiting Cobourg from the Kawartha Lakes in 1822, found that "the Cobourg ladies live in a very smart suitable style. They think nothing of giving fifty or a hundred guineas for a fur muff or tippet. Indeed, fur is much used." Some years earlier Patrick Campbell had been the guest of Joseph Brant in the course of his travels and was much impressed by Mrs. Brant who was

superbly dressed in the Indian fashion. . . . Her blanket was made up of silk, and the finest English cloth, bordered with a narrow strip of embroidered lace, her sort of jacket and scanty petticoat of the same stuff, which came down only to the knees; her gaiters or leggans of the finest scarlet, fitted closely to a stocking, which showed to advantage her stout but remarkably well formed limbs; her magazines [moccasins] ornamented with silk ribbons and beads.

Good clothes existed then, as is further proved by the dresses that have been preserved. How far these are characteristic of day-to-day costume is impossible to say. There certainly had to be warm shawls and cloaks for the winter and the fashion in shoes was for low heels. Since, however, the ladies of the wealthy classes in the towns had neither to wash dishes nor help with farm chores they would have less need for workaday attire than even their educated and refined sisters in the country.

The gentlemen of the towns had not yet succumbed to drab uniformity. In 1799 Alexander Macdonell bought two yards of hair ribbon and tied it on. Later he called in a tailor and instructed him to make a pair of blue pantaloons and a scarlet waistcoat. In the twenties a young man of Sandwich was seen driving in a dog-cart dressed in a black silk velvet cap with gold band, blue jacket slashed with braid, and tight black kersimere pantaloons. There was at least one tailor in each town and in some could be bought ready-made clothes imported from London. One Toronto advertisement in 1836 listed dress coats, frockcoats, trousers, vests, jackets, "waistcoats of Silk Valencia, Velvet, Jean, Plaids, Stripes, etc. etc." There were also moleskin and velveteen shooting coats, and black and white top hats. All these garments came from "one of the first Tailors in London" and were modestly described as "superfine."

There were plenty of occasions on which fine clothes could be worn, at entertainments indoors or sport in the open. Fishing and hunting in many forms were readily available to the townsman and were not necessarily confined to those with larger incomes. Horse-racing was popular and it too could overrun classes, at least for the spectators. The macabre pleasure of witnessing a public hanging could be shared by all those with such a taste. An entertainment hardly less coarse, and not shared by high society, was to watch a brutal kind of fight in what was known as "Virginia fashion," that is in which no methods were barred. Organized games, such as cricket and curling, became popular by the second quarter of the nineteenth century.

For those blessed with education and moderate wealth there were many ways to wile away the long winter evenings. Dancing was popular, but was more formal and certainly more expensive than in the country. One subscription ball held in York in 1800 cost each man $8, a substantial sum. There were "assemblies," too, following the English practice. They were evening gatherings offering usually, or perhaps always, dancing; light chat; and no doubt whist. Plays were performed from early days, sometimes by amateur companies in improvised quarters, sometimes by resident stock companies, but increasingly by visiting professionals in regular theatres. Many different kinds of programmes were given. In 1810 a troupe from London offered "Philosophical, Mathematical and Curious Experiments," together with songs, recitations, and ventriloquism. Not long before that a New York company had come in *The School for Scandal*, and there were comedies and tragedies, sometimes mixed in the same programme, sometimes interlarded with the apparently popular recitations and songs. In 1826 Kingston welcomed the opening of a "small but neat and comfortable theatre" with the first production being the "MeloDrama" of *Timour the Tartar*, performed for a "respectable audience." Some of the early theatres, or rather the buildings in which entertainments were held, must have been pretty uncomfortable, and it was ominous that the public was sometimes assured that the gallery would not collapse. By the thirties, however, there were some good theatres, and in them every kind of show appeared, from Shakespeare to contemporary comedy and puppets.

Musical societies and concerts were to be more common in the forties and fifties but they were not uncommon in earlier days. Some observers found the singing in churches agreeable, but there were not many organs. Some families had pianos, as has been noticed incidentally, but they were expensive. William Proudfoot found that a piano imported from—or perhaps through—the United States cost $232.80 when delivered at his house in London. Various people offered to teach music. In York J. B. Abbott announced his intention in 1810 of opening a school to teach church music or apparently any other kind; but as two years later he secured a license to keep a tavern he had evidently not been overwhelmed by students. In 1831 the church in Cobourg advertised for "a person qualified to instruct a choir in sacred music, and to lead the same during divine service." In the following year Robert McCarrol, a former bandmaster in the militia, undertook to teach all the instruments of an orchestra as well as sacred vocal music.

The gentry occupied and entertained themselves and each other in their houses. The ladies called incessantly, worked at their embroidery, sketched, communed with their dressmakers, and shopped. In the evenings men and women dropped in on friends for tea and conversation. Whist, the only card game mentioned, took up many winter evenings. Letter writing consumed a great deal of time, for polite notes went back and forth by hand in a town and many residents conducted lengthy correspondence with friends and relations in the British Isles. Sometimes these townspeople made the long passage to England; more often they braved the lake schooners and the Ontario roads in visits to their friends elsewhere in the province. In either case their stays were likely to be prolonged.

Some people read widely and the indications are that a great many read fairly regularly. Their choice was wide. First came the local newspapers. Their name was legion but their expectation of life was not good. A personal tone was given by the editor, who was also the publisher and owner and sometimes driven to be the type-setter. Circulation was small and even nominal subscribers could not be depended on to pay. The newspaper of that day offered something different to its successor of fifty or a hundred years later. If its editor was interested in politics he inclined to be a violent partisan and left little space for other subjects. No paper could be a quick purveyor of news in the absence of telegraphic services and even of rapid communication by land or sea. On the other hand a large proportion of a newspaper was often given over to British and foreign news. One explanation is that editors merely lifted large sections from incoming papers, partly as an easy way of filling pages, partly because Ontario was a land of immigrants. Whatever the motive, there is an interesting impression of cosmopolitanism as represented in articles and news stories taken as they came.

Many of the papers that came into Ontario households had something of the character of magazines. They contained articles on a great variety of subjects, book reviews, and books published by instalments. In 1826, for example, the *Kingston Chronicle* was printing Disraeli's first novel, *Vivian Grey*, and in the following year Walter Scott's *Life of Napoleon*. Here was a good start for those of literary bent, and for those who yearned for drama there were the stories of real life. The fashion, it was true, was to adopt a high moral tone and to deprecate any impropriety. These admirable principles, together with the absence of large type, cast a decent veil over the substantive reporting of, say, gory murders faithfully described in every detail though imbedded in phrases such as "we would hesitate to relate. . . ." The first number of the *Canadian Magazine* came out in 1833 but it was a periodical that had a brief life.

Newspapers were imported too, English and American. They came not very quickly but seem to have interested a number of people. There were a good many books in Ontario even in the early days. Richard Cartwright had amongst others in his library in Kingston two copies of Gibbon's *Roman Empire* and a copy of Hume's multi-volume *History of Great Britain*. In York John Strachan and C. J. Robinson both had good private collections. A clergyman of St. Catharines offered for sale both religious and historical works. John Macaulay of Toronto had about two hundred volumes of books and periodicals in 1837; and although this was not a large library the quality and variety in it—apart from a number of legal books—were typical of many of the collections made by men of his class. Amongst the books on political thought were the works of Burke, Locke, and Alexander Hamilton; both ancient and modern history were well represented by, for example, Rollin's *Ancient History* and by Gibbon and Hume; in literature—the largest part —were Shakespeare, Boswell and Johnson's own works, Montaigne, Molière, Fielding, and Sterne; scattered books on philosophy, religion, and economics (including Adam Smith's *Wealth of Nations*). Some men bought their books direct from England but in virtually all towns there were shops that sold books, usually as one section of a more varied stock. From the early nineteenth century the advertisements of books for sale can be taken as some reflection of the public taste, which is seen to be catholic and on the whole serious; but contemporary and recent novels were mixed in with books on travel, religion, history, and indeed almost every imaginable subject.

There were also public libraries of various kinds. Some were started by informal groups either to make books available to anyone or for circulation amongst themselves. An example of the second was the Norfolk Book Society which held quarterly meetings at which agreement was reached on the publications to be bought out of the subscriptions. At one such meeting the following periodicals were chosen: *Blackwood's Magazine*, the *Edinburgh Review*, the *London Quarterly Review*, the *United Services' Journal*, the

Dublin University Magazine, Fraser's Magazine, monthly parts of the *Saturday* and *Penny* magazines, and of *Chambers's Edinburgh Journal,* the *Canadian Magazine,* and the *Upper Canada Farmer.* The City of Toronto Ethical and Literary Society was an example of another type of organization. Its primary purpose was the reading of papers followed by discussion but it planned a library in addition.

The Mechanics' Institutes were modelled on those of Great Britain. About 1830 they were established in a number of towns and were substantially subsidized by the provincial government. The name was somewhat misleading as many of their members, far from being mechanics, were business and professional men. The institutes built up libraries and organized lectures on scientific and literary subjects. There were also "News Rooms" which in fact were libraries. The one in Toronto accepted members at thirty shillings a year but captains and pursers of steamboats were, for some reason, admitted free.

Joseph Willcocks, whose political sins were in part expiated by the value of his diary of life in York, lived in Peter Russell's house. Many evenings were spent by Russell reading from New York newspapers, from magazines, and from books. The books cannot all be readily identified since Willcocks used only approximate titles, but they included *Gulliver's Travels,* "Eudolpho" (Radcliffe, *Mysteries of Udolpho,* 1794), *Peregrine Pickle, Gil Blas* (Le Sage), a history of the Bible, Swift's works, *Don Quixote,* a history of Ireland, and biographies of Charles V of Sweden, Henry VIII, and Charles I. It can probably be taken for granted that these and other books were in Russell's private library since it was a bit early for lending libraries, but how many households followed the practice of reading aloud is not known. Probably many educated families did so.

The fraternal societies, secret and otherwise, were found mainly in the towns. Freemasonry came to Canada with the British regiments in the Seven Years' War and moved into civilian life. There was a lodge in Kingston from 1781 and one in York from 1792. Internal disputes slowed the growth of the order until these were resolved in the forties and fifties, but in the interval a number of lodges were formed. The Orange Order was introduced into Ontario by the Protestant Irish and its numbers swelled by other Protestants. The first identifiable lodge was that at Perth in 1824. By 1834 there were one hundred and fifty-four lodges scattered through more than a dozen counties. In 1837 the estimated membership was 18,000. The St. George's Society was founded in Toronto in 1835, to be an association of Englishmen for social purposes and mutual assistance. The Orangemen and the Irish Roman Catholics with their St. Patrick's Society have been more prominent in Canadian history for their political activities and battles than for their more peaceful and non-political activities. These and other organizations mentioned brought together groups of citizens who found friendship and interest and sometimes mutual assistance. The outlook of any one of the societies may have been in a degree peculiar to itself, but socially and economically they cut across other lines of classes. They had meetings and dinners as well as parades, affording opportunities to the gregarious and the lonely; in their simplest form allowing individuals to get acquainted with each other.

Such were the Ontario towns, and if they did not quite "strike the spectator with wonder and admiration" (to quote again from the *York Directory*) they were well beyond the primitive stage. Towns were the strongholds of the middle class, but the humbler people were vital to their well-being too, and to the latter it is proper now to turn.

CHAPTER FOUR

Body, Soul,
and Mind

IN COUNTRY AND TOWN ALIKE there was an important role for labour, using the word in the conventional sense of wage earners as opposed to landowners, salaried individuals, professional men, and those few who had private means. From early days "choppers" were employed in clearing land for agriculture, even by those who had difficulty in squeezing out a few shillings. Some farm owners could afford to hire men for regular work in the fields and more could do so at harvest time. Some of these workers were residents of several years' standing; others were recent immigrants who needed to earn money as they started farming themselves. Artisans were required in the country, mainly for building, or helping to build, houses, schools, churches, and mills. Most of the farmers, however, were perforce handymen so that they could do a good deal of the routine work, leaving for professionals the more expert carpentry or the construction of stone chimneys.

The main focus of labour is at any period in the towns. Shopkeepers and their assistants stretched from the middle class to the labour group. In the Ontario towns shoemakers and tailors were numerous in days before general factory production. Blacksmiths, carters, and teamsters were essential in the time of traction by horses. Numerous gardeners tended lawns and flower beds. In the small industries were coopers, brewers, brickmakers, wheelwrights, carriage builders, cabinet makers, tanners, and iron workers. For the construction and maintenance of buildings much the largest category of workers was that of carpenters, with bricklayers, masons, painters, and tinsmiths well behind them in numbers. A list of occupations, however, shows an overwhelming majority of "labourers," presumably the unskilled manual workers.

On the subject of domestic servants, in country or in town, came a steady stream of complaints. Many of them were Irish girls and employers frequently described them as untrained and incompetent. Mrs. Simcoe wrote to England (1793) that "the greatest inconvenience in this country is want of servants, which are not to be got. The worst of people do you a favour if they merely wash the dishes for twenty shillings a month." Mrs. Jameson summed up the situation:

The want of good servants is a more serious evil [than the lack of vegetables]. I could amuse you with an account of the petty miseries we have been enduring from that cause, the strange characters who offer themselves and the wages required. Almost all the servants are of the lower class of Irish emigrants, in general honest, warm-hearted and willing; but never having seen anything but want, dirt, and reckless misery at home, they are not the most eligible persons to trust with the cleanliness and comfort of one's household. Yet we make as many complaints, and express as much surprise at their deficiencies, as though it were possible it could be otherwise. We give to our man-servants eight dollars a month, to the cook six dollars, and to the housemaid, four; but these are lower wages than are usual for good and experienced servants who might, indeed, command almost any wages here where all labour is high priced.

John Macaulay hoped that his mother could find him a cook but she did not think "that there could be found in Kingston a good servant man or woman to hire at present." A few months later he told her that "Helen is without a cook. Eliza has been spirited away by some other servants and gets 7 dollars a month from Mrs. Strachan with a promise of 8 if she continues a certain fixed time. Cooks have become scarce and there are families who do not stick at trifles and go beyond their neighbours in wages in order to get their choice."

Writing from York in 1799, Elizabeth Russell said that carpenters were paid nine shillings a day. Some fifteen years later Robert Gourlay gave the average wage as seven shillings and nine pence (Halifax currency). Either wages had gone down or, as is more likely, Miss Russell referred to York shillings. In the thirties Magrath said that on a farm the daily wage was fifty cents plus "diet," and the working day from light to dark in the winter and from six o'clock to dusk in the summer. A short time later Mrs. Traill quoted wages as $10 a month, a much lower rate on the basis of a six-day week. In the absence, however, of accurate figures either as to the cost of living or the value of money in modern terms, little can be drawn from such accounts of wages, even if they agreed.

To the extent that labour, whether in trade, unskilled work, or the domestic category, was scarce the workers had some bargaining power but it was not canalized through organizations to any considerable degree. The place of unions in society was far from being accepted nor were there the concentrations of workers in industry that would give wide support to unions. A few unions existed in the thirties, most if not all ephemeral, but they expressed objectives of some interest. In York and Hamilton unions of typographers were founded but ran into difficulties. Hamilton also had unions of shoemakers and foundry workers for which there appear to be no accurate records. The York Typographical Society seems to have voiced the most comprehensive and modern demands: a minimum wage, ten-hour day, and additional payment for overtime. On the other hand the United Amicable Trade and Benefit Society of Journeymen Bricklayers, Plasterers and Masons, also of York, denied any intention of setting minimum wages but did call for the closed shop. Another approach, and one which apparently had quite wide support, from several groups of artisans, was to demand a protective tariff against American goods.

In 1836 was formed the City of Toronto Mechanics' Association, the object of which was "the protection of Mechanical Labour, either by petition to the Legislature, or to any other branch of Government, for any alteration or extension of duties, by enforcing the law against such as may violate it to their injury, by addresses to the public or to its other members, or by any other lawful means in its power." The meaning of these phrases is far from clear, nor does there appear to be any evidence of activities by the association. One purpose common to any organization of workers, either as part of a programme or frequently by itself, was mutual benefit in case of accident or illness.

Employment was frequently under indenture, that is, under a form of contract by which the employer was required to provide either food and lodging or instruction in a craft, or both, while the employee was obliged to stay in his position, with or without pay, for a specified time. It was far from being a new technique in North America, going back a long way and being later used by Selkirk who brought out workers for his farm in Baldoon under indenture. The more common use of the indenture was in connection with apprenticeship which was the means by which many young people learned a trade. Such an indenture, dated in 1799, has been preserved. It is a printed and solemn form with spaces left blank for the names, duration of apprenticeship, and the particular trade. The apprentice was to serve faithfully and his master's lawful commands gladly to do. He was not to play cards or other such games, frequent taverns, or even buy and sell his own possessions without his master's permission. He was not to absent himself from his master's service. The master, for his part, was called upon only to teach the youth a designated trade. In the middle thirties the Children's Friendly Society began to send boys and girls to Ontario to be indentured apprentices. The society's agent came with such groups, and interested Canadians, who seem to have been members of the society, assisted in placing the young people. In this case the master was required to provide proper food, clothing, and lodging. The same arrangement could be made for a domestic servant. In 1814 a householder in Kingston and another woman signed "articles of agreement," a document similar in language and provisions to an indenture. Under this the woman's son was to be a servant for five years to "perform all such services and business whatsoever" as his mistress might demand. In return he was to receive board, lodging, clothing, and instruction in reading the English language.

It could hardly be expected that such a rigid system as that of apprenticeship under indenture would always work smoothly, and frequently advertisements in newspapers concerning runaway apprentices show discontent, wherever the fault may have been in particular cases. The advertisements are standard, describing the apprentice, offering a reward of sixpence for his "apprehension," and adding a warning such as the following from a Niagara newspaper: "All persons in this Province are forbid harbouring the above described apprentice, under pain of prosecution." How many apprentices ran away, what proportion they were of the whole, and how many employers and employees were satisfied are not recorded.

Critics of this system have described it as close to slavery, but for some years there were also slaves in the technical sense. They are found first on the Detroit River, either Indian or negro. In the early settlements on the upper St. Lawrence and the lower great lakes were a few slaves who had been brought in by the United Empire Loyalists and their contemporaries. It has been estimated that there were five hundred negro slaves by 1793 but this figure is probably too high. Advertisements of slaves for sale or who had escaped constitute one of the few sources of evidence. Several of the best known residents were owners of slaves, who in most cases were domestic servants, and amongst these owners were some who were determined that slavery should continue and others who wanted it to be abolished. The Statute of 1793, the first of its kind in the British Empire, was a compromise as the preamble indicates: "Whereas it is unjust that a people who enjoy freedom by law should encourage the introduction of slaves, and whereas it is highly expedient to abolish slavery in this Province, so far as the same may gradually be done without violating private property. . . ." The gist of the enacting clauses was that no more slaves could be imported, nor could a voluntary contract or indenture be binding for more than nine years. Slaves already in the province were not affected, but from then on a child born into slavery could apply for freedom at age twenty-five.

Simcoe, who would have much preferred simple abolition, wrote to London of the resistance to the Bill: "many plausible Arguments of the dearness of Labour and the difficulty of obtaining servants to cultivate Lands were brought forward." In 1798 the opponents of the Act tried to have it amended so as to allow "persons migrating into this province to bring their negro slaves into the same." The amendment had considerable support and passed the Assembly but was ridden off by the Legislative Council—that body so often accused of being reactionary—strongly urged on by the administrator, Peter Russell, who was himself a slave-owner. With that amendment blocked it was only a question of time before slavery ceased in Ontario. In any case Ontario was not adapted to slave labour as was the American south. There were no plantations, and the character of agriculture did not lend itself to the employment of large numbers of unskilled workers.

For all sorts and conditions of people, rich and poor, living in town or country, physical health was one of the most constant desiderata. Some circumstances in the province were favourable to health, others not. In the towns it was possible for those with means to live in comfortable and heated houses, be looked after by servants, be well clothed and fed. There were opportunities for outdoor exercise through hunting, fishing, and games; and, in the winter particularly, for indoor recreation as well. Even such assets could not form full protection against all the ills that flesh is heir to, and it did not help that some of the people in this category were prone to refined gluttony. Like the upper classes in England and Europe they ate too much and too rich food, washed down by undue quantities of wines and spirits. The less fortunate townspeople did not always have satisfactory housing or a proper diet; nor did they have the same opportunities of taking part in field or indoor games. Lack of interests could lead to boredom and it in turn to excessive drinking of the cheap and crude whisky that was so plentiful. All townspeople were exposed to the likelihood of impure water and the certainty of bad sanitary conditions. In most towns there were no satisfactory arrangements for disposing of garbage and drains were non-existent. A realization of the dangers of this situation was not lacking, and efforts were made to improve conditions. The means of doing so, however, were not easy; public funds were small; and public opinion was not united for reform.

Rural life certainly provided plenty of exercise, though to have it put in that way would have provoked the irony of a pioneer settler battling with a few tools to hack out a farm and knock together some kind of dwelling. Even for the few who had private incomes there was more than enough outdoor work. For all the farming population there was a constant danger of accidents resulting in cuts or broken bones. Many of the early farmhouses were uncomfortable, hard to keep clean, badly heated, and ventilated only by drafts blowing unpleasantly through gaps in the walls. It was possible in the country to raise fruit and vegetables in season and a few people had milking cows; but more common than the bountiful gifts of nature were the endless barrels of salt pork, which might well have appeared on the coat of arms of early Ontario.

In 1831 the Colonial Office sent to each colony a questionnaire from the Royal College of Physicians. The reply from Upper Canada, prepared by an unidentified hand, was incomplete and uninspired, but serves as a starting-point for a list of diseases. Those which it gave were: intermittent and remittent fevers, dysentery, cholera, pneumonia, croup, rheumatism, and pulmonary consumption. To these should be added: burns, fractures, bites of wild animals, rabies, smallpox, scarlet fever, and obstetric mortality. Undoubtedly the affliction most commonly mentioned was "ague," a form of fever, that occurred in both town and country. Isaac Weld, staying at Niagara during his travels in the seventeen-nineties, wrote that "You would expect Niagara to be healthy because it is high, but the reverse is true. There is not a single house without a case of Ague and in some the whole family is ill." Ten years later Thomas Verchères de Boucherville was taken ill at Niagara which he said was a "hotbed of malaria." Hardly a country-dweller who wrote any account failed to emphasize the prevalence of ague. Some years were better than others and seasonally the summer was the worst time. Ague was generally attributed at the time directly to the swamps common before so much forest was cleared and appears as an occupational hazard for the early farmer. On the basis of many contemporary descriptions of symptoms ague has more recently been considered to have been malaria, caused and spread by the anopheles mosquito. As the thick forests were cleared, it is further said, this type of mosquito disappeared and with it malaria. While this may well be the correct explanation it is possible that

Body, Soul, and Mind 71

not all the cases described were of malaria. They may most certainly have been so where considerable numbers of workers were gathered on low ground, for example, in the construction of the Rideau Canal; while in some of the cases in other circumstances the fever may have been some type of influenza. Whatever the diagnosis the affliction called ague was widespread, frequent, and sometimes serious.

For this and other troubles there were some ingenious remedies or supposed remedies. Weld, for example, wrote that "as a precaution against ague we took, fasting in the morning, a glass of brandy in which was infused a teaspoonfull of Peruvian bark. This is deemed to be a certain preventive. You take that and avoid the evening dew." Mrs. Simcoe was satisfied that by drinking buds of sassafras in tea she was freed of the symptoms of ague. Some years later the Langtons were on surer ground when they obtained quinine for themselves and their neighbours. In days when doctors and drug stores were not within hail home remedies and medicine chests were essential. Many of the remedies were herbal and some of these can be traced back for centuries. Roots, bark, leaves, fruit, and seed were the components and often could readily be found in neighbouring woods, as the Indians had long known. From the dried bark of the alder was made a decoction to cure constipation. An infusion from the leaves of burdock was to purify the blood. Smartweed steeped in vinegar was applied to bruises. An infusion of red clover was used for bronchitis and whooping cough. Crushed leaves of plantain were applied to sore feet. A tea made of May Apple was used as a gargle. While many herbal cures were tried and efficacious, imagination went far beyond them. Mrs. Simcoe was told that pounded crayfish applied to the wound cured the bite of a rattlesnake, and that a girl had been cured of consumption by drinking tea made out of "consumption wine." Later a Sandwich newspaper announced that "bathing the part injured with warm strong ley from wood ashes, is an effectual remedy for the Lock Jaw," and that the cure for a wasp or bee sting was to apply an onion.

There must have been hundreds of such medicines and other cures, some effective and others not, but probably few that were harmful. On the other hand there was a tendency, understandable but ill advised, to dull pain rather than remove the cause, and to this end the common aids were whisky, brandy, and opium. It was this weakness, together with a response to ingenious advertising, that was exploited by the manufacturers of the patent medicines that were becoming popular in the thirties and created a major trade in the forties. A few patent medicines were valuable, for example, some cough medicines and others that contained iron; but many of the others were little more than whisky, which could have been obtained more cheaply, or laudanum, which was positively harmful. Persuasive advertisements encouraged people to believe that because they felt better the contents of a bottle had some curative effect.

In physical health as in so many other things the people of Ontario had often to fend for themselves; and with the aid of herbs, various traditional treatments, and what useful medicines could be bought they seem to have done rather well. Many a farmer must have developed skill in setting bones, and there are references to amateurs who successfully pulled teeth. The inhabitants' own efforts, however, were increasingly supplemented by the services of professionals. The first doctors in Ontario were army surgeons on active service or those who had retired. They were followed by civil doctors trained in Britain or the United States. The standard of such men was high; and although they might not have experience of unusual diseases they were well qualified to meet the needs of a pioneer society. Unfortunately there were at the same time a number of quacks, mostly come over from the United States, and other practitioners whose knowledge of medicine and surgery was too limited to be safe for the community. To eliminate the one and test the other a series of ordinances and statutes was passed providing for licence after examination by one or another kind of board. Experience showed that the nets so woven had holes and that undesirable characters were still professing a knowledge of medicine which they did not in fact possess. Although threats of prosecution were made through the newspapers the sparseness of the population, lack of police officers, and the credulity of people who accepted quack doctors as readily as quack medicines enabled these dangerous men to pursue their trade.

The scattered population together with bad roads made it difficult to ensure that medical attention was available to all those who needed it. There were, and have since been, comments to the effect that doctors were reluctant to face the country districts. This may well be true; but to cover a huge area in those days and minister to people who could often make no payment other than in the promise of farm produce was discouraging to a man who had to make a living. Nor were they always without suspicion of the doctor's treatment if it did not accord with ancient traditions. Even in the towns doctors faced difficulties. W. W. Baldwin, who was the first civil physician in York, found that that small place offered not enough patients and so he took up legal practice as a supplement. Doctors were undoubtedly wanted, and people could suffer from the lack of their services. Not infrequently the people of a community would set out to find one. A newspaper of 1828, for example, contained an appeal that "a well recommended Medical Gentleman, of sound British principles, will meet with every support in the vicinity of Vittoria, Township of Charlotteville, London District, the centre of a dense [sic] population." The charges made by doctors seem to have been modest. One near Napanee, for example, sent an account for £5-10-0 for fifteen visits and medication. The doctor was, of course, also a druggist and had to buy the drugs which he himself made up in prescriptions. It was a handicap to the growth of a native medical profession that schools of medicine were late in developing. The first was a private one opened by Dr. John Rolph in York in 1832. It was a successful enterprise, but interrupted by Rolph's involvement in the rebellion of 1837 and his years of exile in the United States.

Hospitals also came slowly into the Ontario scene. One at York received patients in 1829. It was intended for those who could not be properly cared for at home and not for the well-to-do. Those patients who could paid one shilling a day but the really poor were taken free. A second hospital was opened at Kingston in about 1832. Both received substantial government grants. Elsewhere there seem to have been at least no public ones until later. In spite of efforts to establish one, no hospital for the insane appeared until the middle of the century; meanwhile indigent mental patients were placed in the common gaols, which were even more unsuitable for them than for criminals.

Neither home skills, nor doctors, nor hospitals could protect the people against the epidemics that from time to time invaded the province. Smallpox, which had once almost obliterated whole Indian tribes, was still serious but it could be controlled by vaccination which was early introduced. The serious plagues were of cholera and typhus, especially the first. Just as early European visitors had brought with them some European diseases, so the immigrants of the nineteenth century carried others. The appalling conditions in the immigrant ships accentuated and spread whatever germs were taken on by the passengers, and the provisions for medical inspection and isolation at Quebec were quite inadequate to carry the weight suddenly thrown on their scanty resources. There and elsewhere were selfless men and women—doctors, nurses, clergymen, and others—who did what they could and in many cases lost their lives in so doing. Since infected immigrants slipped through the sketchy defences at Grosse Isle the diseases were carried further and further inland, multiplying as they went.

In 1832 alarm and apprehension about cholera were general and even healthy travellers found that doors were reluctantly opened to them. In April a proclamation appointed a day of "Public Fasting, Humiliation and Prayer," exhorting the people of the provinces to pray God "to turn from our people that great calamity with which parts of our Dominion are at this time afflicted." All too little was known of effective treatment and no standing facilities for isolation existed. Every measure to look after those who were ill and to check the spread of the epidemic had to be improvised. The Cobourg *Star* had for some time been reporting the march of cholera across Europe and on to British North America. In June of 1832 it announced that the disease had reached Prescott and, while it did not want to cause alarm, it was sure that some preparations must be made to establish a hospital. As a lake port at which immigrants landed Cobourg was particularly vulnerable and at a public meeting it was decided to set up a board of health on which there were three doctors. The board ruled that immigrants could be landed only at "hospital point" and there be quarantined for three days. Steps were taken to prevent clandestine landing at the main wharf. At many points throughout Ontario boards of health were similarly created, receiving from the provincial government medicines and grants of money. Some months later the epidemic seemed to have subsided and a further proclamation set a day of thanksgiving to the Almighty "for having removed the heavy Judgments which our manifold provocations have most justly deserved." Unfortunately the relief was only temporary and a further epidemic in 1834 took another heavy toll of life among the established residents as well as the newcomers.

Whether or not the series of proclamations justly associated sin and disease as cause and effect, the cure of souls was to many of the people of Ontario no less urgent than the cure of the body. To the extent that the men and women of the province had any positive interest in religion they were Christians. In this period there was no more than a handful of Jews, and the body of Indian beliefs in the supernatural never constituted a religion in the accepted sense. Some of the Indians, of course, were Christians and as such called for the presence of clergy in their midst. The mixture of Christians and heathen (as the non-Christian Indians were commonly described) created a special problem for those clergy of different denominations who lived amongst the latter or visited their communities. No doubt many of the white Christians of Ontario, then as later, were only nominally such; but in the towns, villages, and country districts there were many devout people who wished to worship God in the manner to which they had been accustomed, and to attempt to live in this world in the way to which their beliefs pointed. Often, especially on isolated farms, they had no means other than reading the Bible and other religious books or themselves conducting services within a family or a group of neighbours. They were, however, anxious to worship as members of con-gregations and to have clergymen (using that word in an undenominational sense) to preach to them and administer the sacraments. They wanted build-ings set aside for religious services.

In contrast with the colonial policy of France, the first metropolitan power for Canada, and with the domestic policy of England, the second, Ontario had wide tolerance for the practice of all forms of Christianity. Although there were complaints that the sun of government approval shone on some of the churches and not on others nothing prevented the practice of religion by the less favoured. The first Christian church in Ontario, the Roman Catholic, conducted early missionary work among the Indians and a century later set up parishes along the Detroit River. The destruction of Huronia brought to a tragic end the most promising mission to the Indians attempted during the period of French rule, but the Sandwich area retained its religious as it did its racial character. Meanwhile the services of the Church of England had regularly been read in the posts of the Hudson's Bay Company far to the north. As on ships at sea they were independent of ordained clergy and were more like formalized versions of the family prayers heard in many house-holds in the south. Following the decision made in the mid-eighteenth century Roman Catholics in the Canadas were not only allowed free exercise of their religion but were not subject to legal or political disabilities; indeed their church was subsidized by the colonial administration of a state that had not yet emancipated its Roman Catholic subjects at home. The growth of the Roman Catholic Church in Ontario came not from further French-Canadian settlements but largely from emigrants from the British Isles. Some of these, like the Scottish Highlanders of Glengarry, settled in groups. The southern Irish, who came in substantial numbers in the twenties and in much greater numbers in the thirties, were in some cases settled in groups but the majority found their way to many parts of the province.

It was the migration that began with the American revolution that first brought variety as well as increased numbers to the Christians of Ontario. Nothing even resembling accurate statistics exists to show the adherents of the various churches and sects, and where figures are given they can be accepted only as a rough idea of proportions. Many people, to their credit, went to whatever services were held in their vicinity, and others went to hear famous preachers out of interest or curiosity; but the temptation to do arithmetic on such a basis produces misleading results. The figures for missionary and parish clergy have much more validity since the names of the individuals are known. But except for a particular month of a year it is not even possible to list the churches themselves because of their periodic divisions and unions. In 1820 John Strachan wrote that the Church of England had more members than any other church. When a select committee of the Assembly examined the Christian churches in 1828 it found that estimates of the number of people belonging to the Church of England ranged from one-sixth to one-hundredth of the population. J. B. Robinson said that he did not know the answer and thought that no one did. A later census, that of 1842, gives the percentage of church membership to total population as follows: Church of England, 20.2, Church of Scotland, 16; Roman Catholic, 13.3, Methodists of all kinds, 16.8. The other churches were much smaller. The figures should be treated with considerable reserve but do give an idea of the balance between the churches.

A small population scattered throughout a large area created a problem in providing clergymen and church buildings as it did in the case of doctors and hospitals. The financial difficulty was in part overcome by government grants to several of the churches and by substantial assistance to these and others by bodies outside the province. There were, nevertheless, constant complaints and laments that the number of clergy was woefully inadequate, a weakness fully recognized by those already at work in the province. The ministry was at a disadvantage compared to the medical profession. Doctors could be more or less skilful but at least they were not denominational, and their services were as welcome to one person as to another. The gulf between the Roman Catholic and the Protestant churches could not easily be bridged; but among the latter was a mixture of co-operation and rivalry. Some of the laity, although having a preference, were happy to welcome any clergyman who came amongst them; others were stern and inflexible. Equally there were clergymen who, wishing that their particular church could be built up to cover the whole field, nevertheless appreciated each other's work and were prepared to assist each other in such ways as lending church buildings. Others conducted a bitter rivalry, and spoke as if it were better for the people to have no religious instruction than to be misled by false prophets.

Rivalry was sometimes found not only between Protestant churches but within them. Virtually every denomination in Ontario was at one time or other handicapped by internal dissensions. The story of the schisms, of complete or partial unification, of divisions without administrative breaks, is lengthy and complicated. It is a tale marked as much by strenuous efforts at agreement as by bitterness and bigotry. The details of theological and constitutional debates belong more to institutional history than to the life of the people; but the warring factions and the peacemakers—both including laymen as well as clergy—gave much time and energy to them. Dissension darkened the picture of Christianity in Ontario and seriously impeded the cause of religion.

A distinction between the churches, in part related to what has just been said, was that between those generally conservative and those of the revivalist type. The first group included the Roman Catholics, Anglicans, both branches of Presbyterians, and the British Wesleyan Methodists; the second, with its roots in the United States, was chiefly represented by the Episcopal Methodists and the Baptists. A characteristic portrait of the second as drawn by the first showed irresponsible fanatics infected with republican principles and of uncertain loyalty either to the state or to the established order of society. The second saw the first as stuffy office-holders relaxing in the more comfortable surroundings of the towns and accepting the outlook and the largesse of government. Criticism in such sweeping terms was quite unreasonable; but even in the more subdued language of later writing there tends to be an over-simplified distinction. Since the Church of England and the Episcopal Methodists have been, and are, taken as representing the two schools they may be examined from that point of view.

The Church of England was never established in Ontario in the technical sense but it was in a privileged position because of the great amount of land allotted to it and because it was regarded by government and by some of the leading inhabitants as a necessary factor in maintaining the colony in what they considered to be its proper character. After all it was the Church of England, and it was in a province threatened by the force and influence of the neighbouring Americans who had not long before revolted against the crown and compounded the felony by armed invasion in 1812. Suspicion was strong of those churches which were based on or had come from the United States: a suspicion accentuated by what were regarded as their wild activities in the Ontario countryside. The Church of England found ready support in the towns amongst officials and associates of the oligarchy, many of the other well-to-do citizens, and a portion of the humbler folk. In the farming areas many of the middle-class settlers belonged to that church as did some of the other farmers. It may be a just criticism that too large a proportion of the church's clergy were in the towns, though it is fair to recognize that even the wealthy townspeople had souls; but some energetic parsons did work under the more trying conditions of missionary visits or of huge parishes in the bush. There are, however, too many contemporary comments by those inside and outside the church to the effect that the Church of England clergy did not cover the field to escape the conclusion that, despite the efforts of individuals, the church was by no means meeting fully the challenge of the province.

To John Strachan there was no contradiction between a privileged church and missionary zeal in an undeveloped province. While continuing the battle for church establishment, retention of the clergy reserves, and the presence of the church in education, he was equally anxious that the clergy —starting with the bishop—should "go around the country and spread the Gospel to the people." He himself was no armchair parson, going around the country as much as he could. In 1815 he agreed to take a service each month in York Mills, then a difficult journey from York. He began in November, conducting the service in a dilapidated schoolhouse with rain pouring through the roof, and preached to a congregation of two. In the next year he went there for the ceremony of laying the corner-stone of St. John's Church, a service necessarily out of doors, and again he preached standing in the rain, this time to the only three people who had not run into shelter.

In the eighteen-twenties the Stewart family in the Kawartha Lakes made efforts to get a church built and to secure a resident clergyman; meanwhile the nearest service was five miles away where a clergyman came about once a month. In 1827 they welcomed a clergyman who was also the schoolmaster, and in the next year the whole family rejoiced that they could go to a service on Christmas Day attended by more than a hundred people. Featherstone Osler was the only Church of England clergyman in an area of two hundred and forty square miles; his nearest colleague, more than thirty miles away, was too delicate to do much. In spite of an unfortunate complex about the evils caused by the Methodists he recognized that he could be unpopular as a "book parson" and took to extempore sermons. On his first Sunday he rode twenty-four miles through mud and swamps to hold services in three places and doubted whether he could keep up the pace. Thomas Radcliff, who was critical of the "*easy going* clergy," yet wrote that "The humbler clergymen of our church, when riding through their parishes, in travelling dress, resemble the Irish Methodist Preacher. They carry a valise, containing gown, surplice, books, communion elements, chalice and cup, with a great coat and umbrella strapped over it." There were such men in the Church of England ranks, but too few of them, and friend and foe alike generally argued that the Methodists were making the pace.

To speak of "the Methodists" appears to ignore different origins and to some extent approaches; successes and failures in uniting; and uneven progress toward one Canadian Methodist Church. Such matters took up a great deal of the time of the leaders, but it was the work of the ministers among the people that had substantive importance. Men and women of those days, whether or not attached to a particular church, commonly talked of "the Methodists." In doing so—whether in approval or not—they thought of the message and methods of the church as these came before them; of what the ministers had to say, and of the character of the services. Methodist ministers were early in the field, coming from the United States. By 1806 there were seven stations with nine preachers. It is suggestive that York was not a station until 1818, and that the appointee was an Englishman who remarked that "the brethren from the United States scarcely make an attempt in many of the most populous and important places on the frontier." If the early Methodist preachers were not renowned for their learning they were for their energy in getting into the more unfrequented areas. The "circuit riders" took the Christian message to isolated families and groups who might see no other clergyman from one year's end to the other. The Methodist ministers were commonly known as "preachers" in contrast to "book parsons," and the characteristic preacher of the early nineteenth century was an evangelist of the revivalist type. Sermons were laced with the language of the Old Testament and vigorous emphasis was put on morals and salvation. Mrs. Oille recalled that "one sermon by a Methodist brother who had a 'call' and whose subject was 'The Sin of Pride' said that a woman could no more hope to get to heaven who wore a bow on her bonnet than a toad could climb a greased pole tail foremost."

From 1805 on the Methodists conducted out-of-door revivalist gatherings known as "camp meetings," presumably because, held in the country, they were attended by people from a distance. They lasted for some days, often over two Sundays, and people camped in the woods during this time. On the whole the Wesleyan Methodists disapproved of camp meetings, either opposing them or giving grudging consent. Nevertheless they were frequent and popular for some years, and were commonly regarded as one of the hallmarks of "Methodists," regardless of different schools of thought. This is a description by a friendly hand of one held in 1824:

Before the sermon was ended on Sunday morning, many were cut to the heart, and a mighty cry of penitents went up to God. Before sunset many of them arose rejoicing in the great salvation. . . . The revival was characterized by power [*sic*] and very unusual phenomena. Strong convictions—agonizing struggles—sudden deliverances, and triumphant shouts of victory, marked it almost everywhere. The subjects, who had proved its reality by long years of active and steadfast piety, said they were seized with pain, as if pierced with sharp instruments, and in this agony became unconscious of time and place, till after hours of wrestling they were suddenly filled with all joy and peace in believing.

Many of the camp meetings were extremely emotional, even more so than is indicated by the above description. They were bitterly criticized by some contemporaries and warmly applauded by others. Certainly people attended them in large numbers, though it has been suggested that their motives varied from a simple desire for religious satisfaction, through loneliness and curiosity, to a desire for entertainment. No doubt it is true, as preachers recorded, that some who went to scoff remained to pray; but what is lacking is a study written at the time by someone with a sociological bent, interested not only in the immediate effects of the preaching but also in the effects of gathering together a heterogeneous collection of people living for a week or more in improvised camps. There were regulations for life in the camps and efforts were made by the organizers to exclude undesirables and maintain order. To that end special constables were sometimes appointed. Nevertheless, accusations were made that the meetings created opportunities for what the *Christian Guardian* called "the most disgraceful and pernicious vices." One unfortunate man, who signed by mark, came before a magistrate to complain that his wooden leg had been stolen in the grounds of a camp meeting. Such an incident may be called of little consequence (except to him) but does raise the questions of what order was maintained and what sorts of mixtures of human beings were gathered in a clearing in the bush. The other, and unanswerable, question is how many of the conversions were lasting.

There were thus marked differences in the methods of the churches and in the public response to those methods, but there was much common ground as well. Methodist preachers were justly praised for the energy and enthusiasm with which they carried the gospel throughout the rural areas, and the Baptists, though less numerous and less widely known, did much the same. The difference between the evangelist type and the more conservative one, however, was in this respect one of degree and not of kind. Clergy of all other denominations, Roman Catholic and Protestant, went into the backwoods but not to the same extent. They all travelled on horseback, as did the laity on other business, because that was the easiest mode of travel for anyone not burdened with heavy luggage. Religious services were held in houses, barns, taverns, and schoolhouses simply because these were the available buildings. For the same reason dances were in barns, schools in private houses, and public meetings in taverns. Like other people the clergy lived in the manner of the times; or rather manners, since the more established towns offered an environment far different to that of the remote bush. Many of the country clergy farmed land as a means of supplementing their incomes, and thus had a dual stake in the community. Mrs. Traill wrote of visiting a resident (Church of England) clergyman who lived in a flourishing village and had a farm which produced most of the food for his family. He and his family had started in a wilderness of trees, living in a shanty they threw together, suffering from cold and hunger. He had then himself drawn to the area settlers from Cumberland, which had been his home. A saw mill, a grist mill, and a school had been erected by his initiative. Like the itinerant preacher and the camp meeting, the building of such a community is an example of adaptation to the circumstances of Upper Canada.

The sins of the world as practised in Ontario were denounced with particular and consistent vigour by Methodist and Baptist ministers but were of concern also to the clergy of all the churches. William Proudfoot, Secession Presbyterian minister and tireless diarist, decided that in York there was not so much wickedness as in a town of like population in the old country. In his own area of London he heard a lot of swearing and was told that the people were careless and profane, with no respect for the Sabbath day. Osler concluded that "The Devil, I grieve to say, almost reigns triumphant. Drunkenness, blasphemy, and any species of vice is common; yet there are some exceptions." Most observers, lay as well as clerical, agreed that drunkenness was far too general and a cause of many other evils. The temperance societies that multiplied after 1828 had wide church support, but Roman Catholics and Anglicans were wary of them, especially when they adopted total abstinence. All excesses were frowned on by Quakers and Mennonites who taught simple and peaceful living.

The problems of distance and population that had handicapped doctors and clergymen applied equally to the development of a pattern of schools and colleges. Some of the practical difficulties that had to be overcome were the cost, availability of teachers, buildings, school books, and how best to place the schools within reach of the pupils. Other questions were less tangible and more controversial. Who were to be educated, for what purpose, and in what subjects? Would it be best to concentrate on the few who could be expected to be the leaders of the community or to attempt to spread at least primary education thinly over the population as a whole? Should the curriculum be of a general kind with the classics following the three R's, or should more attention be given to technical education? If the latter were chosen did that mean trades or professions? Where were the native engineers, doctors, lawyers, and clergymen to be trained? That question in turn brought up the question of higher education which was also discussed. Another open question was whether religion should be taught as part of educational programmes, and if so whether it would be on a non-denominational basis. Then, again, was the language of instruction to be English exclusively, or should there be options to meet the needs of the French-speaking groups and the Germans in Waterloo County? Finally, in this forest of question marks, should education be wholly the responsibility of the state, or was there a place for private schools and perhaps colleges?

Private schools were first in the field. One was opened in Kingston in 1785 by the Reverend John Stuart. In 1796 there were two at Newark, one of which gave only evening classes; and a little later another was advertised as taking both boys and girls. At York a school was started in 1798 to teach reading, writing, arithmetic, and English grammar. These subjects formed the basis of most school curricula, and it was commonly promised that the greatest attention would be paid to "virtue and morals." A dozen years later other schools appeared in York. One held only evening classes "for the benefit of Young Ladies (or men) apprentices and others who cannot conveniently attend in the Day time to Study." Another offered either day or evening classes. Both demanded, in addition to payment in money, that each pupil should supply half a cord of firewood for each winter month and that every student bring a supply of candles. As towns grew, similar private schools were opened in many places. All the earliest and many of the later ones were held in private houses. Some were day schools, some for boarders, and others would accept pupils in either capacity. As time went on the curricula became more varied, in some cases by a turn toward such practical subjects as book-keeping; others taught the classics and sometimes one or two modern languages. For girls housekeeping and needlework were standard. Many schools had also optional subjects which were extra.

A great many private schools were started, some succeeding and others lasting for only a short time. Some were for very young children, a few went as far as university entrance, but most seem to have been for what is now the public school range. Both men and women taught, but how many of either had had previous experience in Britain or the United States, and how many had themselves any prolonged education, is difficult to judge in this period. One point that is clear is that the private school was almost always urban, especially after common schools began. Since some of the private schools included boarders those families in the country who had means could send their children to them.

One particular private school merits attention both because it was experimental and because its headmaster was the man who had most influence on the development of the school system of Ontario in the first half of the nineteenth century. John Strachan was a Scot with experience in school-teaching before he migrated to Canada at the turn of the century. Finding that the university in which he had come to lecture was indefinitely delayed he started a school at Cornwall in 1803, and remained in it until he moved to York in 1812. Strachan had been ordained as a Church of England clergyman shortly before he started his school and his concern for the position of the church in education became well known; but of a total of forty-six pupils attending the Cornwall school in 1805 twenty-nine were Anglicans, twelve Presbyterians, two Roman Catholics, and three were listed as independent. The novelty of the school was partly in the addition of science to classics and mathematics, partly in the emphasis on teaching the ability to observe and make judgments in an age in which teaching by rote was often overdone.

Strachan was a complex character who was seen by some of his contemporaries as the defender of a vested oligarchy, of privileges for his church, and of giving to that church a stranglehold on education. Evidence can be found to give substance to these charges but they do not make up a full portrait of Strachan, for he was also, among other things, the chief architect of the common school system. Neither in England nor in the United States was there yet education for the populations as a whole, although in the latter stabs in that direction had been made. Ontario, therefore, was not peculiar in its speculation on what the character of an educational system should be. No one, however, was satisfied that a casual collection of private schools would meet the requirements of even the upper class. The first move toward any kind of government-supported schools came early in the day, in 1797, when the two Houses addressed the king praying that "a certain portion of Waste Lands of the Crown might be appropriated for the establishment and support of a respectable Grammar School in each District—and also a college or University for the instruction of Youth in the different branches of human knowledge." The petition and the resultant grant of more than five hundred thousand acres were significant more in their intention than their result since the land was for long unsaleable. However in 1807 an Act was passed providing for a grammar school in each District, the masters to be paid out of public funds. Although these schools were apparently thought of as filling the role of secondary schools, in fact they were then, and for some time remained, at least in part elementary. The grammar schools were all duly established and the returns of 1827 show 329 pupils in the eleven schools. There were some girls, but most of the students were boys.

Even before the Act of 1807, and then in criticism of it, came demands for a more general network of elementary schools. The fees charged by the grammar schools and their wide geographical spacing precluded attendance by any except those who were nearby or could afford to be boarders. A petition from the inhabitants of the Midland District in 1812 was typical of a criticism that was widespread:

By reason of the place of instruction being established at one end of the District, and the sum demanded for tuition in addition to the annual compensation received from the public, most of the people are unable to avail themselves of the advantages contemplated by the Institution. A few wealthy inhabitants, and those of the Town of Kingston reap exclusively the benefit of it in this District. The institution, instead of aiding the middling and poorer classes of His Majesty's subjects, casts money into the lap of the rich, who are sufficiently able, without public assistance, to support a school in every respect equal to the one established by law.

In 1815 Strachan sketched a comprehensive plan for education in the province which suggests the influence of his Scottish background. Its main points were: continuation of the grammar schools, adding scholarships for poor but promising children; a university, to be established at some future date; grants to teachers of common schools; and a provincial board of education with a paid secretary. All these proposals were in due course implemented. The Common School Act of 1816, with minor subsequent amendments, produced what would later have been called a public school system. What the Act did was to subsidize local effort, for here and there were schools improvised by the co-operation of neighbours and it was expected that others would be started; to provide for the local choice of trustees; and to create appointed District Boards of Education which should have superintending authority and to which quarterly reports were to be rendered by the trustees. The availability of funds would, it was hoped, make possible a sufficient number of schools, and a minimum standard could be imposed. Parts of the structure of thirty years later were thus laid down, but one conspicuous difference between then and later was that in 1816 the only stated qualification of a teacher was that he be a British subject, An unsatisfactory one, however, could be removed by the trustees, subject to the veto of the board of education. Perhaps the way in which the system worked will become more evident by examining the relevant document in a particular case, the date being 1816, that is very soon after the Act came into effect. The statement has eleven signatures.

We the Undersigned Do hereby promise to pay for the number of scholars set down opposite our respective names to be taught in a Common School to be kept at the school House on the premises of Mr. Fairchild in Charlotteville for one year to end and Determine on the last day of May 1817, in fair proportions (according to our Dates of Signature) of the sum of Two hundred and twenty five Dollars hereby agreed to be paid to the Teacher or Teachers of the said Common School, including the Donation of the Statute, for the said term subject to a Diminution in proportion as the number of Scholars hereto subscribed or educated in the said Common School increases--Subjecting ourselves to such rules and regulations as may be made from time to time by the Trustees of the said school with respect to providing Fire wood tor the said School House, Boarding the Teacher for the time being and whatever else may be necessary and right to be done relative to the said school, in pursuance of the Act to Establish Common Schools throughout the province.

The system was an amalgam of private and public initiative not ill suited to the thought and conditions of the day and, though it had imperfections, it did reach the primary objective of providing schooling throughout the province. By 1827 there were 364 common schools with 9,800 students and by 1839 those figures had been about doubled. Universities were for the future, but meanwhile, in 1829, the lieutenant-governor inspired the establishment of Upper Canada College, which was intended to be a superior and advanced grammar school capable of being raised to university level. It should be categorized as a private institution but was heavily supported by public funds. It was non-denominational.

Direct statutory authority for separate schools was not enacted until the early eighteen-forties but there were various opportunities for denominational schools before that time. Private schools could, of course, be so if they wished, and the Roman Catholic bishops did all they could to encourage their priests to teach in addition to their other duties, and to secure funds from the government with which to pay full-time teachers. Bishop Macdonell even paid three schoolmasters out of his own pocket, and by 1826 he had enough public money for nine teachers. He was concerned not only with the desirability of church schools as such but with a situation he believed to exist in which Roman Catholics were "hewers of wood and drawers of water" because of a lack of education. The desire of Macdonell and others of his church was to have Roman Catholic children educated in other than the grammar and common schools, and to a lesser extent a similar point of view was held by some Protestants. What is not clear is whether there were at that time public schools in which denominational religion was in fact taught. Some at least of the common schools had teachers who were also clergymen and it would be surprising if that did not influence their teaching.

Many of the problems met by the schools can be attributed directly to conditions in the province: a scanty and scattered population, crude communications, and scarcity of public funds. Looking at the same relationship from another point of view, it is well to judge the schools by the standards of the day. Probably all the early schoolhouses were made of logs; were ill ventilated, dark, cold in the winter, and ill equipped. But so were the residences of most of the parents and of their children. Teachers and pupils alike had to trudge great distances to school, but such walks were not unusual at the time.

There are two traditional simplifications of the teachers as a whole: the wise and devoted character of the old red schoolhouse, and the old soldier or incapable person who was barely literate. Neither, of course, is characteristic for there was great variety. Some of the private schools particularly had teachers with impressive academic records, and some of the rural schools men or women who could find no other means of livelihood and who moved about from one school section to another. There was the pathetic character bullied by the bad boys of the little school, and there was the muscular one who put a few rebels in their place, leaving them with some aches and pains as part of their education. Every kind of teacher could be found, good, bad, and indifferent. They had little guidance, no training, and such certificates as existed cannot be taken as indicating any standard of skill. The pay was small, "boarding out"—living with families as part payment—was not generally appealing, the school year was long, and most of the schoolhouses uncomfortable. On the other hand few other opportunities offered for those who, without any private means, were either unwilling or unable to face the unremitting physical labour of a pioneer farm.

Although few schools had what they liked to call "scientific exhibits," some globes and a few books, many of them were sadly deficient in all these respects. Then and later many complaints were made by the teachers that they had little of the equipment that they needed. Even blackboards, pens, and paper were in short supply. There were many charges that the schools were more American than British. The Reverend Alexander Macdonell complained of this situation in private schools, writing in 1817 that "boarding schools for young ladies in both the Canadas are kept principally by American women, and every book of instruction put into the hands of their pupils by these school mistresses are of American manufacture, artfully tinctured with the principles of that Government and Constitution." American textbooks were not universal but very generally used. It was said by many teachers that the books they were obliged to use in common schools were not only written from an American point of view but hardly mentioned British North America. In some districts teachers objected that the whole atmosphere was American, that even the children's voices were affected. Apart from this foreign slant, textbooks were often scarce and unsatisfactory from other points of view. In the average common school the curriculum was simple indeed: it had to be in view of the limited education of many of the teachers and scarcity of books. No doubt such feats of memory as learning lists of dates or competing in spelling matches were overdone, and perhaps too much time was spent on penmanship. Too little attention was paid to the training in judgment that Strachan emphasized. On the other hand it is noticeable that in modern times handwriting is frequently illegible, spelling uncertain, and conversation punctuated by admissions of faulty memory.

If the school system of Ontario in the half-century from 1790 to 1840 is taken as a whole any generalization is dangerous. There were many country schools in which the physical conditions, facilities, discipline, and teaching were at a low level, and others in which any or all of these factors were much better. In some private and grammar schools it was possible to get good training in the classics, in mathematics, and some science, in modern languages, and even such fancy subjects as oratory. For girls, in addition to other subjects, there could be drill not only in simple sewing and housekeeping, but in embroidery.

Some attempts were made to introduce technical training into schools but with limited success. Trades such as carpentry, bricklaying, and leather work were learned by apprenticeship. Medical education has been mentioned and legal education will be examined in the following chapter. Little attention seems to have been given to engineering. Training of the clergy was a need that much concerned many of the churches. Until universities were established there was no wholly satisfactory method, but something was done by individuals who took divinity students into their houses on an arrangement not unlike apprenticeship. Both the Roman Catholic church and the Church of England had small training schools.

In the early nineteenth century the school system, with its strengths and weaknesses, provided the only formal education in Ontario, but it was suplemented by lectures, discussions, and reading. In these three last there were differences between the facilities in town and country, but there was also a factor in common so far as the written word was concerned, that in most cases it had to be transmitted by mail. To a degree this was true of the local newspapers; but apart from them and some pamphlets and official notices little was published at this time in the province. Books, periodicals, and additional newspapers were imported, mainly from Britain and to a lesser extent from the United States. The Post Office had a further duty, to carry letters, a duty with a peculiar significance in a province in which so many people were recent immigrants and others who, for personal or business reasons, wished to keep in touch with families or firms in the British Isles and the United States. In days when travel by land or sea was slow and difficult and before the telegraph was in use, rapid and inexpensive postal communication would have solved many problems, but the carriage of mail was subject to the same defects in transportation as were the journeys of individuals. Until 1851 the postal services of all British North America were conducted by the British Post Office, and to the people of Ontario—rightly or wrongly— the main features were the slow appearance of local post offices, the inadequacy of such services as existed, and the high rates for mail. A post office was opened in Kingston in 1789 and one in York in 1799 or 1800, but by 1816 there were only nine post offices between the eastern boundary of Upper Canada and the town of York; four in the Niagara peninsula; and five in the London District (the counties of Middlesex, Oxford, Brant, Norfolk, and Elgin). Of the post offices in the Niagara area the first had not appeared until 1814. It was at Dundas. In places without post offices people had either to go miles to get their letters or else hope that some passing traveller would act as an unofficial postman.

No stamps were used but letters could be prepaid if desired. However the more common practice was to have the postage paid by the recipient, and, unlike so many transactions, only cash was accepted. The rates were high. In 1821 the cost of a single letter from England to Halifax was given as one shilling and eight pence, and from Halifax to York was two shillings and nine pence. From York to Dundas was eight pence. Much higher figures, however, are quoted in contemporary writing, and indeed the House of Assembly claimed in 1820 "that the rates of postage charged in Upper Canada for several years past for the conveyance of letters have exceeded the charges authorized by law." The newspapers regularly printed long lists of letters that had not been called for, in most cases because the addressees could not or would not pay the postage. On her travels in the Talbot country Mrs. Jameson stayed over-night with a widow who kept the post office. She noted that poor immigrants came to get letters but when they found the postage was from three to five shillings they turned away in despair. During a later stop, at Brantford, she saw that forty-eight letters were unclaimed because of the cost of postage. A former postmaster at Oakville told in his memoirs of an Irishman who, finding a letter for him, asked that it be read aloud twice. Having heard it thoroughly he announced that it was not intended for him and went away, thus saving seven shillings. There were various devices of this kind, the simplest being to refuse receipt of what might be a blank page, knowing that its very existence was a message in an agreed code.

Such were the weaknesses of the postal system, but in spite of them a large body of correspondence somehow was delivered. Merchants and shopkeepers sent and received many letters. Records of educated families in town and country contain frequent references to letters, and indeed many of them were later published. Moreover it is noticeable that these contain few mentions of the difficulties of the postal system, a fact which should be set against complaints of the types that have been mentioned. It was for the educated an age of leisurely letters, but they were a limited segment of society. To many of the poorer settlers a letter must have been a novelty, not only because of its cost but because these people, and quite probably their relatives at home, were illiterate. The speed of communications gradually improved. In 1838 the lieutenant-governor wrote to London: "I have the honour to acknowledge,—exactly one month from its date, such is the wonderful rapidity of intercourse with England, Your Lordship's private letter."

CHAPTER FIVE

The Impact
of the State

IN EARLY ONTARIO voluntary interest in the political affairs of the province and of other countries ranged from intense to zero. News of the outside world was often slow in reaching those who wished to follow it, but local newspapers carried many stories and articles on foreign affairs and there were a few subscribers to American and British papers. Newspapers, too, were passed on to friends. In some cases attention was directed to particular countries, for example, by Irish immigrants to developments in their homeland. Of those interested in provincial questions the most obvious persons were employees of the government and members of the legislature. But some others, too, were instinctively drawn towards politics. Regular participation or interest in public affairs was a part of the life of a minority of unknown size.

On nearly everyone, at some time and in some degree, provincial, imperial, or international affairs made some impact; and this was as true of those on backwoods farms as of the prominent citizens of a town. War and revolution had profound influence on the whole early history of the province and of the people who lived in it. At intervals over more than a century the progress of the Hudson's Bay Company in the far north was arrested or stopped by French armed intervention. The French settlers along the Detroit River were originally placed there because of one international situation and transferred to British sovereignty as the result of another. The American revolution caused not only the flow of political exiles, the United Empire Loyalists, into the land of Ontario, but also of non-partisans such as the Quakers and Mennonites, of the so-called "late Loyalists," and of land-hungry people with little interest in politics. As the wars against revolutionary France spread in 1793 to include England and most of Europe the business of Ontario merchants was seriously impaired. Imports became more expensive and their arrival uncertain. From Kingston Richard Cartwright wrote that "As the present Situation of Affairs in Europe has a very unfavourable Influence on the Trade of the Country, I am very much disposed to contract my Business and lye by for a while." What was considered to be a growing threat of American aggression caused concern on the part of the authorities, and no doubt of other observers, as to the position to be taken by the Indians. Joseph Brant, who was having a long dispute with the government over lands, wrote in 1799 to Peter Russell that "the disgustful treatment" the Indians had received might lead to trouble. As it turned out the Indians played a part in the defending forces when hostilities did come.

The effects of the War of 1812 on the population of Upper Canada have yet to be fully studied but the general lines are obvious. The American commanders, fully conscious that the large number of people in the province who were of American origin were by no means all Loyalist and probably not all loyal, directed persuasion and threats in their direction, while the British commanders responded with reassurances and attempts to nullify the enemy propaganda. To Isaac Brock, one of the few competent officers on either side, the home front was worse than insecure; but some of the militiamen kept to their duty with the result that not a few farms, shops, and trades were deprived of their workers, in some cases permanently. Parts of the province were temporarily occupied, and parts were damaged by the incidental effects of hostilities or deliberate destruction. In some respects business was dislocated by these various circumstances, but on the other hand it was stimulated by the heavy British purchasing of food and other supplies for regular and militia regiments and for the construction and maintenance of naval vessels on the great lakes. The Assembly, which played an unheroic part in the war, was at last shaken by "the disgraceful and traitorous conduct of the two members of this House in joining the ranks of the enemy," and was moved to consider legislation directed against cases of treason. No aspect of public affairs is as stark as warfare, and many families in the province were long to remember the loss of life and property, the misery of enemy occupation, and the triumphs that prevented the invading forces from overcoming a province divided in loyalty and ill prepared for the assault. It was a reminder, if one were needed, that world events could not be kept within the covers of a book.

Over a period, however, it was the more down-to-earth aspects of the state that bore on the average resident of Ontario. A limited number of people were interested in the development of political ideas and in association with embryonic parties, but for the average man government spelled administration. He was, willy-nilly, living in a political society in which some of his needs could be met only by government. A man could live in a bush farm with his mind directed toward how to make arable fields, build a decent house, save his livestock from wolves, bring up a family in even minimum comfort; and yet he could not escape the positive and negative sides of government. He might become concerned with the policy under which land was granted because it directly affected him, could object to the laws of marriage, complain about roads because he needed them, demand schools for his children or law and order in his vicinity. Even the reduction of the number of wolves was influenced by the government bounty on them. As the towns developed buildings were burned, rubbish accumulated, vagabonds were at large, streets were impassable. Such were the factors which, in country and town alike, drew almost everyone into the political field in some way. It was not necessary to have an interest in "politics" to have a consciousness of the role of government. Appearing first, as it did for most people, in its administrative capacity government could next be seen in terms of policy and composition if its administrative activities were sufficiently unsatisfactory.

Of the duties of government perhaps the one that has been most generally accepted as essential is the maintenance of law and order, for without them there is chaos. From its first days Ontario was subject to British criminal law, but in the brief period in which it was part of the Province of Quebec it had French civil law, modified in 1785 by authority for trial by jury. When the Constitutional Act of 1791 enabled the legislature of the new Upper Canada to make its own choice of civil law the first statute was one to introduce English law, an inevitable decision in view of the origins and traditions of the colony's few inhabitants. The pattern of courts was several times modified in the course of a generation or more, but its exact form was debated by only a few people who had special knowledge of legal affairs. Provision was made for a court of appeal, superior courts, and so descending to those which were closest to the day-by-day incidents in a community, the Courts of Quarter Sessions of the Peace, made up of the Justices of the Peace (the magistrates).

If there were to be courts there must of necessity be lawyers, and for some time their selection was by means which would seem strange to a later generation, as indeed they did to some people at the time. An Act of 1794 authorized the lieutenant-governor to license up to sixteen persons, a move which led Richard Cartwright, himself a judge, to comment acidly that the appointees would be "without any previous study or training, and by the mere magic of the Privy Seal, are at once to start up adepts in the science of the law." In 1797 it was laid down that both barristers and solicitors had to be on the books of the Law Society and in barristers' chambers or articled. When examinations were first introduced they were confined to Latin authors and mathematics. Specialized education began in 1831.

The body of law introduced into Ontario was, as in Britain and indeed everywhere, harsh on its criminal side. Until much later the death penalty was provided for a large number of crimes. In York an immigrant tailor was induced while drunk to cash a forged order for three shillings and ninepence in 1798 and for this he was hanged. Three years later two brothers were sentenced to death for horse-stealing but this was later changed to imprisonment for life. If there was any public outcry against capital punishment for minor offences it was not voiced by the crowds who watched a public execution. At least one case is recorded of a man receiving twenty lashes in open court. The common law included some enlightened principles such as trial by jury and the writ of habeas corpus—means of protection to the citizen against arbitrary action—but included other features which came to be criticized. There was growing dissatisfaction with the practice of imprisonment for debt long before Charles Dickens wrote his telling attacks on debtors' prisons in England. In Ontario the common gaols were used for debtors, and even set against the standards of the time they were crude buildings, often crudely administered. Improvement in the gaols came slowly, but the Assembly chipped away at the law of debt in a series of statutes that gradually restricted its application. One of the series, for example, was an Act of 1835 which provided that no one was to be arrested for a debt of less than £10, that a man arrested for debt of up to £20 could apply for release after three months in gaol, and for a debt of up to £100 after a year.

An examination of the records of the Courts of Quarter Sessions, which handled a great number of civil and criminal cases, is one means of getting an impression of the state of law and order. There was such a court for each District, and, even if it had to meet in a private house, it was conducted with something of the dignity and ceremony that befitted a British court of justice, reflecting a point of view that was generally and consistently held. Justice was not to be subjected to "democratic" turbulence. Samples taken in two

Districts during the first years of the century show that the highest figure in criminal cases was for assault and battery (including assault of constables), with larceny coming next. Other charges were for trespass, misdemeanours, and extortion. Although it is hard to judge on the basis of a brief record there are indications that care was taken that the trials, which were by jury, were fair, many cases being dismissed for lack of evidence. Fines, ranging from five shillings to twenty pounds, were far more common than gaol terms, for if currency was scarce gaols were even more so. Another form of punishment was being put in the stocks.

Many offences against law and order might be brought before these and other courts but it did not, unhappily, follow that crime was comfortably under control. Even if the courts had been beyond criticism, which they were not, the total means of enforcing law were far from adequate. For years the Ottawa River lumbermen terrorized Bytown. In a letter of 1837 addressed by three magistrates to the provincial secretary the picture looked black:

Bytown being the focus of the lumber trade, is frequented at all seasons by great numbers of raftsmen, among whom are some desperate characters and others easily misled. The inhabitants are dependent upon the lumber trade and upon these men, and cannot, therefore, be prevailed with to act with energy against them.

Those constables who perform their duty are always marked out for punishment. ...

Generally speaking, the persons who commit these outrages are unknown, but if known and warrants issued for their arrest, they fly to the Lower Province (where we cannot touch them) but return again when they please, confident in their strength, and if they are arrested they are immediately rescued or manage to make their escape, from the defect in our constabulary force, and the great distance of the gaol [at Perth].

This was only one of the situations that inspired a long list of proclamations calling for good behaviour and offering rewards for identifying murderers, incendiaries, burglars, and other wrongdoers. In a few cases pardon was offered to informants not directly involved in a crime. The rewards were substantial, £100 being common and a few going as high as £600. There was nothing unique in the use of such inducements for the detection of criminals and the passionate wording of the proclamations could be set down to the style of the times, but the large number of them and the size of the rewards suggest that limited confidence could be placed in such regular agencies as existed for the enforcement of law.

In one way or another local government affected everyone: it met, adequately or inadequately, their local needs, and it imposed obligations in taxes and service. Until after the union of Upper and Lower Canada the system centred on the Courts of Quarter Sessions which were as much occupied in administration as in sitting as a court of law. In the main, therefore, authority was in the hands of the appointed magistrates. In respect of local government the Courts looked in two directions, toward the townships and toward the towns. In the former there was an attenuated version of the New England Town (that is, township) Meeting. Whether it is true, as has been argued, that the Loyalists and other immigrants from the Thirteen Colonies sought the introduction of the whole New England structure or that of the Middle Colonies may be open to question. Some undoubtedly did; but the reluctance to accept such positions as were elective casts some doubt on the enthusiasm of the settlers for local democracy. However that may be, there were meetings in the townships (that is, of the ratepayers in the villages and in the farming areas) at which were elected a number of officials: a town warden, a town clerk, assessors, collector of taxes, poundkeeper, and overseers of highways. These men, who had very limited authority, were answerable not to those who elected them but to the Courts of Quarter Sessions, which also fixed their fees. The Courts also made a number of appointments themselves: for example, the high constable of each District, the constables of townships, the commissioners of highways, and keepers of standards of weights and measures. They directed the incidence of the statutory requirements for labour on roads, received petitions for the construction of roads, and made arrangements for investigations in response to such petitions.

Public confidence in this system no doubt varied according to whether particular results were satisfactory, and perhaps also was limited on the part of those who yearned for the more democratic system of New England. In this latter connection it is appropriate to recall that as emigrants from the British Isles came to take first place in numbers there was a diminishing proportion of people who knew or cared what the New England system was. For better or for worse the scheme of local government dependent on the authority of appointed magistrates together with some elective positions in the townships continued for a long time in the villages and rural areas. Efforts were made both to coerce those who sought to evade the burdens of office and to inform newcomers of the duties that might fall on them. In 1832 the Cobourg *Star* printed a letter over a pseudonym, probably that of a magistrate:

As the inhabitants of the new townships in this district are entirely composed of emigrants from Great Britain and Ireland, who had no parochial or public duties in their native countries, they feel bewildered and at a loss when called upon to perform such duties here. From the ignorance of the nature of such offices, arise, as may be expected, mistakes, wrangles and animosities. To obviate the difficulty of obtaining correct information, and to prevent petty broils and disturbances, an abstract of the numerous Acts, which relate to parish and town officers, and which at present are scattered throughout the whole of the statutes, might be drawn up, sent to the Town Clerks, and directed to be read in every new township for a certain number of years, at the annual town meetings.

Meanwhile "Atticus" added a brief extract of the laws, outlining the duties of the town clerk, assessors, collectors, overseers of highways, town wardens, and poundkeepers.

The Justices of the Peace had responsibilities also for urban government but they proved to be diminishing. A provincial statute of 1792 authorized the Justices in Quarter Sessions to make orders and regulations for the prevention of fires and empowered them to appoint firemen and other officers. A comment on the operation of this regime is found in a petition addressed to the Assembly by "sundry inhabitants" of Kingston in 1816:

We, the Magistrates and Inhabitants of the Town of Kingston, taking into consideration its population and commercial extent, resolve it to be essential to its present and future prosperity, that there should be a well regulated Police established by law. We have found the existing laws insufficient to effect the repairing and improving its streets, keeping them clean, paving the foot-paths and preventing irregularities frequently committed by persons on horseback and in carriages. Much evil has arisen from the want of authority to form Fire Companies, who shall be obliged to attend and work engines at stated periods, to compel the inhabitants to keep a certain number of fire buckets, to repair with them when ever it may be necessary, to oblige individuals to keep ladders to each house, to prevent the danger arising from stove-pipes passing through roofs of buildings, to fix the size of bread, to prevent cattle from running at large in the streets, and many other useful regulations not enumerated.

Your Petitioners therefore beg that Your Honourable House will take into your serious consideration their petition, and pass a law establishing a Police to correct the above mentioned abuses.

The magistrates are the first persons mentioned in the above petition (no names are given for the others) and it is obvious that they did not feel that they were being called upon to criticize their own role in local government or to put in their stead an elected and democratic system of local government. They and the other signatories were saying only that the rules in force were insufficient, and they asked for a "Police." The word was used in a dictionary sense as "the Regulation, discipline, and control of a community." The Police was then the equivalent of a set of by-laws, but at this stage it provided no additional machinery to carry them into effect.

The legislature complied with the petition by passing an Act to provide a police for Kingston, as it did shortly after for several other towns. In that for York, Sandwich, and Amherstburg (1817) it was provided that the magistrates in quarter sessions were to make

such prudential rules and regulations as they may deem expedient, relative to paving, lighting, keeping in repair, and improving the streets of the said towns respectively, regulating the assize of bread, slaughter houses, and nuisances; and also to enforce the said town laws relative to horses, swine, or cattle of any kind, from running at large in said towns, and relative to the inspection of weights, measures, firemen, and fire companies.

In addition to the above duties the magistrates were to raise funds on assessed property and to levy fines on offenders against the rules. Not a word is said about new officials or local bodies. Taking together the Kingston petition and this Act it is evident that, while the people of the towns were concerned to have administration spread over problems which they had experienced, they were not at this time thinking in terms of forms of local government. For some fifteen years only minor amendments were made in these Acts, but at the end of that time elected bodies were created. A statute applying to Brockville (1832) is an early example, and was passed specifically because of the increase of population. Under it there was to be a body corporate, the Board of Police, made up of two members elected in each of the two wards of the town together with a fifth member appointed by the decision of any three of them. These five were then to select one of their number as president. It would now be this corporation which would make by-laws covering the various subjects listed in the earlier Acts, inflict penalties for non-compliance, and raise taxes on assessed property. The corporation, too, was empowered to appoint such officials as it might deem required, to assign their duties, and fix their salaries. With minor modifications this Act was applied to other towns during the eighteen-thirties.

Meanwhile there appeared the first incorporated city. Here again the change was made to meet certain needs and not on grounds of constitutional principles. The Act of 1834 explained that the growth of York demanded "a more efficient system of police and municipal government" than existed, and that no better step could be taken than to erect it into a city, incorporate the inhabitants, and vest in them the power to elect a mayor, aldermen, common councilmen, and other officers. The change thus made was in principle not as radical as that from the rule of magistrates to the rule of a board of police; but it did elaborate and extend both the duties and the structure of municipal government. One important innovation was that the mayor and aldermen were to be Justices of the Peace for the city and to have jurisdiction in it in place of the District Justices. The mayor or aldermen were empowered to order the arrest of rogues, vagabonds, drunkards, and disorderly persons; and the same officials were to constitute a Court of Record having the same powers as the Courts of Quarter Sessions. In one way or another, then, the towns of Ontario had achieved a wide autonomy, whereas local government in the rural areas was little altered before the comprehensive statutes of the forties.

Both provincial and local governments assumed responsibility for the morals of the people. In the instructions of 1791 to Dorchester, as governor of Upper Canada, a paragraph on the subject was included. Existing legislation was to be enforced and additional or amending Acts passed if they were needed, so that "every Species of Vice, Profaneness and Immorality" could be suppressed. Simcoe accordingly issued a proclamation in 1793 repeating in lofty phrases the determination of His Majesty, acting in the best interests of his subjects, to promote virtue and subdue vice. Like other governments before and since, that of Upper Canada had limited success in attaining this high objective, but it did try. The number of moral cases which came before the Courts of Quarter Sessions seems to have varied from one area to another. In early years the court at Newcastle heard few such cases but the London court had several in the first twenty years of the nineteenth century. Four men were brought up for profane swearing and all were convicted, the fines ranging from two shillings and eight pence to six shillings. By what measurement the punishment was made to fit the crime is not recorded: perhaps there were agreed levels of profanity. Four sex cases of various kinds are recorded, one being adultery. Three men were fined three shillings and four pence each for breaking the Sabbath, all on the same day. Another man was accused of keeping a disorderly house and selling liquor on the Sabbath. The early Acts establishing police in towns included in the list of unlawful activities "drawing any indecent words, figures, or pictures, on any building, wall, or fence"; and later Acts added the responsibility "generally to prevent vice." The statue which incorporated Toronto listed as one duty of the authorities "to enforce the due observance of the Sabbath."

There were also a number of statutes aimed at ending or reducing various moral crimes, such as one of 1837, "An Act to make the remedy in cases of Seduction more effectual" by defining certain ways in which the father of an illegitimate child was required to pay for its support. The limited number of constables and the wide spread of the population made all these endeavours more difficult, but in some degree at least they complemented the efforts of individuals, societies, and churches.

It is taken for granted nowadays that the "welfare state" is a recent phenomenon, and that is true enough in the sense of the extent to which the state has assumed responsibility for the poor, the sick, the unemployed, and the old; but the difference is one of degree. Throughout the history of Ontario some public initiative and funds have been devoted to social welfare (in the limited sense in which that phrase is commonly used). At no time was there a complete denial of responsibility for the helpless and the hapless, although there has been a gradual evolution—greatly accelerated in the last generation or so—toward the present concept of birth-to-death protection. At the beginning of the nineteenth century and for long thereafter the public attitude was compounded of a degree of *laissez-faire*, a belief that members of families should look after each other, an inclination to turn to private charity to fill most of the remaining gap, and an understanding that there was a place for governmental action. The last is indicated in the analysis made in 1787 by the magistrates of Kingston of the matters most urgent in that area. "Humanity," they wrote after examining the functions of government, "will not allow us to omit mentioning the Necessity of appointing Overseers of the poor, or the Making of some Kind of Provision for persons of that Description who from Age or Accident may be rendered helpless." It is not unlikely that they had in mind the English poor laws, but when the new legislature of Upper Canada quickly passed an Act introducing English civil law it explicitly excepted the poor laws. This decision may have derived from some budding spirit of individual enterprise, but is more likely to have been taken in the knowledge that the local taxation which fed the English system could not be duplicated in Ontario.

It may well have been a sensible conclusion and certainly in England the laws brought some curious results from a considerable expenditure. The difficulty in Ontario was that, whether or not there was some alternative plan in mind, none was introduced or apparently even suggested, so that the needy were cared for—to the extent that they were at all—through a series of unrelated measures and procedures. One thing they did have in common: they involved little cost. By a statute of 1810 the poor could be housed in the common gaols and by another of 1820 the insane had the same dubious privilege. Parallel with these steps the ubiquitous Courts of Quarter Sessions handled other cases as they arose. They authorized payment for the support of orphans or for children of persons in gaol, for care of the destitute sick, for the maintenance of unmarried mothers, and to bury impecunious immigrants (of whom there were many in the days of cholera plagues). They also applied the system of indentured apprenticeship to abandoned children or to those of parents who were unwilling or unable to look after them, invoking a statute of 1799 which provided that such a child might be bound as an apprentice up to twenty-one years of age with the consent of the Justices of the Peace. A child of fourteen years or more had the option to refuse. This is the minute of a case in 1817:

The Magistrates in General Quarter Sessions, taking into consideration the helpless situation of Alexander Wedge, a boy of about Six Years of age, abandoned by his father and left without an adequate provision by his mother, do order and direct, that the said Alexander Wedge shall be duly indented and apprenticed to James Mitchell Esquire, his heirs and assigns untill he shall have completed His Twenty first Year, He the said James Mitchell his heirs and assigns furnishing the said Alexander Wedge with sufficient wearing apparel and victuals and teaching him or causing him to be taught, to read and write and at the expiration of his apprenticeship to furnish him with two suits of wearing apparel, a Yoke of Oxen worth Fifty Dollars with a Yoke and chain.

So that, while Alexander Wedge would not necessarily have learned a trade, he would at least have been clothed and fed for some fifteen years, had an elementary education, and emerged with a modest capital equipment when he set out on his own.

Although the provincial legislature did not adopt the eighteenth-century English poor laws it seems to have been more attracted to the English Act of 1834 which cut back outdoor relief by requiring that persons who were not sick or infirm must go to a workhouse. A provincial Act to the same general effect was passed in 1837 under which houses of industry were to be created. The Act never came into effect. It was not popular and it came in the year of the rebellion; but the same theory was carried out in Toronto and various towns where houses of industry and refuge were established by private initiative and aided by public funds. Probably no one thought of a general system of pensions, but special ones were devised for those who were wounded in the war of 1812 and for the dependents of those who had been killed.

Again in contrast with modern times, there is also the impression that the state was not active in the economic field; nevertheless, as seen by contemporaries, in a number of ways government had a necessary place in the economic life and the occupations of the people. Such functions started at the beginning in that both French and British governments conveyed groups of settlers to southern Ontario and set them up in business as farmers. In the combination of immigration, settlement, and agriculture, which for long made up the base of the economy, government had a role. In this period it could hardly be said that the provincial government had an immigration policy. It did have responsibility for medical inspection at ports, but its principal duties related to the provision of land and necessary services. Those who criticized the land-granting policy held that it discouraged immigration and encouraged emigration, and to the extent that this was true it delayed development. After the very early years in which government supplied seed and implements it made little attempt to direct agriculture. The encouragement of hemp by bounties and technical advice was an exception. It did intervene at the next stage to protect the grower by setting, as early as 1794, a maximum for the proportion that a miller could retain for his services (one-twelfth). Steps, too, were taken in a series of statutes to protect the consumer. There were Acts appointing inspectors of flour, pot and pearl ashes; and providing for the control of the marking of casks, the weight of the contents, and the quality. Penalties were set for non-observance. There were Acts to control the price of bread and the size of loaves, again with penalties attached. A good deal of attention was paid to ensuring a fixed standard of weights and measures. Governmental encouragement of manufacturing was sporadic, although its progress was a consideration frequently before the Assembly. An Act of 1826 broadly entitled "to encourage the progress of useful arts within the province" turns out to be a procedure for granting patents to inventors.

In respect of both agriculture and industry the greatest contributions that at that time could be made by the state were less direct than intervention in these activities. What everyone connected with them (or with anything else) wanted was better transportation by land and by water. Showers of petitions poured on the Assembly and on the Courts of Quarter Sessions, and although neither could, with the funds available, do more than nibble at the edges of the problem, both devoted a great deal of attention to it. Roads, bridges, canals, lighthouses, and then railways were frequently discussed in the two Houses, if for no other reason than pressure from the citizens. Government intervention took a number of forms: direction of statutory labour, permission to establish companies to build toll roads or canals, subsidies to assist in the construction of roads, and direct participation. In the last category came the erection of lighthouses and other aids to navigation and the building of some main highways. In the financial field were a number of functions important in some ways to many people. The government set the tariff rates and at intervals had interminable negotiations with Lower Canada concerning goods imported by way of the St. Lawrence. Fire insurance companies were incorporated by statute. Reform of the chaotic currency and the establishment of banks affected more than those directly engaged in trade and industry.

Thus there were a great many ways in which the state was a necessary part of the life of the Ontario community: unwelcome ones for the criminal and seldom completely satisfactory to the law-abiding citizen. The former might welcome the fact that the size of the constabulary was small, but the latter could only lament or complain of what might be considered faulty or unfair administration. From such an attitude arose often an interest in politics, varying in the case of individuals from occasional to consistent and intense.

Of the men who participated in the operation of the state the most obvious group was made up of those who held places of profit under the crown. Apart from the minor officials elected locally they were all the beneficiaries of patronage, bestowed in London or in Canada, from the lieutenant-governor to the lowliest clerk, from the chief justice to the town constable. At a time when salaried jobs were few and far between such appointments were generally prized. The second group consisted of the members of the appointed Legislative Council and the elected Assembly. The former, like the senior officials, were selected from a narrow segment of society: men who were generally conservative, "safe" politically, educated, and in most cases from the ranks of the more wealthy and better known. Members of the Assembly were more representative of the population as a whole, far more so than their opposite numbers in the British House of Commons which was in other respects their model. Thirdly, there were the electors, drawn on a wide franchise.

The extent of public interest in political affairs is always difficult to assess. As always, "grievances" appeared, discontent with governmental sins of commission and omission. Sometimes these were pursued no further than some grumbling, sometimes they were the subjects of petitions to the legislature or debates in it, of pamphlets, public meetings, and election programmes. There were a great many newspapers, one or more in each of even the smaller towns. A few of them avoided political controversy, sometimes because they were financially dependent on government printing orders; most of them in some degree, and a portion to a high degree, expressed political opinions. What this proves is a little problematical. Only a few papers had more than a very small circulation, and many of them went under because even the nominal subscribers did not pay up. Thus there is evidence of public interest in public affairs on the one hand, and on the other doubt whether more than a minority of people read the papers at all. Elections often attracted the attention and participation of the public, and elections in those days could be as violent physically as the strident tones of editorials were violent in the literary medium. Before the introduction of the ballot when voting was open the polling-booth could be held by main force by one lot of partisans to prevent their opponents from voting. Such a technique could readily lead to battle.

The principal issue debated was whether the province was to be governed by what its critics claimed to be a self-seeking oligarchy or by those who were regarded by the latter as dangerous republicans. Both accusations were, of course, gross over-simplifications, but they were the sort of verbal weapons used by some extremists in an age when invective was fiercely extravagant. To the Tories it was essential to preserve the British connection and with it the eighteenth-century structure of society. The American revolution, they believed, had been caused by a fatal weakening of the conservative forces. Ontario must be saved from the radicals who would overturn the existing order. The inner circle of the Tories was known as the "family compact," although the common factor was outlook rather than blood. The voting strength of the Tories was spread throughout the province, and included not only the bulk of those of family or wealth but also people in all classes and circumstances. The Reformers found most of their support in the countryside and represented themselves as the friends of "the people." They argued that Ontario was in the grip of a narrow ruling junta which was selfish and unrepresentative, and pointed to defects in the system of granting land, to inadequate schools, bad roads and other matters of general complaint. They were called radicals by their opponents, but when an armed rebellion was precipitated in 1837 the main body of reformers was opposed to it.

How many people in Ontario did sympathize with the rebellion can never be estimated: those who actually took up arms in the abortive march on Toronto, some minor disturbances in the next year, or the attacks from American soil were few in number. The futility of an uprising that lacked effective leaders and strong public support was not, however, at once apparent to people surrounded by alarums and excursions. The ordinary civil life of the province was badly deranged. As in the War of 1812 men dropped their peaceful occupations to join the militia or the insurgents, leaving their families to look after farms and businesses in the midst of wild rumours that flew about. In less than twenty-four hours two hundred militia men set out from Peterborough on the long march toward Toronto. A company was called up in the small town of Fergus and marched off to Galt. The public did not know what the extent of the rebellion was, but old soldiers had knowledge of what fighting meant and others enough imagination to guess at the suffering and misery that come from war within a country. There was apprehension, too, that property and crops would be destroyed, and to guard against that farmers banded together in improvised police units.

The military operations proved to be of little consequence until those rebel leaders who had escaped to the United States succeeded in enlisting there volunteers who undertook to make forays across the border. The resultant invasions were successfully resisted, but no one—whether the officials or the public—could have been expected to know the end of the story beforehand. Rumours again were numerous and wild, of large-scale attacks that were to be made, and of disaffected Canadians at home who would join the ranks of the invaders. A newspaper in Sandwich, close to the border, daily reflected throughout 1838 the preoccupation of the people with the long drawn-out threat. "We have been," the editor wrote in January, "in a state of excitement never before equalled in consequence of the threatening attitude assumed by the rebel blood-hounds and their associates, the *loafers* of Detroit." He told of numbers of men who, fearing prosecution in connection with the rebellion, went unhindered through Windsor on their way to Detroit. Meanwhile he watched Canadian militia men moving toward the defence of the border. Early in December the editor (who was intensely patriotic) reported that "For several nights past the inhabitants of Sandwich and Windsor have been kept on the *qui vive*, marching and counter-marching, patrolling and keeping sentry."

The province was safe from revolution, from within and without, but at a cost. The interruption of peaceful occupations added to the depression that had already been a burden. "In the sad depression of the value of property," the lieutenant-governor wrote in 1839, "and in the deprivation and injurious consequences of turning out all have more or less suffered to a great extent." Casualties occurred in the limited fighting that did take place, and some of the rebel leaders who had not escaped were executed, imprisoned, or transported. There was bitterness on the part of those who thought the punishment harsh and of those who thought that too many had escaped their just due. The whole prolonged affair upset the normal course of life. Immigration had slowed to a trickle. Only when the crisis was at last over could the people of Ontario settle down to their task of developing the province.

CHAPTER SIX

Toward an
Established
Society

FIFTEEN CONSTRUCTIVE YEARS followed the dragging depression of the thirties and the misery and destruction of the rebellion. Ontario can be seen emerging from an age of pioneering and experiment toward the conditions of a settled society with a more rounded economy, greater comfort for the average person, advances in health and education. The period ends in the middle fifties with the first railway age and termination for the time being of large-scale immigration.

Not long after the rebellion, and as a result of the recommendations of the Earl of Durham, Upper and Lower Canada were politically united under the name of the Province of Canada. Although the marriage lasted from 1841 to 1867 it was hardly a happy one and was considered by critics in the western half of the new province to retard progress. In some respects, however, it was a loose union. There was but one legislature for the whole but a large proportion of the Acts applied only to either Upper or Lower Canada (the new names of Canada East and Canada West were seldom used). Education and civil law had separate and different institutions in the two halves of the province, and legislation in many local matters was in everything but name a decision of the representatives of one of the old provinces. Undoubtedly the uneasy balance between the two sections impeded good government, but the effect in the social sphere was less serious than the growing political confusion and turmoil would suggest.

By 1851 there were close to a million people in the province (952,004 to be exact). Since the beginning increase in population had been largely dependent on immigration and the forties made no exception. Famine in Ireland led to a mass exodus in 1846–47, and it is said that by 1848 more than a third of the people of Toronto had been born in Ireland. Total statistics of newcomers are, however, somewhat misleading since some immigrants were interested in Ontario only as a route to the United States and others moved on there after an interval.

Ontario was still, and was long to remain, primarily agricultural. Early signs of a transformation of the rural areas are apparent. Much of the land in the south had been cleared, if not of stumps at least of trees, but it has been estimated that by the middle of the century about two-thirds of the land was still in bush. Wheat had remained the principal crop although it was subject to steep variations in price and to the ravages of the Hessian fly and rust. Some of the land, too, was exhausted from lack of good farming practices. In 1851 wheat took greater acreage than the next grain (oats), and several times that of peas, corn, rye, buckwheat, and barley. The shift toward more diversified agriculture was beginning in the fifties. Mechanization was at an early stage. The first crude threshing machine had turned up in 1832 and the first reaper, the Hussey, was seen in the Cobourg area eleven years later. Both called for so many attendants that their success in saving manpower was limited. The McCormick reaper was in some ways more advanced but the early versions proved to be imperfect mechanically. Horses were taking over from oxen as the stage of making land out of forest receded. Houses and barns on many farms were looking more commodious and comfortable. Tongued and grooved flooring was used to some extent and clapboard for siding.

Settlers on the Ottawa River had favourable opportunities to combine local winter lumbering with farming. David MacLaren, a Scot whose farm was at Fitzroy Harbour, was more ambitious for he spent much of his time at Quebec organizing the lumber trade down the river. It was not at all easy, for in 1837 he found prices ruinously low and sales hard to effect. He reported commercial failures all around him. "It must be desperation," he wrote to his wife, "which drives people to lumber, and madness which continues them in it. Daily labor with potatoes and salt twice a day is a preferable condition." By 1840 he had not yet given up the lumber business, but living on his farm he talked of doing so soon, "as it interferes, I find somewhat with farming operations particularly with clearing land. And is besides a kind of business I do not much admire."

The country people had lagged behind their brethren of the towns in holding responsibility for their own local affairs, but the Acts of the forties, which modified the whole system of local government, brought town and country to much the same point. The essential change was the transfer of administrative and taxing powers from the Justices of the Peace to elected bodies in townships and counties. Local government had now reached what was to be, subject to numerous amendments in detail, its final form. Whether or not it was the result of an overwhelming democratic surge, it certainly was a more workable system in the conditions that existed by the middle of the century. It threw on the rural people the power and responsibility for dealing with the matters that most affected them. No longer would they look to appointed magistrates for a road: it was theirs to build a road and theirs to find the money to pay for it.

Although agriculture predominated in Ontario and the population was still largely rural the pattern of society was changing as the towns became more prominent centres of trade, industry, and finance. By 1851 Toronto had grown to 30,775 people, and the next largest city, Hamilton, to 14,121. Kingston had lost the race in which it had long led, standing now at 11,585. These are still small populations which did not allow for more than minor industries. In Toronto were several small establishments: iron foundries, manufacturers of agricultural implements, of pails, axes, tools, and stoves; paper mills, breweries, distilleries, grist mills, and starch factories. Many of the towns had little industries, and numerous family businesses, such as carriage factories, were scattered throughout the province. There were still far more people employed in saw mills and grist mills than in manufacturing. Trade unions still did not as yet play an important part. Apprenticeship was common and fitted the scale on which so many activities were conducted. A provincial statute of 1847 defined in part the responsibilities between master and servant. Explaining that there was not in force any law to cover this relationship, it decreed that all agreements or bargains for the performances of duty or service, verbal or written, were to be binding; and provided penalties for any employee who did not live up to such an agreement.

The towns were significant more for their importing and exporting agencies, for banking, and for finance generally than they were for industry. The depression of the thirties, spreading from England to the United States, knocked out 618 banks there, but in Ontario the chartered banks miraculously survived. There were not many of them, of course, and they went through an uncomfortable time, but that they did not fail was some token of the soundness of the system on which they had been built. The Gore Bank opened agencies in St. Thomas, Woodstock, Galt, Guelph, and Chatham, but the rate of expansion of banks was not as yet rapid and it is probable that relatively few people, and those mostly in commercial pursuits, were accustomed to making use of banking facilities. Perhaps closer to the public were other types of financial institutions. The Building Societies were evidently popular. A statute was passed in 1845 for the purpose of encouraging such societies in Upper Canada, and they appear to have become more numerous as a result. An advertisement of 1846 gave the prospectus of the Toronto Building Society which was described as having two purposes: a means of investing large or small amounts of money, and to enable individuals to acquire unencumbered real estate. Subscriptions were £100, to be paid in instalments; and a member, by giving a mortgage on his real estate, could borrow from the society when building or purchasing a house. A Niagara newspaper of 1851 carried advertisements of the Niagara District Building Society and the Niagara Permanent Building Society. An Act of 1843 incorporated a somewhat different type of company, the Upper Canada Trust and Loan Company. There had long been insurance companies for fire. Life insurance policies were written by agents of British companies, but in 1847 the first company situated in Ontario (and in British North America), the Canada Life Assurance Company, was established in Hamilton by H. C. Baker, a director of the Gore Bank. The Toronto Exchange was incorporated in 1854, a year after the one in Montreal. There merchants could meet to arrange for purchases and sales, and also to deal in bills of exchange.

Life in the towns was becoming more comfortable. In Toronto a private corporation provided water and gas from 1841, mainly for fire-fighting and street lighting, and a few years later private corporations in other towns such as Kingston, Hamilton, and Brockville followed suit. Professional fire-fighting forces were still for the future. To judge by the advertisements the shops were becoming more numerous and more enterprising: for example, the Nordheimer firm, which opened in Toronto in 1844, carried two of the finest pianos, Broadwood and Chickering. On the other hand there was foreign competition as shown by the advertisements of shops in Rochester and Buffalo. One of the most interesting developments in the retail business was the reaction against the system of credit which was embarrassing and sometimes disastrous to the shopkeeper. An advertisement of 1838 by a shop in Sandwich shows a method of business which has often been attributed to a much later period. It reads:

CIRCULAR.—The subscribers having determined to close their credit business, respectfully beg leave to inform the public that after the first day of April next, they will only sell for current money, payable on delivery of the goods.

As they will thus run no risk of bad debts, and conduct their business with less expense, they will be able to sell at a much lower rate of profit than heretofore; and in all cases the LOWEST CASH PRICE will be marked in figures on the goods, from which no abatement or discount of any kind will be made.

Towns were physically in a state of transition. Visitors noticed remaining log houses and shacks and also solid commercial buildings three or four storeys high. In Hamilton and Toronto some fine houses were built for prosperous citizens by architects. Dundurn Castle, Sir Allan MacNab's fancy on the outskirts of Hamilton, was designed by R. C. Wetherell in the Regency style. It was an exceptional venture, but in the forties other large houses were built in Hamilton in the Italianate manner, classical revival, or Georgian. Limestone from the Hamilton mountain was utilized in a number of large houses. In Toronto residences and public buildings came to assume some distinction under the inspiration of other able architects. John G. Howard was responsible for St. John's Church at York Mills (1843), for the Bank of British North America at the corner of Yonge and Wellington Streets (1845), and for the extensive asylum on Queen Street (1846–49). Kivas Tully designed the Bank of Montreal at the corner of Yonge and Front Streets (1845) and Trinity College (1851). Joseph Sheard planned the Cawthra house on King Street. F. W. Cumberland with various partners contributed to some of the finest buildings in whole or in part: Osgoode Hall, St. James Cathedral, and University College. All these and others were appropriate to growing towns far beyond the pioneer stage.

An inventor in methods of heating was Henry Ruttan of Cobourg who won a first prize at an exhibition of 1847 for his "Hot Air Apparatus," which seems to have been a hot air furnace combined with an oven for cooking. Unhappily for the inhabitants, however, there is no evidence that central heating was adopted as a result.

Townspeople found a wide variety of interests outside their daily tasks and showed a great deal of enterprise in providing for their own entertainment and instruction. Horse races, summer and winter, continued to be popular and autumn fairs were beginning their long reign. Of outdoor games cricket and curling were amongst the most popular and could be followed by supper and social evenings. More towns were coming to have regular theatres and concert halls; but if they lacked them could improvise to house the occasional visiting dramatic company or musician. They drew on local talent too in concerts and in plays staged by the many amateur companies. In Toronto a local Philharmonic Society was organized in 1846, but the high point was the visit of Jenny Lind in 1851, when she gave three concerts (only one had been planned) in the newly completed St. Lawrence Hall. The visit of some distinguished person or the election to the Assembly of a citizen could touch off one of those prolonged dinners at which food, wine, and speeches seemed to have no end. Various societies, of St. George and St. Patrick, the Freemasons and the Orangemen, had meetings, dinners, and other forms of entertainment or ceremonial.

Unless all evidence is misleading there was a considerable demand for books and periodicals. Local papers carried advertisements of book shops in Rochester and Buffalo, and a number of Ontario shops and newspaper offices sold books as a sideline. The *Guelph and Galt Advertiser* printed a long list of books "just received." *Nelson's British Library*, in six volumes, was offered at one shilling and eight pence per volume, and *Chambers's Miscellany*, in twenty volumes, at the same price. There were books on such diverse subjects as astronomy, the Reformation, the papacy, travel, biography, the Irish troubles, beauty, Shakespeare, and some novels. In Niagara John Simpson offered "the most recent and valuable publications" including Bohn's classical library. He also accepted subscriptions for periodicals. Libraries continued to multiply. By the middle fifties Ontario had seventy-two Mechanics' Institutes, each receiving a government subsidy of £50 currency. New private lending libraries were set up by groups of individuals, as in Sarnia in 1839. In 1849 the Hamilton Mercantile Library Association was incorporated, having already existed less formally, for lectures and books. One of the most ambitious projects was the Toronto Atheneum, which was to have a library and a museum, and lectures "in various branches of knowledge advantageous to the said Association and their pursuits in life." Its members decided on incorporation in 1848 and the list of sponsors reads like a society blue book. Another way of reading books was in the newspapers. The *Globe*, for example, was printing *Dombey and Son* by instalments in 1847.

One George Brown, apparently no relation to the editor of the *Globe*, advertised in 1844 that he would consider publishing any book at the risk of any party or jointly with them. He was also interested in the republication of English works with expired copyright. He claimed printing facilities and business connections second to none. A book published by him was reviewed in that year. Books were also published in Toronto by R. Brewer. Publishing in British North America, however, was hampered not only by the small size of the market but by the fact that, while the absence of copyright restrictions enabled Americans to reprint English books (and sell them in Canada) the same freedom did not obtain in the British colonies. The effect, as interested persons saw it, was that the costs were not competitive. The situation was long to obtain.

Rural and urban areas were alike progressing, but one need felt in both was better facilities for transportation. Complaints about bad roads were as frequent and as accurate as they were futile. The cure for the ills of land transport came to be seen in railways and there was much talk of these, but little action until the late fifties. Meanwhile the roads were muddy and bumpy and so they were long to remain in a province of too many miles and too few people. The only major progress was in transport by water. Steamships were now the masters of the great lakes, but the water communication as provided by nature had breaks in the form of waterfalls and rapids. Those on the Ottawa River were overcome by canals, and the Rideau waterway, from Bytown to Lake Ontario, was opened for navigation in 1834. The principal traffic, however, had still to reach tidewater by way of the St. Lawrence and major operations were undertaken to make that route easier. By 1842 steamers could get from Lake Ontario to below Cornwall and in 1848 go on to Montreal. Meanwhile the extended Welland Canal had been finished so that canals filled in the gaps as far west as Sault Ste. Marie.

The carriage of letters had always been in large part dependent on means of transport, but when the provinces of British North America took over the post office in 1851 they moved faster than improvements in travel alone might have suggested. The number of local post offices was rapidly increased; rates were reduced by a third; and stamps appeared. Correspondents were slow to accept the idea that the sender should pay the postage, but the lower rates did result in an increase of 50 per cent in the number of letters. In 1855 money orders and registration were introduced. Meanwhile a new form of communication came in the telegraph. At the beginning of 1847 the *Globe* published Washington news of the previous day as well as the record of the New York Stock Exchange, which, it triumphantly said, had been made up at 7.12 P.M. and received in Toronto at 8.00 P.M. "What next?" asked the editor. He was right in thinking of the telegraph as one sign of a new age, yet public opinion was far more directed to the future railways which were to solve all the nagging problems of bad roads. For this millennium the people still had to wait.

In the forties the familiar problems of health persisted. Emigrant families already weakened by hunger were allowed to leave Ireland when ill and were carried in ships in which the conditions were so ghastly as to beggar description. Neglect by the British authorities and the avarice of shipping companies brought to the St. Lawrence ports the dead and the dying, and others who were to develop typhus, smallpox, cholera, and other serious illnesses as they moved inland into Ontario. The native ague seemed to be no better. Anne Langton, who was not given to exaggeration, wrote in 1847 that she and her aunt had the illness:

They say there has not been such a year as this since the year 1827, when it was still worse. There have been more deaths on the other side of the lake. In some respects we are better off from having four families habitually provided with some medicines. In some settlements there is nobody near to apply to, and the poor creatures having nothing to do but to lie down, and let the fever take its course. . . . Whole families are down with ague or fever, and perhaps no one to look after them but a neighbour, a mile away, herself in a state of ague.

The Langtons kept a supply of quinine which they shared with neighbours but the reign of patent medicine was, unfortunately, at its height. One newspaper printed a typical list of twenty-eight varieties, most of them with impressive names, and few mentioning the ills which they were intended to cure. Perhaps laudanum and whisky would do as well for one as another. One brand with an appealing name and apparently universal use was "The World's Wonder" or "Connel's Magic Pain Extractor." Satisfaction guaranteed or money refunded.

On the brighter side of the medal were some favourable developments. Hospitals were still scarce but more were being opened, as, for example, in Kingston. After years of frustrating efforts an asylum in Toronto for the mentally ill was made ready in 1850 and the patients could be taken out of the old gaol. More doctors were still needed in the rural areas. In the towns frequent advertisements by doctors showed that they were in place but anxiously looking for business. Dentists seem to have been still scarce. One who advertised in a Niagara newspaper in 1851 came there for a part of each month from his place of residence in Lewiston, New York. The long-awaited institutions for the training of doctors began to take shape. Back from political exile, Dr. John Rolph resumed lectures in what he later called the Toronto School of Medicine. In 1850 Drs. Hodder and Bovell planned the Upper Canada School of Medicine. The first became the medical faculty of Victoria University and the second of Trinity University. In 1844 the medical faculty of King's College began its short existence and in 1854 Queen's University inaugurated a faculty of medicine. The appearance of professional schools for the training of doctors did not at once frighten off the quacks any more than legal penalties had done. For a while they competed with the doctors, outside the main towns; but the growing availability of qualified men led to their gradual eclipse. The legislature made its bow to the cause of medical education by providing for dissection the bodies of those dying in public institutions; and to the control of epidemics by designing central and local boards of health. The nucleus of the modern organization for combatting disease now existed.

Some minor advances were made in social welfare and the impetus for them came from two directions. The provincial government was accepting more responsibility as shown by an amendment to the Districts Councils Act under which a township could impose a tax for relief of poor or ill persons. By an Act of 1851 apprentices received more protection. Voluntary effort continued too as in the provision of homes in Toronto and Hamilton for destitute orphans. In addition to these types of welfare was the co-operative one. The British American Friendly Society of Canada, incorporated in 1854, provided relief in cases of age, sickness, or infirmity, this being financed by voluntary subscriptions or contributions. None of these steps introduced any new principle; nor was renewed attention to the conditions of the gaols more than a continuation—though one much needed—of the long series of complaints about them. A statute of 1838 set up a board to examine and report and it found that eight out of thirteen gaols were defective in important respects. A *cause célèbre* developed out of a series of quarrels with and about the Kingston penitentiary, the temperature being raised and publicity enlarged by the fact that criticism and defence of the obviously unsuitable warden were unfortunately associated with party politics. Conditions in the penitentiary, which would horrify public opinion now, were unacceptable even when prison reform had advanced less far. A commission of inquiry, which had a prolonged life, drew out some shocking evidence and was able to introduce a degree of reform. Unfortunately the party manoeuvres which accompanied the case were almost as sordid as the operation of the prison, so that the investigation did not lead to changes as sweeping as might otherwise have been effected.

Slavery within Ontario had long since ceased to be a factor, and by the time that it was abolished throughout the British Empire in 1833 there were, it is thought, only two slaves in Upper Canada. Having long before decided on the gradual abolition of slavery within their own province the people of Ontario were left with two remaining concerns with that institution: opinion, overwhelmingly critical, of its retention in the United States; and the settlement of escaped slaves. The two overlapped, for some of the most ardent Canadian abolitionists took what part they could in the operation of the highly developed system of escape routes known as the underground railway. The United States' Fugitive Slave Law of 1850, which allowed federal officers to capture escaped slaves in the free states of the north caused a sudden migration of apprehensive negroes to Canada and accelerated the social problem of providing for those who escaped and finding for them a place in the communities. By 1852 the newly formed Anti-Slavery Society of Canada claimed that there were about thirty thousand negroes in Ontario, nearly all refugees. The difficulties in absorbing them were in part practical and in part arose out of hostility shown by white inhabitants toward the presence of negroes in their communities. The need for employment was met in some instances by work on farms; training institutes were set up to prepare the men for various trades; and in the fifties negroes secured work in railway construction. One large project was that of the Elgin Association which had powerful support from such men as Peter and George Brown, Alexander Mackenzie, and Oliver Mowat. It secured nine thousand acres in Kent County on which to place negro refugees and this in spite of a "vigilance committee" which tried to block the deal. By 1856 eight hundred people had been installed and a thousand acres cleared. More continued to arrive.

Although there was much goodwill toward escaped slaves and many people spent time and money in helping them there was also resentment at their presence in numbers. Sometimes this was touched off by the behaviour of the odd bad characters who were bound to be mixed in with the rest, sometimes it was naked racial prejudice. Legally the negro had the same status in the province as the white man, but his children were sometimes excluded from the local schools by public opinion, and isolated cases occurred of refusal of service in taverns or of passage on steamships. In the Western District, where there was more concentration of ex-slaves than elsewhere, the council passed in 1849 a resolution expressing alarm that a third of a township was negro and that negroes insisted on their right to vote for the local officials. Fortunately for the reputation of the District the resolution was criticized by other inhabitants of it. None of these problems was settled over-night and particularly the prejudice against negro children in common schools lasted in some places. In many an Ontario town, however, was a substantial group of ex-slaves or the descendants of slaves on good terms with the white population. Close to such groups were their churches, mainly Baptist and Methodist, for religion had been a strength to the slave; and the clergy and members of those and other churches, in particular the Quakers, had been to the forefront in aiding in their escape and their establishment in Ontario.

The churches, like the people and the other institutions, had come originally as immigrants; and like others went through a process of acclimatization. Some individuals, clerical or lay, were consciously influenced by nationalism as applied to institutions within the province; but the dominating factor in the growing independence of the churches was the growth of Ontario in population, wealth, and general social structure. In most areas of the south the pioneering stage was over, or fast disappearing, and as the province thus progressed it became more self-reliant. In conformity with this trend the churches ceased to be dependent on the churches and missionary societies of Great Britain and the United States from which they had sprung; but in the religious as in other spheres it was a change that was gradual and evolutionary. As in so many other things Canadian—whether in government, finance, or social fields—much of the character of the source of imported churches remained.

The pattern varied according to circumstances. The Roman Catholic Church continued as an integral part of the parent body even if its priests from the first adapted themselves to the demands of the Ontario environment. The Church of England in Canada later came to have a more tenuous connection with the church in England, but neither before or after that time did it gain in effectiveness by repeating the English distinction between high and low church. At the same time it borrowed some American practices; the most important was a diocesan synod with lay delegates included, to which, in Strachan's view, "the Episcopal Church in the United States owes almost everything." The Presbyterian churches did not suffer from undue control from outside, but the very fact that they are listed in the plural recalls the external source of a handicap which at times was accentuated in Ontario by bitterness between some individual Kirk and Secession ministers. Even when it became possible to effect a partial union in 1840 the disruption of 1843 in Scotland cut across it again.

In the case of Methodism in Ontario the principal outside forces were those coming from the United States and England. It was to some extent because of particular circumstances as well as of a sense of Canadian identity that both administrative cords were cut. The earliest link, that with the United States, was badly frayed not only by the fact of the War of 1812 but also by accusations that Methodists were disloyal. Years later, in 1828, a select committee of the Assembly vindicated their loyalty; but if the connection had not been broken in that same year it would have been subject to another strain from the events of 1837–38. A union with the British Wesleyans ran into a rock in 1840 when the latter, already considered to have exercised undue control, attempted to have Egerton Ryerson dismissed as editor of the *Christian Guardian* because of a difference of policy. When the English and Canadian Conferences were reunited in 1847, on the initiative of the latter, it was intended, if not put in written terms, that the Canadians should have more autonomy. The Baptist churches, with their emphasis on the individual congregations, found their difficulty in forming an organization to cover the whole, but accomplished this in 1851. The Congregationalists were few in number and allowed even more authority to the individual churches. The Quakers, while self-governing, inherited the American split between the Orthodox and Hicksite branches, with the Children of Peace as a splinter group.

Perhaps the most important requirement for the churches, both in performing their mission and in adapting themselves to the Ontario society, was a supply of locally trained clergy; and the pursuit and accomplishment of this were common to all those which had ministers at all. Fairly early in the nineteenth century there had been improvised arrangements, either by a sort of apprenticeship or through small and informal schools; but it was the establishment of theological colleges that made more organized and more permanent provision for training the clergy, just as similar arrangements were made for other professions.

The work of the churches in Ontario was amongst both the Indian and the white populations. The first was more akin to missionary endeavour in the sense of converting those who were not Christians, although the needs of the smaller groups who had long been so had also to be met. John Strachan summed up the religious care of the Indians so far as his information went. There were, he wrote, two missionaries supported by the New England Society amongst the two thousand Mohawks on the Grand River; a Church of England clergyman with the three hundred agricultural Mohawks on the Bay of Quinte; and a Methodist preacher for the three hundred Chippewas near Lake St. Clair. For the Chippewas on the River Thames there was a Moravian minister in one district and a Church of England clergyman in the other. The five hundred Chippewas of Lake Huron and Lake Simcoe had a Methodist mission and other missionaries visited them occasionally. There had been plans to send a Church of England clergyman amongst the two hundred Mississaugas of the Credit River, but meanwhile the Methodists had got a footing there "and appeared to be doing so much good, that it has not been thought expedient to disturb them." The Mississaugas of Kingston and Rice Lake—both small groups—were being visited by Methodists. Other moves were in mind.

Amongst the white people there were still areas in which missionary work, in the general sense, was called for; but in the southern part of the province a relatively denser and more advanced population needed regular church buildings and resident clergy. The more conservative churches—Roman Catholic, Church of England, and to some extent Presbyterian—found social changes favourable to them, while the evangelical churches, which had so well met early needs, turned to more conservative methods, not so much from doubts of the old on the part of the ministers—although in the forties and fifties more of them had sober theological education—as because of the changing public attitude. There was still room for itinerant preachers, emotional appeals, and camp meetings in the more remote areas, but by 1840 the prolonged camp meeting was not popular elsewhere, a fact which the *Christian Guardian* deplored. The dramatic spectacles of conversion were disappearing. In many sections of the province there were not enough clergy to meet the needs of the people, but the gap was being narrowed.

Although they were not alone in seeking to improve public morals the churches had a distinct part to play. The Quakers and the Mennonites taught a simple and even severe code. The evangelicals were starting to devote a good deal of attention to two causes, temperance and the observance of Sunday. They were followed only part way by Roman Catholics and Anglicans, because "temperance" had turned into prohibition of all alcoholic drinks, and because the Catholics particularly did not accept the Puritan Sunday. About the middle of the century larger temperance organizations, many of them associated with or inspired by similar ones in the United States, began to appear. The tendency now was to move from concentration on the signing of pledges to legislation. The ultimate objective was total prohibition, but intermediate steps were to close the bars from Saturday night to Monday morning and to provide for local option. A statute passed in 1845 was to "avoid profanation of the Lord's Day." No one was to sell anything other than drugs on that day or to perform any labour except works of charity and conveying travellers. There was to be no brawling or profane language, no public meetings; no one could play at "skittles, ball, racket, or any other noisy games," gamble, or have horse races. No bathing could occur "in any exposed situation in any water within the limits of any incorporated city or town." Sales or contracts made on Sunday became void.

One of the most striking changes of the forties and early fifties was the advance made in education, for both schools and universities. The word "advance" is used advisedly since the steps that were taken were, with modifications, in implementation of ideas and hopes widely accepted in the early years of the century but more readily applicable in the stage of development to which Ontario had now attained. In the absence of adequate resources the advantages of education had been open more to those who could attend private or grammar schools than to those who were obliged to rely on the spotty pattern of common schools. The Acts of 1841 and 1843 were imperfect in detail but did contain all the principles that were to govern the school system for many years. They provided for common or public schools supported by public funds, for a Superintendent of Education, and for a Board of Education in each District. There were to be model schools in townships and counties. Robert Murray, the first superintendent, found the first Act particularly hard to administer, but rather for technical reasons than because of its substantive provisions.

By this time the lines of the public school system had been drawn and its weaknesses had been pointed out by Murray and others. To Egerton Ryerson, the next superintendent, fell the task of tidying up the legislation with a view to producing a more workable structure. Ryerson was not an innovator, indeed he introduced no new principles into the common school system, but he was a very able administrator and an enthusiastic protagonist of the common schools. The Act of 1846, which was an improvement on the two previous ones, was drafted by him after an investigation of the schools of the State of New York. Amendments of 1847 made special arrangements for towns and cities.

The schools were to be financed by provincial funds and local taxation, in equal amounts. The direction was put in the hands of an appointed General Board of Education for Upper Canada of which the chief administrative officer, the superintendent, was a member. Each District Municipal Council was to raise the local funds and to appoint a District superintendent. Each school section was to elect its own trustees. In any incorporated city or town the responsibility for raising money and administering the schools was placed in a single board of education.

Public opinion was by no means unanimous in support, indeed more Districts were opposed to the scheme than there were in favour. David MacLaren was unsure whether the Act of 1841 would produce a school satisfactory for the education of his sons. Writing from his farm on the Ottawa River to his brother in Scotland he expressed some doubt:

> Thank you for the kind offer of a home for one of my boys in the event of my sending him over to school. I may perhaps yet avail myself of your good offer but I am at present inclined to wait until I shall see the result of our new school Act. The Provincial Legislature have voted Fifty Thousand Pounds Annually for Common schools, and the people are to be taxed to raise a like Amount for the same object and each child attending school will have to pay 1/3 per month. Every section of a township where 15 children of the age of from 5 to 16 can be collected may take the benefit of this Act, and receive a share of this fund in proportion to the number of children attending school. It is intended to have one of the schools for this township in my "Old clearance" where I have offered an acre of land to build one. The number of children in the neighbourhood are too few however to enable us to support a teacher such as would be desirable, but they are increasing and we look forward with hope. The demand for teachers in consequence of this Act will, I think, be very great. Have you any to spare?

The lasting controversy was whether there should or should not be confessional schools, a question which had obvious social importance. Examining a dispute which at times was pursued in extreme terms (and has never come to an end) he would be a hardy man who concluded that one opinion was right and the other wrong. The position taken by the Roman Catholic Church in regard to religious instruction in schools was an important factor in the whole dispute and at times it seemed as if the argument was about whether there should be separate schools for Roman Catholic children. The legislation, however, was not drafted in these terms. There had always been private schools connected with churches, and it seems evident that in the earliest common schools individual teachers gave religious instruction according to their own points of view. The concept of the "separate" school, however, derives from the Act of 1841 and was modified in subsequent Acts. The formula in the Act of 1846 is as typical as any: ". . . in all cases wherein the Teacher of any Common School shall happen to be a Roman Catholic, the Protestant inhabitants of the Section . . . shall be entitled to have a school with a Protestant teacher . . . and in like manner, when the Teacher of any such School shall happen to be a Protestant, the Roman Catholic inhabitants shall have a Separate School. . . ." This, taken with the wording of the Act of 1841, seems to add up to the protection of a religious minority. There seems to be nothing in the wording to prevent the existence of common schools in which denominational religion was a part of the instruction; indeed it implies that such would be the case. Another form of separate school, and one which the people of Ontario would have liked to forget, was for coloured people. The Common Schools Act of 1850 gave them the "right" to establish separate schools; which, translated, meant that local opinion forced them out of the regular schools. Apparently only three such schools were ever set up, and the last of them was wound up in 1891.

A statistical measurement of the state of education at the half-century mark produces, for 1853, two sets of figures. The first, on the percentage of illiterate in each county, gives the highest figures for Simcoe (53 per cent), Essex and Prescott (52 per cent). The lowest was for Prince Edward (14), with Brant (15) running a close second. The other list is of the percentage of children not attending school. Here the highest figures are for Dundas (43 per cent: 30 per cent illiterate) and Glengarry (39: 38). The lowest are for Kent (14: 19) and Prince Edward (15: 14). Some additional information on common schools applying to the year 1857 may be taken from the report of the superintendent: boys attending, 150,029; girls, 122,608; number of free schools, 1,707. All new schoolhouses had been built of brick.

The available reports made by the inspectors of grammar schools go deeper below the surface. For the eastern section of the province in 1855 there were 895 pupils on the rolls but only 681 were found to be in attendance. As to teaching, the inspector found too much dependence on textbooks and recitation from memory. Some of the buildings were good, some inferior, and one scarcely habitable. The inspector in the western section also found more dependence on memory than on reason, but there were notable exceptions. The masters, he thought, were better than formerly, and more apparatus was in use. There were also union schools, that is, combined grammar and common schools, said to number twenty-one in 1855. The records were not complete for private schools, but for 1855 Ryerson—using, he said, imperfect sources—gave 29 private academies with 1,053 pupils and 278 private schools (a much larger number than previously) with 6,531 students.

The grammar schools in time became secondary or high schools and the common schools were re-named public schools. The effect of the legislation of the forties was to make elementary education available to everyone, although it was not as yet universally free. (That was to come gradually.) As the figures above show, however, the public response belied any theory that all the people of Ontario craved education. The reason why children were kept at home was in some cases poverty, although there was provision for indigents. For others it may have been the distance from home to school. Some farming families preferred to have their children helping with the chores. Other parents thought that education was unnecessary and even undesirable. Mrs. Oille, who lived at St. Catharine's, recalled that a well-to-do farmer there could see no sense in schools and certainly would not send his daughter to one, "for if his gal went to school and learned to read and write she would get so stuck up that she would want to wear shoes and stockings all the year round and would not be willing to hoe the taters." Those who sought to make education general had to convince not only the advocates of education for the few but also the common man who was supposed to be demanding his rights.

The strengthening of the school system was an achievement of the forties, but provision for higher education meant writing on an almost blank page. To have universities in Ontario was an ambition long cherished but the case for it was not so broadly based. The practical argument could be advanced that training was required for doctors, lawyers, clergymen, and engineers; but beyond this was less solid ground. As enrolment in the early colleges showed there was anything but a general demand for higher education. Universities must always be expensive to operate in comparison to schools because of more elaborate buildings, libraries and laboratory equipment, higher salaries, and a different ratio of teachers to students. It would not be correct to say that costs always diminish with larger attendance, but up to a point that would be true. It was not easy to locate schools within easy reach of all pupils, but to do so for universities was literally impossible. The plans for universities were handicapped even more than those for schools by divisions in and between the churches. The dispute over whether denominational religion should be a part of education was carried on no less actively than in relation to schools.

Given all these obstacles it is remarkable that any universities survived or even came into existence at all: but they did both. King's College lived on paper long before it began teaching. Designed by Strachan, it was intended to follow his philosophy of the proper relation between education and the church; but, although it was more liberal than the older English universities, and although no religious tests were applied to students other than those in divinity, the charter (against Strachan's advice) did require them of members of the council and faculty. Even as amended in some respects ten years later (1837), the charter was a design for a Church of England university, and it was as such that it opened in 1843. Meanwhile two other churches had just entered the field of higher education. The Presbyterian Church in connection with the Church of Scotland established Queen's University at Kingston on almost identical principles. In 1842 the Methodists built from their Upper Canada Academy a college which was to be called Victoria. Unlike the other two it imposed no religious tests on the staff, but the church retained authority over appointments, which could produce the same result if that were desired.

Although King's and Queen's were alike in the respects mentioned, it was the former which was bitterly criticized, perhaps because it alone had the benefit of the public endowment. Even after King's had been secularized Egerton Ryerson struck an old note by claiming that it was directed by a family compact. By the Act of 1849 King's College became the non-denominational University of Toronto, and by a further Act of 1853 the university was turned into a governing body with instruction to be given by the University College and any affiliated colleges. The endowment was to be distributed to other universities only after University College had taken what it needed, and not surprisingly there were no such crumbs. Affiliation of these various colleges and universities was much discussed, with the most common formula being that there should be several theological colleges and a single one for secular subjects, all being grouped together in one city. It was argued that economies would result and assumed that the endowment would be shared. In their early years Queen's and Victoria were in serious financial straits, and the small number of undergraduates who attended them was an argument against their separate existences. Queen's started with ten students and after six years had only twenty-five. In 1844 the total enrolment at Victoria was forty-four. No agreement on federation was reached at that time, however. Queen's remained at Kingston, and not until 1890 did Victoria go into the University of Toronto.

When Strachan and his associates lost the battle to preserve King's as a Church of England college he immediately set about the establishment of a private institution which would not have ungodly education. Trinity College received its charter in 1851 and was guided by the strong hand of Strachan. To the protagonists of the Low Church it was a hand that was far too heavy. Led by Benjamin Cronyn, Bishop of London, they withdrew from the corporation and founded Huron College in 1863. The splintering process was even more damaging to Queen's, because it came at an early and critical stage. The division of the Church of Scotland in 1843 forced Queen's to take a side and it chose to adhere to the old kirk, but at the cost of losing trustees, students, and supporters. The Free Church party founded Knox College, which for a time drained off most of the students in theology. Since the Baptists delayed action about university education, the remaining elements in the pattern up to the middle of the fifties were the two Roman Catholic colleges. St. Michael's College, leaning on the strong arm of the Irish Basilians, opened in Toronto in 1852 and federated with the University of Toronto three years later. Assumption College at Windsor began teaching in 1855.

The extent to which this new group of colleges and universities influenced the social structure of the province is not easy to assess. Statistics of attendance, comparable to those for the common schools, would, taken in themselves, suggest that universities were a failure. No one in those days, however, was thinking in terms of higher education for the masses: "masses" being used as a numerical rather than a social measure. No one will ever know what would have been the result of a plebiscite on the question of whether universities were desirable. What people could see was that doors were opened for those who needed professional training and to those with literary, scientific, or philosophical bent. Without men of learning in many fields the province could not achieve full development. Up to that time higher education had had, with few exceptions, to be found in other countries, a method that was expensive and available to few people. Both school and university education must be provided at home if they were to keep up with, and support, the general progress of Ontario.

Part Two

THE LAND
UNFOLDS

CHAPTER SEVEN

The
Railway Age

FOR SOME FIFTY YEARS while the people in southern Ontario had been fully occupied in subduing an untamed wilderness, in cutting farms out of forests, in building towns where there had been isolation, the much greater northern area, once the scene of a busy trade in furs, had been left to sleep and to dream of the past. In the second half of the nineteenth century the old and the new were for the first time combined in the active life of the province. From one important point of view the result came about through movement of people, industry, and capital from the established southern base. As the story proceeded, however, it became evident that—contrary to expectation—this movement was not just a further stage of the territorial expansion that had long been going on, not just adding more thousands of acres for settlement. On the contrary trial and error showed that the north country, the Canadian Shield, was a different kind of land, with opportunities of its own but ones that were not the same as those in the Laurentian lowland.

Thus in the second half of the century there are two main themes. In the south, cities were growing, industries emerging from family shops, prosperous farms showing where not long before grain had been scratched in around stumps, everywhere substantial buildings taking the place of log cabins. In the north, mining and lumbering found their places in a terrain unlike that of the south. Yet the two themes merge at places. Once the essential distinctions had been recognized each area could become complementary to the other.

The province had always been handicapped by an inadequate system of transport; and as the occupied area was extended and economic development became more diverse it was evident that further progress would in part be governed by the means of moving people and goods. Water transport had always been, and continued to be, essential but its limitations were obvious. Canals made great improvements but water courses could not be created wherever they were needed. Furthermore, water travel was seasonal. A local newspaper announced triumphantly that in the winter of 1859–60 the port of Whitby had been closed for only two days but for the most part and in all years the great lakes as well as the rivers and canals were blocked by ice.

Roads were improved but all-weather highways were not built until the second decade of the twentieth century. Nor, indeed, would earlier ones have solved the problem since there was no motive power other than the horse. The first mechanical means of traction on roads that seemed hopeful was the steam traction engine, arousing interest as a supplement rather than as an alternative to railways. In 1867 the *Globe* wrote excitedly about this great machine, which, it said, was in common use in England and had been exported widely. It would be invaluable in Ontario.

The traction engine will supply the want of the back country, namely, cheap transit for heavy goods, at a slow pace. The manufacturers of the engines state that the cost of moving freight by them is one penny halfpenny sterling per ton per mile, so that at this rate it would cost $4\frac{1}{2}$ cents to move a bushel of wheat fifty miles, exclusive of turnpike tolls and the back journey.

James G. Worts went to England to investigate the purchase of a traction engine for the firm of Gooderham and Worts in Toronto. He was much impressed by a demonstration. Downhill the machine would go faster than he could walk and uphill it would pull a heavy load. Even adding 50 per cent to the manufacturers' figures of the cost of operation Worts concluded that goods could be moved at half the cost of hauling them by horses. But if the traction engines were bought for road transport in Ontario they were rare. It is important to keep in mind, moreover, that they were considered for use only for short distances (Worts's estimate was for haulage between Malton and Meadowvale) or as feeders for canals and railways. The railway was the essential answer to the difficulty of land travel and had been seen as such since the eighteen-thirties.

In the south the first lines were short ones going hither and yon, but more ambitious plans were made for railways running broadly east and west, close to the line of the St. Lawrence and lower lakes. These were main or "trunk" lines, that is they were designed to carry heavy traffic for all or part of long distances. They were to be central arteries of commerce, not only of the Province of Canada but also of the United States. The prospectus of the first of them illustrates that ambition. "The Great Western Rail Road is designed not only to facilitate the internal traffic of the Province of Canada, for which its route possesses eminent advantages, but also to form a connecting link in the great chain of Railways from the city of Boston ... to the Mississippi, thus drawing over it an immense and increasing foreign traffic." Those were the days of continental planning based on devoted attention to geography. By 1855 the Great Western was completed from Windsor through Hamilton to Niagara Falls, and from Hamilton to Toronto. It was scarcely under way, however, before it began to fall under the shadow of the Grand Trunk, the first of three great railway companies that came into being in the later nineteenth century. As the Grand Trunk grew to imperial size it absorbed not only the Great Western but also many of the smaller railways that crisscrossed Ontario. Its peculiar and original contribution, however, was that not only did it run, like the Great Western, through the rich lands of southern Ontario to the American border (at Sarnia), but that it went on eastward to tidewater at Montreal and Quebec and to the winter port of Portland, Maine. One handicap of which the commercially minded had been acutely conscious since the late eighteenth century was that Ontario was land-locked. True, salt water lapped the shores of Hudson Bay and James Bay, but there was no way of getting to them from the south, no port if you did, and a hazardous sea route in a short period of the year would be the reward for effort. The St. Lawrence, greatly improved by canals, was an outlet to the ocean for the southern part of the province, but it could not be other than seasonal. Railways had their own solid roads and—even if their early battles with snow often ended in temporary defeat—could be operated all year and could carry people and goods to seasonal or all-year ports.

Probably every town and village in southern Ontario made some effort to have a railway (more than one if its ambition soared) run past its door, believing that its future success would thus be ensured. Many of the calculated results were in the realm of day-dreams but there is no doubt that some urban communities grew larger and others fell into decay depending on whether or not they lay on the line of a railway. It did not follow, of course, that all towns on railways made notable progress, indeed to some extent the opposite was true since the railways made possible concentration of industry in a few places like Toronto and Hamilton. Raw materials could be collected and finished products distributed by rail over distances and to a degree that had hitherto been impossible. Thus railways were essential to industrial development and influenced its geographical pattern.

In the south, where were the main population, commerce, and industry, the railways served a variety of needs. Northward their functions were no less essential but simpler. In this period Ontario, as has been mentioned, was expanding so far as effective use of the land was concerned. The first move was toward the lower part of the Canadian Shield, roughly bounded on the south by a line above Lake Simcoe and on the north by a line eastward from Lake Nipissing. Early railways had been edging up in that direction to carry out lumber. One such ran from Ottawa to the St. Lawrence River at Prescott and another, somewhat to the west, from Almonte to Lake Ontario at Brockville. The main purpose of these lines was to connect with American railways on the other side of the water boundary, thus allowing for the sale of lumber in the United States where it found an important market from the late forties. As both the lumber business and the frontier of settlement moved further northward the railways followed. For both the settlers and the lumbermen the distances to the main waterways, to the towns, and to markets were formidable. Roads of a sort were run northward and to some extent the small rivers could be used for logs but the combination was not good enough to bring this then northerly strip within range. A complex of rail lines was then built running generally northward through the settled area of southern Ontario into the Shield. Several of these were designed to connect with the northern lakes following a concept of integration that has never disappeared from Canadian transportation.

One such railway, the Northern, which ran from Toronto to Collingwood on Georgian Bay, had an additional role to play since it connected with the steamers which for long provided the only transportation to Lake Superior and on to the new west. They lead us to the second area to be developed in the north, one which there has hardly been cause to mention so far. It was the rugged country stretching from Sault Ste. Marie around the north shore of Lake Superior and across the land of forests, lakes, and rocks to Kenora, then still Rat Portage as the fur traders had named it. This is the area now comprised of the Districts of Algoma, Thunder Bay, Rainy River, and Kenora. Ships went as far as Fort William and from there the Dawson Trail (itself a portage and boat system) ran into the interior and westward. The same idea of portage was taken up in this Superior country in the initial stages of the railway to the Pacific, but as the project developed a complete line was put through the whole territory: close to the apparent wilderness on the shore of the great lake and on across an unpeopled country to the provincial boundary and beyond. As interest in mining and lumbering increased the essential part of railways in the exploitation of the region was more obvious. The second transcontinental railway, the Canadian Northern, took a similar route but somewhat farther to the north. The third was the National Transcontinental which was intended to form part of the Grand Trunk to the Pacific coast. Coming from Quebec city it was still farther to the north, being close to the height of land between the Hudson Bay and the great lakes watersheds. By these various means an immense part of Ontario was opened up for the first time since the days of the fur traders.

There is still another chapter in the story of the northern drive in Ontario and one in which the role of railways is no less leading. The desire to make use of the Clay Belt for agricultural settlement focused attention on the area north of Lake Nipissing. The Ontario government built the Temiskaming and Northern Ontario Railway into this new and hopeful land, intending it as a route for the wave of settlers which was anticipated. In fact it was, by chance, the instrument of the discovery of minerals; and mining rather than agriculture was to give its character to this area.

Such in outline were the pattern and significance of railways in Ontario as they developed over fifty years. The effects were so many and so considerable that they cannot readily be summarized: perhaps the best impression is gained by imagining (shutting out thoughts of later highways) what Ontario of the later nineteenth and early twentieth centuries would have been like without railways. One direct effect is obvious, that they created employment, whether in the stages of construction or of operation. Business men and engineers, carpenters, stonemasons, teamsters, and pick and shovel men were all drawn in to the making of a line and the buildings that went with it. Once completed, a railway needed executives, engineers, clerks, stationmasters, train crews, and maintenance men. Farmers were called on to provide food, commercial firms for supplies of many kinds. Ancillary industries grew up to make rolling-stock, locomotives, rails, and to fill a dozen other needs. Lumbermen cut thousands of sleepers and stone quarries were kept busy producing ballast for the right of way. Skilled and unskilled labour, white-collar employees and navvies, found their places on the pay rolls.

From the point of view of the average person in Ontario a railway, regardless of the strategic purpose in the minds of the promoters, could be a community friend meeting local needs. To the farmer or the villager who wanted to travel five miles or ship his product ten miles to market it mattered not at all that a particular railway was really intended to draw into its maw the riches of the American middle west or to satisfy the demands of the government of British Columbia. If it was there to carry himself and his goods in comfort and convenience that was all he asked. The early train, it is true, did not go very quickly. Timetables of 1860 show that it took two and a half hours to go from Cobourg to Peterborough and two hours and fifteen minutes from Port Hope to Peterborough; but compared to the roads of even the late nineteenth century the railway personified speed and comfort. Railways, too, were somehow assimilated into the intimate life of the community. The local station was a meeting place and the stationmaster was everyone's friend. The arrival of a train was not a routine but an event, for the train itself was given a personality. In his *Sunshine Sketches* Stephen Leacock describes the interest in watching the express trains whistling through with all their glamour and the local trains which were so close to the people of the town. Passengers would huddle around the stove of the waiting room chatting idly while the train (an hour late) proceeded on its sedate way. In the summer piles of crates of berries or other agricultural produce waited on the platform for the appearance of the friendly, puffing monster. Lines of buggies and waggons formed a background to what was essentially a community scene.

In the later nineteenth and early twentieth centuries the population of the province which the network of railways served was increasing, although not at a steady rate. Total figures as shown in the decennial censuses are these: 1851, 952,004; 1861, 1,396,091; 1871, 1,620,851; 1881, 1,926,922; 1891, 2,114,321; 1901, 2,182,947; 1911, 2,527,292. In sixty years, then, the population multiplied by roughly two and one-half times.

Looking at the distribution of population first by the main regions of the province it is evident that the northern Districts were still in very small figures but increasing substantially. The lower part of the Shield was barely holding its own. In the south, where the great majority of people lived, the urban population was not only catching up with the rural but in itself becoming more concentrated at a few points. The consistent supremacy of Toronto and Hamilton had a depressing effect on several of the old lake ports. Elsewhere only a few towns and cities were growing rapidly and some were actually declining. Because of urbanization or the unequal progress of towns, or both, a whole series of counties were showing absolute losses of population over the years 1891–1911. To take the extremes: the County of York at 444,234 had almost four times the population of the next largest (Carleton and Wentworth) but at the other end of the line old counties such as Glengarry, Halton,

Lennox and Addington, and Peel (none of which had cities) were around 20,000.

By the turn of the century most of the people in Ontario had been born there. The figures for 1901 were 1,858,787 Canadian-born (principally Ontario) and 324,160 born elsewhere. Immigration was not large in the second half of the nineteenth century—a marked contrast with earlier years —and was not again a major factor until well into the twentieth century. Most of the newcomers were from the British Isles until the northern mines attracted European labour. Americans were coming in only small numbers. The American-born in Ontario were not increasing rapidly. In 1891 there were 42,702. A breakdown of the figure by counties shows that the largest numbers were in those close to the United States. In Essex, for example, there were 3,514 American born, and over 2,000 in each of Kent and Wentworth. Simcoe, on the other hand, had only 921. York had nearly 7,000.

Although there were important Roman Catholic minorities—at first mainly Irish and later increasingly French-Canadian—the province was not only mainly Protestant but could be militantly so. The people were largely derived, even though partly at one remove, from the British Isles. The old drain to the United States had not been plugged and some of the land-hungry were moving to the Canadian west. In both places land was offered to settlers. In the seventies the land commissioner of the Union Pacific Railroad placed advertisements in Ontario newspapers at first offering free homesteads and then land at $5 per acre along the line of the railway. The Canadian west had land aplenty and there are frequent references to the exodus to it. To leave the province, however, was not the only course open to the pioneer and the adventurer, for Ontario had its own north and north-west. The Muskoka–Haliburton area beckoned settlers, and then came the Lake Superior region and the mining country. With growing industrialization in the south there were opportunities for new citizens to work in the factories. In early decades Ontario had been built up by immigrants. Was it still a hopeful land for the intending emigrant? William Davies, who came to Toronto from England in 1854 and made his fortune, had interesting opinions on this point. Here is a passage from a letter of 1875:

My candid opinion is that if the Middle Class want to emigrate there is no better place in America than Ontario and no better city than Toronto, but people of that class should think twice before they start, and as to any *organised* emigration of that class it is all moonshine. It is infinitely better for such to find their way here in 2s or 3s or in Families—new arrivals have to undergo what I call a grinding up, an assimilation. They have 1st a lot to unlearn, and then a lot to learn, you see I speak from experience—of course an Englishman thinks that we know nothing here, that as a mechanic or whatnot he is far ahead of us Canadians, and so he might be if the conditions were the same, and after some time he finds that to suit the changed circumstances he has to adopt our plans. Many a one comes here with means and he does not find this out till his money is gone, then if he is made of the right stuff when he touches bottom, he puts his shoulder to the wheel and begins to rise. . . . But *poor industrious* people are pretty certain to benefit themselves by coming here. They are at the bottom when they get here.

His comment is not dissimilar to the conclusions reached by the wiser immigrants forty years earlier.

Neither immigration nor any other external influence affected Ontario as much as in the first half of the nineteenth century. At the outset its people were almost all immigrants and then for several decades a large proportion were. The Seven Years' War, the American Revolution, the Napoleonic wars, the War of 1812, and the rebellion of 1837 had had various and compelling effects. In comparison the sixty years between the middle of the nineteenth century and the War of 1914 were relatively peaceful; but they were not lacking in incidents and issues, at home and abroad, that aroused interest and sometimes participation. Perhaps the main difference between the two periods is that in the second it was usually possible for people, if they so wished, to go about their private affairs with little attention to public questions.

In the Crimean War individuals offered to enlist and money was raised for a patriotic fund. During the Indian Mutiny a regiment was raised by the United Kingdom authorities in British North America, and in the later imperial crisis in South Africa a substantial number of volunteer soldiers went from Ontario. The military problem closest to home continued for some years to be defence against the United States. To the memories of 1837–38 was added alarm arising out of the American expansionism that was taking effect in the absorption of Texas, New Mexico, and California, and the attempt to buy Cuba. The responsibility for defence, too, was falling more on reluctant Canadian shoulders as British regiments were withdrawn before and during the Crimean War. The Anglo-American tension during the Civil War was bound to have repercussions in Canada and fears were expressed that the triumphant Northern army would become the agent of manifest destiny. Happily the maximum danger faded away but raids by the Fenian Brotherhood, an Irish-American organization, served to disturb the peace intermittently from 1866 to 1871. Such forays as were made were repulsed without difficulty but this could not be forseen, so that British regiments returned to Ontario and the local militia was called out to guard the frontier. On one occasion during the period of anxiety the Cobourg *Star* noted that the volunteers had been relieved of duty and added: "While regretting that the necessity existed for calling so many men away from their every day avocations and adding another item to the public expense, the manner in which the call was responded to throughout the Province is something justly to be proud of." The post-war settlement embodied in the Treaty of Washington, although criticized in Canada, brought an end at long last to the fear of American aggression and allowed arms to be put aside for a time.

The people of Ontario, or those of them who were at all politically minded, had many opportunities of participation or at least interest in civil affairs of state. As communications improved and the population became less scattered news was better disseminated and public meetings could be more readily attended outside the main towns. With railways at hand both newspapers and people could circulate more readily. The proposal in the sixties for union of the provinces found wide support in Ontario, and with confederation achieved the union with Lower Canada was dissolved, leaving Ontario a separate political unit once more, but within the framework of a federal dominion. One effect on the individual was that he was now concerned with three levels of government, federal, provincial, and municipal. There are many indications that, in town and country alike, a respectable portion of the citizens took their political responsibilities seriously. As for playing any direct part in government, more of the people were involved in local government than in the other areas.

The system of municipal government as it applied to counties, townships, cities, towns, and villages, had become elective throughout the southern and smaller part of the province. Up to about the line of the Canadian Shield the land was divided into counties. When northern Ontario began to be developed the same system was judged not to be appropriate for an area which was scantily peopled. For the north there were to be either Districts or unorganized territory. Such Districts (which have no connection with the districts of the earlier nineteenth century) are intended as temporary divisions of thinly populated land for administrative and judicial purposes. Their boundaries do not necessarily have any bearing on those of counties which may later be established over the same area. They have no self-government as such nor have they local officials. Administration rests in the provincial authorities. A District is not necessarily divided into townships, but there may be some townships within it. These may exist only in the sense that they have been surveyed, either around their boundaries or completely within them, and such townships have no administrative organization of any kind. Alternatively townships may be incorporated and in that case have the same institutions as if they were within a county. The difference would be that the next level would be the provincial government. There can also, of course, be cities or towns within a District and then the same situation exists as if they were incorporated townships.

Under the federal system of 1867 municipal government became one of the provincial responsibilities. Education was another, and these, with roads, took the lion's share of effort and expenditure. The people of Ontario, however, having been in the van in pressing for the union scheme, came to have a conception of a province different to that held by them or their leaders when the plan was being evolved. The provincial politicians, and in particular the long-time premier, Oliver Mowat, turned to a crusade for what came to be called "provincial rights." That point of view has been attributed in part to the ambition of provincial politicians but it is significant that it was substantially upheld by the voters. Mowat, who personified this view, stayed in office until he chose to leave it. Not even the formidable John A. Macdonald could dislodge him.

Unless one can assume that the people of Ontario had a devotion to constitutional theories and forms greater than is normal, some other explanation of their attitude must be found. All through the period (1841–67) of the old union both the component parts, Upper and Lower Canada, retained a good deal of their identities. The French people of Lower Canada were consciously concerned with *la survivance*, the preservation of their social characteristics, what Wilfrid Laurier called their "peculiar institutions." Survival for Ontario was a less pressing problem and certainly a less obvious one, but within limits it was pursued. Necessarily expressed in political terms, it was at bottom social. Economic and social development, it was held, should be largely in the hands of those for whom it was intended. There were prejudices and contradictions in Ontario's thought, but somewhere too there was an ethos: a pride of history, a sense of identity and purpose. This it was that underlay the obstinate pursuit of provincial powers, although, of course, other factors contributed to that cause as well.

To many people in the province politics had always been of interest, and for a few a profession. Political parties, provincial and federal, became more highly organized as the century went on and attracted wide attention. The prevailing view on the degree of provincial authority within the federal scheme by no means inhibited people from following or participating in dominion public affairs. Many families and communities became attached to one party or the other; in those days either Liberal or Conservative. Some public questions had special social significance. Tariff policy was hotly debated as is illustrated by the elections of 1891 and 1911. Amongst farmers there was strong pressure for a low tariff while the manufacturing and financial groups generally called for protection. Socialism was not an important factor during this period. Toward the end of it a Social Democratic party had fifty-eight locals in Ontario, but that was a temporary phase for Ontario was still in the tradition of capitalism and individualism.

The province was growing up, but it was still, in the modern phrase, underdeveloped. That was the challenge to the capitalist and to the spirit of individualism. It was a rich land and a varied one, with opportunities for many kinds of endeavour. The great size looked less formidable in the railway age: indeed the time had come, it was agreed, to press beyond the Laurentian lowland into the huge and almost untenanted stretches of the Canadian Shield.

CHAPTER EIGHT

The North Country

THE MARCH OF SETTLEMENT had always been toward the north, and as population increased it seemed appropriate that the process should continue. Attention was turned first to the nearest unpeopled area, that known as the Ottawa–Huron Tract, which lay north of Lake Simcoe, east of Georgian Bay, and south of the Ottawa River. The Nor'Westers had for a few years in the early nineteenth century travelled through the western end of it as a feasible route to the fur trade country during the War of 1812. A series of explorations was made from the twenties on, by military and civil surveyors and, particularly from the Ottawa River, by lumbermen. From their reports government officials and others interested in colonization began to get detailed maps and to deduce the character of the area. Anyone who travelled through it could hardly fail to see that much of it was rocky and unfit for agriculture, but there was a difference of opinion on the proportions of rocks and fertile land. The earliest surveyors gave a variety of pictures. David Thompson mapped and described the Muskoka Lakes and the Lake of Bays. The comments in his diary are too mixed to leave any single impression, but in a letter of 1840 to the provincial secretary he wrote extravagantly of the territory through which the Muskoka River ran. He found thirty-three waterfalls for mills and sixteen hundred square miles he regarded as good for agriculture. That, he said, at five shillings per acre was worth £256,000 currency, and would provide for 5,120 families with 200 acres for each. Another surveyor, younger but better known in his day, was T. C. Keefer, and he in the late forties and fifties was declaring that the Ottawa–Huron Tract was almost all good for settlement. There were others who gave more realistic descriptions, but under the circumstances it is not surprising that government and public alike concluded that colonization could go ahead.

Given that decision a logical next step was to cut colonization roads, and an ambitious programme was undertaken in the fifties, although only in part carried out. The principal road was to start south of Pembroke on the Ottawa River, go through the southern part of what is now Algonquin Park, and eventually connect with Georgian Bay at the mouth of the Magnetewan River (now Byng Inlet). Angling off this northerly main road was to be another headed for Lake Muskoka and thence by the Muskoka River, Go Home Lake, and the Go Home River to Georgian Bay. Other roads parallel to these and a series running north out of the settled parts of the countries were in the general plan. No one had ever had reason to think that road-building in the south was easy and few kind words were said about the results; but in most parts of the Canadian Shield construction and maintenance were both more difficult. Forests were common to north and south, but in the former the rocky terrain and many rivers offered serious problems. Roads still unimproved have told to later vacationers the story of how contractors went around rocks, lakes, rivers, and marshes. In some cases a road can be seen to have just stopped at the edge of a lake. Forest fires destroyed bridges and corduroy. Labour was hard to procure both for original construction and for upkeep.

The relationship between people and roads seldom if ever worked out according to plan. The general assumption was that if there were roads settlers would move into a new area, and once there would provide labour for improvement and maintenance. Thus, it was supposed, population would increase and facilities for travel develop on a principle of mutual aid. The existence of petitions from groups of settlers complaining that they had been misled and that a promised road had never materialized might suggest no more than that the timing was out of adjustment. The difficulty, however, was more deep-seated. There were small groups of settlers here and there who suffered from a lack of roads but it was the paucity of settlers that discouraged the planners from going ahead, both in cutting new roads and in improving the ones that existed.

To some extent the opening of this more northerly area was intended to give opportunities of taking up land to those in the south who could no longer find there good locations or property that they could afford. As the population increased a younger son or the adventurous pioneer could by this means establish himself through muscle and enterprise. The northward drive, however, was not wholly attributable to an existing pressure of population but also to the expectation of a continuing flow of immigrants. Attempts were made, indeed, to stimulate the flow by advertisements and agents in the British Isles, Germany, and Norway during the late fifties. Different methods of granting land were tried. An Act of 1853 (16 Vict., c. 159) provided that there were to be no free grants except ones of up to one hundred acres on or near public roads in new settlements. The reason for the exception, of course, was to have labour at hand. Another means was the well-tried one of a land company. In 1861 ten townships were sold to an English company, the Canadian Land and Emigration Company, on terms which called for a time-table of settlement. Like its largest predecessor, the Canada Company, the new concern ran into difficulties and secured a delay in meeting its obligations. In 1867 the company wrote that it had "used every effort to make known the advantages of settlement in Canada by advertising in that Province, in the United States, in the German and Norwegian papers, and in England. . . ." It had, it claimed, spent more than £10,000 on roads, for the building of saw and grist mills, and for establishment of steam communication. But there had, the writer went on, been unexpected interruptions in securing immigrants: the disturbances caused by the Civil War and Fenian raids, the Austro-Prussian war, and outbreaks of cholera on immigrant ships.

While the company was struggling to reconcile its heavy expenses and scanty income from sales with the payment of any dividend to its shareholders, the newly constituted legislature of Ontario passed, shortly after confederation, an Act (31 Vict., c. 8) which allowed a free grant to anyone who succeeded in clearing a fixed minimum of the lot tentatively assigned to him and in building a house on it, both to be done within a period of five years. Objections were taken by the company to what was regarded as unfair competition although it admitted that the company was itself making some free grants along the roads in its townships. In doing so it was influenced by the same motive as was the legislature but claimed to have a superior method. "The land," it added, "was given upon the condition that the settlers kept the roads free from underbrush. So that there was considerable difference between their free lands and those of the Government; for by the means of their free lands they kept open the roads upon their estates, which the Government did not undertake to do. And so great was the benefit, that all persons who had any money to buy land preferred to buy the land of the company rather than take the free lands of the Government."

Through the combined efforts of public and private enterprise a limited number of settlers moved into the area. The spate of description and comment, in books, diaries, and letters, which throws so much light on early farming in the lowlands seems to have run its course by the middle of the century. Perhaps the novelty of "life in the bush" had worn off; perhaps the market for books about it had shrunk; certainly there was less general interest in emigration from the British Isles to Ontario. For this adventure in the Shield, therefore, the same wealth of evidence does not exist, although contemporary comments of interest were written by immigrants and visitors. Some of them follow rather closely the line taken by thoughtful authors of the thirties, that industrious people would do well and become independent. Mrs. King, herself an immigrant, repeated this advice drawn from her own experience. "Poor ladies and gentlemen form the worst, or at least the most unsuccessful, class for emigration to Canada." The lower classes, she concluded, got on best, and she drew a picture of them on free land in Muskoka. The new settler, after receiving his lot,

with what assistance he can get from his neighbours, . . . clears a small patch of ground and builds a shanty. . . . When he and his family have taken possession, he underbrushes and chops as much as he possibly can before the winter sets in; but on the first appearance of the cold weather he starts for the lumber-shanties, and engages himself to work there, receiving from twenty to twenty-five dollars a month and his food. Should he be of any particular trade he goes to some larger town, and is tolerably sure of employment.

It is certainly a very hard and anxious life for the wife and children, left to shift for themselves throughout the long dreary winter, too often on a very slender provision of flour and potatoes and little else.

When spring at last comes, the steady hard-working settler returns with quite a little sum of money wherewith to commence his own farming operations.

Joseph Dale, writing in 1874 on what he had found in the area, issued warnings against emigration to it from Britain. He had seen little that was good and much that was bad.

Our immigrant having been settled down on the land for eight or twelve months, will now, perhaps, begin to reflect upon his position, which, I venture to say, is a most painful one.

Where now has gone that little capital which he has so industriously saved and got together in England? Wasted upon a worthless block of rock. He has found out at a ruinous cost that the accounts given in books on settlement in the bush in Canada, which were written some years ago, and spoke in glowing terms of settlements rapidly rising around the industrious settlers, and of lands which by labour and self-denial have developed into an inheritance, do not apply to the Free Grant District of 1874.

Both Mrs. King and Dale could have been right, depending on local circumstances. What was as misleading as some of the accounts by early surveyors was the sort of harmful optimism illustrated by the story told after an excursion to Muskoka by the Canadian Press Association in 1872. About 70 to 75 per cent of the land, they claimed, was good for farming in an area with great agricultural capabilities. A more realistic impression was given, much later, by a long-term resident of Muskoka and a warm believer in it. L. R. Fraser, a lake captain and an energetic worker in all local affairs, concluded in his history of the district published in the nineteen-forties that,

> Muskoka, unlike the counties to the south, could not by any stretch of the imagination be considered an agricultural district, but its natural condition was adaptable to several diverse occupations. Beginning at the Severn River the terrain is rugged and wild, broken in places by high rocky ridges and deep ravines, and from an agricultural point of view, forbidding; this condition prevails throughout the greater part of the District; still there are many sections of fine farming land here and there, the most of which was taken by the early settlers and today is yielding crops comparable to the best in Ontario, but the amount of land contained in those desirable sections, when summed together comprise but a small portion of the District's total area.

This is beginning to make sense but it was written too late to influence those who thought of Muskoka as a farming area. At the time there was something like a complex about the superior virtues of colonists as opposed to lumbermen and it was encouraged by the misleading reports and opinions of surveyors. Keefer, for example, in addition to his errors in description, indicated contempt for "the migratory bands of lumbermen." Some farmer-settlers did come, and a portion of them were successful. The conditions in the free-grant system, however, could not by any means be generally met. Looking a little further ahead the records show, for example, that in 1886, 133 persons were located in the District of Muskoka but that in the same year 99 cancellations of grants were made for non-fulfilment of settlement duties. There was undoubtedly good land throughout the lower Shield and there were successful farms, but many other farms were deserted and some families that stayed on in unfavourable locations sank to a very low standard of living. On the whole the attempt to make a second agricultural area out of this part of Ontario was a failure. The population of Muskoka, which in 1891 was 15,666, rose by some 5,000 in the next ten years but by 1931 had lost a part of that increase. Parry Sound, the district north of it, had a somewhat larger population but went through a similar cycle. Haliburton showed a steady decline, as did the County of Victoria which butted into the Shield.

The weakness of the policy of settlement lay not only in a serious miscalculation of the extent and location of fertile land but also in the failure to reconcile the interests of the settlers with those of the lumbermen. Lumbering had long been one of the most important industries. Directly and indirectly it provided employment for large numbers of people, and it was one of the few exports of a province that had to import many manufactured goods. Particularly because of the methods used in the mid-nineteenth century the lumbermen moved rapidly through an area and were now in the lower Shield, for the south was running out of timber as it was of land for settlers. In many ways this part of the Shield was ideal for the trade. Wood chiefly sought was white and red pine and both grew well in light and shallow soil and on rocky terrain where the roots found their way to nourishment through crevices in the rocks. In some parts there were difficulties in getting the timber out to market. At one extremity was the Ottawa River and at the other the upper great lakes but, for much of the area between, these were beyond reach. There the waterways helped but the rivers and small lakes were not continuous and railways were needed to supplement them.

To the traditional sale of lumber in the British Isles was added, about the middle of the century, an additional demand in the United States where the needs of a rapidly growing population could not be fully met from the depleted forests in the eastern states. To Britain went great quantities of squared timber as well as boards; the American chiefly wanted the latter and logs cut into lengths of twelve to sixteen feet. By the middle eighties "saw logs" were shipped in large numbers but squared timber was still produced in quantity. Some of the lumber firms were Canadian, some American. Lumbermen moving in from the Ottawa River were cutting on the eastern side of the area; there were also locations to the west, on the Severn, Muskoka, and Black rivers, and still others in the territory between. Large numbers of men were employed, some only for winter cutting, others for this and for transportation in the spring.

In a perfectly organized society the settler and the lumberman could have been complementary and non-competitive, and to some extent each did serve the interests of the other. The lumbermen had to be fed as did their horses and this could be done at least expense, particularly if rail communication was not close, by farmers in the vicinity. Many settlers depended on the cash income derived from winter work in the woods, and some of them even gave up their land when the lumbering moved beyond reach. For different reasons both the lumberman and the settler wanted to cut down trees, and, depending on the laws in force at the time, the landowner might be able to sell the timber that stood in the way of growing crops. The Canadian Land and Emigration Company supplemented its income in this way. Unfortunately, however, the move into the Shield was far from perfectly organized. To allow people to settle on inferior land, with thin soil and thick rocks, was not only bad for them but closed to the lumbermen areas which were rich in pine. What was even less defensible was the practice of securing land on the pretext of settlement but in reality to hold for a higher price fixed on its value for timber.

Mutual recrimination developed between the two groups. The settler complained that the heavy loads carried over the sketchy roads by the lumber companies cut them to pieces. The lumbermen charged that the settlers destroyed valuable stands of pine by careless and ruthless burning. Both complaints were correct but both misleading. The lumbermen did damage roads but they also took part in building them. The settler was often reckless about fire but he was not the only sinner. When lumbermen had been through a district cutting pine they left behind a floor of branches, discarded logs, and pieces cut off in squaring that together made up an invitation to fire. Neither reforestation nor protection against fire had yet been given sufficient thought and all through the north country there were appalling losses which came from this neglect. The report of a survey in 1886 of part of a township in the northeastern pan-handle of Renfrew County is typical of many sad stories of fires.

The whole township, with very few exceptions, is a brulé; fires at different times have swept over the whole of this and the adjoining townships to the east and west, leaving only standing dead pines and small, second growth poplar, birch, etc. where formerly a vast quantity of valuable pine timber existed. . . . no settlers have yet located within the limits of the work on which I was engaged.

J. F. Way, Crown Timber Agent since 1854, protested in 1867 against the tendency to paint the lumberman as a villain.

It is currently reported that there is a great antagonism existing between the Lumbermen and Settlers. From my own knowledge of the operation of Lumbermen and the Operations of Settlers in the Lumber district, I know the Lumbermen have been a prey to the Settlers. The Regulations have all been on the side of the Settler. The new Townships have been advertised as open for Sale for Timber limits for which lumbermen have paid heavy bonuses, and immediately after such sales the same Townships have been opened for Settlement under Regulations, which allow the Settler to purchase any lot (covered by the Lumbermens license) which he may choose to select.

Very likely Way was prejudiced in favour of the lumbermen, but he did indicate the contradictions that could arise. He was not concerned to show the other side of the medal but his conclusion was to the point.

Under a judicious policy there could be no antagonism between the Lumberman and Settler: They would be a mutual benefit to each other, and if proper restrictions were placed on the Settler, he would increasingly be compelled to seek such lands as would be suitable for agricultural purpose (if any such are to be found) and leave the timbered lands, which are seldom suitable, in the new Townships, to the operations of Lumbermen.

A counsel of perfection, perhaps, and more easily seen after the event. The whole difficulty—and it was seen by a few people at the time—lay in the attempt to reproduce in this northern strip the kind of social structure that had proved to be suitable in the lowlands. In spite of all the errors there were some possibilities of successful farming, and the lumber business grew and prospered in spite of the handicaps described by Way and others. Towns grew up, too, meeting the needs of both farmers and lumbermen and also of the growing business of lake transport. Bracebridge was an example of the possibilities and the limitations of urban development. With a population of only a thousand in 1879 it became the seat of small factories, of banks, newspapers, a Mechanics' Institute, an Orange Lodge, and an Oddfellows' Lodge. In both the few towns and the rural districts there were schools and churches. Some Methodist circuit riders repeated their missionary work in this new field, although in fact they did as much canoeing as riding. The Roman Catholic Church which, as contemporary writers pointed out, had had missions in that area for two hundred years, established a bishopric for Parry Sound and Muskoka. The lower Shield was now assuming its own distinctive characteristics. As an attempted repetition of an earlier experience it was a failure; but on the other hand it began to show part of the great variety that was Ontario.

During the years when the lumberman and the settler were at work in the territory which has just been described another and larger area—that to the northwest and comprising the Districts of Algoma, Thunder Bay, Rainy River, and Kenora—was being drawn into the active life of Ontario. Whether by land or by a combination of land and water travel it was the approach to the western prairies. Something of it, of course, had long been known from the records of the fur trade. The French traders had used a route by way of Kaministiquia since the seventeenth century, but the English firms took an alternative way *via* the Pigeon River at the western end of Lake Superior until that was blocked by American possession. Then the Nor'Westers heard from the Indians of the forgotten northern way and moved their headquarters in 1803 to the place that they re-named Fort William four years later. This, then, became the main station on the trunk line from the great lakes to the prairie. When the fur trade was re-routed to Hudson Bay, Fort William once more fell back into the bush. Nevertheless the line of lakes and rivers remained, and in 1857 S. J. Dawson was appointed to explore from Lake Superior to the Saskatchewan River. He was, then, opening up the old route for the third time, but now for no narrow commercial purpose. Attached to his report was a map "Showing the route by road and navigation for connecting the Atlantic and Pacific Oceans."

This was a land dotted with Indian tribes and white trappers. Dawson met a number of the Indians at Fort Frances. Five hundred had gathered to see him but most had dispersed because of shortage of provisions. He accepted an invitation to attend a grand council.

After their preliminary ceremonies had been gone through with, the principal chief delivered a long harangue. . . . the point he aimed at was to ascertain what object the Government had in view in causing the country to be explored. I replied that I could not say what course might be ultimately adopted by the Government; that they need not fear, however, but that their interests would be consulted; and that we were merely examining the country, to our doing which we trusted they would offer no opposition. . . .

On the following morning they called on me, and said . . . that they had consulted among themselves, and come to the conclusion to allow us, in the meantime, to explore the country as we pleased; but that they trusted no settlers would be sent in without their being consulted.

Dawson in his report expressed anxiety that a clash between the resident Indians and the incoming white settlers or labourers on roads be avoided, bearing in mind the characteristic concern of Indians for the preservation of their hunting grounds. In the event no serious troubles developed. Both the prospectors and the surveyors had dealings with the Indians and regarded them as superstitious. T. C. Keefer wrote that they would not reveal the locations of mineral deposits since these were held to have a sacred character. The surveyors employed Indians in their travels through the wilds. One group in Algoma in 1910 had the misfortune to lose a young white assistant who died from the heat and drinking impure water. As a result eight of the Indians in the party left it and they were difficult to replace. As parts of the area were taken up with white occupation and industries the usual plan of setting aside a number of Indian reserves was followed.

The role of Thunder Bay as part of a route to the west continued to develop. In 1858 a postal service to Fort Garry by way of Lake Superior was begun, but it had to be dropped two years later. In 1870 Dawson was brought back to make a combined water and land route over which could pass the military expedition to the Red River. In 1872 the Sandford Fleming expedition to the Pacific went over this Dawson Trail and G. M. Grant, who was a member of it, described the trip in his diary, later published as *Ocean to Ocean*. Grant, who was a careful observer, gave more details of the mode of travel and of the character of the country than Dawson had been able to do. It took ten days to reach Fort Garry with a mileage he gave as 530. His impression of the first forty-six miles from Thunder Bay would have delighted the few people who lived there:

Everything about this part of the country, so far, has astonished us. Our former ideas concerning it had been that it was a barren desert; that there was only a horse trail, and not always that, to travel by; that the mosquitoes were as big as grasshoppers, and bit through everything. Whereas it is a fair and fertile land, undulating from the intervales of the rivers up to hills and rocks eight hundred feet high. The road through it is good enough for a king's highway, and the mosquitoes are not more vicious than in the woods and by the streams of the Lower Provinces; yet this fine land is wholly untaken up. Not half a dozen settlers are on the road for the first twenty-six miles; and for the next Twenty, not half that number.

He was going across the semi-circle around Fort William into which some settlers were to move during the next thirty years, but further along the journey to Fort Garry he judged that the only land fit for agriculture in a span of 380 miles was that on Rainy River and perhaps around Lake of the Woods. "North and south the country is a wilderness of lakes, or rather tarns on a large scale filling huge holes scooped out of primitive rock." Grant found the journey not a difficult one, and soon afterwards a "line of route" for passengers and freight to Fort Garry was advertised in the Port Arthur newspaper. The charge per passenger, with 100 pounds of baggage, was $10. Additional baggage would be extra, and for machinery and other heavy freight there were special prices. Passengers were advised to take blankets. Meals could be secured at moderate cost.

The passage through what was still a wilderness was a combination of water and portages and a part of a longer seasonal route to the prairies which itself made all possible use of water transport. From Toronto the Northern Railway connected at Collingwood with steamers which went through Georgian Bay, Lake Huron, the American canal at Sault Ste. Marie, and Lake Superior to Thunder Bay. The strategic position of the little settlements at Fort William and Port Arthur (at that time called Prince Arthur's Landing) convinced the residents that the villages were—together or in competition—to be the Chicago of Canada, a belief that was strengthened by the construction of a section of the Pacific Railway begun as a replacement to the route over which Fleming's party had travelled. The railway, as started by the government and completed by the Canadian Pacific Railway Company, was to be the principal factor that stimulated settlement in the early years and became an essential service to the industries that were arising.

For the natural resources of the Huron–Superior area did not stop with its geographical position. From the middle forties there was an active interest in the mineral wealth that was believed to lie in this northern region. The Bruce Mine on the north shore of Lake Huron was discovered in 1846 and from it copper was produced intermittently. From the late forties into the sixties a flow of statutes incorporating mining companies continued. Some of these companies never progressed beyond the paper stage but others acquired properties and began investigations, sometimes followed by production. North of the Bruce Mine the Havilah Gold Mine was worked at intervals from 1892 to 1912. Meanwhile there had been considerable activity in the Thunder Bay section. In 1863 Peter McKellar and his family moved from southern Ontario to Fort William where they built a two-storey house of hewed logs on a stone foundation. He and his brother, in a series of prospecting trips, found both silver and gold, but for the most part the attempts to exploit the discoveries met with small success. In 1868 the Montreal Mining Company sent a party to explore lands it had already acquired and ran into astonishingly rich silver ore on the tiny island of Skull Rock, measuring about 75 by 45 feet, in Thunder Bay. It was appropriately re-named Silver Islet, but the company was slow to appreciate the value of the property and in 1870 sold it to American interests. As much effort had to go into protection against storms as into mining, but it was worked until 1884 when the fuel for the pumps failed to arrive and the mine was flooded. In that time it had yielded more than three and a half million dollars in silver. There was a brief epilogue in 1922.

Other developments appeared on both sides of Fort William. Some distance to the east stories of gold took prospectors to the Michipicoten River, but what they found there in 1897 was not gold but a rich iron deposit. From that came important mines, and ore was taken by ship to the steel plant just at that time being completed at Sault Ste. Marie. Interest was steady: in 1886 alone forty-three patents were issued for mineral lands in unsurveyed territory north of Lake Superior. Some temporary success followed investigations west of Fort William and up to the American border. There were two main groups here, those in the vicinity of Silver Mountain and those near Rabbit Mountain. The most successful was Beaver Mine, in the second group, but by 1892 most of these mines were closed. Further to the west again were a number of gold mines near the Lake of the Woods, and most of them had a brief period of activity in the nineties. The Mikado Mine, forty miles southwest of Kenora, was worked until 1903 and the Sultana Mine until 1906. On the whole the story of mining in that period was one of disappointment, with the exception of little Silver Islet, but it did bring a lot of people into an almost unpopulated area, help to build the towns, and create employment.

If Fort William and Port Arthur were to emulate Chicago, the people of Kenora were prepared to ally themselves with nearby Keewatin to play the role of Minneapolis. Kenora, the Rat Portage of the fur traders and keeping the old name until the end of the century, had sunk to one house but had a dramatic revival with the appearance of the Pacific railway. During the period of construction great quantities of lumber were needed for a number of purposes and before long several saw mills were at work. Lumbering, indeed, was an important industry in the districts of Kenora and Rainy River. By 1890 mills on Lake of the Woods and on the Canadian side of the Rainy River were producing annually ninety-three million feet of lumber. The fact that Canadian firms were blatantly cutting across the border was offset by the inroads of American firms into Canadian territory. In the nineties there was extensive fishing in the Lake of the Woods with shipments to Chicago, Minneapolis, Buffalo, and Denver. The combination of rail transport and water power led to large flour mills. In 1910 a Kenora newspaper announced jubilantly that the mills in that area had a daily output of twelve thousand barrels. A dozen years earlier the Lake of the Woods Milling Company was said to be the largest in Canada. "All history," wrote Miss Nute in her *Rainy River Country*, "in the borderlands about Rainy Lake is divided into two eras: B.D., or Before the Dam; and A.D., After the Dam." It was the dam at International Falls, built between 1905 and 1910, that, in combination with lumbering, brought rapid development to Fort Frances.

The industries and occupations that have been mentioned induced urban or group living, and a line of towns grew up along the southern part of this area of the Canadian Shield. On the eastern end Sault Ste Marie, although by-passed by the transcontinental railways, retained a strategic position on a waterway that continued to carry much traffic even when it lost its unique role. In 1895 a Canadian canal was opened there, making possible a through Canadian route over the lakes. In early years Sault Ste Marie had a larger population than the towns to the west of it. It was a base for the steel industry, and even in 1887 had hydro-electric power. At the beginning of the seventies Fort William and Port Arthur each had a few hundred residents most of whom were dependent on mining, either directly or by providing accommodation, services, and supplies. When one family went to live in Port Arthur in 1872 they reported that it was nothing more than a group of shacks cut off from the world. This first impression was not surprising but was exactly the opposite to that which the residents wished to convey. "Outsiders," complained the editor of the *Fort William Journal*, in 1887, "are of opinion that we live in a barren wilderness, where nothing but rocks abound. The sooner they are disabused of this belief the better it will be for the district." In the intervening fifteen years two crude villages had grown into established towns, nourished by both mining and the railway. It had been exciting to watch them grow and bring in people and business. The editor of the Port Arthur paper, the *Thunder Bay Sentinel*, who had been doing his utmost to represent a great future for the area, pointed out that, even if it was not endowed with good land, it had other assets:

on examination into the position and resources of this portion of our noble Province of Ontario we are constrained to frankly admit that wanting in a great measure is the fertility of soil which distinguishes the large portion of western Canada, and that with the Great Mineral Wealth which undoubtedly exists throughout a vast extent of this District, it is wise to utilize the works on the Great Pacific Railway now in progress in the vicinity, that will render this eligibly and beautifully situated town—the great distributing centre into the more fertile regions of the boundless far west.

The railway was going ahead, and in 1876 the editor of the *Sentinel* rode over several miles in a locomotive. In the following year the Canadian Pacific Railway advertised passenger service to and from Matiwan, though in terms that were hardly alluring. Passengers must travel at their own risk, "the cars not being in the condition for passenger transit." All this time the railway was calling for tenders and some hundreds of men were employed. The railway was always in the news: progress of construction, what officials came to and left the towns, the annual picnics, the later disputes in Manitoba. When the company chose Fort William as a base (greatly to the chagrin of Port Arthur) and built a grain elevator the position of the town as a point of transfer between rail and water was assured.

The towns had their troubles, as witnessed by long lists in the newspapers of property to be sold for taxes, but indications of progress were also visible. Several hotels were patronized by transients connected with mining and the railway; there were shops of all kinds; lumber firms; builders; banks; lawyers; agents for carriages and machinery. To judge by prominent advertisements the people of these towns had a peculiar weakness for sewing machines. They had recreation too. Diverse tastes were met by billiard parlours and public libraries. The Mechanics' Institute of Port Arthur reported an impressive list of books, on shelves or on order, in the fields of history, travel, science, poetry, and fiction. The Canadian Pacific Railway also opened a library in Fort William for its employees, permitting members of the public to use it as well. In 1876 the Good Templars competed with the Town Team of Port Arthur in a spelling match. The Prince Arthur Minstrels and Variety Troupe gave their first entertainment; and not to be outdone the Mechanics' Institute put on an evening of entertainment consisting of songs, recitations, and a play. There were races on the ice for horses and dogs.

Thunder Bay was some two hundred miles from the Sault by the most direct water route, and west of it was another long gap before the next group of towns was reached. Kenora, on Lake of the Woods, with its smaller neighbours, Norman and Keewatin, had been in Manitoba until the boundary decision of 1884. All were summer resorts and in 1894 it was claimed that in a summer the population of Kenora rose from 3,000 to 5,000. In addition to its commercial ambitions it seems to have been a gay place. In the winter there were skating races, a bonspiel, hockey matches, and a dance under the heading of "the calico apron and tie assembly." In summer there were moonlight excursions on the lakes and a regatta, and the rowing club was active. You could enjoy a public concert on the machine recently improved by "Professor Edison, the wizard electrician" or another by the Rat Portage Minstrels; or you could take lessons in drawing and painting. The Sons of England, the Masonic Lodge, and the Knights Templar were all in Kenora in the nineties. From 1892 life was made easier by electric lighting in the buildings. There was a resident dentist, and a visiting "eye specialist" appeared with $2,000 worth of glasses.

Keewatin had about seven hundred people in 1894, that number being doubled by summer visitors. It had shops of all kinds, three churches, a "magnificent new school," and "numerous fine private residences." Norman, mid-way between Kenora and Keewatin, had about eight hundred people at that time and could boast two hotels. It, too, was a summer resort. Fort Frances gained, as has been mentioned, from the building of the dam, and electric light was turned on at that time.

The people who lived in the little towns perched on the edge of the formidable Canadian Shield were uncomfortably conscious that their hinterland was all too commonly described as a barren wilderness. Was it? It was not being opened up by any grandiose governmental plan to turn it into another agricultural area, but there was land to be granted free to settlers and the surveyors were obviously under instructions to report on how much fertile land they found. In reading the reports prepared over thirty years one is first struck by the constant references to the destruction by forest fires. Township after township was described as brulé in whole or in part, with second-growth and inferior types of trees which constituted little asset before the rise of the pulpwood industry. Especially in early years the reports give the impression that the authors were straining to paint the most optimistic picture possible. A few townships were described as wholly unsuitable for agriculture, but in most of them there were said to be parts which had soil of average quality or even as good as could be found anywhere. A cautious note was sometimes struck: that the possibilities for any farming were only fair, or as a surveyor wrote of two townships in Algoma, "In common with most of the northern district, there are no very extensive sections of unbroken good land, though many excellent lots are to be found." It came gradually to be accepted that, in the central area, only a few townships immediately around Thunder Bay had a considerable amount of fertile soil. West of that was a land of rocks and lakes, leaving only three substantial sections that could be used for farming: one between Rainy Lake and Lake of the Woods, one near Kenora, and a third centring on Dryden, some seventy miles east of the latter.

Few of the surveyors were able to report that they had found settlers, or when they did that there were more than handfuls. Some of those they did see were said to be contented and anxious to have more people follow in their footsteps. Yet settlement was slow. The reports by the Department of Crown Lands for the year 1887 on lands sold or bestowed as free grants showed that only fifty-one persons were in that year located in the District of Algoma and of those forty-one were on St. Joseph Island (south of Sault Ste. Marie). In the District of Thunder Bay the forty-four persons located were all in two townships close to Fort William. In the same year the numbers of cancellations for non-performance of settlement duties were thirty-four for Algoma and thirty-one for Thunder Bay. There are no entries at all for Rainy River or Kenora. By 1900 some two hundred persons were settled in Thunder Bay, with little increase in Algoma, and over two hundred in Rainy River. In 1910 the provincial government cancelled scores of land claims in northern Ontario because of failure to comply with regulations. It was evident that many grants had got into the hands of speculators who were holding them for profit.

The progress of the main towns can be seen in the following table:

	1901	1911
Sault Ste. Marie	7,169	10,984
Port Arthur	3,214	11,230
Fort William	3,663	16,449
Kenora	5,202	6,158

Similarly the population figures for the districts as a whole:

	1891	1911
Algoma	13,534	40,962
Thunder Bay	8,000	39,496
Rainy River	2,210	10,429
Kenora	4,084	15,490

The total population of Ontario in 1911 was 2,523,274 whereas that of the immense territory covered by the four districts was only 106,377. No considerable change in the rate of growth took place in the next twenty years. The total figures for the area include not only the towns listed but also the smaller ones, personnel in mines, probably in lumber camps, and perhaps in trapping. No large number of settlers had moved in or were to do so. There had been loose talk of tens of thousands of immigrants making farms in the area, but in fact its characteristics were such as to make its social structure quite different from that of the Laurentian lowlands.

Lying between the two areas which have hitherto been described was a third, that north of Lake Nipissing, west of the Quebec boundary, east of Lake Superior, and reaching into the Hudson Bay watershed; roughly the

Districts of Nipissing, Timiskaming, and Sudbury, together with parts of Algoma and Cochrane. The story begins *pianissimo* in clay and continues *fortissimo* in metals.

The first solid movement into this region was at the southeast corner by way of the Ottawa River and Lake Timiskaming, and at the top of the latter settlers encountered good soil, for they were into the edge of the Little Clay Belt. In the eighties surveyors wrote enthusiastically of what they found. Describing seven townships at the head of the lake, one wrote that there was not "an equal of this tract of land now left in Ontario for settlement." Another in the same area found thirty-seven families with 1,097 acres under cultivation. The crops of hay and oats, he wrote, were as good as anywhere and the lumbermen were buying both at good prices. From the combined efforts of farmers and lumbermen the District of Nipissing grew at a moderate pace.

It was, however, the Great Clay Belt, to the west and north of the other, that attracted the attention of the government of Ontario as suitable for an organized plan of colonization. Forty years earlier they had burned their fingers in a misguided project of extensive settlement in the lower part of the Shield, but now they had solid evidence of a considerable area of good soil. It was, it was true, inaccessible, but by the beginning of the twentieth century it was no longer necessary to depend on roads as it had been in the previous case—nor, indeed, could they have well been built to such far points—since it was possible to extend the railway communications already reaching a large part of the way. The government therefore undertook the construction of a colonization railway, the Temiskaming and Northern Ontario, from North Bay (through which the Canadian Pacific ran) north into the clay belt. The work began in 1902 and reached Mile 102 (Cobalt) by the autumn of 1903. Some settlers did move in, though not in large numbers; but the factor which suddenly gave life to the area was not agriculture—although that was stimulated by rising local needs—but mining. Silver was discovered by accident, first by two railway contractors and then by a blacksmith who, according to the tradition, threw a hammer at a fox and accidentally broke off a piece of rock under which was revealed a vein of silver.

It had been known that there were mineral deposits here and there in this part of the Shield. Individual discoveries had been made, and during the construction of the Canadian Pacific the nickel at Sudbury became known. Production of both nickel and copper began there in 1887 and by the turn of the century was worth about two million dollars. By 1913 the value of the mines was becoming more apparent but the large figures were still many years ahead. Cobalt can be taken as an early example of the hectic, often rough-and-tumble, development which turned the north country into a booming mining area. Turning over the pages of the Cobalt *Daily Nugget* one can see a mining town growing from nothing, the problems and the successes. Evidently this paper's readers had a limited concern with affairs elsewhere but they did have a chance to follow in some detail the opening of new mines over a considerable area and how they progressed. They were also keenly interested in the stock market located in the town. Several stockbrokers were among the advertisers, also mining engineers, land surveyors, firms prepared to do assays and others which offered equipment for prospectors. There were shops of all kinds, too, both for the ordinary needs of life and for such luxuries as gramophone records, candy, and cut flowers. Physicians and dentists and a private detective firm appeared in the paper. The Empire, Cobalt's "high class theatre," had motion pictures and vaudeville. A good deal of attention was paid to hockey, including careful studies of the various players in the amateur teams. The largest hotel made a point in its advertisements that it was equipped with flush-toilets. Early in 1910 the *Nugget* published a picture of an impressive new fireproof office building. Compare this, it said, with the same street in 1906 when there were stumps all over the road. Cobalt at that time was, the paper said, a "rough, raw, unproven mining camp."

Towns grew out of nothing, but not without problems. Certainly provision for sanitation in Cobalt was "rough and raw" enough. In 1909 there were eleven hundred cases of typhoid fever with over six per cent fatal. A year later brought further cause for concern. "But has Cobalt learned the lesson even with its great cost?" asked the *Nugget*. "It is widely known that the water cart men, even after the scourge, were distributing filthy water around the town, because it was easier to get."

The mining frontier with its camps and improvised towns moved northward faster than the rails of the T. and N.O., so that when gold was discovered at Porcupine Lake a space had to be filled by road transport. Stages took three days from Matheson or one day if rushed. The *Nugget* was distressed about the rugged conditions at railway Mile Post 222, where, it said, "an average of fifty men per day are dropped off" on their way north. "Goods are thrown into the snow in hopeless confusion and often when the trains are late passengers have to get off in the middle of the night to shiver around until daylight before arrangements can be made to continue their journey."

Travelling south was no easier, for passengers "have to wait around in the cold for hours without any idea as to when the trains will be along, as there are no telegraphic communications." Once reached, Porcupine Lake had at first little comfort to offer. The postmaster had to content himself with a tent until a shack could be built. "The water in Porcupine Lake is the colour of tea and with a considerable number of habitations around the sheet of water it is of course liable to contamination." With or without houses life was not simple. The prospectors and promoters around Porcupine had their ups and downs, but after a slow start the value of gold produced in 1913 reached more than four million dollars.

Further north again another little town, Cochrane, suddenly appeared. This is a contemporary description, written in 1910:

The town of Cochrane has beaten anything in the north country. On 1 December 1908 what is now the town of Cochrane was a spruce and white birch grove. The sale of town lots took place on 26 November 1908. To-day the visitor will find here a town of stores, hotels and boarding houses, with two soft drink manufactories, with a public school, all the usual Ontario town churches, a moving picture theatorium and another similar place of amusement. There are no blacksmiths' shops nor carpenter shops (that we saw) nor smaller mechanic workshops, because the land was too dear for them.

Additional hotels were being built. The Bank of Ottawa had just moved into an up-to-date brick building and the Imperial Bank planned to go one better.

Such are examples of the towns that mushroomed in the rocky terrain in response to the discoveries of minerals and the creation of camps. A mining camp itself does not readily fit into either the urban or the rural column. It was often dropped into the wilds far from civilization but it was a close community not at all resembling pioneer life in comparably remote districts. The detailed progress of prospecting, the opening of new mines, and the technological development that accompanied the latter make up a large story in themselves but one that is relevant to this study only in its general effects. This part of Ontario, so long neglected, was in the first stage of becoming a source of great wealth, but the main returns were to come later. At the end of the nineteenth century the mineral wealth of the whole of Ontario was a little under ten million dollars. By 1913 that figure had been multiplied by six; but these are small totals compared to the nearly one thousand million dollars in the nineteen-sixties.

The social pattern as well as the economic character of this section of the Shield was taking form. The agricultural portion of the population was overshadowed and was not always large enough to meet the demands of the miners. Miners and settlers together did not add up to any large population in these districts. By 1911 the Districts of Nipissing, Sudbury, and Timiskaming were each a little under 30,000 and the District of Cochrane about 12,000. Not too much, however, should be read into these facts for neither a dense population nor large cities were necessary to the kind of economy that was developing. The people of the district made an interesting mixture. The advance of settlers by way of the Ottawa River–Lake Timiskaming route was on the borders of Ontario and Quebec and no strict provincial distinction was made, with the result that the part of the clay belt which was in Ontario became the home of many persons of French-Canadian origin. Partly to replace labour involved in disputes the mining companies drew in a diversity of people, men from many countries in Europe, adding other tongues and cultures to the scene. In some cases such ethnic groups, whether of farmers or of miners, formed pockets, but this does not seem to have been a general occurrence.

The development of northern Ontario in the late nineteenth and early twentieth centuries, hesitant in some respects, dramatic in others, was introducing a new character for the province. The plans for mass settlement in any part of the Canadian Shield did not, it is true, ever work out on the scale that had been intended but they had indirect results of great importance. The province was now getting depth and the different areas were developing according to their natural potentials. It was not all neat and tidy, of course: there were farmers on land that should never have been ploughed, lumbermen occupying land that was good arable, miners digging where no substantial body of minerals existed. But the economy was shaking down. The increasing diversity of the market for lumber led companies into new townships patiently explored by surveyors. Here and there in the north country, in the clay belt and north of it, the never-ending race of farmer-pioneers could find reward. The exciting game of mining brought fortunes to a few and employment to many, whether they were directly or indirectly connected with the industry.

With all these stirrings in the north the St. Lawrence lowlands more than kept their place as the centre of population, industry, agriculture, and finance. Mineral deposits in the south, apart perhaps from the oil in the southwest, were of marginal importance; and lumbering was constantly moving northward as the forests dwindled. Far from being competitive the north opened a whole new vista before the industry and finance of the south. The cities, and Toronto particularly, now had an economic hinterland, and it was mining wealth that suddenly opened new markets for southern industry and an opportunity to build up a financial centre which could at last compete with Montreal.

CHAPTER NINE

Towns and Farms

VICTORIANISM WAS MODIFIED in southern Ontario by the conditions of the new world but still had much of the character that that word suggests. The little town and the brick farmhouse alike breathed solidity and stability. Individualism no longer struggled in a pioneer setting but it was assumed that progress depended on brains, muscle, and enterprise. Security was a personal achievement, a reward, it was recognized, of hard work. Prosperity was widespread. For the successful it may well have seemed the best of all possible worlds. That there was poverty was not the fault of the economic order, for did you not have the poor with you always?

Neither the townsman nor the farmer felt isolated. Postal, telegraphic, and later telephone, communications were well organized. If roads were on the whole still bad they were adequate for most local purposes, and the automobile was not yet a factor. By 1913 only 23,700 motor vehicles were registered in the whole of Ontario. (In 1960 the total was over two millions.) The railway was the essential means of transport, whether for passengers or freight. Towns and rural areas were more self-contained than in later years. The town and the village, too, were more closely integrated with neighbouring farms. The average family in any one of the three moved within a narrow ambit geographically, but without any sense of being circumscribed for to a large extent the localities were self-sufficient, in work or in play.

By the early twentieth century some villages had declined or even disappeared but they were exceptions. Most of the villages and small towns were intact with their own characteristics, their own commercial and social life. Up to about 1860 many towns were progressing approximately equally and it was not yet evident where the main concentrations of people and commerce were to be. Then the question was answered by a steady drain to a few cities.

This meant that a great many candidates were eliminated in the competition for the first or second rank. Some towns lost old-established industries that moved to cities. The ports on the St. Lawrence and the great lakes saw traffic diverted to railways and at the same time the loss of their ship-building business. But if they did not grow at the rate that any energetic community would like neither were they in danger of becoming ghost towns or deserted villages. Some quite small places did attract new industries and most had a busy enough economic life.

The general appearance of a town was affected by its surroundings: it might be on a lake or a river, in flat or hilly country. But all towns had much in common. In the middle was a Main Street, so called whatever its official name, and on it were shops, banks, a hotel or two, the post office, and perhaps the town hall and a library. Most main streets were singularly lacking in originality or charm as seen by an observer. Without trees, they were hot in the summer. Unpaved roads were alternately muddy and dusty. Yet, with all its defects, the main street symbolized the worldly growth of a town. It represented Progress. The editor of the local newspaper delved deeply into his stock of adjectives whenever a new building was erected or a new business was started.

Beyond the main street was another world. Here were streets lined with majestic maples, elms, or oaks. Here were substantial houses with sweeping lawns, flower beds, lilacs and other shrubs. Shade and thick walls were protection against the heat of summer, and in the winter stoves and open fires made houses snug. Victorianism had full play indoors; not only in red curtains, antimacassars, and what-nots, but in domestic servants and good home cooking. Somewhere in the garden was a swing or a hammock, and at the far end the stable to which children were taken as a treat and allowed to pat the sleek carriage horses. Only a few people lived in this style, of course: the manager of a local factory, tannery, or brewery; a doctor or a bank manager; a lawyer perhaps, or a family with inherited wealth. That some townspeople could afford luxuries is indicated by advertisements in a Perth newspaper in 1876 inviting citizens to spend the winter in Nassau or Jamaica. Concrete evidence is in the many houses that survive.

A large number of people lived in a simpler way but still in comfort. Their houses and gardens were smaller but they lived closer to nature than those in a city, with vegetables and flowers of their own growing, with some hens often and sometimes a horse. They lacked luxuries that for the most part had not been invented, but they had family, neighbours, and animals close to them. Some of the shopkeepers and hotelkeepers lived over their places of business but others might have pleasant houses. So might the school teachers, the newspaper editor, and the postmaster. The real estate or insurance agent (often the same person) could be in the most prosperous group or below it. The clergy had little money but were often supplied with a rectory or a manse, frequently good architecturally and usually expensive to maintain.

Further down the social scale were the skilled artisans and the men employed in any industries that existed. Other inhabitants were shop assistants, barbers, a policeman or two, barmen, and various kinds of labourers. In some towns were negroes who had travelled to freedom over the underground railway.

Retail trade illustrates at once the separate identity of a town and the services it rendered to farmers for miles around. The shopkeepers were men of character, usually competent in their own business and taking responsibility in municipal government, education, and the churches. There comes to mind a particular town as it was in the first decade of the twentieth century. Its shopkeepers were still running family businesses little affected by the years. The baker was a descendant of a man who had come from Berwick-on-Tweed in the middle eighteen-fifties. The shoe and harness store was in the hands of a family which had come from Somerset to that town in 1835. The druggist's forbears were from Scotland, not much later. The hardware merchant, whose fascinating and wandering shop held stoves, tools, and small agricultural implements, had inherited from an immigrant from England of 1847. The spacious dry goods store was owned by a family that had come to the town in 1853. The grocery dated from later, 1870. The clock-maker and jeweller, peering through his magnifying glass in the one lighted corner of a dim and cluttered shop, went back a mere fifty years. In such a town almost anything could be procured, and the mercantile structure existed not only for the one or two thousand people who lived in the town but also for the farmers for miles around.

Dickens could have taken Mr. Pickwick to any one of these towns: to the hotels, to chat at the post office, to the livery stable where friends could gather on benches outdoors or around the pot-bellied stove in winter. The livery proprietors paused then from driving gaily painted buses or sleighs to the railway station to exchange with those who wandered in cryptic comments on subjects of the day, including politics on which apparently unchangeable opinions were held. Long silences were as significant as words.

The small village was less complicated, boasting, perhaps, a church or two, a blacksmith with his roaring flame, and a general store. The latter is not to be taken lightly. It had everything from a door-hinge to an axe, a copy book to a pair of boots, groceries and meat. Barter was still the rule of the day and the storekeeper had to be expert in assessing what was offered and in the market for it. He examined butter with a tube that went into the middle of the keg, and eggs with a light. Like the town the village was the focus for the country immediately around it. The post office was tucked away in a corner of the general store, but that was not the only source of news. Protracted conversations were held between the storekeeper and an unhurried farmer; and the former, like the modern taxi driver, was a mine of information.

Life did not have to be drab or uninteresting. Most small towns had public libraries, and certainly entertainment and sports. Caledonia (Haldimand County) had no less than three circuses in 1856, and in the same year a full programme for the Queen's birthday: royal salutes at sunrise and noon, field sports in the afternoon, fireworks and a brass band in the evening. Haldimand found it necessary to make a schedule of licenses for different types of entertainment. Circuses were $30; wild animal shows, $20; side shows, $6; exhibits of wax figures, $4; puppet shows, $4; jugglers, $10; mountebanks, $10; common showmen, $10. In 1871 Simcoe was offered a programme of "Reading, Tableaux, Music, etc." The tableau was of Mary Queen of Scots signing her abdication, and the evening ended with a pantomime. Admission was ten cents. Dundas was an old town, remaining small because it had been overshadowed by the upstart Hamilton. Featherstone Osler had gone there as rector and his family's correspondence in 1866 speaks of many social events. Two dances were on the list, one being a "grand Ball." For the Queen's birthday a picnic was planned with fireworks and a bonfire in the evening. Croquet parties were frequent and were followed by high tea, the arrival of more guests, dancing and singing, cakes and wine at eleven, an eightsome reel, Sir Roger de Coverley, and finally God Save the Queen.

Church suppers brought all kinds of people together and demonstrated accomplishments in the culinary arts. Those expert in making pies and cakes could also compete for prizes at the fall fairs, as could the keen gardeners, those skilled in needlepoint, patchwork quilts, rag rugs, and sometimes pictures. For the children there were games and for the men judging of horses and cattle. The fall fair, which was a gay and interesting occasion, was an example of local initiative. People created their own entertainment too: playing and singing at home, improvised dances, card games, and anagrams.

Summer or winter, outdoor sports and games were popular. Horse racing was for any season, being on the ice of a river or lake in the winter. Fishing and hunting were close at hand. Hockey and baseball were steadily gaining ground. Skating was widely adopted in the sixties, even by women, shocking as that was to the old-fashioned. Cricket had its ups and downs. In 1857 Dundas had three teams, for small boys, big boys, and men. The last had a "very slap-up uniform." Fergus started a cricket club a year later but it suffered—as did most cricket clubs—from the dominance of lacrosse, long the favourite game in the summer as curling was in the winter.

When, at the middle of the nineteenth century, studies were being made of the amount of fertile land in the Muskoka-Haliburton area it still seems to have been tacitly assumed that all southern Ontario was suitable for agriculture. Most of it was; but if the optimum use of resources had been faced earlier than it was fewer individuals would have suffered and the province would have been richer. The Ontario Agricultural Commission, appointed in 1880 with sweeping terms of reference, was shocked by the disappearance of the forests:

from the day that the first pioneer settler entered Upper Canada until now, a process destructive to our forest wealth has been rashly, recklessly, wastefully, and it may even be said wantonly, going on. . . .
Small blame it is true, attaches to the pioneer in a wooded country if he does cut and slash at all obstructions somewhat recklessly. . . . But it is surprising to see that, even with the bare facts staring them in the face, our farmers who are practically to-day the owners of the remaining timbered lands of the Province in all the settled districts, are in a condition of profound lethargy or innocent unconsciousness of the dangers they invite or the losses they incur.

Property "of fabulous value" had been destroyed, windbreaks were gone, streams had dried up, and even firewood had become scarce. The commission urged economic use of timber and reforestation. Salutary advice, but it was nearly thirty years before more rounded conclusions were drawn: that farming should not be attempted on land good only for trees and that on such land the forest should be restored. This was the argument of the *Report on the Reforestation of Waste Lands in Southern Ontario*, prepared by E. J. Zavitz of the Agricultural College in Guelph after three years of study and published in 1908 by the Ontario Department of Agriculture.

"We have in Ontario," Zavitz wrote, "two classes of land which should be permanently managed for forest crops. First, there are the small isolated patches of non-agricultural soils to be found throughout otherwise good farm lands. . . . Second, there are the large, contiguous areas of non-agricultural soils which exist in many parts of the Province." He gave a few illustrations of the second category: two areas totalling 10,000 acres in Norfolk County, three sand areas in Simcoe County, a belt several miles in length in Lambton County, and a sandy ridge extending through Northumberland and Durham counties. These and others in different counties were made up of blow sand or rock and should be reforested.

Those who attempted agriculture on land unsuited to it had sometimes been misled by a first crop that was good because it was nourished by the humus left on the forest floor. But, once disturbed, this thin layer became dissipated, the blow sand took over, and the land became agriculturally a desert. Other farmers, particularly in parts of eastern Ontario, found too late that they were blessed with more rock than soil. Farms of these kinds either were deserted or maintained on a sub-marginal level. In either case there was personal tragedy of the kind that is only now being slowly eliminated.

This was the liability side of the ledger, but for the most part southern Ontario was adapted to agriculture and in the second half of the nineteenth century the average farmer lived well. He was in a stage between the pioneering conditions that his father had faced and the mechanized agriculture that his son or grandson were to know. Although admitting that the evidence was incomplete, the commission of 1880 concluded that about 45 per cent of the farmhouses were brick, stone, or first-class frame, whereas 54 per cent of the other farm buildings were first class. It was "prudent" to set this priority; it should in time permit better dwellings. How many seriously sub-standard houses there were is not known, but some substantial farmhouses were built in the sixties and later. C. L. Burton tells in his reminiscences of the house of a relative built at that time. Apart from masons and plasterers the house was the work of the family and neighbours. It was quite large, made of white pine grown on the farm, but the total cash outlay was only $800. Here and there were dotted medium-sized stone houses in almost perfect proportion, and everywhere were the brick houses of all sizes that developed from simple Georgian into quasi-Gothic. Large or small, the farmhouses were in part heated by fireplaces but more effectively by various types of wood-burning stoves strategically placed and with long pipes running through upstairs rooms. A "parlour" containing the most cherished furniture, pictures, and nick-nacks was fairly standard, was reserved for special occasions such as weddings and funerals, and only then heated. One or more large barns would be close to the house so as to be accessible in the winter. Within them was another and interesting world of sounds and smells: a warm, reassuring place, with the working and carriage horses, the cows, and the hens invading their sanctuaries. Around the houses flower gardens were becoming more common, and the war against trees was partly offset by rows of maples planted along the roads and groups of pines and spruce placed to break the northwest wind. Of the rows of towering elms only sad skeletons remain.

Conditions were not altogether fixed during this period, of course, but two characteristics did run through: the average farm was no longer isolated but it was a remarkably self-contained little community. For a generation wheat retained its primacy. Production was stimulated by the demand growing out of the Crimean War and the price went up to $2.40 a bushel in Toronto. The depression of 1857–59 drove the price down to 92 cents, but after that came a recovery and the acreage devoted to wheat increased in 1861 to twice that of ten years earlier. Although dropping from that height it continued a general rise until the eighties, along with a shift from spring to fall wheat. Meanwhile other grains, notably barley and oats, were receiving more attention. As late as 1901 Ontario was growing three-fifths of all Canadian grain. Production of wheat, however, had already been moving, together with many Ontario people, to the western prairies. Fruit was taking a more important place, particularly in Wentworth and Lincoln counties. The Niagara peninsula, indeed, became a blaze of blossom in the spring. Livestock of all kinds continued to increase in numbers and dairy products got more priority. Butter and cheese could be made on the farm and sold in nearby towns but cheese factories began in 1864, in Oxford County, and multiplied rapidly. Butter was increasingly made in commercial creameries. The emphasis on wheat gave way to either mixed farming or dairy farming and for a time particularly the former. For people and animals alike such a farm produced most of the food it required.

Methods of farming were improving, aided by the Ontario Agricultural College which opened at Guelph in 1871. Mechanization was limited but it did have some important results. The making of butter and cheese was, as has been seen, moved in large part from farm to factory. Implements were all the time being developed that cut down on hand work. In 1858 the London *Free Press* drew attention to great progress: "The seed can be grown; the plant hoed; the grain cut; the wheat threshed, cleaned and sacked up; the grass mown; the hay made; the rick built; ditches dug; drain pipes laid and all by effective machinery." Implements were made still at a number of factories throughout Ontario, often under American patent; others were imported complete from the United States and sold by agents. These were some of the machines commonly advertised for sale: grain separator, wheel cultivator, grain drill, mower, reaping and mowing machine, reaper, rake. By the seventies there were steam threshing machines and the characteristic mobile steam engine. In the early twentieth century the reaper-thresher was put on the market. Two unusual machines were warmly recommended. One for digging potatoes was advertised in 1858. It was on two wheels with a beam and handle like a plough. On either side of the drill was a "shave" which cast off superfluous earth. In the centre, under the potatoes, ran a shovel flanged at the back. Following that was a forked cylinder over which passed the contents of the shovel. The number of things you could do with the Davis Rock and Stump Extractor was remarkable, and all for $25. This is the description, in 1876:

This machine possesses a combination of advantages, it being Light, Simple, Cheap, Durable, and Effective. It is used for pressing cider and Hay; it makes a Cheap Derrick; it is just the machine to Lay Wall with; it answers for a screw to raise buildings; it can be used for a Windlass in Digging Wells; can be used for a Capstan to move buildings; can't be beat for raising Sick Cattle or for swinging them when butchering; and is useful about many other things when Cheap Labour-saving Power is needed on a Farm, as it can be used in any position without posts.

For threshing machines steam engines took the place of horses, but the early gasoline tractors were too heavy and impractical. Electricity began to become a factor on the farm only at the end of this period. Oxen had faded from the scene but the horse was still supreme.

So indeed was the human, for manual labour was still the order of the day in spite of improved implements, and the farmer needed to be a Jack of all trades, a characteristic which he has never quite lost. Fields had to be cultivated and sown and the harvest reaped and threshed. All the various domestic animals had to be tended and fed and the cows milked. At times a well had to be dug, a building erected, repaired, or painted. Trees needed to be pruned, fences made, firewood cut, eggs collected, animals slaughtered, harness repaired, products taken to market, implements kept in order, and a dozen other things done. The labour for these multifarious activities was supplied by the farmer with assistance from his family, by the co-operative method of the old-fashioned bee, and by the "hired man." The last was sometimes a stable member of the household who might be supplied with a house on the property and remain content with a modest if relatively comfortable and secure existence. In other cases the hired man came and went, putting down no roots. A number of farmers employed boys from the Barnardo Homes in England and some of these boys remained with one family for several years.

A visiting delegate from the English Labourers' Union in the seventies concluded that there was not in Canada a "large body of men who expect to devote their lives to working for wages, as every healthy and sober man can easily become a landholder." There was, of course, a very marked difference between the situation in England where a class of farm labourers existed and that in Canada where a farmer owned, or sometimes rented, his own land; but it was no longer accurate to speak of the ease of becoming a landholder. The province still had, it is true, crown lands from which free grants could be made, but they were not in southern Ontario and experience had shown that it was not easy to make a living by farming in the north. Moreover, a farmer had to have more than land: he had to have a house, implements, and stock. Then, too, an English farm was much larger and its organization was wholly different. In his delightful *Farmer's Glory*, A. G. Street described his father's farm in England on which twenty-three men were employed all year round, with more for the harvest and hay-making. Something like this type of farm was possible in Ontario but it was very much the exception. The hundred-acre farm was almost standard. It was a family affair, but to be prosperous it needed, and normally secured, both one additional regular worker and the aid of the neighbours for certain purposes.

The farmer of southern Ontario did not necessarily spend all his time at the regular work on his own land or in the mutual aid system with neighbours. One additional task, in which he had no choice, was statute labour on the roads. He could, according to his wishes and tastes, take some part in provincial or local government or in the school system. Beyond the public sector he might participate in the affairs of a church, a fraternal society, or any kind of club or charitable work. Then, of course, he had family interests, gatherings with friends, entertainments in nearby towns or villages, picnics, games, and other forms of recreation. There is no such thing as a typical farmer, or a typical anything else; nor do the surviving records of rural life in the second half of the nineteenth century allow for as nearly a composite picture as do those of the first half. What is almost wholly missing from them is the story of the bad or unlucky farmer; of the family hovering on the verge of bankruptcy and subsistence; of the obscure, semi-literate plodder. There were such—there always are—but normally their biography is never written. What can be examined are some samples of small- and large-scale farming operations, together with any available indications of the various aspects of rural life.

David Nelson lived in the Township of Otonabee, County of Peterborough, the setting for many of the best accounts of pioneer days. His post office was Lang, a village which, as the crow flies, is some thirteen miles from Peterborough. He kept a diary—he called it a day book—from 1864 until 1884. His spelling was approximate and his literary style non-existent, but almost every day he recorded, without comment, each event in an energetic and rounded life. Nelson was married, had children, several relatives, and many friends and acquaintances. He was a serious-minded man with a sense of public responsibility, but one too who enjoyed recreation in many forms. Reading his diary is like seeing a motion picture of rural life. One paragraph of it will be quoted to illustrate the variety of interests and activities there could be in a farmer's life. The numbers in brackets are the dates of the month.

September 1875—(1) Very warm weather (2) thrashing at Wm. Nelsons (4) very windy (6) sowing wheat with the Drill (8) finished sowing the wheat (9) sowed Johnsons wheat (12) very cold weather for this time (14) Archd Nelson was here taking of big stones and Aunt Isabella was here (19) very cool weather (20) Tea meeting at Fifes church (21) started to dig a well (22) Georges wife died tonight at Keene (24) Election between Hogan, O'Sullivan and Sargent (26) went to Hastings with the Fullers (28) Mrs. Robert Esson was here (29) went to Peterboro to the Central Show and it is a wet day. October 1875—(1) James Coons and Maggie came down (3) Jane is very sick (5) cold weather (9) started to dig potatoes (12) a hard frost this morning (13) Catherine Nelson was married to Donald Cameron (14) Agness Stewart was here (15) sold the Butter to Campbell McNeill for 20c per lb. (20) pulling carrots (22) pulling Turnips and its beautiful weather (23) Lydia came down from Harvey (24) Lydia and I went down to Dicksons (29) Alexander Speirs married (30) rained all day. November 1875—(1) bought a cow from Father (3) brought the mill over from William Nelsons (4) the ground is frozen hard (8) Frank Nelson started to work (10) went to Peterboro with Mrs. Lang and Mary (11) started to plough again (15 & 16) Thrashed out (20) killed 4 pigs (28) the new Methodist Church opened at Keene and it snowed about 2 in. (29) a very cold windy day (30) a hard frost this morning. December 1875—(1) Mary Ann Lang and I went to Peterboro (2) went to Johns thrashing (4) a fine day and no sleighing yet (7) finished thrashing in the company (8) killed 3 pigs and it is sleighing now (9) took down some chop (10) taking out some wood (11) Frank Nelson left (12) good sleighing now (13) a stormy day and Agness and Bella went over to Langs (14) thrashing at Thomas Nelsons (15) Mr. and Mrs.

Lang and Mary Ann were over (16) took a grist to the mill (17) a cold day and I went up to Hendersons to hire a girl (18) a cold day (19) a very cold day (20) a nice day (21) thawing fast (22) killed 2 pigs and a heifer for James and the snow is all gone (23) muddy roads again (24) chopping (25) went over to James this afternoon (26) a stormy day (27) nomination of Councilors James Miller elected Reeve Thos. Blezard Dep. Reeve and John Lang Timothy Walsh D. McIntyre and Robt. Girvin nominated for Councilors (28) very slippery roads (29) sawing at James W. Speirs (30) went to Peterboro with Bella and Janet (31) we all went over to Langs.

Constant attention to the weather runs all through the diary. So much depended on it: crops and travel. Nelson evidently watched eagerly for the snow and when there was a thaw reported struggling through a foot or so of mud. He was on the roads a great deal in the course of business or pleasure and obviously was relieved when the sleighing was good. He could travel light in a buggy with his team of colts but it was the hauling of building supplies, of products to the market, wood, furniture and many other things that was so much affected by the state of the roads. There is no suggestion that they were improved in these twenty years; but the building of a railway which ran through Peterborough and near the farm partially solved the problem, and indeed was the only social change of importance that appears in the diary. The Nelson family and their friends began to ride in "the cars" and before long were shipping produce from the local station.

The economy of the Nelson farm fairly reflected the reduced priority of wheat in relation to other field crops which has been mentioned together with the growing emphasis on dairy products. Evidently wheat was still his first cash crop but he also grew barley, oats, rye, corn, and hay. Other field crops were potatoes, peas, carrots, beans, turnips, and "Marigold Wurt-zells." The domestic animals included milking cows, beef cattle, pigs, and sheep, as on every farm. Nelson had a wide variety of things to sell for in addition to grains, vegetables, meats, and eggs he had wool and for a time made butter. All these products were marketed in a variety of ways but mainly by driving them to nearby towns: chiefly to Peterborough, occasionally to Keene (which was close) and even to Cobourg (which was a long way). He was not quick to make full use of the railway; perhaps the cost was greater. The record shows that some new implements were acquired: a threshing mill, a reaper, a fanning mill, two ploughs, two drills, and a sulky rake.

In addition to the production of crops, the care of animals, and the sale of both, there were many other tasks to be done on such a farm. Rails were split for fences and gates made or repaired. Two new wells were dug during the period of twenty years. The sugar maple trees were tapped each spring, old stumps were hauled out, and firewood was cut for the house. A good deal of time was spent in "picking" stones off the fields. Drains were dug. The most time-consuming work outside farming itself was on buildings—houses, barns, and sheds—which were erected, torn down, altered, or repaired. Some of the materials were drawn in waggons from nearby towns or villages and the labour was supplied by co-operative effort among neighbours. The bee, indeed, was still an essential factor in rural life. There were raising bees, ploughing bees, stone bees, stumping bees, and—for the women—quilting bees. Threshing too was done by groups of men at one farm after another. Nelson had hired men to help him, even if they changed at short intervals, but for many purposes it was in his interest and that of his neighbours to join forces for the larger tasks.

Nelson found time for many activities other than farming. He took an active part in local government, attending many meetings for the nomination and election of local officials, and himself acting as assessor for the township, and also as school trustee. This last duty was voluntarily extended to work in improving the schoolhouse. He followed provincial politics and in the federal sphere went considerable distances to hear speeches by J. A. Macdonald, Francis Hincks, and Edward Blake. He was apparently an Orangeman since he participated in "walks" on several occasions and he associated with the Grange at least to the extent of attending their picnics. He went to country sales, to ploughing matches, and to many fairs or shows, at Keene, Norwood, Peterborough, London, and Toronto.

The Nelsons were regular church goers, attending services at Keen or Peterborough, at either Methodist or Presbyterian churches, and adding a number of missionary meetings. They also had an active social life with friends and relations frequently at their house and themselves going to parties at other houses. The summer brought picnics, strawberry festivals, an excursion with a brass band on Rice Lake, and some fishing. Neighbouring towns offered organized entertainments: circuses (including Barnum's), concerts, the Swiss Bell Ringers, and oyster suppers. Nelson even seems to have attended a singing school at Keene. His own house was kept in good order and, to judge by the number of visitors, must have been a busy place. At times there were hired girls to help in the domestic work but none of them stayed long. There were doctors at Keene, Campbellford, and Peterborough and they visited the house when illness occurred. Accidents happened every now and then. Nelson must have been a hardy man as on one day in July "I had my hand taken off with the moving machine," and on the two subsequent days he was cutting wheat and hay. More than a month later he went to Rochester for an artificial hand.

In a recent volume of reminiscences, *Farmer Premier*, E. C. Drury describes his family farm in the generation immediately following the point at which the Nelson diary ends. This was in Simcoe County, near Barrie, and was also a mixed farm. The same grains were grown and the wheat was taken by waggon into Barrie to be sold. Cattle were raised too, as were sheep and hogs, all disposed of to buyers in Barrie. Eggs and butter, made on the farm, were cash products. Like the Nelsons the Drurys had many other jobs to do on the farm, making maple syrup, building fences, and all the hundred and one things that people still did for themselves. They were up-to-date farmers, buying new types of implements as they became available. The children played outdoor games and the whole family went to picnics, to church, to concerts, and to the houses of friends. Drury himself came to take the leading part in provincial political life, but that was in a period beyond the range of this chapter.

Such was the mixed farm in the second half of the nineteenth century and the first years of the twentieth; that is, between the stage of the pioneer and that of specialized and mechanized farming. It called for intelligence and hard work, but at its best it offered a comfortable and interesting life, with food, fuel, and other necessities at hand. It was, in fact, as near to a self-contained establishment as can be found in the history of Ontario. The farmer, it is evident, did not need to be a slave or a recluse. On the first count he was his own master, subject only to the vagaries of nature and the prices of his products. On the second he could, as has been seen, spend a good deal of time with friends and in social organizations. His range extended beyond the farmland to nearby villages and towns. The three made up the rural community, a union reinforced by marriages of which those between school teachers and farmers' sons were particularly happy combinations. The farmer could take his part in political and social affairs. Self-government was for the kind of man that has been pictured a very real thing and he saw it at all levels—local, provincial, and federal. He shared responsibilities for churches and schools. Many farmers of the seventies and eighties supported temperance movements and were themselves total abstainers.

From all this one should not deduce that rural Ontario was an ideal society. Many farmers had no interest in public questions, and some farm families lived queer, frustrated, introspective lives, shut out from the world about them. Drunkards, thieves, and murderers were in the country as in the city. It was an imperfect society, but it did have a core of hard working and responsible people who gave it both solidity and moderate prosperity. They were the inheritors and the further builders of a tradition that, in spite of many changes, is still strong.

In addition to the mixed farm there are a few examples of specialized ones, having something of the nature of model farms. One such was that of George Miller in Pickering Township. Evidently its fame was bruited abroad, for in 1860 one J. Mackelcan went from New York State to see it.

Late in the afternoon of the 13th of June, 1860, I arrived at the residence of a Canadian farmer, whose name is well known as one of the best importers and breeders of improved stock the country can boast of. . . . He has 1,100 acres, 300 of which comprise the home farm under his immediate supervision—the rest being farmed by tenants under his direction.

The visitor seems to have been much impressed. He looked at Leicestershire and Cotswold sheep, about a hundred of each. Some imported rams had won prizes in England and the United States. There were choice Dorking fowls imported from England in the previous year. The cattle were Shorthorn and Galloway. A ten-acre field was being prepared for kohlrabi the seed of which had been imported from Scotland. The fields were so well cultivated that weeds were no problem. Grain crops averaged 45–50 bushels per acre and Swedes 1,200 bushels.

In general the farmer of Ontario was the owner of the land, and the owner was the working farmer. Some attempts by English immigrants to change the pattern into one in which the owner directed the work of others were not successful. Two experiments conducted by George Brown, however, went better. As editor of the mighty *Globe* Brown was in no position to live on a farm but he loved the land and all that went with it. He had bought extensive estates in the north of Kent County, which circumstances turned into something more than an agricultural district. When the Great Western Railway built through the property he contracted with the company to provide wood for the locomotives, and at the point where the trains stopped to replenish their supplies he started to build a community. The axemen alone numbered a hundred, and there were opportunities for saw mills and installations to make use of the hardwood and to make potash out of the ashes. Town lots were laid out and beyond them land could be sold for farms. A sizeable village of Bothwell grew from nothing. Brown found that American firms would buy all the hardwood the mills could produce. He retained a personal farm for his own interest.

Then came the discovery of oil, an event which can overnight change the whole aspect of a rural area. Parts of Lambton and Kent counties suddenly experienced an exciting boom in the late fifties. Land acquired a new and blessed value for many poor farmers as small and then larger companies moved in with derricks and all the impedimenta of the industry. George Brown was in the same quandary, though his holdings were on a larger scale, as many farmers in the counties: would land values continue to rise, and should one hold out for a higher price to come in the future? In 1865 he decided to sell to a Scottish syndicate for a large sum in cash together with a block of shares that gave promise (accurately as it proved) of appreciation in value. The oil industry in that corner of Ontario had its ups and downs but turned out to have a successful future.

Despite his involvement in Toronto Brown was a man who could not keep away from the land, and his second adventure in farming was to raise select cattle on a large scale. In 1866 he began to buy property in the pleasant country near Brantford, before long extending it to eight and then nine hundred acres. He bought superior breeds, built model barns, and at the end of ten years had three hundred head of cattle. At the busiest season thirty-five men were employed. In 1876 he decided to extend the scope of the operation and to make that financially possible he turned the farm over to the ownership of a joint-stock company. He himself was the salesman of shares, finding buyers mainly in Scotland. Many visitors from Britain went to see what had become a famous farm, of a kind, of course, that was unusual in Ontario. Bow Park, as it was called, continued to grow as a model farm.

Some unusual cases have thus been noted, those in which landowners could unexpectedly capitalize on the discovery of oil and two model farms in different parts of the province. These, however, were exceptions, for the typical farm before the War of 1914 was a family affair, mixed farming on an average holding of about a hundred acres. At its best this was a going concern and passed from father to son. The degree of success and of comfortable living varied, of course, but all but those on marginal land or those unable to farm effectively were on a standard far removed from that of fifty years earlier. None of them got rich (unless by selling land to an oil company or to buyers of a spreading city) but on the whole this was a good period for the farmer. On the other hand, as urbanization and industry progressed and the wealth that accompanied them became more conspicuous there was growing dissatisfaction with the farmer's share of the provincial income. This was not new: it was a view that had been expressed—and with vigour—by such earlier social reformers as William Lyon Mackenzie, but it came to be channelled into more organized forms than before. Similar agrarian discontent in the United States gave birth to two societies, the national Grange of the Patrons of Husbandry and the Grand Association of the Patrons of Industry. They successively spread into Canada, the Grange in the seventies and the Patrons in the nineties. The Grange found its main reception in Ontario. It was there organized into several hundred "subordinate" groups and for a time had a very large total membership.

There were two avenues to the improvement of the position of the farmers. The one was non-political and consisted of discussions of common problems together with the establishment of co-operative organizations designed to lower costs and assist sales: co-operative stores, insurance companies, and factories for the manufacture of salt being examples. The other method attempted was to exercise influence on governments and legislatures, by representing, for example, the view that high tariffs raised the prices of the articles the farmers had to buy without promoting the value of what they had to sell. The Grange pursued the path of co-operative shops and manufacture; the Patrons followed this route too but, unlike the Grange, they believed also in direct intervention in politics. Only in this way, as they saw it, could they protect their interests. The results were not great. On federal politics they made little impression. In the Ontario election of 1894 they did return seventeen members, but these men were not effective in the legislature and the political arm shrivelled away to nothing. By the end of the century the farmers' movement in Ontario had dropped to a low point.

In 1902 Goldwin Smith's paper, the *Weekly Sun*, asked its readers to express opinions on what type of agrarian association would be most appropriate for the province. The resulting replies, combined with discussion, led to the formation of the non-political Farmers' Association of Ontario, which for a time was the pole attracting farmers who were concerned with reforms. They asked for changes in taxation, control by government of the rates charged by electric power companies, conservation of forest resources, royalties on minerals, the stopping of bonuses to railways, and legislature by initiative and referendum. The Grange allied itself to the new organization.

Even so the Association had very limited success and in 1914 was replaced by the United Farmers of Ontario. It was this body which, in alliance with labour, was to form the government of the province shortly after the war. Then came the opportunity for putting into effect the programme of the farmers.

CHAPTER TEN

Urban Life

IN THE LAST QUARTER of the nineteenth century the growth of cities and towns
began to accelerate on the strength of rising industrialism. In the St. Lawrence
lowlands the locations had long since been established but growth had not up
to this point been striking. At the outset of the seventies most of the towns
had fewer than five thousand people. Seven had between five and ten thousand: Brantford, Guelph, St. Catharines, Chatham, Belleville, Brockville,
and Port Hope. Kingston was somewhat larger. A long way ahead of these
were London, Ottawa, and Hamilton, which ranged from eighteen to twenty-
six thousand. After a still longer gap came Toronto which, with nearly sixty
thousand people, was in a class by itself. At the end of forty years there were
shifts within the group of smaller centres. By 1911 Brantford had shot ahead
of Kingston and Peterborough had nearly caught up to the latter. Port Hope
had an absolute loss. Stratford trebled its numbers. Belleville made a modest
advance but was overtaken by Chatham. At the next level up London slowed
down greatly but Ottawa and Hamilton, having risen into the eighties, kept
their relative positions.

Toronto increased its over-all lead with a population of 376,583 in 1911.
Some explanations of its continued primacy are quickly identifiable: it had
a good harbour, railways from east, west, and north converged on it. For the
rest one can resort to a cliché that success breeds success, or to the metaphors
of snowballs and magnets. Finance, industry, marketing, and business of all
kinds, once having a base, attracted each other. There were still industries
scattered all over Ontario, but the continued growth of many towns was reduced by the drain to Toronto. Hamilton alone remained in the competition,
a fact which foreshadowed the dense complex that was later to be built up
from west of Hamilton to east of Toronto. Meanwhile, however, they were
separated by many miles of peaceful countryside. The age of metropolitanism
was hardly even envisaged.

The difference between the large cities and the small ones was still more of degree than of kind. Like the villages and little towns the small cities and larger towns were largely self-contained communities although that condition was slowly being eroded. They had their own commercial and social life; and if the amenities of the day were often introduced somewhat earlier in Toronto they came before long to share the benefits. The devotees of town planning were all too few. The Canada Company had done some (and there is the improbable tradition that the plans for Goderich and Guelph were reversed by accident) but more commonly the cities and towns grew like Topsy. They were usually laid out on a square grid which might be modified by the presence of a river or lake. Sometimes pleasant open squares might be flanked by a town hall or market. Wide streets were hardly needed and few towns had them; they had enough difficulty in keeping narrow ones in a state of repair. By the middle fifties the main streets in Toronto were paved and so were those in some other centres; but no one had to search far to find plenty of mud. Some towns had parks of which they were justly proud, but these were usually too small, and on the whole the cities were badly off for open spaces to allow for fresh air, clumps of trees, and games. Perhaps the people of Ontario were too accustomed to great stretches of open country to think of a need to rescue parts of it while that was still possible. Examples of foresight in city planning are few. Shores of rivers and lakes were spoiled by factories or railway lines, streets were not widened when that could be done at low cost, beautiful old houses were wantonly torn down in the name of progress. Later on it was not easy to make up for past sins.

The city or town of the later nineteenth century was becoming more comfortable. Some of the earlier crudities—the wandering pig and the garbage that he sought, the reckless horseman, and the uncontrolled fire—were fading, unlamented, into history. Police forces were developed out of the original constabulary; professional fire brigades were taking the place of the volunteer companies; water-supply and sanitation were being taken seriously. Changes were not, of course, instantaneous or universal. As late as the eighties Brantford was relying on fire companies, apparently made up of men with other occupations. Fire-fighting, in common with other needs, was dependent on an adequate supply of water. In 1857 both Hamilton and Toronto were authorized by provincial statute to erect waterworks within twenty miles, to employ people to find pure and wholesome water, to erect hydrants, and to regulate the price of water. They did, to their credit, find water, but it was far from pure and wholesome. More than fifty years later a private company was still selling drinking water by the bottle in Toronto.

The common practice for some time was to place the responsibility for public utilities in the hands of private companies, some of which were later bought out and municipally administered. Thus in Toronto a private corporation was set up in 1841 to provide water and gas. In 1870 Brantford arranged for a company to supply water, Stratford doing the same in 1883 and Belleville in 1886. For the first, public ownership followed in 1874 and for the last in 1899. To progress from wells to pipes and from open gutters to sewers did not automatically solve all the problems. In 1892 the Board of Health of Napanee wrote to the provincial board for advice and help in dealing with "the unsanitary condition of our town as well as the unsatisfactory condition of the water supply which is generally impure and dangerous." The first large slow sand filter was installed in Toronto in 1912.

Streets were lit by gas in some places as early as the forties but more commonly in the fifties. Before then some use had been made of coal oil street lamps. In the eighties municipalities began to turn to electricity as an alternative. Some experiments with dynamos operated by wood or coal did not go well, but by 1887 hydro-electric power was being distributed in Ottawa, Cornwall, Peterborough, and Pembroke. Larger concerns then turned their attention to this source of power, a move which was accompanied by more advanced techniques in transmission over longer distances. Early in the twentieth century the battle began between the supporters of private and of public enterprise. The concern of the municipalities was to secure cheaper power and many of them believed that the rates charged by private companies were too high. A number of them were prepared to co-operate in creating a common supply, financed by themselves, but meanwhile the province was entering the field. In 1903 the Liberal government initiated an investigation into the possibility of public utilities, but action began only when the succeeding Conservative government introduced a bill to create the Hydro-Electric Power Commission of Ontario. Adam Beck, who was its chairman and virtually its author, campaigned vigorously for public ownership and cheap power. With both he was successful. In 1911, while the "Hydro" was still in early days of growth, it was able to supply power to London at four and a half cents per kilowatt hour instead of the previous nine. By 1914 the Hydro was supplying sixty-nine municipalities. Long before then electricity was needed for purposes other than lighting, a principal one being street railways. Windsor began with a line of 1·2 miles in

1886, St. Catharines followed in 1887, Ottawa in 1891, and Toronto in 1892. Another consumer, just coming on the stage, was the telephone. In 1878 a private individual established in Hamilton the first telephone exchange in Ontario, and by the end of the year there were four lines on it.

The external aspects of a town or city were partly old, partly new. Although the roads were indifferent the distances were not great and motor vehicles were rare. Some people had their own carriages, and bicycles were everywhere. Public transportation was provided on street cars, first pulled by horses and then driven by electricity. There had long been cabs for hire. The streets were lit. If pure water was seldom laid on, the public was not yet obsessed with the rules of hygiene. Next to the horse trough was a tap with a metal cup from which people drank. Children waylaid the passing waggon and stole pieces of natural ice which they sucked. Milk was not pasteurized and loaves of bread were carried in the same hands as held the reins. One advantage of the small size even of cities was that no one was far removed from the country, so that there was room for walks and picnics in the summer and snow-shoeing in the winter.

Although probably no country can show a consistent style of architecture, many have, or have at one time had, distinctive forms. Ontario was not in this category. Architecture was an immigrant, and like its human companions, subject to modification in a new environment. The generally Georgian style introduced by the more prosperous Loyalists became less common but continued to be followed so that there are few towns in Ontario which do not have surviving examples. At times Georgian took some strange forms, including an illicit association with a vaguely Gothic influence. Other types of architecture came in: neo-classical, regency, Gothic revival, Norman, and even baronial castles. The complicated imagination of the late Victorians was heavily imprinted on many a public building. At the turn of the century appeared rows of semi-detached houses following no identifiable style, lacking in grace but spacious and comfortable. All had front verandahs, most of them with rocking chairs from which the movements of the human race could be observed. Inside they had ugly but expensive light oak and over-complicated fireplaces. One marked asset of most town building of this period is that what it lacked in charm (and some of it was good) it made up in solidity. Wood was of good quality and seasoned; artisans were skilled; specifications were generous. Nearly every family lived in a house but apartments were just beginning to appear.

Methods of building changed in this period. "Balloon [light] frame" took the place of timber frame construction particularly for houses. Instead of a structure based on heavy timbers having mortise and tenon joints the new method made use of light sawn lumber, generally of 2×4 or 2×6 inches, held together by nails. By this method both time and labour were saved. Nails, which thus acquired a new importance, were made more cheaply; first came machines that cut them from iron plates and later wire nails were introduced. The manufacture of bricks also became mechanized in stages from the middle of the nineteenth century. One of the most ambitious projects in design and construction was that of the buildings to house the provincial government and parliament when they moved to Ottawa before confederation. Planned by a firm of architects in Toronto, they were made of sandstone from Nepean Township on a timber framework. One novelty introduced late in the planning was to have iron and concrete floors as protection against fire and another was a form of hot air central heating.

Technological advances were showing inside houses and other buildings but no more consistently than in other countries. Elevators operated by steam were developed in the fifties and hydraulic elevators in the seventies. Gas installed for street lighting could be piped into houses as could electricity later; however in neither case was early action taken except by a few people. Central heating was being fairly generally adopted by the seventies. In 1873 a shop in Chatham advertised that it would look after hot air furnaces. The victories of piped water over pumps and of indoor over outdoor plumbing have never been charted for Ontario but the turning-point seems to have come in the seventies and eighties. It is understandable that families with small incomes could afford neither, but it is hard to see why others with large houses and adequate means were prepared long to delay the installation of facilities which one would expect to be prized. Ontario was not peculiar in this respect. An Englishman invented a semi-mechanical earth closet in 1860 and decades later the device was being installed in country houses; and even in the United States baths are said to have been far from universal as late as the mid-twentieth century. Yet the time-lag was not caused by lack of human inventiveness. A workable, if somewhat uncertain, water closet, the Bramah, was made from 1778. In 1827 a hotel in Boston had water closets and baths, albeit in the basement. Much more efficient water closets were developed in England in 1870 but not generally adopted. Sigmund Samuel recalled that the house in which he was born in Toronto in 1867 had indoor plumbing with water supplied by the city waterworks, but that the house which his parents moved into a few years later—apparently a larger one—was without a water closet.

Improvements in lighting, heating, and plumbing were available and where they were introduced added to the comfort of life and reduced the burden of domestic work. In general, however, the period was not marked by the appearance of labour-saving devices, nor were they as essential at a time when domestic workers were numerous and inexpensive. There were a few household aids. Sewing machines were evidently widely used. In 1860 the Singer was advertised at $75 and up. A Sarnia newspaper of 1858 carried an advertisement of an "Anti-friction washing machine," which was said to save labour, soap, and damage to materials. "The clothes," it was explained, "are placed in a Frame, made for their reception, and submitted to the action of 200 FLOATING BALLS, which action in a few minutes will make the dirtiest clothes perfectly clean." Even at the price of $8, however, there is no evidence of general enthusiasm for this remarkable (if somewhat incomprehensible) contraption.

In most houses the furniture continued to be a mixture of imported and locally made pieces, the two being often indistinguishable since the makers scattered throughout Ontario made excellent copies of English furniture. The stages of Victorian fashion were dutifully followed in the average middle-class households, not forgetting elaborate what-nots, antimacassars, immense bibles, group photographs in complicated frames, thick wooden curtain rods, and layers of curtains of both lace and red velvet.

Most of the remarks in the last paragraph apply to the more prosperous sections of the community. Urban society, in both the wider and the narrower senses, was getting more complicated and perhaps can best be understood by examining first the occupations that together made up economic life and after that how people related to each other in their leisure hours. The clergy of all denominations were largely out of the missionary stage and settled in parishes of manageable size. Doctors, judges, and lawyers continued to occupy important places. Dentists and engineers were more numerous. School-teaching was the one profession that admitted women. In a few places the staffs of universities lived. Then there was the wide and varied field of business.

A picture of a middle-sized town gives an indication of its economy. In 1867 the estimated population of Peterborough was 4,500. Advertisements show that it had these shops: eight dry goods, two hardware, seven groceries, two watchmakers, two furniture, one harness and luggage, one leather, two boot and shoe, one chemist, one tinsmith, two photographers, one tailor, two book and stationery. The industries were: three carriage factories, one foundry, one manufacturer of agricultural implements. Other advertisements were for two dentists, two banks, a newspaper, a barrister, two insurance agents, and two restaurants. In addition one can assume doctors, school teachers, and clergymen.

One can also look at the scene from the point of view of occupations rather than of particular places. The shops provide a start. They were developing in two directions. On the one hand more were specializing in limited ranges of goods; and on the other were the department stores, the town shops of the early nineteenth century or the later village general store writ large. Barter lingered on even in the urban areas but was gradually disappearing. Credit did not lose its place in spite of the familiar advantages of cash dealings. The formula for cash sales and fixed prices, which has been mentioned as in effect earlier, continued. In 1860, for example, "The People's Cheap Cash Store" in Whitby announced that "Goods at this establishment marked in plain figures, at the lowest CASH price, from which no deviation will be made." The city shops could extend their circle of customers by two means. One was a part of the old practice by which a farmer visited the nearest village; residents of a village visited a town; people of a town a city. In this later period railways facilitated such expeditions. The ladies of a family in Newcastle, for example, were accustomed to go to Toronto for a day's shopping. Setting out by the morning train they arrived close to the shops of the day, had lunch at a nearby restaurant, more shopping, and so back by the evening train. The other means of extending business, by mail order, was not entirely new. It has already been said that shops, including some American ones, advertised in the newspapers of a number of other towns. In the eighties, however, the mail-order sales were promoted in a more orderly and vigorous way by the larger department stores, using both advertisements in newspapers and glossy catalogues. Local shops in smaller places did lose business, or potential business, because of these spider webs but not to a degree that prevented their being healthily active.

The last quarter of the nineteenth century has been described as the golden age of wholesalers in Ontario, this being so because then and well into the twentieth century they were operating in a space between sets of limiting forces. Before that time the function of wholesaling was carried out by the "forwarding" firms of Montreal which imported the goods for shops and exported local farm and forest products. The retail merchants supplemented this channel by direct purchase in England or the United States. The rise of wholesale firms in Ontario signified two changes. One was the availability of more consumer goods from local production and the other was a growing independence of Montreal. Good businesses were built up. Some firms were concerned only with importing—such things as tea, silks, china; others, dealing perhaps in hardware or groceries, bought both at home and abroad. The subsequent decline of the wholesale business, which became serious only in a period later than that covered by this chapter, was caused by the union of wholesale and retail activities, whether by the larger stores or by the new chain stores. In the process the wholesalers were squeezed out, but in the years now under consideration they were having their heyday, influential in several forms of business and in community life.

Montreal still retained, however, much of its place as the financial and commercial capital of Canada. It had an ocean port. The large railway companies had their head offices there and these companies gradually absorbed the private companies that had existed in Ontario. The network of banks, financial institutions, shipping companies, and industries was impressive. This centre of wealth and power, physically reflected in handsome stone buildings, had no counterpart in Ontario. Toronto, the only potential rival, was regarded by Montrealers with anything from contempt to condescension. It was sprawling, crude, an over-grown village, lacking in any sophistication or metropolitan atmosphere. Such criticisms, not well received, were not wholly without validity, but this western outpost was feeling its way toward the stature of a real city, to be the focal point of urbanism in the province. A banking structure was needed and was emerging, but not without difficulties. The banks got themselves heavily involved in real estate and depreciated railway securities in the fifties, to be badly caught when a depression occurred toward the end of the decade. The Bank of Upper Canada collapsed in 1866 as did the Commercial Bank in the following year. "We have been having the worst of times here lately," wrote William Davies in 1859. "The sheriff has been in almost every other house. The Good Times, as they were called, and they were undoubtedly to those who took care, led persons to buy property at ruinous prices on which they paid say 1/10 and the interest killed them. It is now sold every day at low prices and persons lose all they have paid." Banks and public had alike suffered in years of hardship, but both recovered remarkably, and out of it all strong banks came. The Bank of Toronto was founded in 1855, the Ontario Bank in 1857, the Canadian Bank of Commerce in 1867, and the Merchants Bank in 1868.

Stability of banks was attained only after trial and error. One important step in that direction was taken when it was decided to avoid the current American system of many local banks and to have instead the English (and at one time American) plan for large national banks with numerous branches. With the growth of manufacturing and other industries the role of the banks increased. More individuals, too, availed themselves of the facilities of banks for their private affairs.

Other financial institutions also continued to develop. Insurance companies multiplied and in particular the mutual companies were popular. In 1873 one located in Hamilton, the Victoria Mutual Fire Insurance Company of Canada, advertised its principles.

INSURANCE AT ACTUAL COST

A SMALL payment with application covers expense of management.

ASSESSMENTS for loss are payable annually from date of Policies.

As there are no STOCKHOLDERS there can be no PROFITS, each member being called upon to pay the EXACT PROPORTION of losses during the term of insurance.

THE BALANCE of each premium note, or undertaking, is cancelled when the policy for which it is given has expired.

LOSSES BY LIGHTNING are paid by the Company, including Houses and Live Stock, when killed in the fields of owner. Owners of Farm Buildings and contents are paid the full amount of loss on CONTENTS up to the sum insured.

The RATES are as low as possible consistent with PERFECT SECURITY.

HAZARDOUS risks such as Mills, Workshops, Taverns, and Stores, are not accepted in the General Branch.

Life insurance companies, both Canadian and non-Canadian, continued to increase their business, as did the building and loan companies. The change in the latter was from terminating companies, that is, ones which were wound up when the subscriptions were fully paid, to permanent ones as sometimes indicated in the name, for example the Canada Permanent Building and Savings Society. Throughout the province there were branches of banks, insurance companies or their representatives, and a host of societies which would lend money or accept savings. In 1884, for example, Chatham had the Chatham Loan and Savings Company which had money to lend on mortgages and would accept savings deposits, and Richardson's Banking House, Land and Insurance Agency which offered a variety of financial services.

Currency was at last becoming orderly. In 1853 transactions in decimal currency became legal and in 1858 provision was made for government accounts to be kept in it. Shortly after confederation Canadian coinage had general circulation. Strange foreign coins persisted for a time but probably in small volume.

Ontario was in no position to provide all the capital needed for enterprises within its boundaries, nor was Canada as a whole. England was the principal source of capital for development, notably in railways, and American capital (sometimes accompanied by management) came in to finance, for example, mining in the north country. On the home front a uniform currency assisted development and the banks became servants or masters of manufacturing, which itself was the main foundation on which development of urban centres in southern Ontario depended. In 1881 just over 20 per cent of the population was employed in manufacturing. At one extreme the little village industries were disappearing and at the other the larger cities were attracting factories. In between were many towns which were more than holding their own industrially. The County of Perth is an example. St. Mary's had a foundry, flax mills, made agricultural implements, had two planing mills and two establishments for cutting marble. In Listowel were manufactured pianos, furniture, and again agricultural implements. It had also a tannery, a wool mill, flour mills, and a brewery. Stratford had workshops of the Grand Trunk Railway and factories for furniture, threshing machines, and mill machinery. It made fences, cordage, clothing, bicycles, and had a bridge and iron works. Towns put a good deal of emphasis on the need for industry. In 1860 "Observer," a mechanic, wrote to the Whitby *Chronicle* arguing that the town could never achieve an important place without manufacturing. His suggestion was that he and other mechanics start a joint stock company. Another anonymous writer supported Observer. Look, he said, at cities in the United States no larger than Whitby but having manufacturing. Once we got started foreign capitalists would come forward. There was so much interest in this initiative that a meeting was held in the town hall with the mayor in the chair. Resolutions in favour of manufacturing were passed and a committee appointed to study how to get action. Then another meeting was called; but as the story then faded from the columns of the paper it seems that it was easier to pass resolutions than to build factories.

There have been many indications that agricultural implements were manufactured in large numbers and in a great number of places. On the other hand changes in this industry also illustrate the trend toward concentration. The Massey firm began in a village in Durham County, moved to Newcastle, and thence to Toronto in 1879. The Harris firm was at Beamsville, the

Wisner firm at Brantford, and the Patterson one at Richmond Hill. In a series of steps all four were amalgamated by the end of 1891 under the name of Massey-Harris and the whole was located in Toronto. Hamilton, too, was becoming a centre for large-scale industry. A process of mergers produced the Steel Company of Canada in 1910. The Hamilton Cotton Company employed nearly three thousand hands. In 1897 a Canadian branch of the American Westinghouse Company opened there. By 1910 Ontario had 8,001 manufacturing establishments employing five hands or more, with a total personnel of 238,817 and a bill for salaries and wages of $117,645,784.

As physical conditions and the economic structure altered so did the lives of the people. All town dwellers were in some way affected by the changes that were in progress, but some much more than others. The professional men could, like anyone else with the means, take advantage of the growing amenities, and there were more business opportunities for engineers, but otherwise their lives were not much affected. There were other persons, too, such as the small shopkeeper, teacher, and clergyman, who had no great difficulty in adjusting themselves to the new order. The conspicuous social results of the developing economy were the new rich (if that term can be used in a non-derogatory sense) and the industrial wage earners. The former were connected with trade, finance, and industry; and the latter in the main with manufacturing or comparable activities. It was because of the lack of adjustment in the employer-employee relationship to the conditions of an industrial society that the trade union movement received a new impetus.

There were in an urban community of those days large groups with low incomes and often working long hours who were not affected by unionism. Of a whole range of white-collar workers, including clerks in shops, banks, and business houses, many may have believed that their remuneration was inadequate and their hours long; but they gave little if any thought to collective action to secure improvement. Some of them may have anticipated promotion, others welcomed steady employment, and none knew any precedent for clerical unions. Domestic servants worked for long days and at low wages, but they were more in the tradition of the personal relationship, which, as ever, might be good or bad. The class of unskilled workers (excepting those in factories who were in fact unskilled) was, as at other times and in other places, almost untouched by the union movement. A substantial number of workers, skilled or semi-skilled, were either self-employed or associated in small firms or partnerships. Many of them were in a position to set their own hours of work even if they could not change prevailing rates of pay. It was to this group that the middle-class householder turned for the manifold tasks in and around his house. Before the days of the do-it-yourself philosophy an area always had a man to do any job: tend the furnace, shovel the snow, repair or paint the verandah steps, rescue the falling back fence, clear out the eaves troughs, paint a room or two, and so on. These were small-scale operations of some appeal to an energetic and independent man and again had the personal character which had once existed in the small factory or workshop.

The starting-point for a trade union movement was not simply the number of employees, the rise of egalitarianism, or the spread of socialism. The concept of a union did not spring out of Ontario soil in logical response to a stage of industrialization but was imported from Britain and the United States to meet what was a new situation in the province. England, from which so many working men had come, had some half-century earlier been the scene of the testing of *laissez-faire* economics in an industrialization so rapid and sweeping that it has always been styled a revolution; but the fact that by the late nineteenth century when a similar—if smaller—problem became urgent in Canada the union idea was largely accepted in England did not prevent a second round in Ontario. Many employers, probably most of them, resented the intrusion of unions, holding that they for their part should be free to hire workers and that the workers were equally free to accept or reject employment, the terms being automatically governed by the law of supply and demand. It by no means followed that an employer disregarded the well-being of his employees: merely that he could if he wished to, or at least he could be guided by his own views on how they should be treated. What was evident was that, unless there was a serious shortage of labour, the individual by himself had in practice very little bargaining power.

The story of the condition of England question, of the early effects of industrialization, is marked by the personalities of such crusaders as Shaftesbury, Owen, and Place and by the biting criticism in the novels of Dickens and Disraeli. For Ontario—and for Canada as a whole—there was no public outcry and no individual voice or pen to depict in striking colours the miseries of those men, women, and children who were caught up in the grinding wheels of the factory system. It is true, of course, that the stage in Ontario was small in comparison to that in northern England, but for the individuals concerned the effect could be much the same. The description of the condition of Canada question is best found in the reports of two federal bodies of investigation, the "Commission appointed to enquire into the working of Mills and Factories in the Dominion, and the labour therein," which reported in 1882, and the Royal Commission on the Relations of Labour and Capital in Canada, which reported in 1889. Of the two the first is clearer and more informative, the second being repetitive and marred by emotion. Many of the same points are covered by both and the picture that emerges is on the whole a sombre one.

In the report of 1882 some conclusions come out distinctly. One is that there were factories that were well conducted and others that were not. The report is largely concerned with the second group. The commissioners found that in some cases they had difficulty in getting into touch with management and were even refused admittance on the ground that the government should not interfere in matters of trade. On specific questions they noted that of the 43,511 employees of factories visited from Ontario to Prince Edward Island 173 were children under ten years of age and another 2,086 between ten and fourteen. They had been shocked to find that some of the children interviewed did not know their own ages. They were completely uneducated, and indeed it was evident that no children employed in factories obtained any education. They found, however, that the prevalence of child labour was owing as much to the "cupidity" of the parents as to the wishes of employers:

It must not be understood . . . that employers of such [child] labour are more anxious to obtain it than some parents are to force it upon them; the testimony of not a few proprietors and managers at present employing this class of labour leads us to believe that they are quite willing to discontinue its use for the benefit of the children, provided that education be compulsory; as a demand is gaining for intelligent and educated labour in our mills and factories.

The number of adult female employees was high, being 13,059 or 30 per cent of the total. A portion of them were working under very bad conditions.

Female labour is very extensively employed not only in mills and factories but also in private houses and what may be described as workshops, which are very difficult to find, sometimes being in the attic of a four-storey building, at others in a low, damp basement where artificial light has to be used during the entire day, wholesale clothing establishments employing from one hundred to one thousand hands in this way.

Fourteen years earlier, in 1868, the Toronto *Globe* had published the results of a study of female employment in the largest city of Ontario. Of a total population of 50,000, it wrote, about 27,000 were female and of these 5,000 were self-supporting. The largest categories of workers were 1,400 in domestic service and 2,150 in various branches of the making of clothing and hats. Those working at home were often assisted by the rest of the family, including the male members if they had no other occupation, and relatively substantial sums could be made. But the *Globe,* in spite of *laissez-faire* principles, was not oblivious to the weaknesses of the régime.

There is another class of female labourers, whose earthly prospects, though as industriously aided by their own efforts, are not so bright; these are the widows and orphans left by an inscrutable providence to eke out a livelihood at the will of employers, who, even here, with presumably plenty to do for all, do not scruple to extract the last farthing's worth of bodily energy from the dependents of their will.

These women who did piece work at home, with the aid of daughters, might be working from sixteen to eighteen hours a day. In the millinery trade apprentices were required to work for six months without pay but after that had opportunities for good wages. "The majority of those employed are daughters of the better class of tradesmen who prefer to see their girls work until marriage takes them from their control, to having them idle at home." Such girls, who were not dependent on wages, could work at busy seasons. Except for the one barb which has been noted, the *Globe* played down the misery that undoubtedly existed but did allow itself one more critical thought:

How many among the fashionable crowd that "do" King Street on Saturday afternoons, wearing the results of these women's productive energies on their persons, would go to work with equal persistency to keep the wolf from the door if the occasion required, is a suggestive question, seeing the quick strides from penury to affluence and back again to poverty, that are made in this progressive country.

To return to the commissions: that of 1882 found a consensus that ten hours a day was suitable for adults but too much for children. (Seven years later the second commission advocated nine hours for adults.) Its members saw few factories in which there was adequate provision in case of fire, many that were over-crowded, and many that were badly ventilated. They were particularly indignant, as was the second commission, with the sometimes appallingly inadequate sanitary facilities. Taking the two reports together and allowing for a proportion of factories well directed, it is evident that no healthy conscience could leave the factories and mills uncontrolled or wait for reform from within. How, then, was improvement to be secured?

Legislation to control factories was one obvious answer and one that had been given in England. Seven bills were introduced into the Canadian House of Commons and all dropped. In Ontario an "Act for the Protection of Persons employed in Factories" (47 Vict., c. 39) was passed in 1884 and it had intrinsic merit. It placed limitation on the employment of children, insisted on provisions for the health of all employees, laid down detailed rules to ensure against accidents from machines and for prevention of fire, provided for an inspector who should always have access to factories, and for penalties in case of failure to follow the conditions prescribed. But according to the royal commission of 1889 the Act was inoperative, and certainly it proved to be no panacea. Furthermore, important as were the conditions of work, neither the commissions nor the Act ventured into the question of wages. Thus there was a field for trade unions both in supplementing what little was being done by government and in adopting collective action to secure better pay.

Already unions had attempted to achieve objectives sought by their members. The Knights of St. Crispin were established in the sixties to control the application of machinery to shoe factories, an effort which led to disastrous strikes. A more central cause was upheld by the Typographical Union which happened to be the one to raise the question of the obsolete Canadian law on the legality of unions. As part of a campaign in 1872 for the nine-hour day and higher wages the union ran up against George Brown, the editor of the *Globe*, a man whose genuine humanitarianism, which made him a leader in the move to help escaped slaves and in prison reform, was combined with a determined adherence to the doctrines of the Manchester School. In previous labour disputes he had employed strike breakers and now he did so again; but the new step, in conjunction with other master printers, was to have fourteen members of the union arrested on grounds of conspiracy to keep other men from employment. This was possible because Canada was still legally in the position that England had been in the early nineteenth century, when unions were illegal. It was a situation which allowed a Conservative government both to redress a wrong (if somewhat tardily) and to oppose one of its main political enemies. Legislation was passed which caught up with a whole series of enactments passed in England from 1824 to 1871.

Labour unions were now legal and the commission which reported in 1889 laid emphasis on their value, arguing that they had done much to discourage strikes, to improve the skill of artisans, and secure better conditions of work. The commission (which hardly even pretended to be impartial) was overoptimistic concerning unions and strikes but at least it was right in seeing unions as a part of the coming social pattern. However unwelcome to employers, the number of unions and of their members continued to increase, for by 1902 there were 547 locals in Ontario, which was half the dominion total. By that time, too, most of the unions—after a series of trial and error—had formed themselves into larger groups, and followed that by association with the large American Federation of Labor. The union was a child of the urban industrial society and became an integral part of it, even if, as has been indicated, it affected a limited portion of the wage earners. Its writ ran little beyond the boundaries of cities and large towns. The last quarter of the nineteenth century, then, was a period of great significance for the organization of labour, for it saw the legal recognition of trade unions, their grouping within Canada, and their attachment to their American counterpart.

The trade union was one—perhaps the principal—means by which the ill effects of industrialization and urbanization were cushioned. It could not wholly bridge the gap between poverty and riches, nor was it accepted North American doctrine that all should equal be. That there was genuine concern about poverty, and that a limited number of people appeared to share that concern, were both illustrated by a public meeting held in St. Lawrence Hall in Toronto in 1867. The meeting was called

to consider the propriety of providing an Industrial Home, where those in want might get work, and earn subsistence, and where food and lodging might be procured at the lowest cost, thus taking away all excuse for begging, and enabling the decent and industrious with little means, to procure lodging without resorting to disreputable localities, to their own injury and the increase of evil.

The mayor was in the chair, and although only some fifty people attended, the discussion was vigorous. The opening explanation was that "the promoters of the project wished to do away with all excuse for begging, and give several classes of the citizens an opportunity of earning an honest livelihood." The classes they had in mind were women in rags who earned a living by begging, women with small children, men and women who had passed their best days, and "boys and girls on the streets." The police magistrate, who strongly supported the proposal for an industrial home, had nevertheless some reservations as to the effect of moral suasion on some of the people already described. He saw difficulties in expecting the "respectable poor" to stay under the same roof as "outcast females." Giving a grim account of the lives of street children, he urged that a partial solution was compulsory schooling. The meeting ended, as meetings so often do, with the appointment of a committee to explore the possibilities of establishing such a home.

Poverty and misery were recognized by more than the fifty people who took the trouble to attend a public meeting. Indeed, for a class not destitute but on low incomes the growing comfort and variety in an Ontario city or large town brought minimum benefit. For a fairly large segment of society there had been substantial gains. Houses were, or could be, warmer, well lighted, and provided with plumbing. The untrained Irish servants of the early years of the century had been replaced with adequate cooks, starched housemaids, and the occasional butler. The few wealthy people could, if they wished, live in some style, although social standing was not measured in terms of dollars. A "society" could still be identified in any Ontario city at the turn of the century. It would include some but not all of the families long resident there; men from the worlds of finance and industry, whether or not in senior positions; doctors, lawyers, and clergymen; university professors; journalists and other writers; musicians and painters. Such people were brought together by common taste and interests. Other individuals of wealth in vain sought entrée to this group, and still others—rich or poor—were uninterested.

Outside work the tradition of local initiative was still strong in providing a variety of activities and interests. In days when the only mechanical music was that played on a street organ by the picturesque Italian whose monkey solicited pennies, families and groups played and sang in their own houses or organized concerts. In the summer children were taken for rides on the exciting open street cars or to the glamorous visiting circus. Grown-ups went to both concerts and plays, whether amateur or professional. For some decades now visiting theatrical companies had toured Ontario, and as time went on they found better theatres in which to play and large populations from which to draw audiences. Consequently the Ontario cities had the chance to welcome first-class companies. Medium-sized towns often had good theatres and good plays. They also had ambitions, as indicated by an inquiry from the town clerk of Napanee in 1885. Writing to the city clerk of Toronto, where the Grand Opera House with its great stage and baroque interior had been built a dozen years earlier on the site of the burned Royal Lyceum Theatre, he asked what "amount was charged for Opera House Entertainment." Motion pictures were coming in just at the end of this period. They were intriguing novelties not yet competitive with the legitimate stage. A jerky sequence was followed by a notice on the screen: "One minute please while we change the film." A faithful pianist sought throughout the performance to provide atmosphere as the heroine posed in close-ups or narrowly escaped violent death in many forms.

Men's clubs—austerely male in those days—were designed in the London image. The Toronto Club was incorporated by statute in 1863 and the Rideau Club (sponsored by all the well-known politicians and citizens) in 1865. The thick carpets, deep chairs, and subdued sounds were not for those with thin pocketbooks or a weakness for artistic performances. For such the Arts and Letters Club, founded in Toronto in 1907, was more practical and more congenial. Two-thirds of the members were to be professional artists and the remainder drawn from the ranks of other professions and business. Pictures, music, and plays were assembled or performed by the members; and to ensure a sense of simplicity each member was required to carry with him one log of wood as he climbed to the long room over the court house.

Libraries were everywhere numerous and more extensive, and the many book shops also offered a range of reading. Anything could be found from the classics and books on religion to "the most extraordinary book of the nineteenth century: the Bliss of Marriage, the way to the altar. Matrimony made easy; or how to win a lover" (160 pages, $1).

There was widespread interest in outdoor games. Lacrosse long held its primacy, but cricket increased in popularity. In 1872 a team of English cricketers visited Canada and the Toronto press was full of the genius of W. G. Grace, then a young man, but who had in the previous year scored his highest aggregate of 2,739 runs. It was noticed, too, that he was the most active dancer at Government House that evening. Meanwhile, baseball, which was becoming popular by about 1860, was competing both in personnel and scores, for in 1870 A. G. Spalding, the best known American player, visited Hamilton, and in the return match in Illinois the Hamilton team was defeated by 65 to 3 runs. Football, tennis, and rowing all had their devotees and in the winter months hockey took their place. Professional games were just beginning to be popular.

For long the outdoor games for women were croquet and archery with dignified skating in the winter; but as the young women slid past the traditions—not without criticism—into the more active sports of tennis and golf they escaped from the imprisoning bones and multiple thicknesses of cloth that were compulsory in the latter years of the reign of the good queen. In the sixties and seventies the daytime clothes of men, women, and children would seem to an earlier or later age to be incredibly voluminous, leaving only the face to welcome air and sun. From his top hat, past the mutton-chop whiskers, frock coat and striped trousers to button boots the middle-class male exuded dignified respectability. The women seemed to vie with each other in the number of yards and thicknesses of cloth which could be carried on the person, apparently had no feet, and, if they lacked the aid of the best dressmakers, appeared to have carried off some of the curtains and anti-macassars from their Victorian houses. To increase the area which could be covered with material the bustle was run out on a wire frame behind. At the same time many of the dresses had charm of colour and grace of line. The clothes of both men and women were well adapted to cold houses and were not necessarily impractical in days when there were domestic servants. Little can be said in favour of children's clothes of the same period, which too often looked like caricatures of their parents' and unduly restricted their movements. Fur-lined coats and fur caps were fashionable for men, and women used fur in many forms, including muffs.

One institution that had an important place in the calendar of a middle-class family was the country cottage. The programme of events that followed the winter was immutable. First came that alarming ceremony, spring cleaning, conducted by grim-faced and determined women with strange material tied over their hair. Relentlessly they turned everything in the house upside down and inside out, while in the back yard one of the team maliciously beat carpets. Then came some weeks of peace during which father diligently searched for his moveable possessions all of which had been put in the wrong places.

The cycle then moved on to the summer holidays for which Ontario had so much to offer. If a family chose to board in a farmhouse the children had a liberal education in rural life, following the farmer about as he milked or worked in the fields. In the days before bales were used haymaking was particularly delightful. The city language of poultry, beef, and pork was translated into the reality of hens, cows, and pigs. A horse took on a new character when a child could talk to him in a barn or ride on his broad back along the farm lane. The countless lakes and rivers of the province tempted many city dwellers. For those who lived in London the shore of Lake Huron, at places such as Kincardine and Goderich, was popular. At the other end of the province Ottawa saw a mass exodus to cottages on the Gatineau River. Kingston had the Rideau Lakes, the peninsula of Prince Edward County, and the Thousand Islands. At numerous towns on the lower lakes, such as

Brockville, Gananoque, or Cobourg, there were summer houses occupied year after year.

For many families of Toronto and Hamilton a summer holiday meant a cottage among the lakes, rocks, and pines of the Canadian Shield. When the schools had closed in June mother, children, and maid, accompanied by trunks, supplies of food, paddles, and toys, set off by train for the rather uncomfortable but altogether alluring spot on the edge of a lake or on a private island. There was a wide choice: the Muskoka Lakes, Lake of Bays, Georgian Bay, or Algonquin Park after its establishment in 1893. These were years before speed boats, golf courses, cocktail parties, and other accompaniments of advancing civilization. Small children played on the shore and older ones spent timeless weeks in and on the water. In canoes without seats boys and girls, men and women, would paddle for twenty miles, stopping at an unoccupied point to pick blueberries for the pies that came out of a fearsome wood stove which spread heat indiscriminately throughout the frame cottage.

And what of father meanwhile? Apart from his holiday of two or three weeks he camped in a city house in which all the good furniture was draped in dust covers, though leaving him ample scope to offset the spring cleaning. In the course of his usually curious cooking he broke an assortment of dishes and generally proved that he was a helpless male in an age when it was accepted that man's place was not in the kitchen.

CHAPTER ELEVEN

The Individual
in Society

AS THE NINETEENTH CENTURY wore on toward the twentieth the character of
Ontario was changing. A network of railways brought together the communities of the south and gave access to the north and northwest. There were still,
particularly in the clay belt and north of Lake Superior, isolated settlers
whose lives were in many respects similiar to those of the pioneers in the
south fifty or a hundred years earlier; but the mining and lumber camps,
though rugged, were organized and the new towns were well provided with
goods and services. It was a far cry from the farmer breaking land or the
lumberman in the forest to the operative in a city factory, but the isolated
family was becoming the exception rather than the rule. Institutions, governmental and unofficial, were shaking down; the needs of the people were being
more fully and more easily met. The effect, from the standpoint of the individual, was that he was becoming an integrated member of a more complicated society.

Ontario had never been a lawless frontier. The growth of cities added in
some ways to the problem of maintaining order and justice, but on the whole
a denser population throughout the province facilitated their maintenance.
The universities were turning out lawyers whose qualifications were stricter
than in early decades. From this pool, too, could be selected judges for the
various courts. The organization of the courts changed from time to time.
Objection was sometimes taken to the distance that had to be covered by
litigants. In 1868, for example, residents of three townships in Muskoka
petitioned the Legislative Assembly to have a District Court in Bracebridge
and this was promptly granted. Both the civil and the criminal law were made
more humane. Imprisonment for debt came to an end in 1859. In 1865 the
death penalty was abolished for crimes other than treason, murder, and rape.

In spite of the vigorous protests of lieutenant-governors and grand juries, however, the state of the gaols remained thoroughly unsatisfactory. In 1860 the Board of Inspectors sent a questionnaire to sheriffs and to the chaplains and medical attendants of gaols, the answers leading the board to find 'defects . . . of every possible kind . . . defects in superintendence, defects in discipline, defects in construction, in the internal and external distribution of the buildings, defects in the sanitary arrangements, defects, above all, in the means of reforming." In 1886 the City of Toronto was indicted, tried, and convicted of having gaols below an acceptable standard.

Responsibility for the health of the public was divided between governments, private practitioners, groups of citizens, and manufacturers of patent medicines. Both municipal and provincial authorities concerned themselves with various aspects of the prevention and cure of disease, either by regulations or by direct intervention. Civic boards of health struggled to provide satisfactory installations for drainage and water supply. The province joined with private initiative in building hospitals. The crying need for asylums for mental cases had been met first in Toronto in 1850 and institutions followed in Orillia and London in 1861 and Kingston in 1862. After that others were opened at intervals. In many towns and cities hospitals for physical illness were made available. The Hospital for Sick Children in Toronto (1878) was the first in North America exclusively for children. Legislation was passed to deal with particular problems, for example, a series of statutes in the fifties amended the rules for inspection of meat and other foods; and one of 1858 required that any hospital or dispensary in receipt of public funds must keep a supply of vaccine. One day in each week a doctor was to be ready to vaccinate out-patients.

There seems to have been no scarcity of doctors in any part of Ontario for which records exist, this being made possible by the medical schools which had been established around the half-way mark of the century. In those days doctors were frankly looking for business and regularly advertised in the newspapers, as did other professional men. In 1860 a Dr. Carson who had been practising in Whitby put a "card" in the *Chronicle* thanking his former patients for their patronage and recommending Dr. Patterson as his successor. The latter, being left to explain himself, announced "that he is now prepared to treat all diseases, incidental to the human system, acute or chronic, and performs all operations on the Eye and Ear with great success. He will attend to calls either in Town or Country, and the most respectable references given." Organizations under various names were set up to license doctors and in 1869 the College of Physicians and Surgeons was created by statute. There is evidence that dentists were resident in most towns, though in some small centres they spent only part of their time, as, for example, in Port Arthur in the seventies where a dentist from Collingwood advertised that he would spend two weeks. In 1868 the Royal College of Dental Surgery was founded.

To judge by the amount of space given in advertisements the popularity of patent medicines increased until it reached a high point about the turn of the century. The makers vied with each other in their descriptions. It was said of D. Holloway's Pills, for example, that "nearly half the human race have taken the pills," which were for liver and stomach disorders, and that "Many of the most despotic Governments have opened their Customs Houses to the introduction of these Pills, that they may become the medicine of the masses." That one was hard to cap and presumably there was no danger of having to prove any of these remarkable assertions or that the "doctors" who so often appeared in the names of the remedies ever existed. Out of many advertisements, which together might take up a third of a page of any local newspaper, one of "Electro-Galvanic" (1874) catches the eye. Intended to cure headaches and weak vision, this was "a continuous electric current which works its way into the nerves." There is a picture of a man wearing "Galvanic Spectacle" through which the current apparently passed. For several years galvanic electric current was popular as an assumed cure for a remarkable variety of complaints. It is believed to have done neither harm nor good. Without a description of the contents of pills and liquids (which was seldom given and probably never fully) it is impossible to judge whether they were injurious or how fast they were ceasing to be so. One suspects a name like the Canadian Pain Destroyer (1869), but Allen's Lung Balsam was stated to contain no opium, and by the nineties had appeared medicines more familiar in modern times such as Castoria, Carter's Little Liver Pills, and Dodd's Kidney Pills. Some of the later cures went back to traditional herbal medicines with the harmful drugs omitted. Patent medicines constituted a field in which free enterprise had been unfettered, but as governmental controls were imposed it was possible to eliminate the dangerous drugs and to some extent the misleading advertisements.

Social welfare was not a new idea in Ontario for it had been discussed since the first years of the province, but the industrialization of the seventies and eighties increased the need for it. In the largely rural society that had existed up to about the middle of the nineteenth century there were individual cases of the destitute, the old, the infirm, and the fatherless, but many of these could be handled by relatives and others by improvisation even if it was not always satisfactory. The concentration of people in towns and cities brought a difficulty that had formerly been minor: the unemployed. In earlier days farming, building, and then railway construction had mopped up a large proportion of the available workers and sometimes labour had been scarce. Now the immigrants came chiefly to towns. There they might have no friends, and could swell the pool of victims of the business cycle. Even the most convinced devotees of *laissez-faire* were reluctant to argue that nothing should be done, that people could be left to freeze or starve; but on the extent of public responsibility, where it lay, and how it should be met there was no consensus and consequently no single line of action. Governments and public, individually or in combination, built up a network of procedures and organizations that certainly alleviated distress and pointed the way to more elaborate and more coherent plans in the future. By the middle sixties provincial grants to hospitals, reformatories, asylums, houses of industry, orphan asylums, aid societies, and institutions for the deaf and dumb amounted in total to a considerable sum.

Most of the requirements for social welfare were in meeting the same types of problems as had long existed. In 1866 a provincial Act required each county council to have a House of Industry within two years. After confederation this was made optional and in 1903 again compulsory, though adjoining counties might contribute to a single institution. In 1890 provincial grants were made available. Waterloo County was the first to have a home ready, in 1869. The council had sent a committee to study poor houses in the United States and plans were made with that information at hand. A farm was added. A journalist who spent a day there found sixty-two inmates, "a singular gathering of the halt, the imbecile and the blind, the wise and the unwise, the decayed and the decaying of the poverty-stricken of the county, most of them passing quickly to the grave without a thought that can allay the animal happiness of eating and drinking." They were fed, he reported, on porridge and coffee, bread and potatoes, with soup and meat for dinner. He recommended that idiots and inebriates be removed to general hospitals. By 1910 the province had thirty-one county Houses of Industry and Refuge.

There were also private refuges and benevolent societies. Examples of the first were the Orphans' Home and Widows' Friend Society of Kingston (1857), the Ladies Protestant House of Refuge of London (1864); and of the second the reorganized St. George's Benevolent Society (1862) and the St.

Joseph Union Society of the City of Ottawa (1863). What was variously called an industrial school or a reformatory was in these days usually non-governmental. One for boys was opened near Penetanguishene in 1859. It had work and military drill but a modicum of education. The Toronto Female Industrial School was created in 1862 by a number of women of Toronto for the education, maintenance, and protection "of young females, who would otherwise be exposed to evil influences, and to promote and encourage habits of honest industry." In the same year the Boys Industrial School of the Gore of Toronto, which already existed, was incorporated. The objects were "the protection and reclaiming of destitute youths, exposed either by the death or neglect of their parents to evil influences and to the acquisition of evil habits, which, in too many cases, lead to the commission of crime." The Mercer Reformatory for women was opened in 1879.

Some moves were made for the further protection of children. The Humane Society of Toronto was established in 1887 to help both children and animals, and as these objectives were separated the former came to be assisted by the Children's Aid Society. The Charity Aid Act of 1874 listed a number of institutions for children and unmarried mothers and the sums of money granted by the province to them. A statute of 1888 for the protection and reformation of neglected children extended the responsibility of the provincial government over the operations of a number of institutions. Two Acts concerning apprentices were passed, one (1872) to restrict the freedom of withdrawing a boy from apprenticeship and the other (1874) to deal better with complaints made against a master.

Admirable as all these actions were it will be seen that they left great areas untouched. In the absence of a general poor law the municipalities accepted some responsibility for outdoor relief. Reports by the body curiously called "The Committee on Poor and Sanitary" of Napanee reported the expenditure of $22.50 on firewood amongst seven persons in February 1873. In the same year the committee recommended cash grants of 50 cents to $1.50 per week to each of six persons, with this explanation:

Taking into account the large amount of money granted by this Council for to aid and releive the poor of this Town we find it necessary to make strict inquiries so as to be able to do ample justice to each according to there necessities. We find in to many cases a disposition to obtain grants under pretences that will not warrant our recommendation while in other cases we have delt to sparingly.

Unemployment in the eighties brought many hardships for which the remedial measures were wholly inadequate, but it was private institutions that bore the brunt of the load. In one day in 1884 the Young Men's Christian Association, which ran a soup kitchen in London, distributed 122 quarts of soup, 92 loaves of bread, and 17 meals. Goldwin Smith, who contributed generously to many charities of his time, his money, and his pen, was horrified by what he saw in Toronto in that same year. He wrote in *The Week*,

Four hundred and ninety-five applicants for a night's shelter at a single police station in one month, more than eighteen hundred families relieved by two private associations in Toronto in the course of the winter, the street outside the House of Industry blocked by a destitute crowd, and men by scores sent to the city gaol to save them from starvation.

Smith consistently questioned the comforting argument that any one who wanted to work could do so. He was of the opinion that public aid had advantages over private and crusaded for the appointment of a city welfare officer. He at last succeeded in 1893, perhaps because he offered to pay the man's salary for the first two years.

The churches, as ever, played a major part in the non-governmental sector of public welfare. Many of the organizations were sponsored by one or more churches and a number of the refuges and homes were operated by them. The effectiveness of their role in this and the related field of public morals can be judged best in the light of an appreciation of how they were adjusting themselves to the social conditions of the province. One cause of long-standing friction was removed by the secularization in 1854 of the land held as clergy reserves. To ease the financial change the churches which had been benefiting from that source—the Church of England, the Church of Scotland, the Wesleyan Methodists, and the Roman Catholic Church—received capital amounts in commutation of the stipends of the existing clergy. Although this aspect of the Act was criticized by those who did not believe in any connection between church and state, the net effect was to break that connection for the future. Another form of privilege which had long brought controversy was also finally eliminated. In 1857 the provincial legislature passed an Act (20 Vict., c. lxvi) "to amend the Laws relating to the solemnization of matrimony in Upper Canada":

Whereas under the laws now in force in Upper Canada, privileges are claimed with regard to the solemnization of matrimony, by the Clergymen and Ministers of certain denominations, which are partial in their character and offensive to certain other religious denominations and their Clergymen and Ministers. . . .
From and after the passing of this Act, the Minister and Clergymen of any

religious denomination in Upper Canada . . . resident in Upper Canada, shall have the right to solemnize the ceremony of matrimony.

The churches now had a fair field and no favour, but their work continued to be handicapped by the divisions within their own ranks; nevertheless efforts to end this balkanization began to become effective. The Presbyterians united their forces in two stages, in 1861 and 1875, so that by the latter date they were one body throughout Canada. In 1884 the Methodists came together as the Methodist Church of Canada. The problem of the Baptists was somewhat different, to reconcile the autonomy of individual congregations with the existence of some common council. Their answer in 1888 was the Baptist Convention of Ontario and Quebec, a body which was representative but had no legislative functions. Moves in 1905 and 1906 for a union of the Baptist churches throughout Canada were not successful. In the case of the Church of England there was, and had been, no formal division, but the strain between the high and low church parties was an impediment to concerted action. The divergence was shown by the election in 1857 of a bishop to the new diocese of Huron, which was the first occasion on which a bishop was elected rather than appointed. The parties were fairly evenly divided but the low churchmen succeeded in electing their candidate, Benjamin Cronyn. An Evangelical Association was established in the Diocese of Toronto in 1868, merging into the Church Association in 1873. Some of its clergy members were called before the Episcopal Commission but the charges against them were dismissed. Such extremes did not recur but neither was the gulf ever wholly bridged. In practice, however, there were so many shades within the church that the moderately high and the moderately low were not far apart.

The Protestant churches had need of united forces to meet the challenge of the more diversified needs of the Christians of Ontario. The Roman Catholic Church, of course, had not had the same problem of concerted action. In parts of the north, in lumber camps and in sparsely settled agricultural areas, the missionary type of ministry was still needed and to some extent provided. In small towns and villages the complex of churches seems to have been adequate. Solid buildings and resident clergymen had taken the place of log cabins and visiting missionaries. In many of these places the churches formed a focus for social activities and were supported by the efforts as well as the funds of the members. Churches ranged in size from the frame building in the woods, one of two or three charges of a minister, to the substantial brick or stone buildings found in quite small villages. The churches also had to adjust themselves to the industrial society of the larger urban centres where both the wealthy middle class and the factory workmen were in degree new phenomena. The Methodist Church especially included a number of rich business men whose tastes were not in the direction of the emotional revivalism of earlier days. As the cities grew, there were poor parishes too in which selfless clergymen struggled to meet the needs of their people.

At this point the themes of religion and social welfare come close together. A Christian could starve physically as well as spiritually. In their work among the shifting and sometimes hapless people of poor areas and slums the traditional churches were reinforced by the appearance of the Salvation Army whose first Canadian branch was set up in London in 1883. Looking back from 1913 at its work in England the Army's *Year Book* concluded that "In the beginning it was to save souls from Hell that the General [Booth] started his campaign, and ere long both he and his workers saw that many souls could not be saved unless their temporal needs were also regarded. . . . The Social Work is the daughter of the Spiritual." The same combination was apparent in Ontario where the Salvation Army rapidly expanded. It gave food and shelter to those in desperate bodily need and by simple, vigorous, and undenominational evangelism attempted to meet equally the needs of those unconnected with churches, of the drunk, the criminal, and the sinful. Meetings at street corners were more common than in buildings, and the men and women of the Army sought out in their own surroundings those who were at odds with, or in rebellion against, God and society.

The campaign of the Salvation Army conspicuously pointed to the fact that the improvement of public morals was closely connected with religion and welfare: a relationship of which the churches too had long been aware. Human frailty allowed for a wide range of targets but the principal ones chosen were the preservation of the Sabbath and temperance. It was no accident that the former gained additional support as the industrial age progressed and hours of work and leisure were debated. In 1888 the Lord's Day Alliance was organized by Presbyterians, Methodists, and Anglicans and was supported by labour organizations as consistent with the drive for a shorter work week. Legislation was needed, of course, but the first attempt by the province, in 1903, was ruled *ultra vires* by the Judicial Committee of the Privy Council on the ground that it dealt with criminal law. The dominion statute of 1906, the Lord's Day Act, covered a number of activities forbidden on Sunday.

"Temperance" was a word more appropriate to the earlier societies than to those of the later nineteenth century for the aim of the latter was, in fact, prohibition, as was evident in the titles of some of the numerous organizations that came into the field in the seventies and eighties. Their ultimate aim was to make it illegal to manufacture or sell spirituous liquors. The legislatures first of the old province and then of the dominion were pressed by powerful groups to take action and the first success was gained by the passage of the Dunkin Act of 1864 (27–28 Vict., c. xviii) which provided that "The municipal council of every county, city, town, township, parish or incorporated village in the Province . . . shall have power at any time to pass a by-law for prohibiting the sale of intoxicating liquors and the issue of licences therefor." Several counties and townships voted for local prohibition, others against, and some of the first changed their minds later. The Dunkin Act was a complicated one and the next move in local option, the Canada Temperance Act of 1878, was a distinct improvement administratively. From the point of view of the advocates of temperance a Royal Commission appointed in 1892 was a failure since it condemned prohibition. A federal plebiscite of 1898 did produce a majority for prohibition but was held by the government to be indecisive. No better luck was found in Ontario where a referendum showed a majority in favour of a provincial liquor Act. The supporters of prohibition did not give up, but obtained no further results until the peculiar conditions of the first war introduced a new situation.

Such a recital of the bare facts of remedial measures, successful or not, gives little impression of the tragedies brought about by excessive drinking in Ontario, of the strength of opinion in favour of ending them by prohibiting manufacture and sale, or of the determination with which men and women worked toward that end. In earlier chapters several references have been made to the drunkenness which was found in decade after decade; and there is too much solid evidence to dismiss the charge, made by many and diverse contemporaries, that the problem was a serious one. The annual report of the chief of police of Toronto for 1868 showed arrests of 1,701 males and 828 females as drunk and disorderly, that is 5 per cent of the total population. And this was a figure for arrests alone, which does not take account of the deleterious effects of heavy drinking on many others. It was this kind of situation that appalled many people. To some of them prohibition seemed to be impracticable and an unreasonable interference with the private affairs of the majority. To others vigorous methods were needed to cure a serious social evil.

There is, running through the history of Ontario, a stern puritanism that has been an essential part of the character of the province. It is found in all periods and in all types of social circumstances: among rich and poor, in town and country. It has been influenced by, and in part derived from the teaching of some of the churches. Methodists and Baptists, Presbyterians, Quakers and Mennonites have all contributed to it. It is not necessarily connected with or contradictory to the emotional evangelism of the camp meetings of the earlier decades of the nineteenth century. In the second half of the century it could inspire one person to make dramatic appeals for temperance and another to maintain a personal code of moral behaviour. Critics have derided rich Methodists whom they represent as exploiting society while professing principles of ethics for others. That is on the whole a false accusation aimed at men whose ability and energy enabled them to succeed in business and who were at the same time convinced that they were maintaining high principles in and out of their offices. The late nineteenth-century family was another spring of ethical behaviour. In a more settled society than formerly and itself more compact than it was later to be, the family could instil, and to some extent enforce, the moral code built into Victorianism. The puritan influence—if that is the right word for it—has added a toughness to Ontario society: unattractive in some of its aspects to those perhaps no less moral but with different outlooks, but none the less an important element.

By about the middle of the nineteenth century the framework of the educational structure of Ontario had been erected. Taken as a whole it provided, in one way or another, for education from primary school to university. It was not a simple plan, nor did it ever become so, for it reflected the differing views, interests, and needs of the people of the province. A series of compromises had been necessary: between public and private institutions, between free and unfree education, between secular and religious approaches, between a single and multiple languages of instruction, between a standard system and provision for minorities. Not one of the compromises reached could be regarded as stable except for a limited time, and indeed all led to intermittent disputes. The system of education was further influenced by the expansion of settled territory and by the growing complexity of economic and social life. The requirements for education could not be projected from the estimated or actual figures of population since additional factors had to be taken into account: compulsory attendance at school, a larger proportion of pupils continuing into high school, the particular needs of business and professional classes.

In the beginning was the primary school, known up to 1871 as the common school and thereafter as the public school. The chief superintendent's report for 1869 shows that there were 4,524 of such schools with 5,054 teachers. In the rural parts of northern Ontario the schools were still set in traditional pioneering conditions. Reports by inspectors in the seventies describe inadequate buildings, financial difficulties, and teachers lacking knowledge of up-to-date methods; but these were partly offset by the zeal of trustees and other interested persons. Unfortunately for the completeness of the record the inspectors were so fascinated by the scenery and by their own hardiness in travel that they tended to forget to say more than the minimum about the schools. In northern towns and in most parts of the south the public schools were well beyond the pioneer stage. There were many log buildings still in use but more had been replaced and some of the country schools were handsome and well built. No doubt some schools were more successfully operated than others, but an attractive—almost idyllic—description published of the examination ceremony of the school in the village of Claremont in Pickering Township by one of the official visitors in 1860 is appealing.

An examination of the Claremont School . . . took place on Saturday, June 30th. Also in connection with the examination was a very nice tea party under the able management of Mr. Alex. Beaton, teacher. The exercises commenced in the morning at the usual hour, by reading, in which great proficiency was manifested by many of the pupils. The natural philosophy class was also very interesting, and the eagerness with which every one in the class showed to have the honour of answering the questions, by holding up their hands, the little ones reaching up as high as they could, too, in order to attract the attention of the teacher, showed how perfectly they understood what they were doing. After some exercises, an hour's intermission was given. Examination recommenced at one o'clock. The house crowded with the parents and friends of the children, which is a strong proof of the interest which they feel in the cause of education, as well as their appreciation of Mr. Beaton's abilities as a school teacher. The first arithmetic class was thoroughly examined in the different rules from practice to cube root; also a large class in general geography, which was very instructive, as well as interesting and satisfactory. The grammar class was then examined, after which some short but appropriate addresses to the parents and children were given by Mr. McNab, Mr. Wm. Bennett, Trustee, and Mr. Porter. The exercises of the day were agreeably diversified with singing by the children. The conduct of the children also, is worthy of notice—Although there was over a hundred of them nearly all of them small, their behaviour was such as to show the good government Mr. Beaton exercises over his school. At four o'clock the school was dismissed, and we all adjourned to the grove adjoining the schoolhouse, where the tables were nicely spread with such good things as are well calculated to please the palate, as well as the eye, and the tasty manner in which every thing was arranged, reflected the highest credit upon the ladies. . . . On the whole we all passed a very pleasant day which will long be remembered by the children and those present.

Even making allowances for the enthusiasm of the anonymous visitor it is obvious that this was a well-run school and that Mr. Beaton was a successful teacher. Presumably the curriculum indicated was typical, but as for the standard it is impossible to say. There were quite obviously imperfections in the rural schools as a whole, although some of them were as much the responsibility of the parents as the teachers. Compulsory attendance, as required in the School Act of 1871, was not—and perhaps could not be—enforced. Some of the annual reports of the minister show that the gap between the number of children of school age and the number that attended was wide. This was especially true of the rural schools. Whereas in 1869 there were more men than women teachers by the end of the century the reverse was true; and by a kind of Gresham's Law third-class teachers were driving out the second-class. Salaries were too low and the country model schools were turning out immature and inexperienced teachers. Early in the twentieth century such model schools were either placed under provincial administration or replaced by normal schools. The pay of teachers was at the same time increased by provincial bonus.

The regular public schools were the backbone of the whole educational system of the province but they did not take care of all categories of pupils of that age group. Schools for Indians never came under the common school plan. From 1824 until 1867 they were eligible for provincial grants as supplement to other financial sources, that is, the funds of a tribe and support by several missionary societies which from the first had borne the burden of teaching and administration. After confederation the Indian schools became the responsibility of the dominion government which in turn made grants to those remaining under the management of church societies. In addition there were three kinds of "separate" public schools, all supposedly created at the wish of particular groups. To call those few for coloured people voluntary would be pure sophistry. They were made necessary by racial discrimination and had no logical connection with the confessional schools which dated from the forties. The separate schools proper were and are public schools although this is not apparent from even official usage which distinguishes "public" from "separate." Authority existed for a group of local people to establish either a Protestant or a Roman Catholic school. The number of Protestant ones has never been large though it is difficult to trace them in detail since in early reports by the superintendent or the minister of education they are mentioned only in general terms or not at all. In 1895 there were ten, with 520 pupils and 13 teachers. In 1913 there were six, three of which are not in the first list. The total number of pupils had dropped to 420 of whom the overwhelming majority were in the school at Penetanguishene. In detail the methods of financing the separate schools have been complicated and varied, but the general principles have been that parents could be listed as taxed for one or the other and that the provincial government made grants to both.

Separate schools are commonly thought of as Roman Catholic and it is these which make up the large number and have caused the controversies. At first the students were mainly Irish and later increasing numbers of French Canadians were added. Amongst the people of Ontario there were various and conflicting opinions concerning these schools. Of interested Protestants a number were tolerant of an institution that caused no identifiable harm to the general public schools and was considered by some to be slowly fading away from lack of support; others were abolitionists, believing that the whole idea was wrong. To a portion of Roman Catholic parents the common schools were acceptable and an appreciable number of the teachers in them were of that faith. Some Roman Catholics, however—and they included some of the bishops—were accused of making continued efforts to extend the privileges of the separate schools and thus, so their critics said, to sap the vitality of the general schools.

It would be tedious and unnecessary to trace all the steps in a controversy which at times became a hot one: sufficient to note that there was a controversy, and that although the temperature of debate dropped the debate itself did not disappear. The distinction between the separate and the other public schools is not a simple one between religious and secular since it had always been provided that non-denominational Christianity should be taught in the latter. Up to 1884 religious exercises were to be designed by the trustees; after that time teachers were to read from the bible and conduct religious exercises, the nature of which was not clearly defined. Alternatively visiting clergymen could give instruction before and after school hours, leaving parents free to withdraw their children if they wished. To most teachers the whole concept was disagreeable: they, more clearly than the legislators or administrators, seeing how difficult it was to teach a kind of generalized

Christianity as if there had never been differences between Christians on belief and even on interpretation of the bible.

On neither separate schools nor religious teaching in others has there ever been complete agreement, but the school question that most agitated Ontario was not either of these but the use of a language other than English in public schools of any kind. Until the eighties, partly by understanding partly by positive authority, the practice had existed of using French or German as the language of instruction in schools in which children brought up in either of those languages predominated. There was even a list of textbooks in French approved by provincial authorities. This use of languages, unlike the position of separate schools, was not covered by the British North America Act or any provincial legislation, and simply grew up as a means of meeting an existing situation. It was not questioned until the early eighties when a new minister of education was surprised to find that there were twenty-seven schools in which French was used exclusively. He took immediate steps to require that English be taught in every school, but a commission which examined those in which French was used (in the counties of Prescott, Russell, Essex, Kent, and Simcoe) realized that such an order was not easy to enforce, nor was it acceptable to many French-speaking parents. Similar opposition did not appear in German-speaking areas since the parents in them were in general agreed that for practical purposes their children must learn English. A series of further commissions continued to find that progress in introducing a kind of improvised bilingualism was slow. Instruction 17 of 1912–13, issued by the Department of Education, curtailed the use of French as a language of instruction or study to a degree that aroused bitter criticism and positive opposition. Not for another dozen years did new regulations bring even comparative peace.

The issues that have been mentioned did not involve the high schools, as the grammar schools were known after 1871. At no time had there been separate high schools within the provincial system. Two developments only need to be noticed. One was that the number of pupils increased, which was satisfactory since in some of the high schools there had been only a handful of students. The other was the provision in the Act of 1871 for additional grants to certain high schools which were named collegiate institutes: those which, over a minimum size, had a sufficient number of students studying Latin and Greek—"Superior Classical Schools" as they were described in the Act.

Interest in the task of providing adequate primary and secondary schools directed and financed by the province has tended to conceal the lesser but continuing role of private schools. It was such schools that had furnished all or most of the educational facilities in the first years of the province and the demand for them did not disappear when there were alternatives. Small elementary schools were operated for little children by one or two women teachers—"dames' schools" in the old phrase; other schools were quite large and took students from the first grade to university level. Some were church schools, in effect separate schools, and of these the largest number were Roman Catholic institutions which followed on from the separate schools at the primary stage. In the later nineteenth century several new private schools were founded. Some of these were church schools, as in the case of Trinity College School for boys and Bishop Strachan School for girls, which were Church of England institutions, but more were non-denominational. St. Catharines Classical and Commercial School was one that accepted day boys or boarders. In 1863 it could point to success in obtaining scholarships.

By the eighteen-sixties, after many a battle, the elements of the pattern of institutions for higher education had been established. For decades the universities and colleges remained small and struggling, with classes so minute as to amaze later generations. They were, however, accommodating themselves to the needs for more specialized training. Theology, law, and medicine came early, followed by engineering, with discoveries of minerals when they came in northern Ontario giving priority to mining. The Royal Military College at Kingston was opened in 1876 and the Royal Naval College at Halifax in 1910. Business "colleges" were hardly comparable but their multiplication reflected the growing place of business. In 1860 the British American Business College was opened in Toronto for training of clerks, bookkeepers, and stenographers. The Ontario Business College at Belleville dated from 1868, and the Central Business College of Toronto from 1892. Another sign of changing times was the admission of women to universities in spite of suspicions of co-education entertained by some of the most prominent educationalists. Queen's led the way in 1878. Victoria capitulated in 1880, and at Toronto the objections of the president were overruled in 1884.

The intellectual and artistic life of a people cannot readily be either defined or measured, nor can it be said to start at any given moment. Throughout the history of the province there had been individuals interested in reading good literature, hearing music, seeing and possessing pictures, buying fine furniture, studying scientific subjects, and applying their imaginations to the solution of current problems. A small population, living for the most part under simple conditions, consumed more literature, music, art, and science than it produced. The creative side was not wholly lacking but it was not before the second half of the nineteenth century that it assumed proportions sufficient to warrant more than passing reference. It was then stimulated by the presence of more people, expansion of urban life, greater wealth, and the existence of universities around which advanced study and thought could centre.

The boundaries of the subject are elusive. Is imagination in methods of agriculture, in developing new techniques in mining, in designing a bridge less a product of the intellect than a poem or painting? That is a question, of course, that no one can answer objectively. The selection of interests and activities to be examined briefly in the following paragraphs, however, is governed not by any such distinction but by a desire to illustrate the many fields in which people in Ontario were adding to the texture of their lives and in a few instances to the sum of human knowledge.

How are the personalities to be selected in terms of their relation to Ontario? For present purposes those born in Ontario but passing their active lives elsewhere are not included; those born in other countries or provinces of Canada and living a substantial part of their productive lives in Ontario are. It could be argued that a better criterion than place of residence would be some characteristic that gave an Ontario trade-mark. This, however, is a story of the people who lived in Ontario, and, by the grace of God, they have shown some variety. Furthermore the local measure is a dangerous one whether in the arts or the sciences. A novelist often writes of what he sees and experiences. Charles Dickens found his material in England and could not be considered other than English, but no one has listed Rudyard Kipling as an Indian or Joseph Conrad as a citizen of the south seas. That will-of-the-wisp, the great Canadian novel, has yet to be written; but there is no requirement that it has to be about a small Ontario town or farm life on the prairies. Most of us would settle for a Conrad. The yardstick of absolute quality is the one that can be applied in all fields of creation more safely than some attachment to national environment, as witness—to pick names at random—Holbein, Handel, or Chopin.

When D'Arcy McGee was assessing the future of the confederation he had helped to create he was concerned that goals other than material prosperity should not be forgotten, and in 1867 gave a lecture to the Montreal Literary Club on what he called "The Mental Outfit of the New Dominion." He recognized that Canadians generally were readers of newspapers and that they imported books in substantial numbers; but if, he said, he were asked who read Canadian books he would have to answer "very few, for Canadian books are exceedingly scarce." The ones that he did mention did not outlast the fingers of two hands. Some of the descriptive books by early travellers and immigrants were well written, but the tale of imaginative literature produced in Ontario throughout the nineteenth century is brief indeed. Archibald Lampman wrote poetry of quality as did Duncan Campbell Scott. Marjorie Pickthall's poems, published a year before the first war, will stay on the record. William Kirby's *Golden Dog* was an historical novel of some merit. Lucy Maud Montgomery, whose *Anne of Green Gables* became both a classic and a phenomenal best-seller, lived in Ontario for some years but is more justly claimed by Prince Edward Island. Goldwin Smith, not native-born but firmly established in Ontario, was a prolific writer on many subjects and a stylist of distinction in any company.

Stephen Leacock is in a class by himself. His novels could have been written only by one who had both been brought up in Ontario and sensed some at least of its character; they also had something of the quality of all great humour in that there are overtones of tragedy. Ostensibly his novels and short stories are caricatures of life in a small town in Ontario, but not far below the surface lie sympathy, understanding, and a love of the milieu he knew. Of the long list of those who have attempted to portray the Ontario scene no one has come nearer to success than Leacock.

Original thinking in Ontario found its outlet in the spoken as in the written word. Two names stand out in philosophy. George Paxton Young, a graduate of Edinburgh, taught at Knox College at Toronto from 1853 and later at University College. He published sermons on scripture and essays on mathematics but it was as a lecturer that he left a lasting impression. John Watson was a pupil of Edward Caird at Glasgow and came to Queen's University in 1872. As teacher and writer in philosophy over many years in Kingston his influence was felt throughout Canada and he achieved an international reputation as well. In days when university teachers covered a wide range Watson's extended to political economy and in this subject he was assisted by one of his former pupils, Adam Shortt, who became professor of political science in 1891. Shortt's writings on the economic, constitutional, and general history of Canada were pioneer works which helped to establish a foundation in those fields. W. J. Ashley was appointed professor of political economy and constitutional history at the University of Toronto in 1889 and although his stay there was brief (he went on to Harvard) his influence was lasting. Modern history also emerged as an individual subject out of a grouping. Daniel Wilson, president of the University of Toronto, taught history together with English literature, ethnology, archaeology, and anthropology. When he died a separate chair of history was established and to it was appointed G. M. Wrong, who more than any other man in Ontario encouraged the study of history, and particularly Canadian history, based on original research and good style of writing.

Living in a natural and hardly explored laboratory individuals began in the fifties to make archaeological studies of Indian culture, and the process was accelerated by government support. David Boyle, a school teacher, was one of the pioneers, publishing both a number of individual studies and annual reports issued by the provincial Department of Education. The creation of an anthropological division within the Geological Survey of Canada made possible field investigations in 1910 and 1911. The establishment of the Royal Ontario Museum, which was officially opened in 1914, extended the study and portrayal of archaeology beyond Ontario and Canada. Anthropology was to some extent taught in the universities but it was not until much later that a special appointment in that subject was made in any of them.

The past and the present were both demanding scientific examination and the two were combined in geology and more especially in mineralogy, interest being accentuated by a belief in the existence of mineral wealth in northern and northwestern Ontario. In 1841 the legislature of the new Province of Canada voted funds for a geological survey and W. E. Logan was appointed to carry out the task. Until his retirement in 1869 he performed prodigious feats, parts of which are recorded in his *Geology of Canada* published in 1863. Many contemporaries and successors devoted their attention to various aspects of the same general subject: scientists, prospectors, and surveyors. The last, indeed, were expected to be men of almost universal knowledge, for they were required to report on soil, trees, fauna, flora, and water power. Like other humans they were subject to error and at times were the victims of optimism, but their reports taken together constitute an immense volume of information. Much of the record in the realm of science rests on a Canadian rather than a particular Ontario foundation but some residents of Ontario did make notable contributions. In civil engineering T. C. Keefer was particularly known as a hydraulic engineer. C. G. Gzowski built part of the Grand Trunk Railway and the international bridge at Niagara. Alexander

Graham Bell of Brantford was the inventor of the telephone. He also organized the experiment in aviation which led to the flight of J. A. D. McCurdy, a young engineer from the University of Toronto, in the *Silver Dart* in 1909. James Bovell, who studied medicine in London, Edinburgh, and Glasgow, migrated to Ontario in 1848, where he became a brilliant lecturer, a founder of the *Upper Canada Journal of Medical, Surgical and Physical Science*, a pioneer in the study of the effects and cure of drunkenness, and perhaps the best informed doctor in the province. A surgeon in the town of Fergus performed in 1883 the first appendectomy on the American continent. In a stay of only five years in Queen's University George Lawson founded the Botanical Society of Canada (1860). He ranks as the first professional botanist in Canada. William Saunders and his son, C. E. Saunders, did important research in types of grains.

Music has its place in society in composition, performance, and audience. For the first there is, within this period, virtually nothing to record. In the second there was great activity, much of it inconspicuous, and particularly effective in choral work. The one organization that attained international distinction was the Mendelssohn Choir, founded in 1894 by Augustus Vogt and conducted by him until 1917. Educational facilities in music developed throughout Ontario, and some of the great orchestras and individual artists came to cities. Music did play a part in the lives of the people but Ontario had little to show that was original.

With few exceptions painters in Ontario who achieved any distinction began their work after 1860. A few portrait painters demonstrated competence but nothing more. Painting in Ontario, as elsewhere in Canada, was largely of landscapes. For most of this period the subject was southern Ontario and work of lasting value was done by such men as L. R. O'Brien, Daniel Fowler, and Homer Watson. George A. Reid was an early painter of murals. Art schools and art leagues helped to develop new talent and to spread interest. In the early twentieth century a number of artists turned their attention, as did other people, to the new areas of northern Ontario. The first, and the unsurpassed, of these artists was Tom Thomson, whose joy was the forest of Algonquin Park. The members of what came to be called the Group of Seven—J. E. H. MacDonald, Arthur Lismer, Franz Johnston, F. H. Varley, Frank Carmichael, A. J. Casson, and Lawren Harris among them—put on canvas the spirit of a wide area of the Canadian Shield. It was work of inherent quality but also as novel in its effects upon its audiences as the discovery of silver at Cobalt, both in style and subject. It largely escaped the appellation of "derivative," that supposed sin in Canadian art (as if there were art wholly lacking in that characteristic). The Group of Seven aroused so much interest that it led to unfortunate consequences: a swarm of unskilled followers, and an illogical belief on the part of many people that landscapes showing the Canadian Shield were "Canadian" whereas those of the softer scenes in southern Ontario were not.

Publications and organizations drew together and recorded much of the artistic and scientific accomplishment of the times. There were outlets in books and in articles printed in such Ontario periodicals as the *Canadian Magazine*, and Goldwin Smith's *Week* which first appeared in 1883, edited by Charles G. D. Roberts. The painters found a forum in the Ontario Society of Artists, founded in 1872. Leading men of Ontario in the literary, scientific, and social science fields joined with their fellows from other parts of Canada in the Royal Society of Canada which was chartered in 1881. An older institution, the Royal Canadian Institute, was born in Toronto in 1849, and its charter is an interesting reflection of the mood of the day. It was to be a society,

for the encouragement and general advancement of the Physical Sciences, the Arts and Manufactures, in this part of our Dominion; and more particularly for promoting the acquisition of those branches of Knowledge which are connected with the professions of Surveying, Engineering, and Architecture: being the Arts of opening up the Wilderness and preparing the country for the pursuits of the Agriculturist, of adjusting with accuracy the boundaries of Properties, of improving and adorning our Cities and the habitations of our subjects, and otherwise smoothing the path of Civilization. . . .

The emphasis of study was on the sciences but the membership drew on a much wider field of professions and business. In 1913 the Institute began a series of public lectures intended to be of popular interest and which indeed quickly became so.

As people were brought together by scientific, literary, and artistic interests so they were in various other ways. The fraternal societies continued to expand. The Masons settled down in 1858 after a period of internal divisions and were active at many points, north and south. Newspapers carry many references to other societies. In London, for example, a lodge of the Independent Order of Foresters met weekly. In 1867 a Cobourg newspaper noted the annual picnic of the St. Patrick's Society and the annual meeting of the St. Andrew's Society. In the same year there was a large gathering of Orangemen in Cobourg on July 12. Streams of waggons converged on the town and a train brought another thousand or more. A Fort William paper recorded the formation of a lodge of the Knights of Pythias in 1890.

The Farmers' Institutes, which date from the eighties, were sponsored and subsidized by the provincial government and were concerned with the technique of agriculture. They did not survive long, but out of them grew the Women's Institutes which began at Stoney Creek in 1897. The purpose was "to promote that knowledge of household science which shall lead to the improvement in household architecture, with special attention to home sanitation, to a better understanding of the economic and hygienic value of food and fuels, and to a more scientific care of children with a view to raising the general standard of the health of our people." Branches were added throughout Ontario and as time went on the Institutes grew in membership and in the scope of their interests. Such extension beyond the domestic scene was characteristic of the growing participation in public affairs by women. Not until the second and third decades of the twentieth century were they able to influence the course of government by voting and by membership of parliament, but meanwhile they were to the front in the cause of temperance and in a variety of charitable organizations. It was becoming increasingly obvious that many women were not prepared to stay at home and leave public matters to men.

The Young Men's and Young Women's Christian Associations were directed to people interested in religion but who also had need of educational and cultural development. The associations were of particular significance in the cities to which young people came without friends and needing social focus. There were clubs for many purposes: purely social, literary, athletic, and dramatic. The industrial wage earner, who was not likely to be a member of many of the above organizations, might be a member of a trade union, and some of the unions had social as well as business sides. From 1858 to 1900 the manufacturers had tentative arrangements for consultation and in the latter year the modern Canadian Manufacturers' Association was founded. Farmers were considering better means of joint action to further their interests. People were brought together in common purpose at schools, universities, and churches. They met at plays, concerts, picnics, horse races, agricultural shows, and political speeches.

For most of the people of Ontario the old isolation had gone, and that in two senses. A denser population in the south and largely grouped settlement in the north combined with somewhat better roads, with postal and telegraphic services, and particularly with railways to bring people together physically. They were also, or could be, members of organizations of the various kinds that have been mentioned. The net result was not to eliminate rugged individualism and *laissez-faire* but merely to chip at the edges. Governments were still far from assuming the main responsibility for social welfare, from directing the economy by means other than tariffs, from subsidizing farm products, and all the many ways by which they intervened in social life in the mid-twentieth century. For the bulk of people there was no such protection, whether they were manufacturers, industrial workers, farmers, or professional men. There was still a world for adventure in the north, and to the southerner the doctrine of Horatio Alger could bring the North American message of opportunity.

Part Three

THE WAY WE
LIVE NOW

CHAPTER TWELVE

The Modern
Province

IN THE FIRST DOZEN YEARS of what Laurier hopefully called Canada's century Ontario had its full share of optimism and of growth. The signs of progress were solid enough. In spite of a serious drain of people to the United States, immigration and natural increase together raised the population figure by some 16 per cent to a total of more than two and a half millions. Manufacturing was going ahead well. Banks and other financial institutions showed new strength. In the north old dreams of a great mining industry were beginning to turn into reality.

Yet if a magic carpet could take a present-day observer back to the province of 1914 he might well think it to be as much of the nineteenth as of the twentieth century. The rural population was not much less than the urban and there were no great cities. Toronto had outpaced the others but was neither large nor complicated. It had pleasant residential areas, so much so that families came from elsewhere to spend the summer there. The countryside was near at hand and the little towns in neighbouring counties were associated more with surrounding farms than with the city. To reach them by road was an endless adventure. The few expensive motor cars were viewed with awe but the family Ford was nevertheless an exciting innovation. It was exciting in more ways than one for it was subject to many maladies. If it finally collapsed in silent indignation the passengers could, if evening had come, sleep on the seats or in the ditch. Punctured tires were normal incidents on a journey, to be repaired on the roadside; and the flame that vulcanized the tire shone like the camp fire of earlier travellers.

And then there were the roads. Certainly they had improved for horse-drawn vehicles, but there were few paved miles and for the rest the spring mud was unconquered. It was normal for a car to be stuck at this time of year, even on the principal routes, but the old fences yielded up stout rails to be used for a surface or as levers. So eventually the destination was reached —that day or perchance the next.

The imaginary visitor would not be much impressed by the methods of travel, although at the time they seemed much better than formerly. Steam railways were well developed and extensively used for long or short distances. Complementary to them were electric railways, often known as "radials," which reached their height of popularity in Ontario and at about this same time. Several hundred miles of lines were being operated for both passengers and freight, mainly for quite short runs. From Toronto one line ran to Lake Simcoe, serving the intermediate towns and holiday spots on the lake. Another went westward to Guelph. Hamilton was a centre for radials, through the Niagara peninsula, and also to Brantford and thence to Kitchener or Port Dover. London was connected with Lake Erie at Port Stanley, as was Chatham at Erie Beach. With the development of hydro-electric power in the province a great future was seen for electric railways; but just as they grew and flourished when travel by road was difficult, so they waned and perished when reliable motor vehicles were placed on adequate roads. Later the radial car was to be reincarnated as the diesel "dayliner," again a friendly and neighbourly conveyance that stopped at every crossroads.

Then, too, people were more self-propelled, whether on their feet or on bicycles, and bicycles were both numerous and safer in the absence of heavy motor traffic. They converged on schools, but in the country children more often walked. In retrospect both the daily walks (with chivalrous boys carrying the school bags) and the little red schoolhouse have been represented as romantic and even heroic. They had, of course, no such character at the time. Children on a farm could have found plenty of exercise in more productive forms, and among the outspoken admirers of the schoolhouses today are those who want to introduce better lighting, heating, and plumbing before living in them.

Whether education in the second and third decades of the century was better or worse than in later years must be a matter of opinion; but clearly it was less general. In both town and country a much smaller proportion of children went further than public school and fewer again to a university. In 1917 there were only 34,000 pupils enrolled in the secondary schools of the province, and in 1921 just over 9,000 undergraduates at the few universities and colleges. Little universities in little cities loomed larger than big universities in big cities. Their staffs were well laced wth "characters"—men who were famous beyond the college walls and active in community life.

If only a low percentage of young men and women received higher education was that because of a conscious policy of excluding the masses, of maintaining a privilege for the few? If it was, the basis for it is not obvious, nor is there much evidence of protest against it. In several faculties—such as· theology, medicine, dentistry, or engineering—the governing factor was later employment. In the humanities and social sciences there was more representation of the middle class, sons and daughters of families that had traditionally believed in university education. Many other young people were undoubtedly prevented by lack of funds from attending; but on the other hand costs were modest, even taking into consideration the changed value of money. Tuition fees were nominal, residences and boarding houses, for those who came from out of town, were inexpensive, and few students of that era ever thought of owning motor cars. In such subjects as literature, history, or philosophy the relationship to employment was less clear. Young men and women who intended to teach in high schools entered various courses, but commercial employers were less impressed by the advantages of general education. Even in the thirties a leading bank could tell an applicant for employment that university degrees were of no interest.

The War of 1914 brought out much of the best and some of the worst in the people of Ontario. In spite of—and to some extent because of—immigration in the previous few years the province was still strongly British, conscious of the United Kingdom and the empire as major interests and guide lines. Response to the German threat was immediate, general, and positive. During the years of war 242,655 men enlisted in Ontario in the Canadian Expeditionary Force, well over a third of its total. Others joined the Canadian navy or the British forces. Women knitted socks and Balaclava caps; men and women worked in munition factories. In the long casualty lists were written the tragedies of hundreds of families but to win the war remained an overriding objective. Internal dissension arose over conscription to which there was substantial minority opposition, but a more divisive force for the country as a whole was the bitter dispute on this policy between Ontario and Quebec. Impressed by the necessities of war the people of the province of Ontario resented what they regarded as the failure of Quebec to play its full part in the Canadian armed forces. On this theme, and on the concurrent one of the use of the French language in Ontario public schools, old prejudices were bitterly voiced. All the stops were pulled out, anti-French and anti-

Catholic. No indictment can be laid against a people as a whole, but in Quebec the sensational statements were the ones that were read, just as in Ontario people saw the words of a Bourassa. That neither province made any effort to understand the point of view of the other and that spokesmen in each resorted to extremes are all too evident.

Then, as before and after, serious charges have been laid against the people of Ontario and their successive governments: that they never understood, or attempted to understand, Quebec; that they were overbearing and intolerant; that by leading the crusade for "provincial rights" they distorted the original plan for a strongly centralized state. How much validity lies in such accusations must remain a matter of opinion. All that can be said with certainty is that time has blunted the edges of particularism and obscurantism. The people of Ontario, certainly, proved not to be disciples of the exact constitutional views dominant in 1867, but they never lost faith in the united country which they had led in founding. They have thought in terms of the province and the dominion, but never—as some recent observers claim—of an English-speaking bloc and a French-speaking one together making up Canada. Almost alone of the provinces Ontario has never harboured a serious movement for secession, fundamentally because that would mean seceding from itself.

It is a comment on the extent to which the province had grown that, in spite of a large diversion of manpower into the armed forces of the First World War, it proved possible to grow more food and to initiate new industries, particularly those for the manufacture of munitions and their components. Business men and engineers were enterprising in turning to wholly new fields and the ranks of factory workers were swelled by large numbers of women. To some extent the availability of capital, management, and labour came from unused capacity resulting from the recession that had begun in 1913. In the financial sphere the first federal income tax was imposed in 1917, and the Victory Loans, floated with some hesitation by the Canadian government, were over-subscribed. The war accelerated the trend toward a more mixed economy and in particular toward industrialization. If it brought to many men compelling and dangerous duties it spelled wealth for a few and prosperity for many.

The mood of the crowds that milled in city streets on the day of the armistice comprised relief, satisfaction, and a sense of finality; for had not the threat of German domination been removed in a war that was to end all war? There was to be disillusionment later, but meanwhile reaction from the strain of the war years showed in personal expenditures and a strain of careless gaiety. Jazz music, coon coats for young men, daringly short dresses for young women, and battered motor cars seemed to symbolize a state of mind. Underpinning a generally high standard of living was the continued health of the economy, broken only once in the next decade. The experience gained in manufacturing munitions was transferred to the production of consumer goods and the level of employment remained satisfactory.

Not everyone was conscious of living in the best of all possible worlds, and those who were were alarmed by discontent and the appearance of radical ideas. The general strike in Winnipeg in 1919 was worrying but not too close to home. Two years later the most radical branch of political and social philosophy found a footing when the Communist Party of Canada was founded in an Ontario barn. Meanwhile the traditional rhythm of politics was upset when, in 1919, the United Farmers of Ontario, making common cause with labour members, formed the provincial government. These were disturbing elements, but business was good and protest movements making only temporary headway. The stock exchange exercised a fascination over people who had previously only heard of it. Thousands of people dabbled in penny stocks and made paper fortunes. Teachers, doctors, and housewives stopped to "telephone my broker," indulging in the agreeable game of buying stocks without paying for them, oblivious of what "margin" meant.

They found out—suddenly and sadly—when the bubble burst loudly in the autumn of 1929 and Ontario, with the rest of the western world, was plunged into an economic depression. Per capita incomes dropped by close to a half. Between 1929 and 1933 foreign exports from Canada as a whole were reduced by two-thirds and construction by almost as much. In Ontario the number of persons employed in manufacturing was a third less. Over the same period the cost of living dropped by 27.3 points, bringing apparent gain to those with private means or on salaries; but the private means dwindled with reduced returns on investments and salaries were cut or at best pegged. In some of the skilled trades wage levels were maintained but this was of benefit only to those who could find jobs, and unemployment in Canada as a whole jumped from a low of 65,000 in 1928 to 826,000 in 1933. It was more common for people to take what little pay they could get.

For white-collared workers and wage earners alike it was difficult to find or to retain jobs, and often impossible. To say that there were few people who did not have to reduce their standards of living hardly suggests the loss of possessions and savings, the hardships mounting close to starvation. Unshaven and embittered men stole rides on freight trains, looking for jobs somewhere and seldom finding them. Even for those who did not experience the extremes of the depression the long, grinding pressure of worry and frustration left marks that did not fade but were in no wise understood by the generation that followed.

During the years of depression those who were interested watched numbly while the international situation went from bad to worse until it erupted in a second war. That ended the economic depression it is true, but it introduced in turn another kind of abnormal situation. Again the people of Ontario threw themselves into the struggle, with 397,808 men enlisting in the armed forces of Canada and women serving in the forces too. There was a grimness about this mechanized war that was unenlivened by patriotic songs or tales of individual exploits. Heavy demands for food, goods, and labour led the federal government to introduce strict controls by taxation, maximum prices, and rationing. The profiteering on government contracts that unfortunately existed in the first war was almost eliminated in the second. The public— apart from those whose relatives were serving in a battle area or braving the North Atlantic passage—were at worst inconvenienced. The rationing was not severe, for in most cases supplies were not far short of demand; but most consumer goods were kept to the minimum to allow for the manufacture of war materials. As gasoline was short and no new cars or tires were for sale some drivers of Cadillacs surprisingly turned up on bicycles or walked to street cars. Meat and butter were not plentiful and substitutes were found for tea. A male civilian might have to search widely for a new shirt and a housewife for a kettle. Trains were desperately crowded. Doctors were overburdened. In some urban areas housing became very scarce. In Ottawa it was said that people watched death notices in the hope of finding dwellings. Many people were obliged to economize carefully, but not in the negative atmosphere of the depression. There was more than enough work to be done, and if there were minor hardships for civilians they were directed to a purpose. As the war began without song so it ended without cheers. A job had been done but for the rest the future was uncertain.

It had been a curious period, for through twenty out of thirty years extraordinary conditions had been imposed by events outside the control of the people of Ontario. The years of hostilities had seen accomplishments of a kind, both in the contributions of the province to the armed forces and in the growth of the economy under forced draught. On the other side of the ledger were limited immigration, delayed housing and public works, and in general diversion of attention from the normal needs of a community. The social lessons of the depression, which will be examined in detail in a later chapter, bore their main fruit after the second war. In a sense then the modern period of Ontario covers no more than the last twenty years; but in that short time came rapid growth and change, and with them the problems that were their almost inevitable accompaniments.

The most obvious and basic development in these years has been the increase and diversification of the population. From 1941 to 1951 the rate of growth was 21.4 per cent, twice that of the previous decade, and from 1951 to 1961 it was 35.6 per cent. It pushed the total well over six millions. Who were these people? Of the three original ethnic groups the Indians were more numerous in Ontario than in any other province but their numbers were still small, being 48,074 in 1961. Some of the Indians lived on reservations and some not. Of the various occupations of the latter, who had by great majority rural residence, the most spectacular was in the construction of high steel buildings, at which the Mohawks became especially famous. Apart from agricultural Indians the first farmers in Ontario were French. There had not been many people of French race in Ontario until the late nineteenth and early twentieth centuries and immigration from Europe did little to add to their numbers, but the total in 1961 was 647,941. The main increase is explained by migration from Quebec.

The distribution of the French remained uneven. Using again the 1961 statistics, two counties on the Ottawa River, Prescott and Russell, were overwhelmingly French (83.6 and 73.2 per cent), and those immediately inland from them, Glengarry and Stormont, were about half French. The remaining river counties, Carleton and Renfrew, were considerably less French. At the southwestern corner of the province, Essex County had only 21.4 per cent in spite of its long French history. Several of the remaining southern counties, including the heavily populated Wentworth and York, had less than 5 per cent of French origin. There had long been a substantial migration from Quebec to northeastern Ontario. By 1931 the three Districts of Cochrane, Nipissing, and Sudbury had more people of French than of British descent and the same remained true in 1961. In the latter year, in fact, Cochrane was half French with, of course, various other ethnic elements as well. In northwestern Ontario, however, the situation was different. Thunder Bay, Rainy River, and Kenora each had about 10 per cent of people of French origin. Summing up the position in 1961, people of French origin made up about one-tenth of the population of the province but were largely concentrated in the southeast, northeast, and to a lesser extent in the southwest. Only in those areas was there any equivalence between ethnic origin and mother tongue and in them it was marked. In most of the other counties where there were people of French origin only a third to a half of them had the French language as mother tongue.

The descendants of the second white people to settle in Ontario, the British, have been continually reinforced by further waves of immigrants. In the period from 1936 to 1945, years of depression and war, the whole immigration flow was small but of what there was about one-third was from the British Isles. In the next twenty years the proportion ranged from one-fifth to one-half. Even combined with natural increase within Ontario that was not sufficient to maintain the proportion of persons of British origin, which in 1941 had been approximately two-thirds of the total. By 1961 it was not much more than a half. That change was caused in part by the influx from Quebec but more by the immigration of Europeans, particularly from Germany, Italy, the Netherlands, and the Ukraine.

The people of Ontario are, then, for the most part of British and European extraction. Indians constitute a small element and there are only a few Asians and Negroes. Superficially this is a description which could apply to much earlier times; it is the balance that has altered. In the twenty years after 1941 the proportion of native-born became markedly smaller. In 1961 those who had migrated to Ontario since the second war made up about one-fifth of the labour force. The white-collar categories were filled more by those from Britain than from elsewhere. Many Europeans, notably those from Italy, went into the construction business or into other unskilled or semi-skilled work. The ranks of all services, trades, and professions, however, were well supplied with recent immigrants. Apart from a number of Dutch farmers who came in the fifties relatively few immigrants have been engaged in agriculture but they are well represented in mining. Apart from the last, it is the cities which have been most affected.

This is a development which can be seen from two points of view, that of the immigrant and that of the native-born. Some of the newcomers, including political exiles and skilled workers from Britain, returned to their native lands, either from dissatisfaction or because they had never intended to stay permanently. It can never be an easy adjustment to move from one country to another, and to add to changed circumstances there have been some cases of exploitation. An Ontario royal commission reported in 1962 some shocking abuses by employers in construction firms who had evidently taken advantage of either the ignorance or the helplessness of immigrants. Whether or not this has occurred in other fields is not evident but it appears that at least the majority of newcomers consider that they have gained by migration.

Those with deep roots in Ontario have mixed feelings about the new ethnic pattern. They do not need to study statistics to be aware of it, for everywhere they hear foreign tongues or run into clerks and artisans and waiters who have crossed the Atlantic. Canadians have never pursued the policy of the melting pot but they at times speculate on the results of the ethnic mixture; on whether some measure of social unity can be preserved. The advantages of the varied cultural traditions brought by the immigrants from Europe are generally recognized, but any inclination to look too much to countries of origin or to live in blocs in the new land can give cause for concern. Most of the immigrants from Europe find it necessary, for purposes of employment, to learn at least some English; but other languages are used in many of their homes, and in 1961 there were 98,820 persons in Ontario who spoke neither English nor French. The second generation in Ontario for the most part learn English. In 1967 there are 65 newspapers and periodicals published in foreign languages in Ontario and their circulation, together with some originating in other provinces, is estimated to be about 300,000.

Ontario was becoming a predominantly urban society. In 1961 more than three-quarters of the people lived in centres of one thousand or more while less than 9 per cent lived on farms. Of the town dwellers much the largest number were in cities with populations of 100,000 or more. In 1961 the population of Metropolitan Toronto had reached 1,576,000. For the first thirty years of the twentieth century the number of persons engaged in farming remained almost constant at about 300,000, but after that time it fell. At the same time, however, production increased since mechanization and improved methods allowed a greater output by a smaller number of men.

Distribution by areas followed much the same lines as before. By 1961 the largest city in the whole northland was Sudbury (80,120); the next group— Fort William, Port Arthur, and Sault Ste. Marie—were in the middle forties. Northeastern Ontario with its clay belt and more especially with its mines passed the half-million mark in that same year, but the Lakehead-north-western region was less than a quarter of a million. More than four-fifths of the population of the province live in southern Ontario which has less than one-quarter of the land area.

The average density continued to rise. In 1911 the number of persons per square mile was 6.91; in 1921 it was 8.02; in 1951, 13.36; and in 1961, 18.12.

The density varies greatly from one part to another. In the early fifties three counties—York, Halton, and Peel—contained about 29 per cent of the population of the province. Density was lowest in parts of the north and nearest to average in some of the less populated counties of the south. Before leaving the analysis of population one or two additional points might be mentioned. In the decade 1951–61 the figure for natural increase (births less deaths) was 953,493 while that for immigration was not far behind at 817,292. The birth rate fell during the depression but after that it was higher than before. The part of the population aged 65 and over has shown a marked increase. Comparing 1961 with 1931 the average woman lived to 74 instead of 62 and the average man to 68 instead of 60.

From counting heads one naturally turns to the family, which has commonly been regarded as the foundation of the social structure. Of the changes that have taken place only a few can be described with certainty. In 1961 the average size of the Ontario family was 3.6; the marriage rate jumped from 5.9 per thousand of population at the depth of the depression to 10.9 just after the second war, and settled back to 7 in 1961; people married and had children at a younger age than formerly. In 1941 about one out of each twenty married women had paid employment but twenty years later one out of five had. Grandparents seldom form part of the modern family unit. Apartments and small houses without domestic servants and from which both parents may be away all day do not lend themselves to the care of older people. To some extent provision is made for them by the state and by voluntary organizations; and as life expectancy rises there are more older people. The number of divorces has risen steeply in Ontario. At the turn of the century there were 2; 208 in 1929; and 3,474 in 1964.

Beyond these few facts, or indeed in making deductions from them, it is wise to move with great caution. There is a widely held view that the family as an institution has decayed from what it was at an unidentified date in the past; that parents contribute less to building the character of their children; that children have less respect for their parents, who "do not understand modern youth" (that time-worn phrase). Much of this comment is hard to pin down, nor are comparisons easy. Earlier in this book, referring to the beginning of the nineteenth century, it was noted that children were apprenticed as a means of getting them away from parents who would not or could not look after them. Later in the century gangs of children were reported to be ranging the streets of Toronto. On the other extreme there are at the present time ideal families in which parents and children respect and help each other, are companions, and in general act as human beings with interests and affection in common.

Perhaps such cases, early and late, are all exceptions. There is some evidence of a causal connection between broken homes and juvenile delinquency, and certainly the last has become a more serious problem. It is well, however, to keep in mind the great variety of family circumstances. They are different in town and country and within each. It cannot be automatically assumed that the low rate of divorce in earlier years betokened congenial relations and happy homes for children, or that a home will be the same if the parents are both preoccupied with paid employment. Labour-saving devices, including processed food, simplify housework and cooking. Whether in town or country children get to school without effort. Modern techniques make possible a mode of life not within reach of the Victorians. Is it one too mechanized for the maintenance of relations within a family? In Ontario, as elsewhere in the world, there are evidences of changes in social behaviour, with at least a segment of youth accepting less discipline and fewer traditions. The manifestations are both too obvious and too varied to call for description; but the relevant question in this context is whether the family in its modern form is cause or result of that state of mind. Perhaps both?

The sedate pace of education changed in the middle forties to a hectic rush. School and university authorities had nightmares in which huge multitudes of students knocked in vain on the doors of institutions never intended to receive such numbers. There were two main reasons for the sharp increases in pupils. The most obvious, of course, was the speed in the rise of population and the higher birth rate. The second was the new stress placed on education by employers. This stress applied in many fields. The advance of mechanization left less and less space for unskilled workers. Young people were encouraged to carry their education further and adults to attend technical courses. At the university level industries which had once preferred "practical men" looked for graduates whose minds were trained to the point at which they could be taught the particular techniques of a business. People talked of the "crisis" in education. In its submission to the Royal Commission on Canada's Economic Prospects the government of Ontario estimated that the cost of elementary and high schools in 1975 would be about twice what it was in 1954. In higher education it tentatively multiplied costs by five. Later studies did nothing to pare these estimates.

The needs were obvious: buildings, books, equipment, teachers—and money. Provided that the taxpayer did not rebel buildings could be put up, even at rising prices, and books could be published or republished. Teachers, however, could not be manufactured or employed at will. Higher salaries—that is, higher in relation to the cost of living—proved to be an attraction, and in a sellers' market and with the equivalent of unions in some cases teachers have been in a position to secure better rates. Scholarships have facilitated advanced studies. Equally important has been a new interest among young men and women in the teaching profession in preference to other careers. These factors cannot ensure an adequate supply of teachers but go some way toward doing so.

New school buildings shot up everywhere, and in the country hundreds of yellow buses buzz like bees along the roads, picking up children at farm gates or carrying pupils from villages to high schools. With transportation no problem schoolhouses could be located according to other considerations. The pattern of schools remained. Public and high schools continued to provide for the large majority. Of the separate schools the Roman Catholic ones had increased enrolment but the Protestant schools dwindled. Parallel with the provincial system, at either elementary or secondary level or both, private schools, the pioneers of education in Ontario, more than maintained their relative position. Parents who chose private schools were not relieved of taxes for public schools and had in addition to pay fees swollen by the change in the value of the dollar. Scholarships and bursaries to these schools could take care of only a limited number of pupils who would not otherwise have been able to attend. Apart from financial considerations there are, on the one hand, parents who prefer that their children should attend public and high schools as being more representative of Canadian society, and on the other hand those who argue that smaller classes together with more opportunity for games and other extra-curricular activities outweigh the former consideration. Cities and towns are the main feeders of private schools.

One matter has been re-examined that relates to a controversy some seventy years old, the use of French as a language of instruction. Within limits this has long been permitted in public schools, and private schools have always been free to teach in French if they wished. Recently experiments in using French have been made in private schools for young children in Toronto. For the first time a provincial government has adopted a policy of extending the use of French to secondary schools. This important change, forecast in general terms, would apply in areas in which a sufficiently large French-speaking group made it appropriate.

The cloistered peace of the universities was mercilessly broken by large-scale invasion after the second war, the contrast being underlined by the fact that the universities could do little more than mark time during hostilities. First came the veterans, older in years and much older in experience, whose serious attitude made possible classes of two or three times the size of pre-war days, addressed by professors reluctantly attached to microphones. But this was just the beginning, since not only did the group of undergraduate age expand but those in it who proceeded to higher education increased in proportion by some two-thirds in a few years. The few existing universities in the province grew rapidly; but for them to absorb the whole body of students would make them of unmanageable size and at the same time accentuate the old difficulty of going great distances to college. Two expedients were adopted. One was to establish additional colleges some miles from an existing university but within reach of lecturers to be sent from it. The other was to create universities, either *de novo* or on the basis of existing institutions. They were widely spread throughout the province. The most northerly ones were at Sudbury and the Lakehead. Others were at St. Catharines, Guelph, Waterloo, Peterborough, and in the northern part of Toronto.

The problem of numbers has been the most compelling but by no means the only one demanding attention. The proper place of technical education at both secondary and college levels has been debated by a generation in which technology has recognized importance. Experiments have been made with television but without conclusive results. After prolonged study the method of examination at grade 13 in the high schools has been altered. In universities the relation between teachers and students—the basic question in higher education—has been re-examined. So also has been the place of both in the structure of university government. The students too have been studied —especially by a puzzled public. The inclination to revert to the beards and tight trousers of their great-grandfathers, to the gay colours of the eighteenth century, and to the long hair of the seventeenth, is in curious contrast with bursts of political radicalism. Oliver Cromwell would have been embarrassed if he had been mistaken for King Charles I. By some students, no doubt, more attention is paid to non-academic than to academic matters, but amongst the majority the pursuit of learning is as earnest as ever. On the whole, too, and in spite of the weight of numbers, standards have been maintained, but it has not been easy.

The role of the churches in post-war Ontario is much harder to assess, as they themselves are well aware. There is on the part of a number of people an assumption that the churches have relatively fewer members and less influence than was once the case. Statistics in the Canadian census are of limited value since few people list themselves as having no religion—in 1961 only 24,759 people in Ontario did so—and others are only nominal members of churches. The figures, such as they are, do show an absolute increase in numbers and a somewhat greater diversification. The Roman Catholic, United, and Anglican churches, in that order, have remained much the largest, with Presbyterians at about a third of the first, and Baptists and Lutherans at about half the figure for Presbyterians. The presence of substantial numbers of Greek Orthodox and Ukrainian (Greek) Catholics on the one hand and few Confucians or Buddhists on the other indicate the supremacy of European immigration over Asian.

The geographical distribution of church membership is broadly in conformity with the ethnic pattern of the province. Northeastern Ontario is about one-half Roman Catholic and northwestern Ontario about a third. The four counties in the southeast have a heavy Roman Catholic majority and Essex has close to a majority. In the remaining counties the churches are more evenly represented. Urbanization is one factor that has modified the character of churches, but there are still the many small towns and villages, the farming areas, and the thinly populated regions, especially in the north. The social conditions, the needs of parishioners, the financial resources of a congregation, their outlook, and the physical conditions under which a clergyman works will differ from one part to another.

Two main trends are apparent. One is toward church union. The chief accomplishment so far has been the formation in 1925 of the United Church of Canada, a merger of the Methodists, Congregationalists, and such of the Presbyterian congregations as chose to join the new body. The decision was not made easily for there are few subjects that can raise temperatures as quickly as this. In many a town there were fevered arguments and bitter controversy when the matter was under discussion. A split appeared only amongst the Presbyterians, for they preferred to vote by congregations, many of them opting out.

A second and much later proposal was in line with the œcumenical thinking at the middle of the century. In 1964 a committee representing the United and Anglican churches met to discuss the basis for a union between the two bodies and reported a series of principles on which they were agreed unanimously. There were to be "constitutional" bishops, a mutual recognition of ministries, and a single list of sacraments. The principles were approved almost unanimously by the general synod of the Anglican Church, the primate taking occasion to represent such a union, once accomplished, as a step towards a more general one, to include both Protestant churches and the Roman Catholic and Orthodox churches. There were critics too, more noticeable in the United Church, but the latter as a body did accept the principles somewhat later. It was stressed by those concerned in the negotiations that final action could not be expected before the end of several years.

The other trend has no such simple lines: it is the consideration of the proper policies and practices of the churches in society as it now is. In the sixties it seems a far cry to one of the most dramatic campaigns on behalf of fundamentalism, that led by T. T. Shields, minister of a Baptist church in Toronto in the nineteen-twenties. The issue over fundamentalism, however, has not disappeared from the Baptist and some other church bodies; and other indications of religious conservatism, in both town and country, are not lacking. The emphasis, however, has been on taking account of change. The Roman Catholic Church, traditionally considered conservative, has been in the van of the reformers, one important example being the decision—generally implemented in Ontario—to replace Latin with the vernacular. The Anglicans analysed themselves through a series of controversial books. The results of that exercise are not apparent, as yet at least; but the most striking reform has been the acceptance of remarriage after divorce, under conditions canonically defined.

Individual churches of various denominations have experimented with unorthodox or at least novel techniques thought to be agreeable to "modern" youth. "Rock and roll" music, for example, has been tried, and it is claimed with success. The churches, too, either as individual congregations or in their central bodies, have on occasion debated or taken positions on public affairs, national and especially international. The airing of opinions on such matters has, inevitably, received more publicity than continued concern for social problems.

The population of the province has been shown to be more widely, though unevenly, distributed. By covering a larger area it became in that sense more spread out. On the other hand the opposite effect was much more significant, that is that people were closer together. Mathematically this closeness took the form of density and concentrations. From another point of view it was caused by the fact that the centripetal forces set up by better transportation and communications were stronger than the centrifugal forces created by wider distribution. This was the reverse of the situation as it had existed up to late in the nineteenth century. Earlier the balance of advantage between one form of transport and another had shifted from time to time but before the middle of the twentieth century all the older means had improved and new ones had been added. Every method, with the exceptions of gravity and flowing water, of moving persons or objects from one place to another depends on a combination of locomotive force and a surface to carry the weight. If the two are out of adjustment the results are unsatisfactory. Travel can be on water, under water, on the ground, under the ground, or in the air. All these came to be utilized in Ontario with the exception of underwater travel which nowhere has been found useful, except in the form of tunnels, for civil purposes.

The latest and longest step in improving transportation by water was the St. Lawrence Seaway, opened in 1959. It allowed for 27-foot navigation from Montreal through the Welland Canal to Lake Erie. Beyond that vessels could continue to Lake Superior within the limits of the lesser depth of the Sault Ste. Marie Canal. In 1964 about 5,000 vessels passed through all or part of the seaway. Some (1,259) were ocean-going which meant that Ontario now had ocean ports in addition to those on Hudson Bay.

The railway, the *deus ex machina* of the later nineteenth century, fulfilled the requirements that have been mentioned: the rails made a surface and the steam engine provided locomotion. Technical improvements made the railway more effective, and it had one advantage over its rival the waterway in that it could be placed almost anywhere. It was a pioneer of the north country and turned like a homing pigeon to new mines or wherever else there was business to be found. But it was losing its character as an intimate member of the community. Passenger traffic dwindled and many little stations were pulled down, with the loss of one of the old centres where people gathered, chatted, and watched the trains. It used to be fun for small boys to put pennies on the tracks and count the cars on freight trains, but these high-speed monsters that disdained the local station were machines not characters. Somehow it seemed harder to personify the diesel than its predecessor—so much so that private railway societies conducted nostalgic excursions on special trains pulled by the last surviving steam locomotives. If the railways were becoming more and more restricted to long-haul freight they were still essential in that role, nor did they merit undue pity for resorting to what has always been the most profitable side of their operations.

It was the modernization of the road that was one of the main causes of this change in the business of the railway. Road transport has always had the peculiarity that the surface can never keep up with the traffic or the means of locomotion. For horse-drawn vehicles and in the overlapping days of the early motor car the roads were of low quality regardless of the volume or speed of traffic. As passenger cars, trucks, and buses increased in number, and as they became more demanding because of their weight and speed, good roads were built but never ahead of the vehicles that sought to use them. Nevertheless the modern highway with easy gradients and curves, up to twelve traffic lanes, and cleared of snow looks as if it came from another world in contrast with the mixture of mud and logs that passed for a road during much of the nineteenth century. But the demands on it are heavy. In 1964 there were 2,381,219 motor vehicles registered in Ontario. In heavily populated areas and on main highways it was an uneven race between new construction and traffic. Fortunately for the road builders their task has been facilitated by great machines which can perform any duty from shaping a simple gravel road to transforming the surface of the land to allow for new highways.

Whether for business or pleasure the network of roads has had a radical effect on the social life of Ontario. Large and small trucks carry freight from door to door, across the continent if need be. Buses cover more routes than it was ever economical for a railway to do, touching at almost every little town. Perhaps the bus station will some day be a place for chat as was the old local railway station. All that the bus needs is a whistle and a bell. Roads have been cut through hitherto inaccessible parts of the north. The Trans-Canada Highway took the old fur trade route by the Ottawa and Mattawa rivers to North Bay, hugged the shore of Lake Superior as far as Fort William, and thence inland through Kenora. The enterprising Highway 11 chose a far northerly line close to the Canadian National Railway, turned south to Fort William, and on to Fort Frances. Supplementary to these were connecting highways and access roads to mines and paper mills.

The aeroplane added a new dimension to transportation. It has the peculiarity that, apart from fields or bodies of water for take-off and landing, it needs no surface on land or water. It travels on the air which, like water, may be affected by weather; but there need be no fixed routes and there is no construction or maintenance between the points of departure and arrival. In this case, then, the equation between the vehicle and the element on which it moves is quite different from that in any other form of transportation.

Effective aircraft were first used in the War of 1914 and after it were turned to civil purposes in the northern parts of Ontario; the type of machine then existing was not suitable for inter-city traffic, nor was there a demand for this, but in the hands of the adventurous bush pilots it was ideal for many purposes in the north. Such aircraft were used for exploration and mapping, to convey many kinds of persons on their lawful occasions, and to carry freight to and from remote mines. A distance could be covered by air in one day instead of two or three weeks. As larger and more refined aeroplanes were developed they were employed on regular flights between cities, allowing passengers, goods, and mail to be transported with a saving of time comparable over long distances to the superiority of the railway over the stage coach. The prospector could now be landed with his equipment in a far part of the north or a business man of Toronto could fly to Montreal for a meeting and return in the same day.

Developments in transportation are important components of the process of mechanization. Mechanization, or technology to look at it from another angle, has applied across a broad front, particularly in the last generation. The farmer and the manufacturer were offered machines to take the place of manual labour. Mining benefited both from mechanical aids and from hydro-electric energy. The household accumulated a great number of labour-saving devices. "Automation"—the use of mechanical processes—was not in itself a new phenomenon in western countries. It had, for example, been an essential factor in the industrial revolution in England and had caused social disruption as well as efficiency in production. At that time, however, Ontario was too young to have any comparable experience. To some extent, of course, mechanization was known in the province in the nineteenth century, for instance in the introduction of steam threshing machines, but large-scale mechanization came only after the first war, gathering speed in the next decades.

Human ingenuity in exploiting the energy found in gasoline and electricity brought many obvious advantages: greater comfort in home life, widened opportunities for travel, speed in industry and agriculture. In a large province in the course of development the new means of accomplishing public works and facilitating private industry were of particular value. On the human side, however, the results were not all immediately beneficial. There was supposedly a neat sequence by which mechanization would reduce hours of labour and so make greater allowance for leisure. To some extent this worked out, but reduction in the demand for labour could also lead to unemployment. In particular the need for unskilled labour decreased as machines appeared to dig ditches, sweep the streets, pick up and carry objects, reap the crops, and so on. One remedial measure was to restrict the admission of unskilled labourers from other countries and another was to increase the facilities for technical education to the end that young people particularly would be equipped with various skills, ready for the new circumstances.

Distance contracted through communication as well as through transportation. The newspaper is the oldest form of communication in Ontario but over a century and a half its character has been steadily modified. Once the newspaper was distinctly local, not necessarily in the subject-matter of its columns, although that was true of some, but in its circulation. Moreover there were more newspapers in any one place and far more in comparison to population. A quite small town might have two or three newspapers and each would bear the personal imprint of the editor. And the same was true of cities. In 1892 Toronto had seven general newspapers (as well as many specialized ones), three of them having morning and evening editions. The pattern was then altered by two factors. One was the tendency toward large-scale business with amalgamations, and the other was the ease of transportation. Many small centres retained their own papers but if so their range narrowed to local affairs and they became secondary to the city papers which were delivered by train, truck, or aircraft over hundreds of miles. A resident of Ottawa, for instance, can read the one Toronto morning newspaper at his breakfast table.

The most radical change in communication came from the invention of radio and television. Radio broadcasting began in the nineteen-twenties. Techniques improved rapidly and coverage widened. By the fifties television was coming into common use. Radio particularly, and television only in lesser degree, could reach all but a small portion of the people of the province. Together they contributed to the ending of isolation. They brought news, domestic and foreign; educational programmes; political speeches and election results; entertainment of all kinds from westerns and simple comedy to music, ballet, and drama. An invalid could hear church services, a farmer the latest advice on methods of agriculture, those of all ages could see a hockey game or the opening of parliament. For children there are cartoons and stories.

Radio and television are not only additional forms of communication but have other features that are peculiar in this age. News and thought of other parts of the world have always come to Ontario through newspapers of the province, but can be selected or explained in them so as to relate to the interests and tastes of their readers. Only a very few people have been accustomed to purchase British or American or foreign-language papers. In the case of radio and television the same alternatives exist but, for technical reasons, in different proportions. Radio and television stations can, and do, broadcast programmes of non-Canadian origin which they themselves chose; but those who possess receiving sets (and most families in Ontario do) can readily turn to entertainment or ideas at their source. Through short-wave radios many parts of the world can be tuned in, but it is more common to use radios with limited range or television. The result will vary from one part of Ontario to another, but in some parts, including the Toronto-Hamilton area, users of both media have access to more American than Canadian stations.

Through these forms of communication, as in many other ways, southern Ontario is constantly exposed to American cultural influence. The question that arises here is not whether that influence is in itself undesirable—and indeed some of it, notably music, is in an international language—but rather its effect on the ethos of Ontario. To build an iron curtain that would exclude foreign productions would, to lovers of music and the arts, be an illogical form of self-denial. The more adult answer for a society as advanced as that of Ontario lies in encouraging and strengthening native genius. One of the obligations imposed on the Canadian Broadcasting Corporation when it was created in 1936 was that it should be predominantly Canadian; and it, together with the private stations, has means of promoting Canadian endeavours in the cultural field. The printed word, whether in the newspapers, periodicals, or books of Ontario, is another powerful factor to balance what is imported. In an earlier chapter D'Arcy McGee was quoted as lamenting the absence of books by Canadians. A century later the book shops of Ontario are rich in volumes on many subjects, written and published in the province. In painting and music there is a flowering of ability and occasionally of genius. It is an indication of the strength rather than the weakness of the native contribution that the symphony orchestra in Toronto should have in the late 1960s a Japanese conductor.

Ontario did not lose its identity when it joined with other provinces in the union of 1867 or subsequently because of the external pulls of the British Empire and the United States. In later years its ethnic composition has become far more mixed, but this has enriched rather than distorted the basic character of the province. It remains determinedly Canadian, but as a unit in a federation which is different to the Atlantic or western provinces or to Quebec. Some of its people think that it leans too much this way or that: too British, American, or French; or alternatively too little of any of the three. To a casual visitor its cities look identical with those of the United States, but the superficial is misleading. The nature of a society cannot be expressed in a word or a phrase, least of all in a large province with wide variation in conditions. Critics have called Ontario prejudiced, smug, or dull. It depends on the point of view. Those who live in the modern province draw—largely unconsciously—on the themes of the near and remote past: of the frontier pioneer, the stern moralist, the engineer, scientist, soldier, man of learning; on the North American spirit of enterprise and the British concept of justice. The result, of course, is an amalgam, for no society has a single characteristic. But it is an amalgam peculiar to Ontario and recognized by those who maintain its continuity.

CHAPTER THIRTEEN

Cities of the South

THE CITIES OF SOUTHERN ONTARIO are in appearance North American; and if they lack the interest found in ancient buildings and winding streets they have been fortunate in growing in an age in which the problems that bore so heavily on the cities of Britain and Europe—order, cleanliness, and public services— could more readily be solved. Ontario cities have no long history in comparison with those of the old world from which their people came, but long enough to build up identifiable and differing characteristics and increasingly to lead citizens to study the past. For those looking back to earlier times the visual record has been depleted by the destruction of fine buildings of the nineteenth century; even though the province had never had Roman remains, Gothic cathedrals, or examples of Wren's genius there were houses worth preserving. Nor was any Ontario city fully planned like Washington or redesigned like Paris. Some of the very early schemes for what were more villages than towns showed imagination and foresight, but as the places grew improvisation all too often took over.

Of the twenty-five cities of southern Ontario most are quite small and the great majority are either on Lake Ontario or not north of the line of the lower lakes. Only one has a population of more than half a million. Their rates of growth have varied. One or two have actually decreased, some moved forward slowly, and others rapidly. Minor cities have retained a relatively simple and consistent structure; a few of the major ones have become metropolitan areas.

"Metropolitanism" is a word which has been used with various connotations, and is sometimes hardly distinguishable from urbanization. In the present connection it is taken to describe two related conditions. One, extension of influence into a region beyond municipal boundaries, will become evident in the later study of towns and rural districts. The other is at once the magnitude of urban concentration and the development of a different form of municipal government because of that. Thus "Metropolitan Toronto," created by provincial statute in 1953, was a combination of the city itself (which retained its entity) and twelve suburban municipalities. They were united federally with the suburbs keeping local authority and being also represented on the metropolitan council. It was a device designed to improve and make uniform such public services as police, transportation, water supply, sewage, parks, planning, and finance in a geographical area in which there were no breaks in building and where such services had been uneven in quality or had suffered from fragmentation. Other large metropolitan areas are Ottawa, Hamilton, and London.

A city proper is in the centre with the metropolitan area around it. Beyond that may be a planning area. In the case of Toronto a planning area meant adding five townships, the whole then covering some 720 square miles. Even this was not the end for there can be suburbs that do not fall even within the planning area but are tied to Toronto by economic bonds. For those cities which may not have reached the metropolitan stage in the sense of form of government the territorial spread into the surrounding countryside has a manner and an extent unknown until after the end of the second war. The large cities themselves have little increase of population, their growth being in the outlying districts. By the middle sixties as many people lived in the suburbs of Toronto as had been in the city itself before the second war.

Suburbs are, then, important factors in urban life. They are not always distinguishable. Starting from the centre of a city a visitor may drive through the older residential parts and beyond them into others which are marked by non-Victorian and newer houses and by smaller trees. At some point he leaves the city proper and so goes into suburbia. The transition may not be at once apparent but soon the scenery will change. There are two distinct types of suburbs, as may be seen in the leading case of Toronto.

One has developed out of what was formerly an independent and self-contained village or town, such places as Cooksville, Brampton, Oakville, Markham, or Whitby. They did not originate as suburbs (which, indeed, were not known at the time) and they went about their own business and created their own societies. If life in them differed from that in Toronto it was not because they were suburbs but because they were small. As business expanded in Toronto men were drawn to it for daily employment, going at first by train and later by bus or automobile. The next stage, and it was a gradual one, was metropolitanism in the form of overshadowing of the local community. Local retail business was in part absorbed and the city physically spread out and surrounded the towns. The net result was a compromise. In some respects the town lost its own character but a part of it was preserved. Local governments adjusted themselves as best they could to the inrush of inhabitants. It was sometimes impractical to expand public services and schools at a rate sufficient to meet the needs of all the intending residents so control was maintained by restricting the number of building permits. The little towns, partly overwhelmed, stood as a mixture of the old and the new, keeping something of their traditions and their identity.

The other kind of suburb is an entirely new creation. Open farmland is invaded by an army of men and machines and before long roads and houses spring out of nothing and are followed by shopping centres. There is no existing nucleus, social or administrative. A magic wand has been waved by the developer, producing houses which, in the opinion of purchasers, may or may not be well built. New suburbs tend to vary in direct ratio to the cost of the houses in them. Paved roads sometimes come quickly, otherwise plain mud persists for months. Drains, street lighting, and transportation are good in some, inadequate in others. Motives for moving into suburbs are several. A common one, especially for those limited to low-price houses, is that small houses within a city are scarce, and if available at all too expensive. For such people it is not the appeal of suburbia as such that draws them but the fact that houses can be found there. Other families seek to escape from apartments and crowded streets into surroundings more suitable for children. The more expensive suburbs are deemed to offer good addresses.

All types of suburbs added together account for a large proportion of an urban population but fall into no single social scheme. Some of the people living in the formerly separate towns may be from families which have been there for two or three generations, have established houses with gardens, and enjoy the advantages of full public services, shops, movies, clubs, and friends. They are joined by others who are attracted by such amenities or are just seeking shelter wherever it can be found. In the newer suburbs, especially in the lower-priced ones, a much larger proportion of the people have made no conscious choice of *milieu*. Financing their houses, even with small down payments and mortgages, is a heavy burden for many. For such people, rather than for those in the older and more restricted suburbs, there can be worry and a sense of isolation. Some residents of the higher-class suburbs, on the contrary, resent what they consider to be an over-developed sense of community spirit in suburbia and retreat into the anonymity of a city. For all suburbanites the factor of transportation looms large, consuming time and money and patience. Yet it may be transportation that holds the key to the future. If that could be sufficiently improved the distinction between the outer fringes of a city and its nearby suburbs, marginal in any case, might disappear completely.

Buildings throughout the urban areas fall into no simple categories. In fast-growing cities, large or small, new construction and new styles are more evident than old, notably in business districts and suburbs. Landmarks disappear overnight and great new districts are added. The most conspicuous feature is the high building, whether for commercial or for residential purposes, and the height continues to increase year by year. Less obvious is the parallel trend toward lower buildings, for factories and related purposes, schools, and suburban houses. To some extent the high building is explained by the value and scarcity of ground space, but not altogether so for large complexes of apartment houses spring out of the mud of distant fields. It is, however, generally true that height prevails where space is at a premium. The construction of both kinds has been facilitated by machines that quickly dig out the foundations, whether deep or wide. Skyscrapers have been made more possible by enormous cranes and other devices. The availability of air conditioning has allowed for modification in floor plans, for with it there can be rooms without windows. With better lighting, ventilation, and plumbing factories escaped the criticisms formerly made against them.

The apartment is now a common feature of urban life but a comparatively new one. At the beginning of the century there were hardly any apartment houses in Ontario and it was not much before the middle of the twentieth that they became common. The sight of so many of them now has tended to conceal the fact that far more people live in detached houses than in any other kind of dwelling. In 1961 Toronto was the only city in Ontario in which there were more apartments than houses, but if the metropolitan area be taken the proportion changes to that obtaining in other large cities, about half as many. Old houses do not survive in cities as often as in the country, but all cities have some, whether in good style or in bad. That earlier outlet for self-expression, the so-called mansion, became rare after the twenties. When smaller houses in central residential areas became scarce, large ones with large gardens or wide frontage (but no domestic servants and long tax bills) were torn down, making room for several semi-detached ones. This type of house, once popular and then for long unfashionable, achieved new respectability by being re-named "town house," but was given a more substantive dignity by a return to quasi-Georgian lines. The main explanation of the large number of houses, however, is to be found in the miles of streets stretching farther and farther from the centre.

Building and purchase of houses has depended on mortgage lending. For this there are three sources: banks; life insurance, loan, and trust companies; and the federal government. The last entered the field initially through the Dominion Housing Act of 1935 with the dual purpose of reducing unemployment and providing houses. A series of subsequent Acts included one of 1945 which established the Central Mortgage and Housing Corporation, to be primarily an agency for administering the National Housing Act, as it had been re-named.

New dwellings were delayed first by the depression and then by war, and it was only after both that the rush to build houses and apartments got under way. By that time there was a serious shortage, aggravated by the return of military personnel from overseas and by the growth of population. One result of delay followed by intensive action was that a considerable proportion of buildings were new; and if they showed no general flowering of architectural genius on the whole they were not unpleasing. Taking old and new together the level of equipment was high. Four small cities in different parts of southern Ontario will serve as examples. In three of these few dwellings were without baths although some were shared between families. In all four most dwellings had indoor flush toilets and many had more than one. The pattern in large cities was similar. That most dwellings were so well provided indicates general comfort, but the fact that there were exceptions points to the presence of sub-standard housing.

Housing faces two principal problems. One is the continuation of over-all shortage, as the number of dwelling units continually lags behind the growth of population. It is a question which has received increasing attention by provincial and municipal governments. The other is the existence of slums in parts of the cities, a situation which seems inconsistent with the generally higher standard of living, though by no means new. A special advisory committee set up by the Board of Control of Toronto in 1934 on the suggestion of the lieutenant-governor, Dr. H. A. Bruce, turned their attention to two districts in Toronto that were known to have slums, Moss Park and the Ward. After examining 1,332 dwellings the committee concluded that 96 per cent fell below a minimum standard in respect of central heating, lighting, freedom from vermin, inside plumbing, and cooking facilities; that 75 per cent fell below a minimum standard of health; that 59 per cent had no baths, 20 per cent no inside toilets, and 55 per cent were verminous. This was in the middle of the depression. Ten years later a committee of citizens made a submission to the city council describing the housing situation in Toronto as unsatisfactory and calling for a low-rental housing programme financed publicly. They then argued not on the ground of charity but of public interest:

Figures from many reports from Great Britain, the U.S.A. and Canada have shown clearly the connection between bad housing and the breakdown of decent social standards in a community. It is clear that juvenile delinquency, crime and vice thrive in an environment of bad housing. In terms of taxes, for the taxpayer this means increased police, fire protection and health rates and a high cost for private social service agencies, in relation to better housed areas. On this score many of these surveys have indicated clearly that it is the slum that makes the slum dweller, not the slum dweller the slum, and therefore with the elimination of the slum one tends to get the elimination of lower social standards.

The major experiment in rehabilitating a slum area was in Regent Park, a portion of the Moss Park area in the southeastern part of Toronto. Plans were made for a housing centre to cover several blocks and including apartment houses, houses, a community hall, and playgrounds for different ages. By 1951 part of it was occupied and by 1957 the whole was completed. There were 56 houses in rows and 1,233 apartments. The historian of Regent Park, Albert Rose, is satisfied that the evidence shows a marked degree of rehabilitation from the beginning. It was not all immediate. To the surprise of almost everyone concerned juvenile delinquency increased at first but, to their relief, decreased sharply in most of the immediately succeeding years.

Initiative in housing has remained primarily in the private sector but slum clearance and the more recent projects of the Ontario government for making available serviced lots are public services. With such exceptions as telephone and gas, public services have long been the responsibility of municipal governments. They include street lighting, policing, water, sanitation, collection of garbage, and fire protection. It is only when unusual circumstances interrupt any one of them that it becomes evident how dependent a city is on services which normally its citizens take for granted. During part of the War of 1939 electricity was so much in demand that it became necessary to cut off the supply to residences for some hours in each day. Citizens dashed to shops or their summer cottages for oil lamps, stable lanterns, or candles and it was a strange sight to walk along a city street and see houses lit only by flickering candles. Thunder or ice storms occasionally produce the same result, depriving houses of light, heat, and capacity to cook. Any pleasure from the thought of a return to the hardy life of the pioneers is quickly cancelled out by the inconvenience.

Transportation is in part a private and in part a public responsibility, but the latter is the more essential. The number of motor cars and trucks is limited only by the whims or pocket books of the owners, but their useful operation is governed by the inadequacy of the roads, by traffic control, and snow clearance. What was earlier noted as the situation on highways is true also of city streets: it is well nigh impossible to provide enough road space to accommodate the vehicles. In rush hours seemingly endless lines of cars imprison their occupants for protracted periods and the pursuit of parking places becomes a national sport. The private motor car, in spite of its many advantages, is the chief obstacle to the rapid movement of people and goods since it occupies on the streets the maximum space for the number of passengers. The problem before city planners, then, is to provide public transport that will not only cater to those without cars but attract as many as possible of those who have them.

Toronto has had the most varied experience as well as the largest number of people to carry. In 1921 the nine separate transit systems were amalgamated under the Toronto Transportation Commission, and in a matter of weeks the first buses appeared on the streets. They were double-deckers, and with solid tires must have kept awake even the most sleepy riders. From then on street cars and buses divided the load until the first subway line was completed in 1954, after having been proposed in 1910. Travellers within Metropolitan Toronto now had a wide choice but cars from the suburbs still clogged the roads in great traffic jams. To overcome this the provincial government in co-operation with the Canadian National Railways built a new suburban rail service known as "Go" trains. The experiment was an immediate success but it would be impossible to calculate how many cars it took off the road. What it certainly did was to afford effortless journeys for those who chose to use it.

Such are some of the principal physical characteristics of the cities of southern Ontario at about the middle of the twentieth century. One of the interests in the actors on this urban stage is in the variety of ethnic strains. Cities were not equally affected. Some medium-sized ones—London, Kingston, and Brantford for example—are still predominantly British. Hamilton is more mixed and Windsor more so again. Toronto, the largest, has come to be only half British. In it there were 77,898 Italians in 1961 and the number has increased since that time. The three other largest groups—Polish, Ukrainian, and German—were each about a third of that size.

The word "group," commonly used in this context, could imply a series of separate blocs in the sense of people of similar racial origin living close to each other or gathering for social purposes. To some extent both do happen, more especially in the lower income brackets. Sections of cities come to take on a particular ethnic colouring with shops catering to the habits of the people concerned. Associations, churches, and foreign-language newspapers are aimed at people of various European origins. On occasion the recent arrival finds himself in this sense segregated. A young Italian, to whom it was suggested that there were many of his countrymen in the same city, replied suggestively "too many." The ideal balance between retention of inherited culture and adaptation to the life of the new land is not easily reached.

European immigrants of the first generation and the smaller numbers of the second are found in most occupations: in the professions, as artisans, labourers, shopkeepers. A large hospital is an ethnic laboratory in itself. A patient reported being cared for by a Scottish head nurse, another nurse clearly from Yorkshire, an Iranian intern, German orderly, Japanese barber, and West Indian housemaid. Restaurants have sprung up to provide the food of many countries. Hairdressers and barbers speak many languages. A customer of a barber shop may learn about Tunisia or the Netherlands, about football in Europe, or the restoration of Florentine art treasures from the omnipresent Italian. Taxi drivers seem to come from most parts of the world and the ominous ticking of the meter can be stilled by a lecture on the present state of Hungary. The ranks of cleaning women seem to be filled largely by the wives of recent European immigrants working to get the homes they all want. Because they often have little or no knowledge of English they inspire halting excursions into foreign tongues by employers. To the universities of Ontario come teachers and students from around the map, the latter normally for temporary residence. In this setting, as in music, the arts, and the drama the larger Ontario cities have been enabled by the presence of foreign residents or visitors to approach more nearly to cosmopolitanism than at any time in the past.

The economic life of a city is complex and the occupations in it correspondingly varied but there are limits. It cannot participate directly in agriculture, fishing, mining, or the forest industries, although these are indirectly important to its financial and manufacturing functions, which are perhaps the two economic hallmarks of a city. Financial institutions absorb a considerable segment of executive and clerical workers. The commercial banks have followed the trend toward large-scale organization. In 1901 there were thirty-four in all Canada and by 1966 only eight, all operating to some extent in Ontario. Partly as a result of the size and strength of the banks the risk of insolvency disappeared, the last failure being in 1923. In the same sixty-five years, however, the number of branches in the province rose from 349 to 2,022. Your "friendly" and your "neighbourhood" bank popped up everywhere, offering to lend you money in implied competition with the small loan companies that were also to be found everywhere. Financial needs in commercial or personal affairs were filled out by various institutions including insurance companies, trust companies, and stock brokers. All these various organizations also account for the employment of many people.

Not all manufacturing is in the southern cities but the lion's share is in them or in their vicinities. In its various forms manufacturing calls for many categories of personnel from managers and engineers to those on hourly wages. Other large numbers of people are involved in meeting demands that arise out of finance and manufacturing, and in doing so not only swell the population but themselves create further demands. The professional classes embrace doctors, dentists, lawyers, clergy, teachers, and architects. The building industry is on a large scale and has many sides, it too occupying a variety of people. The whole complex of municipal services involves many men and women.

Retail trade is prominent in any city and is one of the principal agencies of metropolitanism. The transition of shops from small individual enterprises into the realm of big business has long been evident but reached major proportions only after the second war. The independent local shop did not disappear and remained the favourite of a limited number of people, but it was overshadowed and in many cases absorbed by the other types: department store, co-operative, and chain store. Up to 1941 the proportion of business conducted by those of the second group did not increase greatly, but the figures for twenty years later are very different. In 1961 the smallest shops in the province had together sales of approximately $27 million and the largest had over $2,000 million. These big shops took over much of the wholesale as well as the retail functions and were centred in the main cities. In the chain stores, which handle principally food, housewives trundle little carts into which they drop goods picked off the shelves, thus achieving exercise and, they are satisfied, economy. The department stores have apparently not suffered from the success of the chain stores, partly because the lines of goods are not on the whole competitive. The former continue to provide free delivery and credit.

The above are some examples of the multiple occupations in a city. For those who wish to explore in more detail the goods and services available a full list can be found in the Yellow Pages of a telephone directory. A dip at random into the Toronto directory opens it at the letter P and these are some of the principal items under it: packaging and packing, paint and painters, parts manufacturers, paper (with many sub-divisions), parcel delivery, parking areas, pastry shops, patent attorneys, paving contractors, pawnbrokers, pens, perfumes and cosmetics, personnel consultants, pet shops, pharmacies, photocopying and photographs, physicians and surgeons, pianos, picture frames, plastic products, plating, plumbing, power transmission equipment, printers, publishers, pumps, and pyjamas. By adding the other letters of the alphabet one would have a bewildering array of forms of employment.

One occupation that is not welcome to society is that of the criminal. The published statistics of offences apply to the province as a whole. They have shown a rise, though not on the face of it a startling one, in the last few years. There are, of course, large numbers of convictions in connection with the operation of motor vehicles; but it is such crimes as burglary and assault that particularly affect the lives of city-dwellers. The impression is general that cities are less secure in such respects than they used to be. Women have learned to be cautious about walking alone after dark in residential districts once considered safe. Petty thefts, purse-snatching, and more serious crimes are thought to be more common. Citizens have been held up on the streets by men carrying knives or revolvers. Robberies of shops and banks are frequently reported in the newspapers. There has been increasing talk of the existence of "organized crime." The police forces have gained certain advantages such as rapid transport, radio communication, and scientific laboratories, but on the other hand the criminals have been opportunists in respect of technical aids. If it is true that society is less secure against those who prey on it there is little indication that communities accept the challenge. The police have been reported as finding a lack of support from the public.

In a happier vein is the record of those who make positive contributions to society in the realms of learning and the arts. The cities have had no monopoly, but in them are universities, governments, head offices of large corporations, art galleries, museums, music halls, theatres, and concentrations of people interested in, and supporters of, endeavours in these fields.

From small beginnings there emerged in the universities of the province new studies of the history, government, and economy of Ontario and of Canada as a whole. A number of important books embodying new research and interpretation stimulated further study by students, and so a self-perpetuating school of scholarship has created a deeper understanding of past and present.

Similarly, within and without the universities, examinations were made of the physical make-up of the province—soil, minerals, and climate; the habits of animals, birds, and fishes; problems of the human body and mind; the social behaviour of the people. A further stage was the application of scientific investigations to the proper treatment and use of soil and preservation of forests; control of insects and other enemies of agriculture; sanitation, medicine, and care of the mentally defective. Amongst the rich results of such applied studies was the discovery of insulin, a means of controlling diabetes, by Sir Frederick Banting and Dr. C. H. Best in 1921.

Recognition of the growing place of science and technology in industry caused the provincial government to establish the Ontario Research Foundation and a number of private companies to devote increasing attention to research and experiment. West of Toronto the Ontario Research Community at Sheridan Park began in 1963 to accommodate the Foundation and the research centres of a number of firms. The objective was to draw together thirty companies and 6,000 research workers on one site. Other experimental laboratories have been planned or instituted at Hamilton, Sarnia, and elsewhere. These and related activities constitute Ontario's answer to the challenge that industry must be up to date, must be technically advanced, if it is to compete successfully in the modern world.

The application of learning and experiment in such ways as have been mentioned is directed toward having a better informed, a healthier, and a prosperous people. It is more difficult to categorize another group of the fruits of the human mind, those sometimes labelled as "culture," a word which has too many meanings and interpretations. Music and the arts are traditionally related to advanced civilizations, and for some of the artists are ends in themselves. It is from such a selfless spirit of creation that one might expect timeless portraits, musical compositions, or verse. It is only realistic to admit at once that Ontario has had few such productions that measure up to the highest international standards. The comforting theory that such relative failure is explained by pioneer conditions, by emphasis on building the country, is without conviction. Few of those who have lived in the province in the last two or three generations ever saw pioneer life or consciously devoted their whole energies to building the province or the nation. It would be more accurate to say that the genius of the people lies more in the physical, in the practical. From amongst them have come more engineers and scientists of distinction than artists. The majority can, for example, live happily without good music; and it would be hard to find one who would forgo dinner in order to pay for a ticket to the opera as did the Viennese during the depression.

In the story of a people, however, it is less important to award marks in imaginary international competitions than to explore the ways in which their lives are enriched by participation or interest in those arts which portray nature and man in beauty and ugliness, which inspire emotions and reflection, which amuse or depress, which convey loveliness or grim reality. To describe music and the arts as entertainment may seem to be depreciation but they have little meaning divorced from listeners and audiences. They are educational within their own orbits but essentially are intended to please, amuse, or edify the public. The distinction between the professional and the amateur is blurred. Some of the best poetry has come from the pens of men and women who had other occupations; musical composition and performance, however, have rested largely in the hands of those not otherwise engaged.

Ontario writers have been prolific in most fields, although least in the gentle and sophisticated art of essay writing. There has been a notable increase in the number of periodicals, some of comment, some literary, and others learned journals. The shelves of novels and poetry have grown long. Though more tributes have been paid to the poets, the novelists of the fifties and sixties have shown greater versatility than formerly. For both media the range of subjects has been wide, but, as in other parts of the world, a large number of writers have given all or part of their attention to their province and their country. The approaches have been as varied as the land itself and the interests of the authors, as a few examples will show. In the nineteen-twenties Mazo de la Roche began, with her prize-winning novel, *Jalna*, a series of studies of rural Ontario. Over the same period Morley Callaghan wrote, in a very different mood, about the cities of central Canada. Robertson Davies recaptured, in a critical vein, aspects of the life of a small Ontario city. Of E. J. Pratt's narrative poems two are on major historical themes. *Brébeuf and his Brethren* is the story of the martyrdom of the Jesuit missionaries in

Huronia, and *Towards the Last Spike* of the national enterprise of building a railway across the provinces, recently joined politically.

The drama was popular from the earliest days of the province, but commercial theatres lost ground as motion pictures matured. Where they survive they subsist in the main on visiting road shows with a few Canadian performances added. That appreciation of good plays performed by professionals has not died is demonstrated both by the continued existence of large city theatres and by the success of the Stratford Shakespearean Festival which was organized in 1953 by a group of practical idealists. Starting with the production of Shakespeare's plays in a tent they found that they had rapidly become an institution attracting visitors from all over Canada and beyond it. The tent was replaced by a large theatre and the repertoire was extended to include other playwrights, opera, ballet, and music. Elsewhere a large number of theatres have been built, or more often improvised. In some of them are local professional companies but the bulk of the participants are amateurs ranging from undergraduates to experienced actors and actresses. There are summer theatres, some of them in barns, some in cities. They perform tragedy and comedy, old plays and new, some of the latter being written by Ontario playwrights. The Dominion Drama Festival, originated in 1933, has since then been a focus of amateur activity and is preceded by regional competitions. Radio affords another medium for reading plays and has been extensively used for that purpose. Television, with obviously greater possibilities, has been less utilized.

The theatre, then, has been maintained as a professional art while providing as well a hobby for many amateurs. The same is true of painting and sculpture. In the National Gallery in Ottawa and the Art Gallery of Ontario in Toronto there are examples of many schools of foreign and Canadian painting. The opportunity to look at pictures, in these and smaller galleries, both public and commercial and in private collections, is the form of participation accepted by the largest number of people and can be a mixture of education and enjoyment. The majority of professional artists in Ontario have painted landscapes. Some of these subjects have been found in other countries and some in Ontario from the bleak north to the cities and the gently rolling farmland of the south. In style and subject artists have varied from forms of the traditional to the non-objective. Amateur painters have produced results good, bad, and indifferent. Some of them have natural gifts enhanced through lessons. The point, however, is not so much to judge the quality as to recognize another interesting hobby. A stockbroker, a widow, or a university professor finds equal enjoyment in painting, whether or not he or she ever exhibits.

In music the amateur is less seen as a performer. Forty or fifty years ago it was customary for children to have lessons on the piano (sometimes with agonizing results) and for accomplished amateurs to join together for the performance of choral or instrumental music, or to entertain themselves around the piano at a casual gathering in a private house. This pleasant practice was reduced by the gramophone, but is being restored in a somewhat different form by music in the schools. At the same time professional orchestras, string quartets, individual instrumentalists, and singers have developed within the province and have found wider support. Some good, if not great, music has been written by Ontario composers and is performed in the many concert halls or over the radio by local organizations. People in the cities, too, have the pleasure of listening to singers, instrumentalists, or orchestras from other countries. Thus the urban people of Ontario, while losing something of value that they once had in the making of their own music, will by other means be found to have music as no lesser part of their lives.

Ballet is the newest of the arts in Ontario, having aroused wide popular interest only in the last twenty years or so. In addition to amateur and semi-professional groups is the National Ballet Company which is the ranking organization in the province. Visits by ballet companies from other parts of Canada and from other countries indicate the growing audiences.

As the cities of Ontario grew older and larger they became more complicated in the sense that more kinds of people chose different modes of life. The ordered society of the turn of the century faded less quickly in the smaller cities than in the large. In a little city like, say, Woodstock or Stratford or even in a bigger one like Kingston a recognizable "society" (in the narrow sense of the word) continues to exist. In Toronto this broke down completely under the very weight of the population and the variety of people who had come to live in it. The families who from the days of old York had been the leaders of society did not cease to exist: they faded with little regret into the background of their friends and interests. The new pattern had its own appeal just because it was not all of one piece. Europeans are everywhere evident. Toronto shares with Montreal the domicile of some three-quarters of the Jews of Canada, people who have come to take a more active part in the city than formerly. A growing consular corps adds a near facsimile of diplomatic life. Wealth in a degree previously unknown is another element. The pattern might most aptly be compared to a series of circles based on common interests, wealth, ethnic origin, location, background, sheer accident, or any combination of them. The circles can overlap but normally do not; on the other hand they are seldom in competition with each other. A visitor armed with introductions will probably fall into one circle; another, with a different set of letters, will move in a second circle. Toronto, like all large cities, should socially be thought of in the plural.

The same is found true by applying the economic measure. There are rich, moderately wealthy, adequately provided, and positively poor inhabitants. Lines of broken down, bug-infested houses stand in grim contrast to the great houses on large grounds or even to the modest comfort of the average middle class or artisan family. The former linger as the skeleton in the urban cupboard which is pushed shut by those who do not want to see and pressed open by those who urge reform. The average standard of living, however, is high, and it is neither the very rich nor the very poor that are typical.

This great middle group may live in a city or its suburbs, in flats or in houses. Conditions of living are influenced by a series of developments over the past generation. More members of a household have paid jobs. The division of labour between the man who earned the daily bread and the woman who looked after the house and the children has become less fixed. Women of the type who were once domestic servants were siphoned off into industry and trade, with their places only partly taken by the cleaning woman employed by the day. Almost gone, too, are the handymen of the early part of the century, those who stoked the furnace, cut the grass, put on the double windows, cleared the snow, and did minor repairs.

Into the breach marched first the man of the household whose five-day week left room for other than paid work. Young fathers learned the mysteries—hidden from their fathers—of the care of small children, of cooking and housework. They turned their hands to gardening, painting, and carpentry. Usually the "do-it-yourself" practice originates in economy but often continues as a hobby. And team work extended to many tasks. A man and his wife can share the duties of putting the children to bed and then both reach for paint brushes to restore the walls.

Their ally is technology. They cut the grass themselves but with a power mower. The furnace feeds itself. The house is full of machines and gadgets. Mother can toss the clothes into a washer, place the dishes in another, pull the vacuum cleaner out of the cupboard. Father can start the day with an electric shaver and on return from his labours cut the joint with an electric carver. After watching television he brushes his teeth electrically before laying his exhausted frame under an electric blanket. Wakened next morning by a tune on the radio he consumes the products of an electric stove and a toaster, pushes the button to open the garage door, sets off in a car which all but drives itself to commune with a computer or nurse a machine in a factory. The children having gone to school, mother checks on the frozen food and mixes, sets the stove with its built-in brain, and departs to her job.

Styles in clothes are less subject to technology than is their means of manufacture. At the time of the first war women's clothes had long since lost the complications of Victorian style, being in general severely simple with high necks, long sleeves and skirts. Men's clothes changed little except that the frock coat was turning into a morning coat and, with the top hat, being relegated to very special occasions. In the twenties costume for women was in tune with a general reaction against convention. For perhaps the first time in modern western history evening dresses were made with high necks and short skirts, an unorthodox balance continued into the day time by the disappearance of the female head into the cloche hat. During the depression these designs gave place to the return of some conservatism modified by the liberation of the human form from what came to be considered undue covering. Bathing dresses for women shed enough yards of cloth to permit of swimming, and men won the right to appear on public beaches in shorts. Children were at last given more sensible clothes which allowed sun and air to play on their legs and arms. In the fifties and sixties young men rejected matching jackets and trousers, and in the sixties for young women the imported mini skirt became the mode.

Leisure has increased with shorter hours of work. Some of the time saved is devoted to domestic tasks but there is opportunity for recreation too. Sport is one form. Golf can be an expensive game but is not necessarily so. Tennis, bowling, and curling have many adherents. Ski-ing became well known in Ontario in the twenties and has the advantage of being a family game in which youngsters (being apparently made of rubber) threaten to outclass their parents. Hockey and football are played at schools and universities and the former especially is variously sponsored in innumerable leagues for all ages up from toddlers. But the greater amateur clubs of the twenties have faded into history. Both hockey and football became big business for the entertainment of the public, financed by immediate spectators and television rights. Hobbies from crossword puzzles to pottery, from chess to barbecues in the garden, appeal to different tastes.

Life in a city can be seen as offering comfort built on facilities and services, with a wide range of occupations, and with many different ways of spending leisure time. To a portion of the people who live in one the choice is of a quiet home life with perhaps informal gatherings with friends and the occasional movie. For others there are gay restaurants, theatres, or dances. One citizen may eagerly watch professional hockey and another follow lectures on archaeology; one turn to weekly bowling and another to his comfortable chair and a good book. Yet what to many seems flexibility is to others artificial and conventional. A mystic, a poet, or an artist may withdraw from what seem to him intolerable routines into a carefully guarded corner, to be in the city but not of it. Less unobtrusive is another form of minority, the so-called "hippies," whose programme for a better world has as yet to be more exactly defined for the ordinary citizen to understand. Such groups, however, seem to be essentially urban.

A more common reaction to city life is claustrophobia. In serious cases this drives the sufferer to villages or more rarely to farms. But the average case is mild, and can be cured by intermittent doses of the open air. As always, the summer cottage on the Rideau Lakes, Lake Huron, or in Muskoka is the summer resort of a family, even if the teen-age members may be absent on summer jobs. For those without such bases or wishing to be in the country over a longer part of the year parks within driving distance may be the answer. "Park" perhaps suggests something more restricted and formal than are the Conservation Areas which are being opened up in many parts of the province. Conservation, of course, is not designed exclusively for recreation: it includes flood control, water conservation, management of fish and wild life, and reforestation. Consistent with these objectives, however, is freedom to range over unspoiled country. Within reach of Toronto, for instance, are Conservation Areas of from 150 to nearly 1,000 acres. Visitors may go by the day or camp there for protracted periods. The Areas are provided with picnic tables, washrooms, and refreshment booths. They offer swimming, boating, fishing, and nature walks. Many of the areas are open in the winter for ski-ing, sleigh rides, and snowmobile trails. Heated buildings have open fires and changing rooms. The provincial parks constitute a parallel network of recreation areas. Many of them are in northern Ontario but by no means all. They too are—in the words of the Ontario government—"to provide for the people of Ontario outdoor space in which they may enjoy the kinds of recreation usually associated with the natural environment such as camping, swimming, boating, fishing, hunting, hiking, skiing, and the general enjoyment of nature." That they meet a real demand is shown by the nine million people who visited them in 1964.

Another, and increasingly popular, cure for claustrophobia is to buy a farm or part of one within reach of a city. Those—the minority—who daily go to their urban places of work would resent being called suburbanites. They, together with the majority who are week-enders or travel to and fro only throughout the summer, are in search of the simple life (with some added luxuries). Sometimes farming is attempted (at a financial loss); more often a bit of gardening, tree-planting, house-painting, and the hundred and one forms of manual labour that compensate for desks and apartments.

All these forms of exodus to the outdoors, of some participation in rural life, might together be thought of as one of the pleasanter forms of metropolitanism, in personal rather than financial terms. But it would be a mistake to think of that great Ontario beyond the southern cities as the playground for the cities; it has its own life and its own interest.

CHAPTER FOURTEEN

Beyond the
Main Cities

METROPOLITANISM in the sense of influence by a large urban centre over smaller ones and over rural areas has existed for many years but in minor degree. The bank in a small town was a branch controlled by a distant headquarters. Railways, planned as far away, could make or break a town. Little industries were sucked off to the cities. Eaton's catalogue has always been required reading on many farms. The enlarged force of metropolitanism, however, as it was known by the mid-twentieth century, was made possible by new factors: the trend toward large-scale enterprises, the merging of wholesale and retail functions, and—above all—the efficiency of road transportation.

The principal medium of metropolitanism is retail trade. The geographical range is wide. In Muskoka and Georgian Bay the supply boat was a victim. No longer can children (and grown-up children) run down to the dock at the sound of the supply boat's whistle and have the fun of exploring a floating shop. Much farther north the Toronto department stores—though rarely the chain stores found in Toronto—are represented in cities and towns from Timmins to Kenora. In the south both department stores and chain shops are everywhere, the former through order offices. The final blow to the old régime is an order office blatantly occupying a dignified building which was once a station hotel, the meeting place of travelling salesmen, the forum for political debate.

The effects of the invasion are widespread and considerable; but they are not simple. They do not result in complete domination or altogether overpower the local economy. Walk along the main street of a little town. You pass a bank or two, but they were always there. Here at intervals are two chain stores and a co-operative, but between them are local grocers, a butcher,

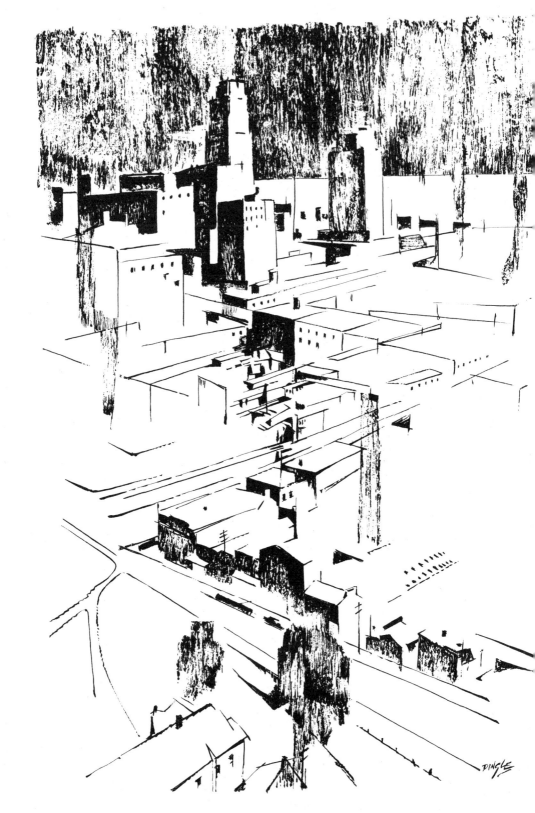

and a hardware merchant. Across the street from each other are the order offices of Eaton's and Simpson's, but nearby are independent shops: one selling women's and another men's clothes, a third furniture, and a fourth television sets and radios. A large slice of business has certainly been taken by the outsiders but many of the native shops survive in apparent good health. The latter seem to be up to date and competitive in price, and they are sustained by more than local pride. Even in the chain stores at least the majority of the employees are people of the town.

Agricultural implements come now from a city instead of from the old factory at the end of the town, but the agent must know the locality and be of it. The reaper he sold to Farmer Jones (and he knows the Jones farm well) has broken down in the most critical period of the harvest. An immediate rescue operation is in order. There are two independent lumber dealers in the town, both doing good business. Many other services are rendered by residents: by doctors, dentists, lawyers, insurance and real estate agents, funeral directors, hairdressers and barbers, builders, plumbers, and electricians.

Drive on to a crossroads village. The general store is still there and owned by the same family as have run it for fifty years and more. It has shopping carts now and some customers remember to use them. But not far behind the façade of a grocetaria is tucked away the remarkable assortment of goods that have always been there. The family live in the same building and if you are lucky you may be invited in to hear the fiddler who has played at square dances for longer than anyone can remember.

The community has more meaning in the small town or the village than it can have in a large city, and it has continued as a real social factor in spite of the ease of travel and the spread of city shops and city people; the latter, indeed, may well be caught up in it. Local projects such as community halls, parks, and fairs are undertaken by people of a locality. In the summer of 1967 it was striking to see the energy and initiative devoted to centennial projects in small places. Prizes for beards gave a new look to the men; parades, dances, and sports were organized; nineteenth-century costumes were resurrected from old trunks. A great deal of imagination and effort went into these schemes. They depended on local interest, on the ability of people to get together, to plan and organize, rather than on the expenditure of great sums of money. The community in this sense is made up not only of those living in a town or village but of farmers for miles around.

Perhaps it is because most of them work hard that the country folk play with energy, and because the town and the rural areas are drawn together economically that the community embraces both. Of the rural occupations fishing does not take a large place. In the fifties and sixties only some 3,000 to 3,500 men were engaged in it. The total yield and value were increasing but some individual regions declined. Lake Ontario showed small gains and Lake Erie considerable ones. Lake Huron and Georgian Bay went first up and then down; Lake Superior was decreasing. It is agriculture that is the principal occupation in the rural parts of the south. Farming in the last fifty years has not been all of one piece. The stimulus given by the first war was checked in the years of depression. Prices of agricultural products, as of virtually everything else, dropped badly. Even well-established farmers were forced to leave their cars and tractors in the barn and revert to the buggy and the team of working horses. Labourers were glad to accept low wages in the summer and board and tobacco in the winter. Men and women were on the move, looking for employment and seldom finding it. A kindly farmer might give a meal to some wandering unfortunate but he himself had little to spare.

The second war, with again a heavy demand for foodstuffs, restored markets and prices. Concurrently with this revival came some changes in the scheme of agriculture. There were fewer farms—150,000 in 1951 as contrasted with 192,000 in 1931. A part of the decline was due to owners dropping out, either through sale of the property or unwillingness to go on working what in some cases was unrewarding land. Another explanation lay in the increased size of farms. Between 1921 and 1951 came a steady rise in the number of those over 100 acres. Taking provincial agriculture as a whole there has been no radical change in the use of land; on the other hand there is more specialization on individual farms. For those concentrating mainly on dairy products or beef cattle the field crops are for forage. Others specialize in fruit, vegetables, tobacco, or poultry. Soya beans have increased in acreage but still take a small part. Fall wheat remains about the same but there is more mixed grain in proportion to oats.

Even with somewhat reduced acreage and substantially fewer persons engaged in agriculture total production nevertheless rose. It follows that the individual worker was more productive; indeed the index (1935–1939 = 100) stood at about 190 in 1953. Several factors have combined to produce this result: abandonment of sub-standard land; more liberal use of fertilizers; larger farms; and more mechanization. The first is self-explanatory. The second follows from scientific studies of soil and its chemical needs. Another new use of chemicals is large-scale spraying against weeds. In the case of corn, for example, some farmers by this means avoid the time-consuming task of cultivation during the growing period. Mechanization is another aspect of the application of technology.

It was after the first war that farming began to be materially changed as a result of the development of effective machine processes. First credit must go to the gasoline tractor, produced in a lighter form than the earliest versions and at a lower price. It gradually came to replace the horse as means of traction and could also be used as a source of power. The combination of the two is illustrated in the process of manuring a field. A lift attached to the tractor loads a spreader, whereupon the tractor changes its role and pulls the spreader. The gang plough, that is one with more than a single ploughshare, had long been used to a limited extent but required three or four horses, not always available on a single farm. With a tractor such a plough is normal, usually cutting three furrows at a time and saving further hours by the fact that it does not have to stop for rest (nor does the farmer often since he is sitting instead of walking). The value of the tractor was enhanced by elaboration of the machines to which it was attached, and even if these antedated the tractor they could be pulled by it faster and for longer hours. On a beef cattle farm, where the hay crop is large and essential, an energetic farmer may be seen jumping off and on machines from dawn and working under electric lights until on into the night. The days of good weather are too precious to be wasted. Some of the more sophisticated machines such as the combine may be either self-propelled or drawn behind a tractor.

Electric energy is second only to that derived from gasoline or diesel motors, but its general adoption was late in coming. In 1930 fewer than 20,000 farms had electricity but by the early fifties the figure had risen to nearly 150,000: in other words most of the farms were so equipped. Some of the uses of electricity, such as lighting houses and barns, were conveniences but others have become essential or desirable in the actual farming operations. A modern dairy farm could not be operated without electric milkers. On the—fortunately rare—occasions when the electric power fails, the cows (to their unconcealed disgust) cannot be milked, not only because it would take so long to do it by hand but because the modern cow has never encountered such an archaic procedure. Other uses for electricity are for water pumps, elevators in barns, mixers for food (as used in large pig farms), automatic barn cleaners, and machines for grinding grain.

The work of the farmer is also speeded up by improved means of transportation. Animal or vegetable products can quickly be taken to market. In the last few years fluid milk has been picked up by tanker trucks which, by means of power pumps, draw the milk from the farmer's vat, a process in contrast with the manhandled cans which contained eighty pounds of milk each. Seated on tractor, truck, or car the farmer moves rapidly about his business, whether that be on his own farm, that of a neighbour, or to a nearby town.

Mechanization has done much to enable the farmer to do his work without additional help but there are limits. The cost of some implements may be too high except on very large farms, though to some extent this may be overcome by employing men who take their machines from farm to farm, combines, for example, or corn cutters. Moreover there is some residual need for manual labour. It has not been easy to find such assistance as is needed since for both full-time and seasonal workers a shortage has existed. The federal and provincial governments, co-operating through the Federal-Provincial Farm Labour Committee, have taken steps to improve the situation. Workers have been recruited in the Atlantic provinces, in Quebec, Indians in northern Ontario, and experts in the southern United States for the tobacco harvest. Little success has resulted from efforts to bring farmer immigrants from the British Isles and Europe. Financial assistance is offered for construction of housing for seasonal workers. Daily workers are transported from Toronto and Hamilton to nearby farms.

The farmer, however, is not wholly dependent for help on what used to be called "hired men," for other members of his family take as ever active parts in farm operations. On some nine-tenths of the farms the wife and children participate to some degree in chores, milking, the harvest, and other jobs. Summer vacations leave boys of school age free to add very materially to the pool of labour and at a time of year when help is most needed. There are also four-footed assistants. Those innocent-looking cats and kittens romping on the barn floor are tough professionals in the destruction of mice. And then, of course, there is the farm dog. One of these, a Border Collie named Laddie, a personal friend of the writer's, is very busy indeed. Twice a day in the summer he collects the milking cows, and with a dog's extraordinary sense of time hardly needs to watch for his master to start for the barn. He wages successful war on invading ground hogs and rabbits, and—most important of all—supervises all the activities of the family. A misleading pose of deference thinly hides his consciousness of responsibility.

It has often been remarked that in modern times the rural family lives in much the same way as the urban one. Certainly there are more similarities than there were. Happily it is a subject on which information is provided both in the census and in a *Special Study of Farm Homes and Homemakers* made in 1959 by the Ontario and Canadian Departments of Agriculture. Nearly all farmhouses are detached and most are owned. Unlike urban ones the great majority were built before 1920 and a substantial number are more than a hundred years old. Many need minor, but few major, repairs. Installed water, baths, and toilets are not as general as in urban dwellings but are found in about two-thirds of the farmhouses of the province as a whole and would be in greater proportion in the south. Houses are adequately heated though sometimes by stoves instead of by the methods found in cities.

Of the 352 farmhouses, in every county and district, on which the *Special Report* is based 320 were found to have electricity in both house and barn. The percentage of these houses having labour-saving equipment was at the time as follows: power washing machines, 98; electric or gas refrigerators, 95; vacuum cleaners, 87; electric or gas stoves, 85; electric freezers, 56; electric floor polishers, 41; automatic clothes dryers, 11. Automobiles were owned by 88 per cent of the families, so that most of them had ready access to shops, churches, doctors, and dentists. In some remote areas a few families were as much as forty miles from a doctor and sixty miles from a dentist. Rural delivery of mail is a convenience that is widespread.

All this sounds much like urban living but the differences are marked too. A farm is a little kingdom which must be guided and governed by its owners and which cannot be neglected or left at any time to its own devices. Urban workers can stop work for one reason or another; have regular holidays; may lock their doors and go to a restaurant for dinner. Not so on an Ontario farm, or at least on one that has livestock of any kind. There can be, and have been, group protests but strikes are impractical and holidays are possible only if there is someone left at home. Rural families share with urban ones risks of ill health and accident, less vulnerable, perhaps, to the first and more to the second. A city worker may lose his job but it is difficult to imagine a farmer unemployed and collecting unemployment insurance. In the country the weather is always a factor. Hundreds of acres of hay may have to be burned because it has rotted, a sudden storm flattens the fall wheat so that it cannot be harvested, a drought keeps the corn at miniature size. Finally, the farm family must be more self-contained. In degree this is not as true as it once was but is still so in comparison with a city. Even on a specialized farm the owner has to be a bit of a carpenter, mechanic, and plumber. For major work on his machines he will call in an expert, but there are so many little things that turn up day by day, indoors and out.

Life in the country has many attractions and the standard of living for most farm families has risen appreciably. Yet it is still hard work over long hours and the financial rewards are understandably considered to be out of line with those for comparable urban dwellers. All societies, and therefore all governments, aim at having cheap food and it is proper that they should; but how are low prices to the consumer to be reconciled with adequate profits to the producer? It is well, too, to recall that not all farms are successful. There are rural slums as well as urban ones. The cause may be unproductive soil, continued bad weather, ill health, or inefficiency. Some farm families live in decaying houses, heavily in debt, with few crops, and not enough cash for food and clothes. More farms on blow sand or rock will have to be abandoned and presumably some provision made for the evacuated families. To reduce the farm population would be to exaggerate a decline that has already caused some concern. It has been a traditional lament that children leave their parents' farm for jobs in a city. Many of the daughters, of course, marry young farmers. In some cases sons take over from their fathers after a period of working with them. Others acquire farms of their own. If by some strange change in outlook they should all wish to do so there would not be enough land to go around, but the practical issue is that the farm population is lower than its optimum figure in relation to the people who have to be fed.

Much of what has so far been said about agriculture applies to the province as a whole, but it should be added that conditions in the north have at all times been different in some respects to those in the south. In the Laurentian lowlands the pioneer was a farmer and for a long time agriculture and related activities absorbed the largest part of the population and were the chief sources of income. In the north, on the other hand, the pioneers were wood-workers and miners, with farmers being subsidiary and largely dependent on them. In the nineteenth and early twentieth centuries the provincial government had found to its sorrow that the story of the south could not be repeated in a land of rock and lakes. How much fertile soil exists in the Canadian Shield has been so variously estimated that no sure conclusions can be drawn. It has earlier been seen that inaccurate reporting was in part responsible for the misguided project of extensive agricultural settlement in Muskoka and Haliburton; and an epilogue was added in the nineteen-twenties when the Ontario government offered to settlers then in certain parts of northern Haliburton alternative land in the Clay Belt together with free transportation.

A number accepted. In that large break in the rocky terrain there are un-doubtedly opportunities for raising good crops, but the optimism that led to the construction of the Temiskaming and Northern Ontario Railway as a means of access by great numbers of settlers has yet to be justified (however useful the railway turned out to be in other and unforeseen ways). One of the first problems put before the Farmer-Labour government in 1920 arose out of complaints by men in the soldiers' settlement at Kapuskasing that their lot was intolerable: that the land was hard to clear and that the promised paper mill at which they could find employment to eke out their scanty gains from the land had not materialized. A commission sent to investigate supported the complaints and proposed that any settler who wished might be moved and recompensed for the work he had done (a curious contrast with the contemporary move in the opposite direction already mentioned). Looking back at the episode the then premier, E. C. Drury (himself a farmer), commented that "the land, it is true, was moderately fertile, but clearing was too costly and the climate, with its late springs, short summers, rainy harvest time, early falls, and long cold winters was suitable only for a very limited and specialized agriculture, to supply some of the needs of nearby mining and paper towns."

The future of the Clay Belt was not to be as discouraging as the temporary failure at Kapuskasing might indicate, but the connection drawn by Drury between northern agriculture and its markets was well founded. There were smaller tracts of fertile land near Sault Ste Marie, at the head of the lakes, near Rainy Lake and Lake of the Woods, and innumerable pockets throughout the northland. Persistent efforts were made by the provincial government to effect orderly settlement and to avoid scattered farms which could be provided with neither roads nor schools. To that end new townships were not opened for settlement until others were at least partially occupied. In the early years of the twentieth century, those of heavy immigration of persons prepared to undertake pioneer farming, the number of acres located in free-grant townships (which were in the north) was running around 200,000. This fell sharply during the first war, revived in the early twenties (to over 100,000), but by the forties was down to a fragment.

Conditions of living for the northern rural family varied considerably. In some areas settlement was fairly compact, with the amenities of neighbours, schools, churches, and adequate roads. On the other extreme were odd families—or sometimes small groups—scratching out of clearings in the bush crops which were supplemented by fish and game. Theirs was the sequel to the log-cabin story of the early pioneers in the south. More characteristic, however, were the agricultural districts which formed the hinterland to urban centres and which were the results of them. Given the cost of transporting products to markets outside the Shield—or of bringing them into it—it would seem logical that the northern farmer should feed the northern industrial worker. Only up to a point has there ever been this nice balance. The farmer has not always grown what the townsman wanted, nor do local conditions always assure regular, or indeed, any crops. In fact considerable importation of food from the south has occurred.

The farmer of the north country had followed in the path of the miner and the lumberman and the relations between them have extended beyond producing and consuming food. As had happened farther south the settlers both sold timber to the lumber and pulp companies and worked for them during the winter. This source of cash income was in some cases too attractive, leading to neglect of the still primitive farms, but in others the winter work eased the costly first period of settlement. From the point of view of the companies the availability of additional labour was as welcome as a supply of food or hay, though in recent years the changing techniques in the forest industries have sharply reduced the need for seasonal employment. Meanwhile, however, there has been a drain from agriculture to industry, with immigrants and others who went in as settlers moving to the towns or to lumber and mining camps. Between 1951 and 1961 the farming population of all the northern Districts declined absolutely. In Algoma the change was marginal but in all the others very substantial. In Cochrane the farm population was halved.

The main activities in the northland, in old time and new, have been connected with exploitation of the the gifts of nature. First was the trade in furs, and although this has shrunk and has been supplemented by raising fur-bearing animals in captivity, there are still trappers ranging the forest. Fishing has been in most parts of the north a minor occupation. Timber, first for lumber, and then also for pulp and paper, involves the use of a crop which, under skilful planning, will be self-repeating. When, however, minerals are extracted from the surface or below there is no process of replacement. This fact is illustrated by the phrase "mining the soil," referring to a type of farming which does not allow the ground to recover its productive captivity. The same criticism is made of wood cutting which takes no account of the need for new growth. For soil or trees, however, restoration is possible but a mine, once drained of its marketable minerals, has no further value. In the early days of mining in Algoma and Thunder Bay a number of mines were opened but in most cases turned out to have short lives. When large-scale mining started in the twentieth century the process was not essentially different although a number of mines were started which turned out to be heavy producers and some of them for protracted periods.

The stages are familiar: first the prospectors working under difficult conditions, often in virgin territory. Of the claims staked and recorded many turn out to be worthless. Occasionally comes a dramatic discovery of rich ore, and particularly in the case of gold this brings a mad rush of fortune hunters, scrambling over the rocks and over each other to find locations. A few gain prizes and of them a portion are agents for those with capital, are "grub-staked," and draw only modest returns. Where the results of tests are encouraging a set of crude shacks rises on the surface while shafts are run below it. If no rich veins are found, or if they prove to be short, the little community becomes a ghost town and the frame buildings are left to subside into the ground. When better results are secured the mine and processing plant make a break in the land of trees and rocks and a crude village turns into a comfortable town in due course. Most of such places continue to thrive for in a good area one mine will run out and another take its place. It is a story of adventure, of prospectors who are often explorers, of many failures and some successes; of life underground, never becoming free from danger in spite of technical improvements and safety regulations; of many simple miners, of capitalists losing their gamble and a few others making millions. All this raw material for a drama awaits another Robert Service.

Mining is not one of the industries which directly employs large numbers of people, and as methods have been improved and mechanization further utilized less manual and more skilled labour have come to be required. On the other hand the ramifications of the industry are wide. "It has been estimated," states a pamphlet issued by the Mining Association of Ontario, "that for every person employed in a mining operation, six others are employed in industries and services which supply mining companies." Seen from the point of view of the province as a whole the mining industry thus stimulates a range of business activities and creates a principal export for a country the prosperity of which depends on selling abroad. The value of mineral production in Ontario has risen with few set-backs. In 1928 it was approximately $100 million and by the middle sixties was moving toward $1,000 million. From the point of view of the persons directly employed in mines, in mills, smelters, and refineries much of the drudgery has been taken over by machines; health and safety measures have steadily advanced in spite of penetration to greater depths.

Neither the proportions between minerals produced nor the locations enjoying particular success have any consistency over a period. Changes came from the availability of ores, methods of processing and separating them, new discoveries, application of capital, or the state of markets and prices. To take the position in a recent year, 1965, nickel was substantially ahead of other metals (32·42 per cent of total production of metals), with copper coming next (16·61 per cent), iron—a late starter—at 9·18 per cent, gold down to 7·48 per cent, and silver at only 1·6 per cent. Looking at areas it is evident that the eastern one retains much of the primacy it secured after the collapse of most of the early projects near Thunder Bay and Kenora. Prospecting extended from the camps at Cobalt and Porcupine to Kirkland Lake and Timmins. Sudbury is an important mining centre. Cobalt is an example of successes and failures. A boom in silver was followed by trouble when the world price declined and the richest ore ran out. For a time the town struggled along by selling the mineral after which it was named and then reverted under more favourable conditions to silver. A glance at the list of gold mines that have existed in the Porcupine area shows that eight of those originating between 1910 and 1940 were still in production in 1965 but twenty-one, some of which had been important, had ceased production. The discovery of a great new body of ore (copper, lead, zinc, silver, and other minerals) in 1964 proved that the days of mining rushes were not over. Prospectors madly staked claims in and around it, and in the Toronto Stock Exchange new records for numbers of shares traded were chalked up.

Farther to the west some important discoveries were made. One such was at Red Lake, far to the north of Kenora, where there was a characteristic gold rush in the winter of 1926. Red Lake was of particular interest not only because it turned out to be a rich field but because for the first time aircraft were used for transportation. At first the promoter chartered them from the Provincial Air Service and then a commercial line was established. It was to be some time before large aeroplanes capable of carrying heavy equipment were available, but for passenger traffic to a remote area the use of air travel was revolutionary. Another of the more interesting new discoveries was at Manitouwadge, midway between the Canadian Pacific and the Canadian National railway lines. Here again the story began with prospecting in unfamiliar country by canoe; and in this case a new field, where copper, zinc, and silver were found, attracted transportation to it. In pursuit of business the railways built from north and south, and access roads were opened, one south from Highway 11 and the other north from Highway 17. A model community mushroomed in the midst of the forest.

The production of iron reached significant proportions only after the second war. In southern Ontario the enterprise started at Marmora in the early nineteenth century was revived in 1949. The main action, however, was in the north. One spectacular engineering feat was to drain Steep Rock Lake (northeast of Fort William) in order to get at the iron that lay underneath it. A river system was diverted to prevent replenishment and in six months one hundred billion gallons of water were pumped out. A recent additional source results from the development of a process by which iron can be recovered as a by-product from the ores in the Sudbury area. One final example of mining may be noted, the discovery and production of uranium. Over 9,000 claims were staked in short order east of Sault Ste Marie in 1952, and from a few of them came the mines around which was built the town of Elliot Lake, another model community springing up where there had been nothing. The demands for uranium were as new as the mines which supplied them and for a time the market was brisk; but the ups and downs of the mining business are always unpredictable and for a time there was apprehension that Elliot Lake would become another ghost town.

Mining had its early and small beginnings in southern Ontario but it reached magnitude only much later as it spread across the Canadian Shield. It grew into a complex industry of which the actual extraction of ore from the earth is only one part and the processing plants another. To these were added demands for transportation, hydro-electric power, machinery, and lumber; financial support, the professions, and labour; all the diverse goods and services that are required where people are gathered together. Probably most of the men and women whose livelihood depends in whole or in part on mining have never been down a shaft or have any knowledge of the techniques that produce metal from ore.

As a major industry mining is comparatively modern but forestry, the other principal economic interest of the north, goes back to early days in the lowland. The lumberjack, pictured in a red shirt and high boots, with great strength and an immense appetite, is one of the characters of Canadian history. Lumber was always in demand for domestic purposes and was one of the few important exports. Lumber companies used local labour where they could but they were migratory. As cutting reduced the forests in the south the industry moved northward, up through the lower Shield and so to northern Ontario proper. Thinking in terms of endless trees they cut without consideration for the future. The wood industry of the last fifty years is part of a long story but has important new characteristics.

The forest industries now fall into two main divisions, the one being lumber and the other pulp and paper. In the first the principal processes are cutting saw logs and making lumber from them in mills. Railway ties, mine timbers, and the manufacture of plywood and veneer are other parts of the business. Several kinds of trees are used but pine is, as always, overwhelmingly the favourite. Others are spruce, birch, hemlock, maple, and poplar. The value of sawmill products has varied. In 1959 it was close to $60 million. The pulp and paper industry, a relative newcomer, has overtaken the lumber business in both quantity and value. In this case the wood principally used is spruce, with jack pine, poplar, and balsam in much smaller amounts. In 1959 the value of pulp produced was well over $200 million.

Over the last generation methods in the forest industries have changed materially. Machines have wholly taken the place of the horse and in part of manual labour. Mechanical saws, loaders, and self-propelled vehicles have become general. The picturesque spring drive of logs takes care of only part of what is cut, the remainder being taken to mills by train or more often by truck. In place of indiscriminate cutting careful conservation is followed by co-operation of the companies and the provincial authorities (since most of the limits are on crown land). Fire protection and war against pests and diseases have been increased. The general principle of preservation is that the forest resources should not diminish, the means of maintaining them being both reforestation and natural growth. Another means of avoiding waste is the use in mills of chips and sawdust as raw material.

For the lumberjack—the man who cuts down trees and starts them on their way to a mill—conditions of labour and living have steadily changed. As mechanization has developed his output has become greater but he has had to become skilled in handling more than an axe and a saw. As late as the nineteen-thirties, however, the old régime was still largely in effect. Many of the camps operated by small jobbers could have been taken for those of a much earlier age. Camps were generally small, for twenty-five men or less. The buildings were crude, with walls and often roofs of logs. Even the floors were made of poles, making cleaning almost impossible. Windows were too small and ceilings too low. Stables were often placed under the same roof so that if a horse (which was a valuable property) got loose or kicked he could be heard. Sanitary arrangements were primitive and provision was seldom made for isolation of sick lumbermen.

By 1940 conditions were improving. Some bunkhouses were made of sawn lumber or prefabricated panels. One large camp had running water, with a washroom in each bunkhouse, and separate rooms for kitchen, dining, and recreation. Baths, laundries, and electric light (manufactured by gasoline engines) followed. But so long as the lumber camp was in fact a camp, with a life of some three years, there was inevitable reluctance to increase capital expenditure. It was one thing to abandon rough log cabins but quite another to leave well-constructed buildings to rot. Several companies therefore experimented with portable buildings. One type could be mounted on skids. It had to be small to get through the forest roads and light enough to be pulled by machines then available. The other was prefabricated, to be taken to pieces in sections and loaded on trucks. Both methods were quite widely employed, but a second difficulty then arose: how to move water, sewage, and electric installations.

The old shanty camp was no longer acceptable to employees, but to convert it into modern living conditions and then abandon the whole was impossibly wasteful, although to move it was not proving very practicable. Some of the companies then turned to permanent structures such as one camp —if it can still be called that—on the Abitibi River which has modern two-storey buildings equipped with most of the urban comforts. This fits in well with the changed concept of labour, which in turn has arisen not only out of discontent with the old rough living conditions but also out of the altered processes in the forest industries. The need of the companies now is for skilled workers employed through all or most of the year. Good quarters, means of entertainment, and better diet attract the kind of men that are wanted. The lumberman has always been famous for his appetite but the meals, if impressive in quantity, used to be lacking in variety. A modern dinner menu shows how this latter deficiency could be overcome. It consisted of pea soup, pig's feet, stew, roast beef, sausage, cold ham, head cheese, chocolate walnut pie, sugar pie, apple sauce, prunes, custard, lemon pie, cake, biscuits, milk, tea, and coffee. Served in a comfortable dining room, and perhaps accompanied by soft music on the radio, this could hardly be bettered.

There was one more alternative, to eliminate camps altogether. In at least two areas of northern Ontario the workers live with their families in modern houses placed in neat communities and are daily transported to and from the woods.

Emphasis has been laid on the changing life of the lumberjacks, but they have come to be a small portion of the labour force in the forest industries. The others directly involved are listed in the census under "manufacturing industries," some of the largest categories being those in saw mills, planing mills, and—much the largest—pulp and paper mills. In addition are all those who in one way and another supply goods and services.

If the economic pattern of northern Ontario has developed in a way quite different to that of the south it was nevertheless consistent with the history of the area over the course of a hundred years. By the mid-twentieth century forest and mineral products had more than realized early hopes; and these two industries were interdependent with the two principal services, transportation and electric power. These factors together with the natural characteristics of the region—climate and terrain—go a long way toward explaining the social structure of the northland. It has produced wealth, but on a narrow economic front and with a small population. In 1961 the aggregate population of the eight northern Districts was not much greater than that of Toronto without its suburbs. Kenora and Timiskaming each had about the same number of people as the city of Sarnia; Sudbury, the most populated of the Districts, was roughly equivalent to London; Rainy River had no more inhabitants than did Galt. In the whole Patricia Portion of Kenora (until 1927 a separate District) that ran up to and along the western shore of Hudson Bay there were only 12,341 persons, and that included Red Lake. In size northern Ontario dwarfed the south: in population it was dwarfed by it. Yet the healthy growth of the first no more depended on numbers of people than did that of the second on numbers of square miles.

In some ways the north resembles southern Ontario at a much earlier stage and in others it is distinctly modern. It contains very large areas which are almost unoccupied, and elsewhere has modern industry and modern cities. It has been an open field for technology. The effects of mechanization on the mining and wood industries have been mentioned. For them, for the people engaged in them, and for the population generally, radical changes in transportation and communications have largely put an end to isolation. The proportion of rural population is greater than in the south although the urban centres hold a distinct majority. Since, however, "rural" in the census definition refers to everything less than communities of one thousand it would include groups of men living together in mining and lumber camps.

About half the Indians of Ontario live in the north. Ojibways are most numerous, followed by Crees and Saulteaux. In some Districts the majority live on reserves and in others the opposite is the case; but the total Indian population is not large, being about 23,000. Reserves are of different sizes but in sum they run into hundreds of thousands of acres. Several of them are on or near Lake Superior; others, the largest, are in the far north. The biggest reserve (89,600 acres) runs toward Albany, and another of 64,000 acres is on the north shore of Lake Eabment. These two, and many of the others, are of the same size as when they were originally laid out. They offer no barriers to settlement.

The rural population, then, is in the main made up of Indians, lumberjacks, farmers, miners and prospectors, trappers, and fishermen. That some parts have virtually no residents is indicated by the existence of "unorganized" land, that is not organized into townships or even surveyed as such. In the District of Rainy River, for example, there are many townships to the west of Fort Frances and a few to the east, but most of the eastern half is unorganized. Scattered people live in unorganized territory but they are very few, not enough to justify detailed surveys and municipal institutions.

A few of the cities and towns in the north area are on the sites of fur trade posts but the others can be attributed more readily to particular causes than is the case in the south. This does not mean that the location of southern towns was casual but that it came as the result of a series of migrations. A mining town, however, sprang up at any point where the early exploitation of a find was encouraging enough to draw in numbers of men first to dig for the ore and then to feed and render other services to the diggers. Such a place might begin with an indiscriminate collection of tents and ugly shacks and then either take its own unplanned course or be built by a company or the government. An interesting example of the latter is Manitouwadge the story of which has been written (L. Carson Brown, *Manitouwadge: Cave of the Great Spirit*). Following the discovery of minerals there people moved to the site—and so did the Ontario government as town planner. The scheme which was implemented provided for separate residential, commercial, and industrial areas. Houses might be owned by individuals or rented from one of the mining companies. There is a hotel, a hospital, three churches, public, separate, and high schools, and a recreation centre with facilities for games and meetings. That centre, together with an addition to the high school, was contributed by a mining company. Continued direction was made possible by the fact that the town was an Improvement District, that is to say, governed by a board of three trustees appointed by the province.

The experiment at Manitouwadge was so successful that a similar operation was carried out not long after at Elliot Lake. It too was carefully laid out in several areas, commercial and residential, and likewise made an Improvement District. In this case the area included a group of townships and totalled nearly 400 square miles.

There are also "company towns," that is ones built, owned, and managed by mining or pulp companies. Carefully planned with pleasant houses, public services, and community facilities, they stand out as modern urban centres in striking contrast to the forest which stretches out on every side. From the point of view of the people who live in them they have many advantages, but there are criticisms too. Some of the residents feel that they are too much dominated by the company, and resent what they see as a kind of paternalism. An individual who retires may find it difficult to stay in a house in which he has lived for years but does not own. In some cases independent fringe areas develop beyond the town limits. In them living conditions are much less good but the cost is less and there is freedom from controls.

The cities of northern Ontario are neither large nor numerous. By the 1961 census there were only five and Sudbury, with 80,120 people, was much the largest. In Thunder Bay Fort William and Port Arthur, old rivals, were neck and neck at just over 45,000. The Districts of Cochrane, Kenora, Rainy River, and Timiskaming had no cities and their towns were not large. And yet urban life in the north is in many ways very much the same as in the south. If the climate is more severe that means only a bit more fuel and snow clearance. Types of dwellings are similar. Single detached houses predominate, although in Sudbury a third of the dwellings in 1961 were apartments. Whether living in houses or apartments few of its families are without television sets and most have motor cars. Much the same amenities are to be found in Kenora, a smaller place. Sophisticated urban life with a backdrop of forest is of the very essence of the northland.

CHAPTER FIFTEEN

Poverty,
Prosperity,
and Security

THE THREE CONDITIONS mentioned in the title of this chapter have at all times affected the lives of people, but in the last half-century the combinations and contrasts between them have been particularly striking. For a decade prosperity reigned without security; for another poverty without either; and for the last twenty years prosperity and security have gone hand in hand.

The passage from the first to the second of these periods was not a transition, it was a revolution. A few far-sighted individuals had forecast trouble but the prevailing mood had been one of unadulterated optimism. Any thought that the average person gave to the morrow was coloured not by caution but by expectation of continued good fortune. He was not much concerned about security when fair weather seemed so firmly established. Suddenly and inexplicably the bottom dropped out of the economy after the collapse of prices on the stock exchanges in the autumn of 1929. Before long it became evident that this was not a brief, if violent, collapse. It was crushing, interminable. The issue was not one of convenience but of survival. People of all kinds and in most occupations were in serious difficulties but the greatest social problem was the shrinkage of employment for wage-earners.

For Ontario the most detailed study of unemployment (by H. M. Cassidy, *Unemployment and Relief in Ontario*) applies to the year 1931. Bearing in mind that the depth of the depression was not to be reached for another two years the figures were already sufficiently alarming. Of the Ontario cities with populations of more than 10,000 the worst hit were the manufacturing centres of Oshawa (39.4 per cent of males unemployed) and East Windsor.

The northern cities of Fort William, Port Arthur, and Sault Ste. Marie were all slightly over 30 per cent. In the rest of the south there was a wide range from a group around 20 per cent, through Toronto (19.4 per cent) to the fortunate Stratford (9.5 per cent). The professional and clerical classes came off relatively lightly; unskilled workers were the hardest hit; and the skilled ones took a lesser but still a heavy loss. Neither depression nor unemployment was new to twentieth-century Canada, but the peculiarities of the depression of 1929 were its severity and particularly its length. Those of the unemployed who had saleable possessions—and they were a distinct minority —ran out of their resources in spite of doubling up in housing and of adopting other economies. As the depression lengthened and deepened there were more and more families and unmarried men who had no employment, little expectation of it, and either not enough to live on or simply nothing at all. Either work must be found for them or they must be supported out of public and private funds. All three expedients were adopted.

None of them was new. Not long before, in 1925, for example, the provincial government and municipalities had co-operated in the provision of public works to relieve unemployment and in the distribution of food, fuel, and clothing to the needy. Private organizations had never ceased to give assistance in these and other ways. In the mounting crisis that began in the autumn of 1929 governmental and private efforts to help those who suffered from it were for the most part complementary. The principal forms of government aid were direct relief (that is, the old poor relief) and public works. The first consisted for the most part of food and fuel. Employment was created by undertaking municipal works such as the erection of buildings or putting in sewers. The province launched a programme of new highways in northern Ontario, making camps to accommodate men drawn from many parts of the province. A large number and variety of private organizations, many of them with long experience in social work, gave some direct relief in their soup kitchens and hostels, but more of their attention was devoted to the areas in which governments were less active, such as rent and clothing. As experience was gained more co-ordination between them was effected, as it was with governments. From such integration came a more equitable distribution of aid. Inevitably there were on the one hand individuals who improperly claimed benefits or who went the rounds of the soup kitchens; and on the other families who were too proud to admit the straits they were in or who had not long enough residence to qualify for government aid.

Given the degree of improvisation required, the gap in legislation, and the shortage of public and private funds, the way in which the emergency was met reflected no little credit on those who organized assistance and on the generosity of the public. There were, however, deficiencies. The municipal projects were designed to absorb the maximum manual labour and because of that they proved in many cases to be very expensive ways of doing things, and that at a time when the municipal authorities were at their wits' ends to find money to meet the many new burdens thrust upon them. The northern road camps were on the whole successful experiments, but at that time it was not easy to prove that the roads were really needed. They took care of some men, particularly unmarried ones, but were carried on for a limited period. Opinion was divided as to whether the food supplied to families was sufficient to maintain their health but the majority of informed contemporaries claimed that it was not.

Immediate and pressing effects of unemployment were followed by others. Those who had savings saw them converted into debts and people were unable to meet instalments on houses and furniture. The rates of suicides went up steeply and there was evidence of increased mental disorder which did not quite reach that stage. Dislocation of families, fall of morale, and frustration among younger people ready to enter the labour market were common. It was the wide extent of hardships that marked the thirties. Apart from those without any work were others on part time or on wages so low as not to provide for the necessities of life. Thousands of experienced workers who would ordinarily have taken employment for granted were deprived of it and were looking at a future which seemed bleak indeed.

The depression was ended by an extraneous force, the second world war. Shortages of manpower and of consumer goods took the place of unemployment and over-production. The state undertook the control of the economy to a degree not known before. Whether or not it could be reasonably assumed that the lightning would not strike again, that economic life would remain vigorous after the termination of hostilities, the tide was running strongly in the direction of fuller protection of the individual against circumstances largely or wholly beyond his control. The horrible experience of the thirties was not the only force pressing toward that end, for there was a general modification of social philosophy both at home and in countries with which Canada was closely associated. The doctrines of *laissez-faire* had proved to have too many loopholes both for the industrial society of southern Ontario and for the vulnerable wheat economy of the western prairies. At the same time the ogre of government intervention in business had become less fearsome through the experience of the war years. A body of opinion remained unsympathetic to the new trend, seeing no good in mollycoddling individuals who, it was argued, could look after themselves if they had energy and enterprise. The effective majority, however, was prepared to go a long way in diverting public income to guarding citizens against the exigencies of modern life. Individualism retreated before the advance of security.

There is no absolute distinction between social welfare before the second war and after it. No new principles were invoked. The differences in method and degree, however, are so wide that they have been seen as creating a difference in kind. Be that as it may, if the state was writing with a wide pen it was not on a blank page. Both continuity and novelty can best be judged by an outline of the successive governmental measures in the main categories of social welfare. Since the purpose is to show only how the lives of the people of Ontario were changed the constitutional aspect of the question need not be examined in detail, important as that was from other points of view. It is, however, necessary to take note of the extended place of the federal government, not only because that was an important development in itself but because it allowed for the deployment of greater resources and a degree of consistency through the country.

In 1929 a provincial Royal Commission on Public Welfare was appointed to investigate institutions and activities, most of which had been in some form among the earliest welfare responsibilities accepted by the province. They included various kinds of hospitals, penal and corrective institutions, gaols and industrial farms, houses of refuge, and agencies for the care of children. The report, rendered in 1930, was in part approving and in part critical. It urged co-ordination under a Department of Public Welfare, training more social workers, detailed inspection of institutions, and urgent expenditure (some $25 million immediately) to relieve overcrowding and for other purposes. The proposed ministry was established and placed under it were the Children's Aid Branch, industrial schools, the Mothers' Allowance Commission, houses of refuge, orphanages, the Soldiers' Aid Commission, and the Old Age Pension Commission.

Some of these organizations and the matters with which they dealt have been touched on in earlier chapters. Of the more recent ones the Mothers' Allowance Act was first passed in 1920 and its application broadened by an amendment of the following year. Its main purpose was to provide monthly allowances to mothers and foster-mothers of dependent children where such help was needed. By 1929 the list of those being assisted amounted to 5,357 families and 15,984 children. The federal Family Allowance Act of 1945, the "baby bonus," allotted a small monthly sum for each child, money which was to be spent on the child's welfare.

The reference to pensions is to those arising out of the Canadian Old Age Pensions Act of 1927, a plan to be administered by such provinces as wished to do so. The federal government contributed half the sum and this was raised to three-quarters during the depression. It was not a large amount: $20 a month, which could be increased to $25 by a province on the same sharing arrangement. It was provided on a means test to those over seventy years of age who had lived in Canada for twenty years. The Act of 1927 was at the time a radical departure but it came to be increasingly criticized as theories of social welfare changed. In legislation of 1951 the means test was preserved in extending coverage to the 65–69 age group but for those over that it was dropped. Finally (if there is any finality in this field) was added the Canada Pension Plan which came into effect in 1966. It was a contributory system for employed persons, intended after an interval to come into effect at age sixty-five.

Meanwhile efforts were made to fill the gap which was the worst in the depression of 1929, the absence of unemployment insurance. The first move was as a part of R. B. Bennett's "new deal," a programme put forward in 1935 to meet certain outstanding problems of the day. The Act to provide a contributory plan for unemployment insurance collapsed when the courts ruled that it was not within federal competence; and it was not until 1941 and after a constitutional amendment that a measure of unemployment insurance was put into effect. It was based on contributions from employers, employees, and government and provided about two-thirds of the worker's average wage with a supplement for dependents. In 1945 it was said to cover 2,300,000 out of 3,000,000 wage and salary earners.

Advances in medicine, surgery, and sanitation improved the health of the population but the problem was to make these benefits available to as many people as possible. A good deal had already been done. In 1914 the legislature of the province passed an Act to compensate workmen injured in the course of their work. It covered free medical care as well as compensation for loss of wages. Another group was helped by the Ontario Medical Relief Scheme, initiated in 1935 in the midst of the depression. It superseded municipal plans but its operation was conducted by co-operation between the provincial and municipal authorities and the Ontario Medical Association. Persons unemployed or on relief might obtain, on application, medical care and drugs without charge but hospital treatment was not included. A few years later the arrangement with the Medical Association was extended to all recipients under welfare programmes. These arrangements remained in effect until the initiation of the Ontario Medical Services Insurance Plan in 1966. The province had long either operated hospitals or contributed to their expenses, and in 1937 had a survey made of the hospital system by two American experts. The report was not encouraging. The provincial institutions, it stated, had been brought to "a lamentable state of incapacity." General overcrowding had produced an intolerable state of affairs that needed to be remedied quickly. Accommodation, doctors, and nurses were all insufficient. Whereas Massachusetts had 13.1 nurses and attendants per hundred patients and New York State 10.5 Ontario was down to 6.5.

Whether or not all these criticisms were justified it did prove to be virtually impossible, even with the best intentions, to keep up with demands, far less to run ahead of them. In the ten years from 1946 to 1956 the number of patients in the Ontario medical hospitals increased from fifteen to twenty thousand, and from 1944 to 1954 active treatment hospitals had comparable experience. Meanwhile the cost of construction and operation soared. As one physician put it, no one could afford to be ill. In the mood of the day there could be no question as to the priority of the public's health over additional government expenditure. It was, therefore, both in spite of and because of rising costs that in 1959 the Ontario Hospital Insurance Plan was put into effect. Membership was optional and for those who joined a small premium was required.

Even before the hospital plan was introduced it was noted that 49 per cent of the charges made by 145 principal hospitals in Ontario were paid by insurance organizations on behalf of patients. They were of various kinds including such private ones as the Associated Medical Services, which began in 1937, and the Blue Cross. Other persons were covered under plans to which they and their employers contributed. While in recent times governments have taken the largest and most conspicuous part in providing social security theirs is by no means the only one. Proportionately the place of private initiative in this field has declined but in absolute terms it has increased. In northern Ontario experiments in supplying doctors and hospitals in "company" towns began some years ago. Retirement or pension plans are far from new in principle but they have come to take a much larger place than they did. Salary-earners have been talking of security of tenure while wage-earners have in effect sought to become salaried, that is, to have a guaranteed annual income. In recent years more contracts between employers and employees have contained clauses concerning pensions, medical insurance, and sick leave.

There is much talk of the "welfare state." What does this mean? Sometimes welfare is equated to social security; sometimes it is still thought of as charity, or at least as related only to the lowest income brackets. The welfare of mankind has no evident boundaries, but the word is sometimes given a quasi-technical meaning, referring to a few basic necessities such as food, shelter, clothing, and medical care. This line of thought, however, seems to explain only one side of what is commonly called the welfare state. The word "security" may be more comprehensive. Nowadays the public appears less interested in a career open to talent than in one open to the minimum risk. "Security," too, applies more to society as a whole. And that is important, for one of the most significant facts is that the measures respecting pensions, housing, and medical care have been steadily extended to all the people of the province rather than confined to those in particular need.

All this is too new to allow for anything approaching a final judgment on the nature and extent of change in the lives of the people of Ontario, but some effects seem obvious, if only in outline. The amount of effort devoted to human needs is formidable. Private organizations have by no means vacated the field because of the breadth of government intervention. Their attention is directed to many social problems: those of the blind, the care and adoption of children, rehabilitation of unmarried mothers, broken homes, drug and alcohol addicts, social misfits—the list is a long one. Through a combination of official and private action has come what has been aptly styled cradle-to-grave insurance. For a very large segment of society there is an incalculable gain, and not least for that portion of the population which could not be rated as rich or poor. Protection against the threat of expensive illness and inadequate resources in old age can make the difference between misery and peace of mind.

Such radical departures could hardly fail to have liabilities as well as assets. In protecting the individual against society there is a risk of not protecting society against the individual. If life is made in some respects easier there is a temptation to make it easier still. Unemployment insurance was based on the assumption that people wanted to work but unfortunately that is not universally true. Anyone who has at least touched on the margins of social work will have observed cases in which unemployment insurance was abused.

This, perhaps, is the price to pay for providing a fair deal to the great majority.

Under the old régime the cautious saved money against the possibility of illness and the certainty of old age. To the extent that that has become unnecessary family finances can either be carefully modified or pushed to an extreme in which the future is mortgaged. Why save money for a rainy day if free umbrellas are supplied? Is such a latter course within the intent of social security? There is no simple answer, partly because each case is different. All that can be suggested here is that a drastic social change can hardly be free from problems of adjustment, no matter how great the net benefit.

The welfare or social security measures which have been outlined constitute one explanation of the higher standard of living now enjoyed by the average person. Another is found in better conditions of work and enhanced rewards. The focus of attention has been on wage-earners or "workers," generally considered in a rather broad generalization to be the most vulnerable and least privileged category. Whether or not such an opinion would be valid at all times it was so during the depression of the thirties. Some indication has been given of the extent and results of unemployment. It could be regarded as an achievement to have any kind of job in those difficult years, but the returns were sometimes meagre. Up to 1929 wages had been steadily rising from the time of the first war. The index (with 1913 as 100) climbed to 192.7 in 1929. For the same two years the cost of living index stood at 100 and 160 respectively. In the twenties there were categories in which wages were abnormally low and hours long, but it was the depression which halted most of what advances had been made and on the average forced wages down and hours up.

The report of the Royal Commission on Price Spreads, the reincarnation of the Select Committee of the House of Commons (the Stevens committee) was published in 1935 and contains some shocking information on conditions of employment. Granted that the committee and commission had a particular purpose and slant and that they dealt only with chosen sectors of the economy, it can probably be assumed that the factual material used was in itself accurate. "In certain industries," the report reads, "the sweat shop still survives in Canada . . . unemployment and low wages have reduced many workers to a state of abject poverty." The commission found, within the industries which it chose to examine, long hours and depressed wages. In both respects it branded certain sections of the clothing industry as "deplorable." The employees of a number of baking concerns in Ontario were in many cases receiving less than $15 a week. For those employed in firms making agricultural implements earnings had decreased by 32 per cent since 1929. In the principal departmental stores of Toronto slightly more than half of the female staff received more than $10 per week. Hours of work were in some cases extreme, running to sixty or more in a week. While it appears that some trades were able to hold the line better than others, yearly earnings for wage-earners in manufacturing establishments of all kinds in Canada as a whole fell from $1,040 in 1929 to $787 in 1933.

It was from this low point that the position of the wage-earners improved steadily over a generation until it reached today's level. The first obvious cause of change was the revival of the general strength of the economy and with that a demand for labour. The recession that it had been feared would follow the second war never took place and unemployment did not exist to a serious extent. The second factor was the new power of the trade unions. During the thirties they had been weakened not only by lack of bargaining power but also by dissensions within their own ranks and by disputes between the federations. Internal peace was coincident with the return of prosperity rather than caused by it. During the forties and fifties a series of integrations took place together with a sharp rise in membership of the trades unions as a whole (from 359,000 to over a million).

The writ of the unions, however, had had limited range both by types of occupation and by area. In 1961 (taking total Canadian figures) their membership was about half the labour force in transportation, logging, public utilities, and mining; about 40 per cent in manufacturing, and somewhat less in construction. In trade the figure was under 5 per cent. Farmers are, with possibly some exceptions, outside the union picture. Some unions, such as those including carpenters, plumbers, or electricians, increased their size more in cities than in the country or small towns where many of the artisans have preferred to settle their own conditions of work. Such independent skilled workers may feel no need of assistance, but some others—particularly outside the unions—are less fortunate. For them particularly legislation, both federal and provincial, has been beneficial. It has dealt with a number of subjects: minimum rates of pay; maximum hours of work; government supervision of apprenticeship training; technical training; barriers against discrimination on grounds of race, creed, colour, nationality, or sex; machinery for conciliation proceedings; and compulsory safety rules.

More than any other segment of the population labour is affected by mechanization. Like the office worker the wage-earner may have labour-saving devices in his house, but in addition his work is coming to be more and more changed. Perhaps there will arrive a day when the shovel and pickaxe, the hand saw and drill, will, with the hod, qualify only for museums; for already machines threaten to make unskilled labour anachronic. So fast are techniques changing that concerted efforts are being made to provide technical training, particularly for young people. Without that, it is urged, there will be no place for them in industry.

The trade union movement will perhaps have to be renamed. It originated and developed in days when it could include only factory workers, artisans, manual workers, and similar groups. In modern times, however, collective action and bargaining have attracted those who had previously refrained from such methods. Now white-collar workers, notably civil servants and school teachers, have seized on the means so successfully used by wage-earners; have adopted collective bargaining, contracts, and strikes to further their interests. The movement may well go further.

Although the improvements in income and working conditions for wage-earners are especially noteworthy the general rise in the standard of living in Ontario is hardly less marked. In the *Submission of Ontario to the Royal Commission on Canada's Economic Prospects* (1956) there is an interesting summary:

As measured by personal expenditure on consumer goods and services, the standard of living of Ontario residents may be estimated to have gone up by 35 per cent since 1942 and nearly 53 per cent since 1939. These figures exclude both the rise in consumer prices and the increase in population; in other words, they are per capita figures adjusted for price change. They mean that, in terms of the goods and services he buys, the Ontario consumer is half again as well off as he was in 1939.

Ontario's higher real income is not, of course, limited to the things the consumer buys for himself. Improved public services contribute to higher real incomes too, although they do not appear in the figure for consumers' expenditures. Better educational facilities, better streets and highways, public buildings of all kinds, waterworks, improved sanitation and measures to improve health and care for the sick are examples of the many public services which enable the people to lead healthier, more comfortable lives.

A substantial rise in personal income per capita, resulting from the high productivity of labour and the full employment which the war and the post-war years have seen, is the basis of the increase in living standards. A large element in personal income is wage and salary earnings. In Ontario, the average weekly wage or salary per employed person in manufacturing, expressed in 1949 dollars, rose from $37.55 in 1939 to an estimated $58.00 in 1955, an increase of 57 per cent, after price changes are allowed for. During the same period, the average length of the work week declined from 47 hours in 1939 to 41 hours in 1955—a reduction of 13 per week. In terms of both increased pay and increased leisure, Ontario citizens have made considerable progress.

A standard of living is both a mathematical measurement and a personal concept. For a general analysis it is valuable to have, as in the passage just quoted, figures of income and expenditure. The individual, however, is more likely to think in terms of what he has learned to expect, or perhaps of what he considers he deserves. In specific terms this would be related to what is from time to time available. No one, for example, would demand electric light before it was invented. But having got that, people could presumably live without the appliances which come from it, such as radios, televisions, or washing machines. Given the means of public transport they could in many cases get on well enough without private motor cars. When electricity and automobiles were new they were in the hands of only a few people. By the times of the census of 1961 there were in Ontario 1,640,750 dwellings. Of these 1,350,483 had television sets and 1,085,575 had passenger cars. One way of assessing a standard of living is to watch the transfer of items from the category of luxuries to that of normal possessions.

There are, of course, factors far more basic that go to make up a standard of living: housing, food, clothing, and health for example. But again something of the same approach is not inappropriate. A century ago it was unusual to have water piped into a house or to have anything like modern central heating. Now it is the exceptional dwelling that does not have them both. That spells, as it were, an absolute difference; but the relative one is that more families are able to reach or rise above the contemporary minimum.

A standard of living is primarily the degree of physical well-being of the average person living under average conditions. To that may be added less tangible gains, mental and moral. Better facilities for education and entertainment, for example, allow for a fuller life. In reality, of course, there is no average person as measured in worldly goods, any more than there is in tastes. People are in varying degrees above or below the average: a consideration which inevitably leads to an attempt to divide society into sections. That can be done according to income, and would tell you something: that people may be so poor as to find even subsistence a problem; that others can just make both ends meet; that a larger proportion live in some comfort; and that a smaller one has more than ample means. Evidently, then, some people can, and others cannot, build large houses, travel abroad, collect rare postage stamps, go to the theatre, or become amateur farmers. What it does not tell you is whether they do any or all of these things. Perhaps, again, in their leisure hours they choose between race tracks, bowling alleys, restoring antique cars, or listening to gramophone records. In short, the financial measure does not tell you what sorts of human beings they are.

It is more customary to divide society according to classes, and from that to deduce manners and modes of life. Although income is an element, the class division must not be confused with the money division. There is a "working" class, but its composition is by no means clear. No doubt it includes manual labourers, artisans, factory employees, and such domestic servants as still exist. But should one add clerks, shop assistants, barbers, and service station operators? If not they must go into the only place left, the so-called middle class. Middle between what? In Europe and Britain the middle class came into existence as an urban and commercial one inserted between feudal landowners and peasants. As industrialization progressed it became larger and more complicated, and in England had to be split into upper and lower middle class. In Ontario there have been few candidates for the role of feudal landowner and no more for that of peasant. If there is, or has been, an upper class it has been based not on land or money but on a subjective and ill-defined code of background, tradition, and behaviour.

The middle class, then, is of uncertain size and composition. It includes professional men and women, those in business (although the lower limit of this is not fixed), and families with short purses and long pedigrees. It apparently does not include farm owners, for whom there seems to be no place in this set of categories. Even admitting, however, a serious lack of precision, there is within—if not throughout—the middle class a list of values, habits, and outlooks which has marked it from the early days of Ontario. It is easier to observe than to describe, but can be seen running through letters, books, and newspapers from the time of the first villages and towns.

Whatever the social groupings may be called—and it is idle to expect any neat pattern—it is evident that in some respects the boundaries are becoming more fluid. Larger incomes for artisans in some of the skilled trades, combined with scholarships, offer opportunities for advanced education for their children. It is noticeable, especially perhaps in older-settled parts of the south, that the children of parents who may have had little formal education attend high school and some of them universities. It is not intended to suggest that such cases are the rule or even common, but they do exist and over a period may multiply. Distinct boundaries to such a movement will long remain. A large segment of the population is not financially equipped to take advantage of education, whether technical or not, as a widening road to more profitable or more agreeable forms of employment. Nor are traditions changed over-night, and that of advanced education has not in the past been widespread. Nevertheless in this urban and mechanized society there are new forms of the flexibility and change which have marked the past.

Our Odyssey ends. It has been a journey through more than two centuries of history, across a thousand miles of land and water from north to south, from east to west, in a territory ever rich in variety and contrast. Now in the Laurentian lowlands the footprints made by the early settlers as they advanced from the shores of the rivers and lakes into the dark forest are buried deep beneath mile after mile of urban complex, the fringe of which steadily encroaches on towns, villages, and farms. Beyond the flat farmland near the lower lakes—or what is left of it—lies the gently rolling and fertile country, in modern dress but retaining many of the traditions of the Ontario of a hundred years ago. Then come the lower reaches of the Canadian Shield revealed by Champlain, the tireless explorer. Beyond that again is northern Ontario where the Adventurers of England perched on the shores of Hudson Bay, harassed by those adventurers of France who knew the northland well. Mines and mills invade the stillness of the forest but have not conquered it.

The diversity of Ontario can be seen, too, in terms of time as well as space for its whole history is laid out for those who look. Pioneer farmers still live in solitary cabins in the wilderness. The little villages and towns are only superficially changed. The city is but the early commercial town writ large. The farmer is, as ever, governed by nature and its vagaries. Then there is a record of the work of men's hands: buildings, roads, and boats; furniture, glass, pottery, and works of art.

This has been the history of a people who have lived in all these various environments, uncovering riches hitherto unknown, planting a civilization modified by the years. They came from many lands or were born in the province. They worked and played, fought and prayed. Rich and poor, happy and miserable, clever and stupid, muscular or intellectual, saints and sinners: all have passed across this stage. A few became famous, most are forgotten. But social history is not biography of the great; rather it is a composite portrait of a diversity of creatures. And to all who helped to build Ontario—the leaders and the obscure—this book is a salute.

BIBLIOGRAPHY

Bibliography

THE WRITTEN RECORD available for a study of the social history of Ontario is both voluminous and uneven: uneven both in what it covers and in quality. Statistical information, for example, is incomplete and often uncertain for the earlier periods but generally satisfactory for the later. On the other hand the letters, diaries, and other contemporary sources so valuable for the first half-century dwindle after it and have no parallel in the twentieth century.

An attempt has been made to select for this bibliography those items which have proved to be of substantial value, but in some cases mediocre books have had to be included in the absence of anything better.

The bibliography is arranged with convenience rather than convention in mind. Only three points seem to call for explanation. The first is that most of the documentary material will be found in the first part and published volumes which deal exclusively or primarily with subjects of the second part are placed there. Secondly, subjects are omitted from Part Two either because they are less central or because not enough is written specifically on them. Thirdly, it should be borne in mind that topics inevitably overlap each other and are also dealt with in part in general books or collections of papers. To make a comprehensive list for each one would produce a bibliography of monstrous length.

1. GENERAL

DOCUMENTS

MANUSCRIPT

Manuscript collections on social history are few and thin compared to those on political history. Some of the best, too, are adequately represented in published volumes and are not mentioned here in their original form.

Ontario Archives: Canada Company Papers, Cartwright Papers, Macaulay Papers, F. P. Smith Papers, Records of the Courts of Quarter Sessions.

Toronto Public Library: Elizabeth Russell Papers, St. George Papers, Baldwin Papers.

Public Archives of Canada: Oille Memoirs (in J. C. A. Campbell Papers), David MacLaren Papers, Thomas A. Keefer Papers.

Copies from local historical societies: David Nelson (Peterborough); F. L. Walsh, Miscellaneous (Norfolk); Benson Papers, Napanee Municipal Council, Joseph French (Lennox and Addington).

PRINTED GOVERNMENT RECORDS

The massive bulk of government publications forbids anything like a comprehensive list.

Ontario: Statutes of Upper Canada, of the Province of Canada, and of the Province of Ontario; Journals of the Legislative Councils and Assemblies, Appendices and Sessional Papers; reports and other publications of departments and agencies; "Proclamations by Governors and Lieutenant Governors of Quebec and Upper Canada" (*Report of the Bureau of Archives for the Province of Ontario*, 1906); *Submission of Ontario to the Royal Commission on Canada's Economic Prospects*, Toronto, 1956.

Canada: Statutes; Census of Canada; *Canada Year Book* (preceded by *Statistical Abstract and Record* from 1885 to 1903 and *Statistical Year-Book* from 1903 to 1905); reports and other publications of departments and agencies.

PRIVATE COLLECTIONS

The Champlain Society has published for the Government of Ontario a series of volumes of documents. The following have been principally used:

Firth, Edith G., *The Town of York, 1793–1815: a collection of documents of early Toronto*. Toronto, 1962.
———— *The Town of York, 1815–1834: a further collection of documents of early Toronto*. Toronto, 1966.
Johnston, Charles M., *The Valley of the Six Nations: a collection of documents on the Indian lands of the Grand River*. Toronto, 1964.
Lajeunesse, Ernest J., *The Windsor Border Region, Canada's Southernmost Frontier: a collection of documents*. Toronto, 1960.
Murray, Florence B., *Muskoka and Haliburton, 1615–1875: a collection of documents*. Toronto, 1963.
Preston, R. A., *Kingston before the War of 1812: a collection of documents* Toronto, 1959.
Preston, R. A. and Lamontagne, Léopold, *Royal Fort Frontenac*. Toronto, 1958.

OTHER PUBLISHED COLLECTIONS:

Cruikshank, E. A., *The Correspondence of Lieutenant-Governor John Graves Simcoe, with allied documents relating to the administration of the government of Upper Canada.* 5 vols., Toronto, 1923–31.

Cruikshank, E. A. and Hunter, A. F., *The Correspondence of the Honourable Peter Russell.* 3 vols., Toronto, 1932–36.

Sanderson, Charles R., *The Arthur Papers: being the Canadian papers confidential, private and demi-official of Sir George Arthur in the manuscript collection of the Toronto Public Libraries.* 3 vols., Toronto, 1957–59.

Innis, H. A., *Select Documents in Canadian Economic History, 1497–1783.* Toronto, 1929.

Innis, H. A. and Lower, A. R. M., *Select Documents in Canadian Economic History, 1783–1885.* Toronto, 1933.

Papers of William Proudfoot, printed in part by the London and Middlesex Historical Society in 1915, 1917, and 1922; and in part by the Ontario Historical Society in 1931, 1933, 1934, 1936, and 1937.

NEWSPAPERS

Newspapers constitute the most important single source. Original files, usually incomplete, may be found in several archives and libraries. Many papers have been microfilmed, though again the files are seldom complete. They are listed and described in the *Catalogue of Canadian Newspapers on Microfilm* published by the Canadian Library Association.

An immense number of newspapers have been published in Ontario, some of them for very short periods, and they have been preserved in part for almost every locality in the province. Some are more political than social but all are rich in advertisements.

PERIODICALS

Bibliographical information will be found in the *Review of Historical Publications relating to Canada* and in its successor, the *Canadian Historical Review*; in *Ontario History*; and, for a more limited field, in the *University of Toronto Quarterly*. Articles concerning the social history of Ontario appear from time to time in the *Canadian Historical Review* and regularly in *Ontario History*, as they have done in the preceding publication, *Ontario Historical Society: Papers and Records*. Several of the many local historical societies publish, or have in the past published, relevant articles.

Numerous gazetteers and almanacs have come and gone since early in the nineteenth century and are packed with factual information. *Morang's Annual Register of Canadian Affairs for 1901* was replaced by the *Canadian Annual Review of Public Affairs* (1903 to 1937–38) and then by the *Canadian Annual Review* (1960–   ).

FOR REFERENCE

Canada and its Provinces, edited by A. Shortt and A. G. Doughty (23 vols., Toronto, 1913–17) is still valuable, both for some of the general articles and for the two volumes devoted to Ontario. Other helpful works are:

Story, Norah, *The Oxford Companion to Canadian History and Literature.* Toronto, 1967.

Wallace, W. Stewart, *The Encyclopaedia of Canada.* 6 vols., Toronto, 1936.

——— *The Macmillan Dictionary of Canadian Biography.* London and Toronto, 1963.

Encyclopaedia Canadiana. 10 vols., Ottawa, 1957.

Urquhart, M. C. and Buckley, K. A. H. (eds.), *Historical Statistics of Canada* Cambridge and Toronto, 1965.

BOOKS AND ARTICLES

One part of the general history of Ontario has been admirably written by Gerald M. Craig in *Upper Canada, the Formative Years, 1784–1841* (Toronto, 1963). Another volume in the same series, *The Union of the Canadas 1841–1857* by J. M. S. Careless, was not available when the present book was written. There is no comparable work for the whole period. The four-volume *Province of Ontario: a history* by J. C. Middleton and Fred Landon was published in 1927. Half of it is taken up with short biographies and much of the remainder with a series of individual and unrelated articles on various subjects. It is necessary, therefore, to piece together the outline of the story as well as to follow the social side. The books that follow here are either on general themes or on questions not dealt with separately in the second part of this bibliography.

Burton, C. L., *A Sense of Urgency: memories of a Canadian merchant.* Toronto, 1952.

Canada one Hundred, 1867–1967. Ottawa, 1967.

Careless, J. M. S., *Brown of the Globe.* 2 vols., Toronto, 1959, 1963.

Clark, S. D., *The Suburban Society.* Toronto, 1966.

Due, John F., *The Intercity Electric Railway Industry in Canada.* Toronto, 1966.

Easterbrook, W. T. and Aitken, Hugh G. J., *Canadian Economic History.* Toronto, 1961.

Glazebrook, G. P. deT., *A History of Transportation in Canada.* 2 vols., Toronto, 1967.

Gourlay, Robert, *Statistical Account of Upper Canada: compiled with a view to a grand system of emigration.* 2 vols., London, 1822.

Grant, George M., *Ocean to Ocean: Sandford Fleming's expedition through Canada in 1872.* Toronto and London, 1873.

Guillet, Edwin C., *Early Life in Upper Canada.* Toronto, 1933.

———— *The Story of Canadian Roads.* Toronto, 1966.

Herrington, Walter S., *The History of the Grand Lodge of Canada in the Province of Ontario, 1855–1930.* Hamilton, 1930.

Joynt, Carey B., "Social Change in Huron County, 1880–1945" (*Western Ontario Historical Notes*, vii, 3).

Kerr, W. B., *The Orange Order in Upper Canada*, n.p., n.d.

Landon, Fred, *Western Ontario and the American Frontier.* Toronto, 1941.

Ontario Historical Society, *Profiles of a Province: studies in the history of Ontario.* Toronto, 1967.

Putnam, Donald F., *Canadian Regions: a geography of Canada.* Toronto, 1952.

Robertson, J. Ross, *The History of Freemasonry in Canada, from its Introduction in 1749.* 2 vols., Toronto, 1900.

Ross, Murray G., *The Y.M.C.A. in Canada: the chronicle of a century.* Toronto, 1951.

Royal Ontario Musuem, *Modesty to Mod: dress and underdress in Canada, 1780–1967.* Catalogue of 100 items in the exhibition May 17 to September 4, 1967.

Royal Society of Canada: fifty years retrospect. n.p., n.d.

Severance, Frank H., *An Old Frontier of France: the Niagara region and adjacent lakes under French control.* 2 vols., New York, 1917.

Smith, William, *The History of the Post Office in British North America, 1639–1870.* Cambridge, 1920.

Spelt, J., *The Urban Development in South-Central Ontario.* Assen, Netherlands, 1955.

Stanley, G. F. G. (ed.), *Pioneers of Canadian Science: symposium presented to the Royal Society of Canada in 1964.* Toronto, 1966.

Taylor, Griffith, *Canada: a Study of Cool Continental Environments and their Effect on British and French Settlement.* Toronto, 1947.

Wallace, Elisabeth, *Goldwin Smith, Victorian Liberal.* Toronto, 1957.

Wallace, W. Stewart (ed.), *The Royal Canadian Institute: centennial volume, 1849–1949.* Toronto, 1949.

LOCAL HISTORY

There are a great many local histories—of townships, counties, towns, cities, and other areas—but few of them have more than marginal historical value. Those that offer substantial fare include the following:

Bertrand, J. P., *Highway of Destiny: an epic story of Canadian development*. New York, 1959. On the area north of Lake Superior.

Fraser, L. R., *History of Muskoka*. n.p., n.d.

Hamil, Fred Coyne, *The Valley of the Lower Thames, 1640 to 1850*. Toronto, 1951.

Herrington, Walter S., *History of the County of Lennox and Addington*. Toronto, 1913.

Johnston, C. M., *The Head of the Lake: a history of Wentworth County*. Hamilton, 1958.

Johnston, William, *History of the County of Perth from 1825 to 1902*. Stratford, 1903.

Kerr, Donald and Spelt, Jacob, *The Changing Face of Toronto: a study in urban geography*. Ottawa, 1965.

Masters, D. C., *The Rise of Toronto, 1850–1890*. Toronto, 1947.

Mathews, Hazel C., *Oakville and the Sixteen: a history of an Ontario port*. Toronto, 1953.

Nute, Grace Lee, *Rainy River Country: a brief History of the region bordering Minnesota and Ontario*. St. Paul, 1950.

Robertson, J. Ross, *Landmarks of Toronto: a collection of historical sketches of the old town of York from 1792 until 1833 cnd of Toronto from 1834 to 1893*. 6 vols., Toronto, 1894. Articles reprinted from the Toronto *Telegram*.

Robinson, Percy J., *Toronto during the French Régime: a history of the Toronto region from Brûlé to Simcoe, 1615–1793*. Toronto, 1965.

Scadding, H., *Toronto of Old*. Toronto, 1873.

Templin, Hugh, *Fergus: the story of a little town*. Fergus, 1933.

Toronto Transit Commission, *Transit in Toronto, 1849–1967*.

Walker, Frank N., *Sketches of Old Toronto*. Toronto, 1965.

TRAVELLERS AND SETTLERS

Many accounts by travellers and settlers were printed at the time or later. Few relate to any period after 1850. Some are of considerable value but many others are either too opinionated or do little more than repeat what was in earlier books. The following have been found most useful:

Authentic Letters from Upper Canada, including an Account of Canadian Field Sports by Thomas William Magrath: the whole edited by the Rev. Thomas Radcliff: Illustrated by Samuel Lover and introduced by James John Talman. Toronto, 1953.

Campbell, Patrick, *Travels in the Interior Inhabited Parts of North America in the Years 1791 and 1792.* Edited by H. H. Langton. Toronto, 1937.

Dunlop, E. S. (ed.), *Our Forest Home: being extracts from the correspondence of the late Frances Stewart.* Montreal, 1902.

Innis, Mary Quale (ed.), *Mrs. Simcoe's Diary.* Toronto, 1965.

Jameson, Anna Brownell, *Winter Studies and Summer Rambles in Canada.* n.p., 1943.

Langton, H. H. (ed.), *A Gentlewoman in Upper Canada: the journals of Anne Langton.* Toronto, 1950.

Moodie, Susanna, *Roughing it in the Bush.* Toronto, 1962.

Samuel, Sigmund, *In Return: the autobiography of Sigmund Samuel.* Toronto, 1963.

[Traill, Catherine Parr], *The Backwoods of Canada: being letters from the wife of an emigrant officer, illustrative of the domestic economy of British America, to which is appended an account of the country of the Oregon.* London, 1846. Published anonymously,

Warr, G. W., *Canada as it is: or the emigrant's friend and guide to Upper Canada.* London, 1847.

Weld, Isaac, *Travels through the States of North America and the Provinces of Upper and Lower Canada during the years 1795, 1796 and 1797.* London, 1799.

2. SUBJECTS

INDIAN SOCIETY AND RELATIONS WITH EUROPEANS

Barbeau, Marius, "Asiatic Migrations into America" (*Canadian Historical Review*, xiii, 4).

Clark, Ella Elizabeth, *Indian Legends of Canada.* Toronto, 1960.

Innis, Harold A., *The Fur Trade in Canada.* Toronto, 1962.

Jenness, Diamond, *The Indians of Canada.* Ottawa, 1932.

Macgowan, Kenneth, *Early Man in the New World*. New York, 1950.

Martin, Paul S., Quimby, George I., and Collier, Donald, *Indians before Columbus: twenty thousand years of North American history revealed by archaeology*. Chicago, 1947.

Morris, J. L., *Indians of Ontario*. Toronto, 1943.

Morton, Arthur S., *A History of the Canadian West to 1870–71*. London, n.d.

Parkman, Francis, *The Jesuits in North America in the seventeenth century*. Boston, 1867.

Quimby, George Irving, *Indian Life in the Upper Great Lakes, 11,000 B.C. to A.D. 1800*. Chicago, 1960.

Rich, E. E., *The History of the Hudson's Bay Company, 1670–1870*. 2 vols., London, 1958–59.

Rivet, Paul, *Les origines de l'homme Américan*. Paris, 1957.

Rogers, Edward S., *The Round Lake Ojibwa*. Toronto, 1962.

Scott, Duncan C., "Indian Affairs, 1763–1841"; "Indian Affairs, 1840–1867" (*Canada and its Provinces*, vols. 4 and 5).

IMMIGRATION, LAND POLICY, AND SETTLEMENT

Calendar of Durham Papers in *Report of the Public Archives for the Year 1923*.

Cruickshank, E. A. (ed.), "Petitions for Grants of Land in Upper Canada, 1796–99" (*Ontario Historical Society, Papers and Records*, xxvi).

———— "Petitions for Grants of Land, 1792–96" (*Ontario Historical Society, Papers and Records*, xxiv).

———— "Records of Niagara: a collection of documents relating to the first settlement" (*Niagara Historical Society*, 38 and 39).

———— *The Settlement of the United Empire Loyalists on the Upper St. Lawrence and the Bay of Quinte in 1784: a documentary record*. Toronto, 1934.

"Emigration" (Documents in *Report on Canadian Archives*, 1900).

"Grants of Crown Land in Upper Canada, 1792–1796" (Documents in *Report of the Ontario Archives for 1929*).

"Indian Lands on the Grand River" (Documents in *Report on Canadian Archives*, 1896).

Paterson, Gilbert C., "Land Settlement in Upper Canada, 1783–1840" (*Report* of the Ontario Archives for 1920).

Rich, E. E. and Johnson, A. M. (eds.), *Moose Fort Journals, 1783–85*. London, 1954.

"Special report to His Excellency the Governor-General by Mr. R. D. Harrison on the excessive Appropriation of public Land under the name of 'Clergy Reserves' " (C. P. Lucas, *Lord Durham's Report on the Affairs of British North America*, vol. 3. Oxford, 1912).

"United Empire Loyalists: enquiry into the losses and services in consequence of their loyalty" (*Report* of the Ontario Archives for 1904).

Cartwright, C. E., *Life and Letters of the Late Hon. Richard Cartwright.* Toronto, 1876.

Coats, R. H. and Maclean, M.S., *The American-born in Canada: a statistical interpretation.* Toronto, 1943.

Cowan, Helen I., *British Emigration to British North America: the first hundred years.* Toronto, 1961.

Ermatinger, C. O., *The Talbot Régime: or the first half century of the Talbot settlement.* St. Thomas, 1904.

Gates, Lillian F., *Land Policies of Upper Canada.* Toronto, 1968.

Hamil, Fred Coyne, *Lake Erie Baron: the story of Colonel Thomas Talbot.* Toronto, 1955.

Herrington, W. S., *Pioneer Life among the Loyalists in Upper Canada.* Toronto, 1915.

Hill, Daniel G., "Negroes in Toronto, 1793–1865" (*Ontario History*, lv, 2).

Jamieson, Annie Straith, *William King, Friend and Champion of Slaves.* Toronto, 1925.

Kirkwood, A. and Murphy, J. J., *The Undeveloped Lands in Northern and Western Ontario.* Toronto, 1878.

Landon, Fred, "Social Conditions among the Negroes in Upper Canada before 1865" (*Ontario Historical Society, Papers and Records*, xxii).

Macdonald, Norman, *Canada, 1763–1841, Immigration and Settlement: the administration of the imperial land regulations.* London and Toronto, 1939.

Martyn, Lucy Booth, "The McNab in Upper Canada: a feudal experiment of the Maitland régime." Unpublished M.A. thesis, University of Toronto, 1936.

Pease, William H. and Pease, Jane H., "Opposition to the Founding of the Elgin Settlement" (*Canadian Historical Review*, xxxviii, 3).

Richmond, Anthony H., *Post-War Immigrants in Canada.* Toronto, 1967.

Riddell, R. G., "The Policy of Creating Land Reserves in Canada" (*Essays in Canadian history*, edited by R. Flenley).

Riddell, W. R., "The Official Record of Slavery in Upper Canada" (*Ontario Historical Society, Papers and Records*, xxv).

———— "The Slave in Canada" (*Journal of Negro History*, v, 3).

Rosenberg, Louis, "The Demography of the Jewish Community in Canada" (*Canadian Jewish Population Studies*, no. 2).

Tasker, L. H., "United Empire Loyalist Settlement at Long Point, Lake Erie" (*Ontario Historical Society, Papers and Records*, ii).

Wilson, Alan, "The Clergy Reserves: 'economical mischiefs' or sectarian issue?" (*Canadian Historical Review*, xlii, 4).

Withrow, W. H., "The Underground Railway" (*Royal Society of Canada, Proceedings and Transactions*, 1902).

AGRICULTURE

Ontario Agricultural Commission: Report of the Commissioners. 3 vols., Toronto, 1881.

Report on the Reforestation of Waste Lands in Southern Ontario. Toronto, 1909.

Brownell, Evelyn and Scott, S. G., *A Study of Holland Marsh: its reclamation and development.* Toronto, 1949.

Drury, E. C., *Farmer Premier.* Toronto, 1966.

Fowke, Vernon C., *Canadian Agricultural Policy: the historical pattern.* Toronto, 1946.

Innis, H. A. (ed.), *The Dairy Industry in Canada.* Toronto, 1937.

Jones, R. L., *History of Agriculture in Ontario, 1613–1880.* Toronto, 1946.

Macdonald, Norman, "Hemp and Imperial Defence" (*Canadian Historical Review*, xvii, 4).

Special Study of Ontario Farm Homes and Homemakers. Prepared by the Ontario and Canadian Departments of Agriculture and published in a series of mimeographed reports from 1959 to 1964.

Talman, James J., "Agricultural Societies of Upper Canada" (*Ontario Historical Society, Papers and Records*, xxvii).

TRADE, INDUSTRY, AND FINANCE

Report of the Royal Commission on the mineral resources of Ontario and measures for their development. Toronto, 1890.

Ashworth, E. M., *Toronto Hydro Recollections.* Toronto, 1955.

Breckenridge, Roeliff Morton, *The History of Banking in Canada.* Washington, D.C., 1910.

Brown, L. Carson, *Cobalt: the town with a silver lining.* Toronto, 1965.

——— "The Golden Porcupine" (*Canadian Geographical Journal*, January 1967).

——— *Ontario's Mineral Heritage.* Toronto, 1965.

——— *The Red Lake Gold Field.* Toronto, 1966.

Calvin, D. D., *A Saga of the St. Lawrence: timber and shipping through three generations.* Toronto, 1945.

Canadian Pulp and Paper Association, *The Pulpwood Harvest.* n.p., 1963.

——— *From watershed to watermark.* n.p., 1967.

Carruthers, George, *Paper-making.* Toronto, 1947.

Chalmers, Robert, *A History of Currency in the British Colonies.* London, 1893.

Collard, Elizabeth, *Nineteenth-century Pottery and Porcelain in Canada.* Montreal, 1967.

Cruikshank, E. A., "A Country Merchant in Upper Canada, 1800–1812" (*Ontario Historical Society, Papers and Records,* xxv).

Denison, Merrill, *Harvest Triumphant: the story of Massey-Harris.* Toronto, 1948.

——— *This is Simpson's.* Toronto, 1947.

Fox, William Sherwood (ed.), *Letters of William Davies, Toronto, 1854–1861.* Toronto, 1945.

Gibson, Thos. W., *Mining in Ontario.* Toronto, 1937.

Glover, T. R. and Calvin, D. D., *A Corner of Empire: the old Ontario strand.* Cambridge, 1937.

Golden Jubilee 1869–1919: a book to commemorate the fiftieth anniversary of the T. Eaton Co., Ltd. Toronto, 1919.

Hamilton, W. J., "Silver Islet" (*Thunder Bay Historical Society,* 1912).

"History of Crown Timber Regulations" (*Annual Report of the Clerk of Forestry,* Ontario Sessional Paper no. 36, 1899).

Hughson, John W. and Bond, Courtney C. J., *Hurling down the Pine.* Old Chelsea, Quebec, 1965.

Langston, John Emerson, *Canadian Silversmiths and their Marks, 1667–1867.* Lunneburg, Vermont, 1960.

Lower, A. R. M., *The North American Assault on the Canadian Forest: a history of the lumber trade between Canada and the United States.* Toronto, 1938.

——— "Settlement and the Forest Frontier in Eastern Canada" (*Canadian Frontiers of Settlement,* edited by W. A. Mackintosh and W. L. G. Joerg, vol. ix, Toronto, 1936).

McIvor, R. Craig, *Canadian Monetary, Banking and Fiscal Development.* Toronto, 1958.

Masters, D. C., "The Establishment of the Decimal Currency in Canada" (*Canadian Historical Review*, xxxiii, 2).

Miller, W. G., "Mines and Mining" (*Canada and its Provinces*, vol. 18).

Mining Association of Canada, *What the Mining Industry Means to Canada.* Toronto, 1966.

Neufeld, E. P. (ed.), *Money and Banking in Canada: historical documents and commentary.* Toronto, 1964.

Plewman, W. R., *Adam Beck and the Ontario Hydro.* Toronto, 1947.

Ross, Victor, *A History of the Canadian Bank of Commerce*, 2 vols., Toronto, 1920–22.

Stevens, Gerald, *Early Canadian Glass.* Toronto, 1960.

Tanton, T. L., *Fort William and Port Arthur, and Thunder Bay Map-Areas, Thunder Bay District, Ontario.* Ottawa, 1931.

Treadwell, William, "The Pellet Makers" (*Canadian Geographical Journal*, June 1966).

Trigge, A. St. L., *A History of the Canadian Bank of Commerce*, vol. 3. Toronto, 1934.

Wilson, Pearl, "Consumer Buying in Upper Canada, 1791–1840" (*Ontario Historical Society, Papers and Records*, xxxvi).

LABOUR

Report of the Commissioners appointed to enquire into the Working of Mills and Factories of the Dominion, and the Labor Employed Therein. Ottawa, 1882.

Report of the Royal Commission on the Relations of Labor and Capital in Canada. Ottawa, 1889.

Creighton, D. G., "George Brown, Sir John Macdonald, and the 'Workingman' " (*Canadian Historical Review*, xxiv, 4).

Forsey, Eugene, "History of the Labour Movement in Canada" (*Canada Year Book*, 1957–58).

Kennedy, Douglas R., *The Knights of Labor in Canada.* London, Ont., 1956.

Logan, H. A., *Trade Unions in Canada: their development and functioning.* Toronto, 1948.

Watt, F. W., "The National Policy, the Workingman, and Proletarian Ideas in Victorian Canada" (*Canadian Historical Review*, xl, 1).

JUSTICE AND LOCAL GOVERNMENT

There are few studies of either subject which are satisfactory for historical purposes. There is a chapter (xx) in Middleton and Landon's *Province of Ontario* on the courts of Upper Canada, and in volume 18 of *Canada and its Provinces* a brief account of the judicial system from 1774 to 1913. In the latter volume there are chapters on municipal government from 1791 to 1867 and from 1867 to 1913. Most, if not all, of the more recent accounts of local government deal with southern Ontario only. The following will be found useful.

Minutes of the Court of General Quarter Sessions of the Peace for the Home District (1800–1811) and for the London District (1800–1809, 1813–1818), are printed in Reports of the Ontario Archives for 1932 and 1933. Minutes for other districts may be found in manuscript.

Aitchison, J. H., "The Development of Local Government in Upper Canada, 1783–1850." Unpublished Ph.D. thesis, University of Toronto, 2 vols., 1953.

Elliott, John K., "Crime and Punishment in Early Upper Canada" (*Ontario Historical Society, Papers and Records,* xxvii).

Jones, James Edmund, *Pioneer Crimes and Punishments in Toronto and Home District.* Toronto, 1924.

EDUCATION

Hodgins, J. George (ed.), *Documentary History of Education in Upper Canada: from the passing of the Constitutional Act of 1791 to the close of the Reverend Doctor Ryerson's administration of the Educational Department in 1876.* 28 vols., Toronto, 1894–1910.

Report of the Royal Commission on Education in Ontario. Toronto, 1951.

Calvin, D. D., *Queen's University at Kingston: the first century of a Scottish-Canadian foundation.* Kingston, 1941.

Hodgetts, J. E. (ed.), *Higher Education in a Changing Canada: symposium presented to the Royal Society of Canada.* Toronto, 1966.

Jubilee Volume of Wycliffe College. Toronto, 1927.

Phillips, Charles E., *The Development of Education in Canada.* Toronto, 1957.

Prang, Margaret, "Clerics, Politicians, and the Bilingual School Issue in Ontario, 1910–1917" (*Canadian Historical Review,* xli, 4).

Purdy, Judson D., "John Strachan and Education in Canada, 1800–1851." Unpublished Ph.D. thesis, University of Toronto, 1962.

Reed, T. A. (ed.), *History of the University of Trinity College, Toronto.* Toronto, 1952.

St. John, J. Bascom, *Separate Schools in Ontario*. Reprinted from the *Globe and Mail*, Toronto, 1963.

Sissons, C. B., *Bi-lingual Schools in Canada*. London and Toronto, 1917.

————— *A History of Victoria University*. Toronto, 1952.

Spragge, George W., "The Cornwall Grammar School under John Strachan, 1803–1812" (*Ontario Historical Society, Papers and Records*, xxxiv).

————— "Elementary School Education in Upper Canada, 1820–1840" (*Ontario Historical Society, Papers and Records*, xliii).

————— "John Strachan's Contribution to Education, 1800–1823" (*Canadian Historical Review*, xxii, 2).

Walker, Franklin A., *Catholic Education and Politics in Upper Canada: a study of the documentation relative to the origin of Catholic elementary schools in the Ontario school system*. Toronto, 1955.

Wallace, W. Stewart, *A History of the University of Toronto, 1872–1927*. Toronto, 1927.

HOUSING AND FURNITURE

The reconstruction of early nineteenth-century villages is an aid to the study of both buildings and furniture, and examples of the latter may also be found in museums and private houses. For modern housing the following list may be supplemented by the Census and by publications of the Central Mortgage and Housing Corporation.

Architectural Conservancy of Ontario, *Victorian Architecture in Hamilton*. Hamilton, 1967.

Arthur, Eric R., *The Early Buildings of Ontario*. Toronto, 1938.

————— *Toronto, No Mean City*. Toronto, 1964.

Macrae, Marion and Adamson, Anthony, *The Ancestral Roof: domestic architecture of Upper Canada*. Toronto, 1963.

Rempel, John I., *Building with Wood*. Toronto, 1967.

Ritchie, T., *et al.*, *Canada Builds*, Toronto, 1967.

Stewart, John R., *A Guide to Pre-Confederation Furniture of English Canada*. Toronto, 1967.

Whebell, C. F. J., "Pre-Confederation Houses in Norfolk County, Ontario" (*Ontario History*, lviii, 4).

Wright, Lawrence, *Clean and Decent: the fascinating history of the bathroom and the water closet*. Toronto, 1967.

RELIGION AND MORALS

Moir, John S. (ed.), *Church and State in Canada, 1627–1867: basic documents.* Toronto, 1967.

Spragge, George W. (ed.) *The John Strachan Letter Book, 1812–1834.* Toronto, 1946.

Alfred, Brother, *Catholic Pioneers in Upper Canada.* Toronto, 1947.

Brown, George W., *Canada in the Making.* Toronto, 1953.

Burkholder, L. J., *A Brief History of the Mennonites in Ontario,* n.p., 1935.

Burnet, J. R., "The Urban Community and Changing Moral Standards" (*Urbanism and the Changing Canadian Society,* edited by S. D. Clark, Toronto, 1961).

Carroll, John, *Case and his Cotemporaries, or the Canadian itinerants' memorial; constituting a biographical history of Methodism in Canada, from its introduction into the province, till the death of Rev. Wm. Case in 1855.* 5 vols., Toronto, 1867.

Clark, S. D., *Church and Sect in Canada.* Toronto, 1948.

———— *The Developing Canadian community.* Toronto, 1962.

Dorland, Arthur Garratt, *A History of the Society of Friends (Quakers) in Canada.* Toronto, 1927.

Fitch, E. R. (ed.), *The Baptists of Canada: a history of their progress and achievements.* Toronto, 1911.

Garland, M. A. and Talman, J. J., "Pioneer Drinking Habits and the Rise of Temperance Agitation in Upper Canada prior to 1840" (*Ontario Historical Society, Papers and Records,* xxvii).

Grant, John Webster (ed.) *The Churches and the Canadian Experience.* Toronto, 1963.

Gregg, William, *History of the Presbyterian Church in the Dominion of Canada.* Toronto, 1885.

Ivison, Stuart and Rosser, Fred, *The Baptists in Upper and Lower Canada before 1820.* Toronto, 1956.

Lewis, James K., "The Religious Life of the Fugitive Slaves and Rise of Coloured Baptist Churches, 1820–1865, in what is now known as Ontario." Unpublished B.D. Thesis, McMaster University, 1955.

McNeill, John Thomas, *The Presbyterian Church in Canada, 1875–1925.* Toronto, 1925.

Millman, Thomas R., *The Life of the Right Reverend, the Honourable Charles James Stewart, Second Anglican Bishop of Quebec.* London, Ont., 1953.

Moir, John S., *Church and State in Canada West: three studies in the relation of denominationalism and nationalism, 1841–1867.* Toronto, 1959.

O'Dwyer, William C., *Highways of Destiny: a history of the Diocese of Pembroke, Ottawa Valley, Canada.* n.p., 1964.

Sanderson, J. E., *The First Century of Methodism in Canada.* 2 vols., Toronto, 1908.

Silcox, Claris Edwin, *Church Union in Canada: its causes and consequences.* New York, 1933.

Sissons, C. B., *Egerton Ryerson, his Life and Letters.* 2 vols., Toronto, 1937, 1947.

Somers, Hugh Joseph, *The Life and Times of the Hon. and Rt. Rev. Alexander Macdonell, D.D., First Bishop of Upper Canada, 1762–1840.* Washington, D.C., 1931.

Spence, Ruth Elizabeth, *Prohibition in Canada: a memorial to Francis Stephen Spence.* Toronto, 1919.

Waddilove, W. J. D., *The Stewart Missions: a series of letters and journals.* London, 1838.

Wilkinson, Anne, *Lions in the Way: a discursive history of the Oslers.* Toronto, 1956.

Vernon, C. W., *The Old Church in the New Dominion: the story of the Anglican church in Canada.* Toronto, 1929.

HEALTH AND SOCIAL WELFARE

Anderson, H. B., "An Historical Sketch of the Medical Profession of Toronto" (*Canadian Medical Association Journal*, vol. 16).

Canniff, William, *The Medical Profession in Upper Canada, 1783–1850: an historical narrative, with original documents relating to the profession, including some brief biographies.* Toronto, 1894.

Cassidy, H. M., *Social Security and Reconstruction in Canada.* Toronto, 1944.
—— *Unemployment and Relief in Ontario, 1929–1932: a survey and report.* Toronto [1932].

Dunham, B. M., "The Waterloo County House of Industry and Refuge" (*Waterloo Historical Society*, 1948).

Elkin, Frederick, *The Family in Canada: an account of present knowledge and gaps in knowledge about Canadian families.* Ottawa, 1964.

Heagerty, John J., *Four Centuries of Medical History in Canada, and a sketch of the medical history of Newfoundland.* 2 vols., Toronto, 1928.

Morrison, Jean (ed.), *The Canadian Congress on the Family.* Ottawa, 1965.

Riddell, W. R., "Popular Medicine in Upper Canada a Century ago" (*Ontario Historical Society, Papers and Records*, xxv).

Rose, Albert, *Regent Park: a study in slum clearance*, Toronto, 1958.

Splane, Richard B., *Social Welfare in Ontario, 1791–1893: a study of public welfare administration*. Toronto, 1965.

Wallace, Elisabeth, "Goldwin Smith and Social Reform" (*Canadian Historical Review*, xxix, 4).

———— "The Origin of the Social Welfare State in Canada" (*Canadian Journal of Economics and Political Science*, xvi, 3).

Youth, Marriage and the Family: prepared for the Canadian Youth Commission. Toronto, 1948.

LITERATURE, MUSIC, AND THE ARTS

Brown, E. K., *On Canadian Poetry*. Toronto, 1943.

Collin, W. E., *The White Savannahs*. Toronto, 1936.

Harper, J. Russell, *Painting in Canada*. Toronto, 1966.

Harris, Lawren, "The Group of Seven in Canadian history" (*Canadian Historical Association, Report*, 1948).

Hubbard, R. H., *The Development of Canadian Art*. Ottawa, 1963.

McInnes, Graham, *A Short History of Canadian Art*. Toronto, 1939.

MacMillan, Ernest (ed.), *Music in Canada*. Toronto, 1955.

MacTavish, Newton, *The Fine Arts in Canada*. Toronto, 1925.

Pacey, Desmond, *Creative Writing in Canada: a short history of English-Canadian literature*. Toronto, 1961.

Smith, A. J. M. (ed.), *The Book of Canadian Poetry: a critical and historical anthology*. Toronto, 1953.

———— *Masks of Fiction: Canadian critics on Canadian prose*. Toronto, 1961.

Smith, Leo, "Music" (*Encyclopaedia of Canada*, edited by W. S. Wallace, vol. 4).

Index

AGRICULTURE: Windsor area, 17–18; pioneer, 33–35; southern Ontario, 108, 165–177, 264–266; lower Shield, 142–147; northern, 154, 156, 158–159, 268–270

Architecture, styles of, 111, 181

Art, 216–217, 256–257

BANKING. *See* Finance

Baptist churches, 118, 204

Brant, Joseph, and Indian lands, 26–27, 92

Brown, George: escaped slaves, 116; his farms, 172–175; and labour union, 192

Buildings: construction of, 31–32, 36, 37, 46, 54, 55, 181–182; general description, 111, 166, 181, 247–249, 267, 277–278

Buller, Charles, and land policy, 29–30

CANADA COMPANY, 23–24, 179

Canadian Land and Emigration Company, 142, 146

Canadian Pacific Railway, 132, 150, 151, 152–153

Cartwright, Richard: trade, 49, 92; and lawyers, 94

Chisholm, William, 45

Church of England: position and outlook, 77, 78–80, 117, 204; missions to Indians, 118–119; education, 123–124; clergy reserves, 203

Clothing, 38–39, 59–60, 195–196, 227, 259

Congregationalist churches, 118

Courts of Quarter Sessions: judicial, 94–95, 99; administrative, 96–98; and welfare, 101

Currency. *See* Finance

DAWSON, S. J., surveys, 148–149

Dentists, 114, 154, 157, 200

Doctors. *See* Health

Drury, E. C.: farming, 173; on the north, 269

EDUCATION: general, 18, 82–83, 207–212, 233; schools, 83–89, 116–117, 120–123, 208–212, 224, 233–234; university, 123–125, 212, 224–225, 235; legal, 94; medical, 74, 114–115, 199; divinity, 118

FARMERS' ASSOCIATION OF ONTARIO, 176–177

Farming. *See* Agriculture

Finance: early methods, 49–50; banks, 51, 109–110, 185–186, 252; other institutions, 110, 186

Fire, protection from, 53–54, 110, 179

Fisheries, 264

Food, 11, 39–40, 58–59

Forests. *See* Lumbering; Reforestation

Freemasons, 64, 112, 153, 217

Furniture, 32–33, 46, 55–58, 183

Fur traders, 6, 7, 8–16, 148, 270

Methodist churches: camp meetings, 41, 80–81, 119; work of, 80; developments in, 117–118, 204; missions to Indians, 118–119; education, 124; clergy reserves, 203

Metropolitanism: in general, 244–245, 252, 262–263; metropolitan areas, 245–247

Mills, 41–42

Mining: early, 46–47; northern Ontario, 150–152, 156–159, 269–273

Moodie, Susanna, on life in Upper Canada, 25, 38

Morals, 82, 99–100, 119–120, 205–207

Music, 61–62, 112, 216, 242, 257

NATIONAL GRANGE OF THE PATRONS OF HUSBANDRY, 176

Newspapers, 62–63, 104, 241

Northern Railway, 132, 150

OIL INDUSTRY, 175

Orange Order, 64, 112, 147, 217–218

Osler, Featherstone: lending library, 40; religious duties, 79; public morals, 82; in Dundas, 164

PAPER, manufactured, 46, 274

Pedlars, 40

Plumbing, 157, 182–183, 248–249, 267

Police forces, 179

Population: in 1812, 21; in 1821, 24; in 1851, 107; 1851–1911, 134–136, 178; since 1914, 229–232, 244–245, 250–251; urbanization, 109, 134, 231; northern Ontario, 155, 159, 276, 278. *See also* Immigration

Post office, 89–90, 113, 161, 218, 267

Presbyterian churches, 117; union of, 204; education, 124–125; clergy reserves, 203

Proudfoot, William: on people of Ontario, 38; on winter clothing, 39; on public morals, 82

Public services, 110, 179–181, 249–250

Pulp and paper industry, 273–276

QUAKERS, 20, 118, 119

RADIO, 241–242, 256

Railways: early, 130–134, 171; modern, 238; street railways, 180–181; radials, 224. *See also* under names of companies

Rebellion of 1837, 104–106

Recreation, 40–41, 60–65, 111–112, 153, 164–165, 172, 195–197, 256, 259–261

Reforestation, 165–166, 274

Religion, 13, 76–78, 81–82, 117–120, 203–207, 235–237; church union, 236. *See also* under names of individual churches

Retail trade, 47–49, 110–111, 163–164, 183–184, 252–253, 262–263

Roads: characters of, 3–31, 113, 130, 161, 171, 223–224, 238–239; in lower Shield, 141–142, 146; northern Ontario, 149, 157, 239

Roman Catholic Church: position in Ontario, 76, 77, 117; education, 87, 121, 125, 210; clergy reserves, 203
Ryerson, Egerton, 118, 120, 124

ST. GEORGE'S SOCIETY, 64, 112
St. Patrick's Society, 65, 112, 217
Salvation Army, 205
Sanitation, 53, 180
Schools. See Education
Selkirk, Earl of, Baldoon settlement, 21, 68
Simcoe, John Graves: and immigration, 21; slavery, 70
Shipping: in French régime, 6–7; on Hudson Bay, 9, 12; in nineteenth century, 43–45, 113, 150
Shops. See Retail trade
Slaves: in Ontario, 17, 69–70, 115; escaped slaves, 116–117
Smith, Goldwin: agrarian organization, 176; welfare, 203; as writer, 214
Sports. See Recreation
Strachan, John: and Church of England, 77, 79; synod, 117; and education, 84–85, 123–124; missions to Indians, 118–119
Suburbs, 245–247

TALBOT, Thomas, and colonization, 21–22, 37

Telephone: invention of, 215–216; first exchange, 181; 161, 218–219
Television, 241–242, 256, 289
Temiskaming and Northern Ontario Railway, 133, 156
Temperance, 82, 119, 205–206, 218
Theatre, 61, 111–112, 157, 194, 256
Trade unions, 68, 188–189, 192–193, 218, 287–288
Transportation, 30–31, 43–45, 102–103, 113, 129–134, 237–240, 250, 265–266, 271–272. See also Railways; Roads

UNEMPLOYMENT, 201, 202, 227, 279–281, 283
United Empire Loyalists: migration, 18–21, 30; land grants, 28, 29

WARS, of 1812, 92, 102; of 1914, 225–226; of 1939, 228, 281
Welfare, social, 100–102, 115, 193–194, 200–203, 205–206, 248–249, 280–286
Wholesale trade, 49, 184–185, 252
Women's Institutes, 218
Wright, Philemon, lumbering, 41

YOUNG MEN'S CHRISTIAN ASSOCIATION, 203, 218
Young Women's Christian Association, 218